MCSE

TESTPREP

Windows NT
Server 4
Enterprise

MCSE TestPrep: Windows NT Server 4 Enterprise

By Jay Adamson, Emmett Dulaney, William N. Matsoukas, Brian Komar, Kristin Wahlquist, and Kevin Wolford.

Published by:
New Riders Publishing
201 West 103rd Street
Indianapolis, IN 46290 USA

Printed in the United States of America   2 3 4 5 6 7 8 9 0

Library of Congress Cataloging-in-Publication Data

97-81027

ISBN: 1-56205-827-4

Warning and Disclaimer

Associate Publisher   *David Dwyer*

Executive Editor   *Mary Foote*

Managing Editor   *Sarah Kearns*

Acquisitions Editor
Danielle Bird

Development Editor
Kezia Endsley

Project Editor
Gina Brown

Copy Editors
Amy Lepore
Julie McNamee
Tom Stevens

Technical Editors
Brian Komar
Christoph Wille

Team Coordinator
Stacey Beheler

Manufacturing Coordinator
Brook Farling

Book Designer
Glenn Larsen

Cover Designer
Dan Armstrong

Cover Production
Casey Price

Director of Production
Larry Klein

Production Manager
Laurie Casey

Production Team Supervisor
Vic Peterson

Graphics Image Specialists
Sadie Crawford
Wil Cruz
Marvin Van Tiem

Production Analysts
Dan Harris
Erich J. Richter

Production Team
Lori Cliburn
Kim Cofer

Indexer
Kevin Fulcher

About the Authors

Jay Adamson is a Senior Network Analyst for a multinational computer consulting firm. He has been teaching in the computer industry for the past eight years, and has been specializing in Microsoft networking for the past four years. His certifications include MCSE for both Windows NT 3.51 and 4.0 and MCT. He greatly appreciates the support and understanding of his wife Sherri and two sons Matthew and Devon. He can be reached at `jaysher@autobahn.mb.ca`.

Emmett Dulaney is a consultant for DS Technical Solutions. An MCSE and CNE, Emmett is also a LAN Server Engineer, and frequent magazine contributor on the topics of NT and certification.

William N. Matsoukas is a Certified NetWare Engineer, and works as a Senior Consultant for an international firm. Bill makes his home in Colorado with his wife Teri and their three children. Living in Colorado affords Bill and his family to concentrate on the more important things in life: bicycling, hiking, mountain climbing, and hockey.

Kristin Wahlquist a CNA, MCSE, and MCT has spent close to six years as a senior technical support professional at WordPerfect and Novell. She has consulted and assisted in network and applications installations for various clients throughout the country. Currently Kristin is an instructor with GSE Erudite Software based out of Phoenix, Arizona. Kristin teaches core NT and several back office courses on the MSCE track.

Kevin Wolford is an MCSE, MCT, Master CNE, and CNI. He has had several careers, including technical writer, pension actuary, and trainer. He is the lead NT trainer for GSE Erudite Software in Salt Lake City, Utah. You also can see Kevin in training videos produced by Keystone Learning Systems of Provo, Utah. Kevin enjoys explaining complex, technical things in a simple manner.

About the Technical Editors

Brian Komar is a trainer and consultant with Online Business Systems. He holds a Bachelor of Commerce degree and several professional designations, including Microsoft Certified Trainer (MCT), Fellow Life Management Institute (FLMI), and Microsoft Certified Systems Engineer (MCSE). Brian's six years of experience in the Information Technology industry is supported by strong business skills and a background in accounting and actuarial services. Online Business Systems is a consulting firm with offices in Winnipeg, Minneapolis, and Calgary. Online develops complete, practical computer solutions. Brian can be reached by e-mail at `bkomar@online-can.com`.

Brian would like to thank his wife Krista for putting up with him for the past few months as this book was produced. He would also like to thank Kezia for assisting with the development of this book as he switched hats between technical editor and author.

Christoph Wille, an MCSE and MCSD, has an extensive background working with OLE, MFC, Microsoft SQL Server, Microsoft operating systems, and Access. He is currently developing web sites with integrated e-commerce as well as working as a consultant for companies that want to connect their private networks to the Internet and who need someone to design their Internet presence.

Trademark Acknowledgments

Contents at a Glance

Contents

3 Managing Resources   109

Introduction

The *MCSE TestPrep* series serves as a study aid for people preparing for Microsoft Certification exams. The series is intended to help reinforce and clarify information that the student is already familiar with by providing sample questions and tests, as well as summary information relevant to each of the exam objectives. The series is not intended to be a single source for student preparation, but the series is a review of information with a set of practice tests—used to increase your familiarity with the exam questions and thus increase your likelihood of success when taking the exam.

Who Should Read This Book

MCSE TestPrep: Windows NT Server 4 Enterprise is designed for network administrators and network engineers who are considering certification as a Microsoft Certified Systems Engineer (MCSE) or as a Microsoft Certified Product (MCP) Specialist. The Enterprise exam ("Exam 70-068: Implementing and Supporting Microsoft Windows NT Server 4.0 in the Enterprise") tests your ability to implement, administer, and troubleshoot systems, as well as your ability to provide technical support to users of the Microsoft Windows NT Server 4 operating system.

How This Book Helps You

In addition to presenting a summary of information relevant to each of the exam objectives, this book provides a wealth of review questions similar to those you encounter in the actual exam. This book is designed to help you make the most of your study time by presenting concise summaries of information that you need to understand to succeed on the exam. The review questions at the end of each objective help reinforce what you have learned. The final exam at the conclusion of each chapter helps you determine if you have mastered the facts.

At the end of the book are two full-length practice exams. For further information on certification and certification exams, check the following:

Microsoft Education: Call (800) 636-7544

Internet: `ftp://ftp.microsoft.com/Services/MSEdCert`

World Wide Web: `http://www.microsoft.com/train_cert/default.htm`

CompuServe Forum: `GO MSEDCERT`

How to Use This Book

You should use this book to make sure that you are ready to take the exam after you are familiar with the exam concepts. Use this book for a final review before taking the test to make sure that all the important concepts are set in your mind, as well as for taking the practice tests at the end of each chapter and at the end of the book. See Appendix B, "All About the Exam," for more information about taking the Microsoft test.

Understanding What the "Implementing and Supporting Microsoft Windows NT 4.0 in the Enterprise" Exam Covers

The "Implementing and Supporting Microsoft Windows NT Server 4.0 in the Enterprise" exam (#70-068) covers six main topic areas, arranged in accordance with test objectives. The exam objectives, listed by topic area, are covered in the following sections.

Planning Objectives

The exam topic areas and their respective objectives include the following:

- Plan the implementation of a directory services architecture. Considerations include:

  - Selecting the appropriate domain model

  - Supporting a single logon account

  - Allowing users to access resources in different domains

- Plan the disk drive configuration for various requirements. Requirements include choosing a fault-tolerance method.

- Choose a protocol for various situations. Protocols include:

  - TCP/IP

  - TCP/IP with DHCP and WINS

  - NWLink IPX/SPX Compatible Transport Protocol

  - Data Link Control (DLC)

  - AppleTalk

Installation and Configuration Objectives

- Install Windows NT Server to perform various server roles. Server roles include:

  - Primary domain controller

  - Backup domain controller

  - Member server

- Configure protocols and protocol bindings. Protocols include:

  - TCP/IP

  - TCP/IP with DHCP and WINS

- NWLink IPX/SPX Compatible Transport Protocol

- DLC

- AppleTalk

- Configure Windows NT Server core services. Services include:

  - Directory Replicator

  - Computer Browser

- Configure hard disks to meet various requirements. Requirements include:

  - Providing redundancy

  - Improving performance

- Configure printers. Tasks include:

  - Adding and configuring a printer

  - Implementing a printer pool

  - Setting print priorities

- Configure a Windows NT Server computer for various types of client computers. Client computer types include:

  - Windows NT Workstation

  - Windows 95

  - Macintosh

Managing Resources Objectives

- Manage user and group accounts. Considerations include:

  - Managing Windows NT user accounts

  - Managing Windows NT user rights

  - Managing Windows NT groups

  - Administering account policies

  - Auditing changes to the user account database

- Create and manage policies and profiles for various situations. Policies and profiles include:

  - Local user profiles

  - Roaming user profiles

  - System policies

- Administer remote servers from various types of client computers. Client computer types include:

  - Windows 95

  - Windows NT Workstation

- Manage disk resources. Tasks include:
  - Creating and sharing resources
  - Implementing permissions and security
  - Establishing file auditing

Connectivity Objectives

- Configure a Windows NT Server for interoperability with NetWare servers by using various tools. Tools include:
  - Gateway Services for NetWare
  - Migration Tool for NetWare
- Install and configure multiprotocol routing to serve various functions. Functions include:
  - Internet router
  - BOOTP/DHCP Relay Agent
  - IPX router
- Install and configure Internet Information Server.
- Install and configure Internet Information services. Services include:
  - World Wide Web
  - DNS
  - Intranet
- Install and configure Remote Access Service (RAS). Configuration options include:
  - Configuring RAS communications
  - Configuring RAS protocols
  - Configuring RAS security

Monitoring and Optimization Objectives

- Establish a baseline for measuring system performance. Tasks include creating a database of measurement data.
- Monitor performance of various functions by using Performance Monitor. Functions include:
  - Processor
  - Memory
  - Disk
  - Network
- Monitor network traffic by using Network Monitor. Tasks include:
  - Collecting data
  - Presenting data
  - Filtering data

- Identify performance bottlenecks.
- Optimize performance for various results. Results include:
  - Controlling network traffic
  - Controlling server load

Troubleshooting Objectives

- Choose the appropriate course of action to resolve installation failures.
- Choose the appropriate course of action to resolve boot failures.
- Choose the appropriate course of action to resolve configuration errors. Tasks include:
  - Backing up and restoring the Registry
  - Editing the Registry
- Choose the appropriate course of action to resolve RAS problems.
- Choose the appropriate course of action to resolve connectivity problems.
- Choose the appropriate course of action to resolve resource access and permission problems.
- Choose the appropriate course of action to resolve fault-tolerance failures. Fault-tolerance methods include:
  - Tape backup
  - Mirroring
  - Stripe set with parity
- Perform advanced problem resolution. Tasks include:
  - Diagnosing and interpreting a blue screen
  - Configuring a memory dump
  - Using the Event Log service

Hardware and Software Recommended for Preparation

MCSE TestPrep: Windows NT Server 4 Enterprise helps you review concepts with which you already have training and experience. To make the most of the review, you need to have as much background and experience as possible. The best way to prepare is to combine studying with working on real networks by using the products on which you will be tested. This section gives you a description of the minimum computer requirements for a good practice environment.

The minimum computer requirements to study everything on which you are tested are: one or more workstations running Windows 95, Windows NT Workstation, and two or more servers running Windows NT Server—all connected by a network.

Windows 95 and Windows NT Workstations require:

- Computer on the Microsoft Hardware Compatibility List
- 486DX, 33 MHz (Pentium recommended)

- 16 MB of RAM (32 MB recommended)
- 200 MB (or larger) hard disk
- 3.5 inch, 1.44 MB floppy drive
- VGA (or Super VGA) video adapter
- VGA (or Super VGA) monitor
- Mouse or equivalent pointing device
- Two-speed (or faster) CD-ROM drive
- Network Interface Card (NIC)
- Presence on an existing network or use of a hub to create a test network
- Microsoft Windows 95

Windows NT Server requires:

- Two computers on the Microsoft Hardware Compatibility List
- 486DX2 66 MHz (or better)
- 32 MB of RAM (64 recommended)
- 340 MB (or larger) hard disk
- 3.5 inch, 1.44 MB floppy drive
- VGA (or Super VGA) video adapter
- VGA (or Super VGA) monitor
- Mouse or equivalent pointing device
- Two-speed (or faster) CD-ROM drive
- Network Interface Card (NIC)
- Presence on an existing network or use of a hub to create a test network
- Microsoft Windows NT Server

Que Corporation

The staff of Que Corporation is committed to bringing you the very best in computer reference material. Each New Riders book is the result of months of work by authors and staff who research and refine the information contained within its covers.

As part of this commitment to you, Que invites your input. Please let us know if you enjoy this book, if you have trouble with the information and examples presented, or if you have a suggestion for the next edition.

Please note, however: Que staff cannot serve as a technical resource for Windows NT Server 4 or for questions about software- or hardware-related problems. Please refer to the documentation that accompanies your software or to the applications' Help systems.

If you have a question or comment about any Que book, there are several ways to contact Que Corporation. We will respond to as many readers as we can. Your name, address, or phone number will never become part of a mailing list or be used for any purpose other than to help us continue to bring you the best books possible.

You can write us at the following address:

Que Corporation
Attn: Publisher
201 W. 103rd Street
Indianapolis, IN 46290

If you prefer, you can fax Que Corporation at:

317-817-7448

You can also send electronic mail to Que at the following Internet address:
certification@mcp.com

Que Corporation is an imprint of Macmillan Computer Publishing. To obtain a catalog or information, or to purchase any Macmillan Computer Publishing book, call 800-428-5331 or visit our web site at http://www.mcp.com.

Thank you for selecting *MCSE TestPrep: Windows NT Server 4 Enterprise*!

CHAPTER 1

Planning

This chapter helps you prepare for the exam by covering the following Planning objectives:

- Select the appropriate directory services architecture for given scenarios (considerations include selecting the appropriate domain model, supporting a single logon account, and allowing users to access different resources in different domains).

- Plan the disk drive configurations for various requirements. Requirements include fault tolerance, stripe sets, and volume sets.

- Select the proper protocol for various situations. Protocols include:

  - TCP/IP

  - TCP/IP with WINS and DHCP

  - NWLink IPX/SPX Compatible Transport Protocol

  - Data Link Control (DLC)

  - AppleTalk

1.1 Selecting the Appropriate Directory Services Architecture

To prepare for this part of the exam, you need to recognize which domain model is appropriate for a given network environment. You need to know how to set up the trusts for each of these models and how to assign groups to give permissions across the trust relationship.

A. Goals of Windows NT 4 Directory Services

A logical grouping of servers and clients in Windows NT is called a *domain*. Domains can be linked together to enable users from one logical group to access servers in another logical group. Administering the accounts in domains and providing links between domains are the main tasks of directory services.

A single domain maintains all the directory database information in the Security Account Manager (SAM). The *SAM* contains all user accounts, Windows NT computer accounts, group accounts, and any account settings assigned in the domain, all of which contribute to the SAM's size. Microsoft recommends that SAM not exceed 40 MB. Table 1.1.1 shows the size of each account or group included in the SAM database.

Table 1.1.1   SAM Database Limitations

SAM Database Item	Size Per Item
User accounts	1.0 KB
Local groups	512 bytes per group plus 36 bytes per user
Global groups	512 bytes per group plus 12 bytes per user
Computer accounts	0.5 KB

The maximum size of the SAM is a physical limitation of the domain. Domains are also often broken into logical units, such as departments within a company. The organizational chart and political influences usually need to be addressed in the design. Individual departments may require control of their own resources.

Directory services are implemented to help you administer and maintain a consistent network environment throughout a WAN or LAN. The main goals of directory services are:

- One user, one account
- Universal resource access
- Centralized administration
- Directory synchronization

1.   One User, One Account

Each user in your network should not have more than one account name or password. Administration is simplified with only one account per user. With one account per user, you can easily assign permission to a single user for resources located anywhere on the network, you can audit your system for any type of access by this user, and it is easier to modify the permissions of a user because the account is located in one place. Having one account is also easier for users because they have to remember only one username and one password.

> BackOffice applications also can use Windows NT usernames and passwords so that you maintain the goal of one user, one account.

2.   Universal Resource Access

With this single account, users should be able to access all resources, regardless of physical location. This is known as *universal resource access*.

By having universal resource access, a user from one domain can access resources in other domains without having a separate account in these resource domains. However, users may not even be aware that they are accessing resources outside of their own domain. When the administrator configures permissions correctly, universal resource access should be transparent to the user.

3. Centralized Administration

The goal of centralized administration is to consolidate the administration of user accounts and resource access to one central location. It's easier to manage user accounts when they are in one central place than when they are scattered on different servers throughout the enterprise.

4. Directory Synchronization

All directory services information must be available to all the computers in the network so that users can access resources whenever they need. This information is copied to all domain controllers through *directory synchronization*. Directory synchronization is automatic within domains in Windows NT Server 4. By using trust relationships (discussed in the next section), domains communicate with each other to share the database information.

Setting up a trust relationship does not synchronize one domain's accounts with another. Rather, a trust allows one domain's directory services database to be accessed from another domain. Accounts are not copied from one domain to another; the domains cross-reference the other domain's databases through the trust.

B. Trust Relationships

A *trust relationship* is a secured communication link between two domains implemented as a Remote Procedure Call, or RPC. One of the domains acts as the trusted domain, and the other is the trusting domain. The trusting domain permits users from the trusted domain to access its resources.

Because a user can access resources in another domain through the trust, the user doesn't need a new account in the resource domain. This one account can access resources throughout the network on different domains as long as trust relationships are properly configured. Accounts can be administered in one central place while still allowing access to remote resources. With more than one domain in the network, using trust relationships is critical to meeting the goals of directory services.

1. Trusted Versus Trusting

Every trust relationship has a trusted and a trusting domain. The trusted domain is the domain that contains the user accounts. The trusted domain is also referred to as the *account domain*.

The trusting domain uses the accounts from the trusted domain. Located in the trusting domain are the resources that you need to share. The trusting domain assigns security permissions to any user in its SAM and any user in a trusted domain's SAM. By creating a trusting domain, departments can maintain control of their resources while still allowing the users to be administered centrally. A trusting domain is also referred to as a *resource domain*.

2. Graphically Representing a Trust Relationship

When drawing trust relationships, domains are represented as circles and the direction of the trust relationship is depicted by an arrow. The direction of the arrow always points to the trusted domain. One way to remember the direction of the arrow is to always point to whom you can trust. The arrow head in a trust diagram points to the trusted (account) domain.

A trust relationship always involves two domains. One domain contains user accounts. The other domain has resources, such as files, printers, or applications, that users in the account domain need to access. The account domain is known as the trusted domain. The resource domain is known as the trusting domain, so in a trust diagram the trust arrow points from the resource domain to the account domain. If you become unsure during the test, try drawing the trust relationship on paper.

3. Planning Trust Relationships

Administrators from both domains in a trust relationship must configure their domains to participate in the trust. A trust relationship cannot be established from one domain. The requirements for setting up a trust are the following:

- The trust relationship can only be established between Windows NT Server domains.

- The domains must be able to make an RPC connection. Basically, the PDC from each domain should be able to make a network connection. However, the PDCs cannot have an existing network connection when you try to establish the trust.

> **You can use the following command to terminate all sessions with any other computers:**
>
> ```
> net use * /d
> ```

- The trust relationship must be set up by a user with administrator access.

- The number of trusts and type of trusts should be determined prior to the implementation.

- Determine where the user accounts reside; this is the trusted domain.

- Determine where the resources reside; this is the trusting domain.

Always define the role of your domain before configuring the trust. When implementing a trust, you must specify in the interface which domain is trusted and which domain is trusting.

4. Establishing Trust Relationships

Establishing a trust relationship must be completed by an administrator from each domain in the trust relationship by using the Trust Relationships dialog box. This dialog box is accessed from User Manager for Domains by selecting Trust Relationships from the Policies menu.

This dialog box has two different sections. The administrator specifies in the dialog box the relationship of the other domain in the trust relationship. The name of the administrator's own domain never appears in the Trust Relationships dialog box; only the name of the trust partner appears:

- The trusted domains section is filled in by the trusting domain.

- The trusting domains section is filled in by the trusted domain.

You can configure the trust in either order; however, Microsoft recommends the trusted domain initiate the trust by entering the name of the trusting domain. When the trusting domain completes the trust by entering the name of the trusted domain, a message "Trust Successfully Established" is displayed.

If the trust relationship was established in the opposite order (trusting domain initiates the trust), it can still be completed; however, you receive a dialog box warning that the trust could not be verified. In this case, the trust is not immediately established (it can take up to 15 minutes), and you need to manually verify the trust later.

The steps needed to establish a trust relationship are as follows:

1. From a command prompt, type **net use** to see if you have any connections with the PDC in the other domain. If you have connections, type the following in the command prompt to end these connections:

   `net use * /d`

2. From the trusted domain, start User Manager for Domains, and then select the Trust Relationship command from the Policies menu.

3. From the trusted domain, add the name of the trusting domain. A password for the trust can be entered, but is optional.

4. When the trusting domain has been added into the Trust Relationships dialog box, the trusted domain can then close the screen.

5. From the trusting domain, open the Trust Relationships dialog box and add the name of the trusted domain. Type the password specified by the administrator in the trusted domain.

6. After the trusted domain is added, you should see the "Trust Successfully Established" message.

When a trust is established, Windows NT changes the password that was used to establish the trust. The domain controllers in both domains know the new password, however it is not visible to the users. Frequently, this password is changed by Windows NT for added security. If one of the domains in the trust relationship was to break the trust, the trust could not be reestablished without breaking both sides and starting the trust relationship from the beginning. This is because the administrators do not know the current correct password.

---

a.   One-Way Trusts

A *one-way trust* is a trust relationship with a single trusted domain and a single trusting domain.

The accounts exist in the trusted domain, and the trusting domain has resources that are assigned permissions to users in the trusted domain.

b.   Two-Way Trusts

A *two-way trust* is nothing more than two one-way trusts. In a two-way trust, both domains are trusted domains and trusting domains. This type of trust is necessary because each domain has user accounts and also has resources that users in the other domain need to access.

c.   Non-Transitive Trusts

Trust relationships are non-transitive, in other words you cannot pass through one trust into another. A trust relationship involves only two domains. The domain with user accounts must be explicitly trusted by the domain with the resources the users need to access.

Assume an environment in which DomainA trusts DomainB and DomainB trusts DomainC. Because trusts are not transitive, a user from DomainC can access resources in DomainB, but cannot access any resources in DomainA, even though DomainB and DomainA also have a trust relationship. There isn't a trust relationship between DomainA and DomainC, which are the two domains in question. DomainA must trust DomainC if a user in DomainC wants to access resources in DomainA.

5.   Removing Trusts

You remove a trust relationship by removing the name of the other domain from the Trust Relationships dialog box. If either domain, trusted or trusting, removes the opposite domain, the trust is broken. If the broken half of the trust tries to reestablish the trust, the trust fails because the password assigned to the trust relationship has been changed by Windows NT.

A trust also can be broken if the domain name of one of the members of the trust relationship is changed. The trust relationship will not be reestablished even if the name of the domain is changed back.

> **When the domain controllers in a domain are stopped, the trust is temporarily broken. If any domain controller for the domain comes back up, the trust is reestablished.**

6.   Accounts in Trust Relationships

When a trust relationship is established, you have access to accounts in trusted domains as well as your own domain accounts.

You can create two types of user accounts, but only one of them can be used across a trust—global accounts.

a.   Global Accounts

A *global account* is the default user account type. Every user account is a global account unless you specify the type of account as local. Global accounts are designed to be used across trusts and can be assigned access in the local domain and all the trusting domains.

b.   Local Accounts

A local account is a special account type with some limitations:

- Cannot be given permissions across trusts, thus they are only used for accounts in non-trusted domains.

- Do not support interactive logon processes.

- Require their own passwords. Users will not be able to automatically synchronize passwords from one local account to another.

The local account cannot be used across trusts and is used only locally in your own domain. This type of account can be used to assign permissions to a user who only needs access to one domain in your enterprise. You, for example, can use local accounts for temporary employees who only need to access specific applications or resources. Because the temporary employees are set up as local accounts, they can never access resources outside the domain the account is created in, which provides additional security. Users from another domain can use a local account if they connect to a share by specifying the local account's username and password.

To specify a local account, select the account options in the User Properties dialog box, and select the Local Account option.

c.   Global Groups and Local Groups

Microsoft recommends using groups for assigning all permissions. Users then inherit permissions from the groups to which they belong. Assigning permissions through groups is preferred to assigning permissions directly to individual users.

In Windows NT Server, the two types of groups are local and global. Local groups are restricted to being used where they are created, such as within a domain for local groups created on a domain controller. On the other hand, global groups are designed to contain users used across trusts.

The recommended strategy is to collect users together in global groups and to assign permission to local groups. Users get permission to use resources when global groups they belong to are added to local groups for resources they want to access. Users could be placed in global groups based on job function, department membership, or a common need to access certain resources on the network. Local groups are created where the resource is located. Resources could be file shares, printers, or applications. Permissions to use the resource are assigned to the local group. Then, the global groups with the users are added to the local groups with the permissions.

If you need to have different levels of access for one resource, you need to create more than one local group. If, for example, you wanted users of an application to have read rights while allowing administrators full control rights, you would create one local group with read permission. The global group with the application users would be assigned to this local group. You would also create another local group with full control permission. The global group with the application administrators would be assigned to this local group.

This method of granting permissions enables resource administrators to control access to their resources without having to control which groups users belong to. Assigning users to groups is typically done by account administrators. The resource administrator just controls which rights are given to a local group and which global group is added to the local group.

However, the resource administrator does not control who belongs to this global group. The membership of global groups is controlled by the administrator in the accounts domain. The resource administrator must "trust" the account administrator to assign the appropriate users to the global group. Because the resource administrator is controlling permissions, all the accounts administrator needs to do to give a user rights is to add that user to the appropriate global group. To take rights away from a user, the administrator removes the user from a global group.

Built-in groups are automatically created in a Windows NT domain. Table 1.1.2 shows the built-in local groups and Table 1.1.3 shows the built-in global groups.

Table 1.1.2   Built-In Local Groups

Local Group	Initially Contains	Rights
Administrators	Domain Admins, Administrator	Administrator account, to manage and maintain the entire system.
Users	Domain Users	Access resources, day-to-day operation of computer system.
Guests	Domain Guests	Guest account disabled by default.
Server Operators	None	Share and Stop sharing resources. Shut down/Lock servers. Stop and Start services. Server Maintenance. Backup and restore server.
Print Operators	None	Share and Stop sharing printers. Manage printers.
Backup Operators	None	Backup and restore server.
Account Operators	None	Create and manage user and group accounts.
Replicators	None	Used for the Directory Replicator service.

Table 1.1.3   Built-In Global Groups

Global Group	Initial Accounts	Member of...
Domain Admins	Administrator	Administrators
Domain Users	Administrator	Users
	All accounts created in domain.	
Domain Guests	Guests	Guests

Remember that only global groups and global user accounts can be used across trust relationships.

d. *Assigning Permissions Across a Trust*

Assigning permissions across a trust uses Microsoft's strategy to give users rights—global groups with users are added to local groups with permissions. When trusts are involved, a global group from a trusted domain is added to a local group in a trusting domain. Adding global groups from another domain to a local group is done in much the same way as adding global groups from the same domain. Create or edit the local group in User Manager, and then choose the Add button to add members to the group. Then, select the trusted domain from the List Names pull-down menu. The global groups and users from the trusted domain are listed and can be added to the local group.

Local groups and local accounts cannot be seen from this view because local accounts and local groups cannot be used across trusts.

7. The NetLogon Service in a Trust

After trust relationships are set up and permissions assigned, users from trusted domains must be authenticated to get access to the resources in a trusting domain. Similar to logging on to a domain, the user account must be verified and the security permissions must be assigned to the user account. The NetLogon service is responsible for handling logon requests and authentication. When requests are made across a trust, the action is called *pass-through authentication*.

a. Pass-Through Authentication

Pass-through authentication enables the trusting domain to handle the logon request, but it looks into the SAM of the trusted domain to verify that the account is valid.

If a user is using a computer in DomainB to log on to DomainA, the request to validate the logon must be passed on to DomainA from DomainB because DomainB does not have any record in its SAM for this user account. The communication between the two domains to validate the user is called pass-through authentication.

C. Windows NT Server 4 Domain Models

Windows NT domains can be organized into one of four different domain models. Each of these models supports the goal of directory services. Although there are other ways to combine domains, these four domain models (single domain, single master, multiple master, and complete trust) are the ones Microsoft expects you to know for the exam.

1. Selecting your Domain Model

When you are selecting a domain model, you should consider a number of points:

- Number of user accounts
- Number of organizational, or departmental, domains required
- Whether centralized account administration is required
- Whether centralized or distributed resource administration is required

Responses to these questions help you select the correct domain model.

2. Single Domain Model

The single domain model is the easiest to implement. It places all users, groups, and resources into a single domain. The single domain is the starting point of all the domain models; in any implementation you must ensure that each domain can function as a single domain before you should consider any of the other models.

The single domain model is ideal for smaller organizations. The benefits in a single domain model are as follows:

- Simple installation; just install the first server as a Primary Domain Controller and you have a single domain model.
- Centralized administration of accounts because there is only one domain database.

- Centralized administration of resources because all the resources are in one domain.

- No trust relationships to establish.

The limitations of the single domain model affect larger organizations that have a distributed WAN environment. The limitations of the single domain model are as follows:

- Can only support a SAM database of 40 MB, which is the maximum size Microsoft recommends for a single domain.

- No departmental administrative controls (decentralized administration) can be assigned because there is only one domain database for assigning security permissions.

- Browsing is slow if the domain contains a large number of servers and resources.

The total size of a domain is determined by the number of user, computer, and group accounts. The size of each of these accounts is discussed earlier in the section "Goals of Windows NT 4 Directory Services."

3.   Single Master Domain Model

The single master domain model has one domain with user accounts and other domains to control access to resources. This model maintains the centralized administration of user accounts while allowing decentralized management of resources.

These resource domains can maintain their own resources and permissions, with all user accounts residing in the master domain. From a user's perspective, the domain appears to be one large system, every user logs on to the master. The users can connect to other domains in the environment without requiring additional user accounts or passwords.

The benefits of a single master domain model are

- Centralized administration of user accounts.

- Resources can be distributed and administered throughout resource domains.

- Each resource domain can have a domain administrator to maintain its resources, without giving access to the master domain.

- The trust relationships are fairly easy to implement.

- Maintains one user, one account goal of directory services.

- Global groups can be maintained from the master domain.

The limitations of a single master domain model are similar to those of the single domain model. The single master domain model still uses one domain database for all the users, so the number of user accounts this model supports is limited. The limitations of the single master domain model are

- Local groups must be defined in each domain, both master and resource domains.

- Maximum number of users is limited by the 40 MB maximum size of the SAM database.

- Resource domains have no control over group memberships of global groups from the master domain.

- Trust relationships have to be established in the proper direction to maintain the directory services structure.

The single master domain model is best suited for organizations with less than 20,000 users that require some departmental resource administration. This model is excellent for companies with locations spread across a WAN, because the trust relationships allow for the centralized administration of user accounts.

a. Trusts in a Single Master Domain Model

The trust relationships in a single master domain model are relatively easy to implement. In this model, the master domain holds all the user accounts and global groups, and may also have resources. The other domains in the organization become resource domains. The master domain is the trusted domain, whereas the resource domains are the trusting domains. All resource domains trust the master domain.

b. Accounts in a Single Master Domain Model

All user accounts in this model reside in the master domain, so all the global groups for the organization must also be defined in the master domain. Users or global groups from the master domain can then be accessed by any of the resource domains.

At the resource domains, local groups must be created with permissions for resources. Global groups and users from the master domain are then added to these local groups to give users access to the local resources. Remember that Microsoft stresses adding global groups rather than individual user accounts to local groups.

To assign administrator rights for the resource domains, administrators from the master domain are added to the resource domain's local administrators group. The simplest way to do this is to add the Domain Admins global group from the master domain to the local administrators group in each of the resource domains.

4. Multiple Master Domain Model

The multiple master domain model is designed for very large organizations that have users distributed across multiple domains. In this model, there is more than one master domain. Each master domain contains user and global group accounts to be used by all other domains in the environment. In this model, account administration can still be centralized. For all administrators to manage accounts, the Domain Admins global group from each master domain must be added to the local administrators group in each master domain.

The multiple master domain model is the most scaleable of the domain models. Each master domain can be the maximum recommended size of 40 MB. Additional master domains can be added to this model to enable the network to expand to include an unlimited number of users. The number of master domains available in this model is not limited.

The advantages of the multiple master domain model are the following:

- Scaleable to networks with a large number of users.

- Resources are grouped into resource domains to enable distributed resource management.

- Each master domain can have a domain administrator, or can be grouped to achieve centralized administration.

- User accounts and global groups are maintained in the master domains.

The limitations of the multiple master domain model are the following:

- Complex trust relationships have to be configured to maintain this domain model.

- User accounts are distributed across multiple master domains.

- Global groups may have to be defined multiple times, one in each master domain.

The multiple master domain model requires more planning than the single domain or the single master domain models. Domain planners must decide how the master domains are divided. Master domains can be based on geographical areas or different parts of an organization, such as unique business units. Centralized account administration can still be achieved in this model by adding the global Domain Admins group from each master domain into the local administrators group in all the other master domains. The trust relationships are more complex in this model.

a. Trusts in a Multiple Master Domain Model

The trust relationships in a multiple master domain model are configured similar to the single master domain. All resource domains trust the master domain. However, the multiple master domain model has more than one master domain so each resource domain must trust *all* master domains. Each master domain must have a two-way trust with all other master domains. There are no trusts between the resource domains.

You can determine the number of trusts required for a multiple master domain model by using the following formula:

```
M*(M-1)+(R*M)
```

M is the number of master domains, and R is the number of resource domains. The formula indicates that every master domain must trust every other master domain (M*M–1) and every resource domain must trust each master domain (R*M).

> **Remember that two-way trusts are actually two one-way trusts.**

b. Accounts in a Multiple Master Domain Model

The accounts in the multiple master are distributed across multiple master domains. Each user still has only one account; however, global groups may have to be duplicated in all the master domains. If, for example, an organization has members of the marketing department spread across both master domains, a marketing global group must be created in each master domain because users can only be assigned to global groups in their own domains. To give these marketing users access to a resource, the marketing global group from each master domain must be added to the local group for that resource.

The key points to remember regarding accounts in a multiple master domain are the following:

- User accounts are located in one of the master domains.

- Global groups are defined in all the master domains.

- Local groups are defined in resource domains, and contain global groups from all the master domains.

The multiple master domain model is best suited for large organizations that have more than 20,000 users and want to maintain centralized control of user accounts, while allowing resources to be administered departmentally.

5.   Complete Trust Model

The complete trust model enables each domain to maintain their own control of users and resources with the opportunity to assign permissions to users of any other domain in the model. The complete trust model implements two-way trust relationships between every domain in the environment. Each domain is both an account domain and a resource domain.

This model is scaleable and flexible because domains can easily be added and removed from the model. However, the model does not allow for centralized administration of user accounts or resources.

a.   Trusts in a Complete Trust Model

The complete trust model requires more trust relationships than any other domain model. Every domain has a two-way trust with every other domain.

You can use the following formula to determine the number of trusts required in a complete trust model:

```
N*(N-1)
```

N is the total number of domains in the model.

b.   Accounts in a Complete Trust Model

Every domain is responsible for administering the user accounts and global groups in their own domains. The local administrators are also responsible for creating local groups and assigning members to them. This domain model makes it difficult to centrally manage the user accounts, and is designed for environments that do not require centralized administration.

1.1.1   Exercise: Selecting the Appropriate Directory Services Architecture

The type of questions you will see on the enterprise exam will be scenario-based questions. The questions will supply you with some basic information and you will have to select the appropriate domain model for a given situation. Try out a few questions to determine whether you understand the directory services architecture:

1. ABC Corporation has locations in Toronto, New York, and San Francisco. They want to install Windows NT Server 4.0 to encompass all its locations in a single WAN environment. The head office is located in New York, and all user accounts will be created at that location. In Toronto and San Francisco, ABC has numerous applications and resources that users from all three locations may need to access. What is the best domain model for ABC's directory services implementation? Pick only one answer.

    A. Single domain model

    B. Single master domain model

    C. Multiple master domain model

    D. Complete trust domain model

2. JPS Printing has a single location with 1,000 users spread across the LAN. They have special printers and applications installed on the servers in their environment and need to be able to centrally manage the user accounts and the resources. Which domain model would best fit their needs? Choose one.

    A. Single domain model

    B. Single master domain model

    C. Multiple master domain model

    D. Complete trust model

3. Worldwide Training has locations spread across the world. The North American headquarters are located in Seattle, the European headquarters in London, England. Smaller locations are distributed throughout the world. All the user accounts would be maintained from the two corporate headquarters, but each location needs to manage their own resources. Which domain model would best fit their scenario?

    A. Single domain model

    B. Single master domain model

    C. Multiple master domain model

    D. Complete trust model

4. ABC Corporation has a single domain model to maintain the directory services in its Toronto location. They manage all users and resources for their current network. ABC Corporation is merging with DEF Corporation. The two companies will still run as separate companies, but want to share network resources. Each domain would be completely responsible for user accounts and resources in their separate domains. Which domain model would allow the two domains to maintain account and resource control, but still allow access between the two domains?

    A. Single domain model

    B. Single master domain model

    C. Multiple master domain model

    D. Complete trust model

1.1.2 Exercise: Synchronizing the Domain Controllers

Exercise 1.1.2 shows how to manually synchronize a Backup Domain Controller within your domain.

1. Click Start, Programs, Administrative Tools, and select the Server Manager.

2. Highlight the BDC (Backup Domain Controller) in your computer list.

3. Select the Computer menu, then select Synchronize with Primary Domain Controller.

1.1.3 Exercise: Establishing a Trust Relationship Between Domains

Exercise 1.1.3 shows how to establish a trust relationship between multiple domains. To complete this exercise, you must have two Windows NT Server computers, each installed as Primary Domain Controllers in unique domains.

1. From the trusted domain select Start, Programs, Administrative Tools, and click User Manager for Domains. The User Manager for Domains application starts.

2. Select the Policies menu and select Trust Relationships. The Trust Relationships dialog box appears.

3. In the trusting domain section, click Add and enter the name of your trusting domain. You can leave the password blank.

4. When the trusting domain information has been entered, click OK and close the Trust Relationships dialog box.

5. From the trusting domain, start the User Manager for Domains.

6. Select the Policies menu and select Trust Relationships.

7. In the trusted domain box, click Add and press Enter. Type in the same password that you entered in step 3, and then click OK. If you left the password blank, do not enter a password here.

8. A message should appear stating that the trust relationship was successfully established.

9. To test the trust relationship, log off from the trusting domain. When logging back on, select the drop-down list from the Domain section of the logon screen. You should see the name of the trusted domain and your current domain.

1.1.4 Exercise: Designing a Network Domain Model

Exercise 1.1.4 steps you through the planning phases of your Windows NT domain model. Look at the situation below, then work through the planning of a domain model.

Situation: The ABC Corporation has a building in Los Angeles, a production department in San Francisco, and a satellite location in San Diego. The Los Angeles location has 1,500 users and holds the central IT department that is responsible for all network administration. The other two locations, San Francisco and San Diego, each have a local administrator who is responsible for network servers and resources but does not need administrator access in Los Angeles.

Answer the following questions to help step you through the planning phases of your network.

1. How many domains would you require for this situation?

2. Which domain would hold all the user accounts?

3. Sketch the domain diagram for the scenario; make sure you include all trust relationships in the diagram.

4. What groups would the local administrator for the resource domains need to be placed in?

1.1 Practice Problems

1. ABC Company has 500 users located in a single location. The MIS Director wants to administer the accounts and resources for the network in one central place. Which domain model is best for this situation?

    A. Single domain model

    B. Single master domain model

    C. Multiple master domain model

    D. Complete trust model

2. The Acme Corporation has 20 locations. Administrators at each location want to manage the user accounts for their location. Resource access will be controlled by departments at each location. Which domain model is best for this situation?

    A. Single domain model

    B. Single master domain model

    C. Multiple master domain model

    D. Complete trust model

3. Riverton City wants to install an NT network. They have 600 employees located in five divisions. The network administrator wants to manage all the user accounts, but will allow administrators in each division to control access to their resources. Which domain model is best for this situation?

    A. Single domain model

    B. Single master domain model

    C. Multiple master domain model

    D. Complete trust model

4. Mid-Size Inc. has 30,000 users who each have an NT Workstation for their desktop computers. The network needs to have centralized control of user accounts

while allowing branch offices to control their resources. Which domain model is best for this situation?

    A. Single domain model

    B. Single master domain model

    C. Multiple master domain model

    D. Complete trust model

5. Big Company has 20,000 users who each have a Windows NT workstation. For their domain, the MIS Director wants the MIS department to maintain user accounts and to manage the resources on the network. Which domain model is best for this situation?

    A. Single domain model

    B. Single master domain model

    C. Multiple master domain model

    D. Complete trust model

6. XYZ, Inc. has 100 users scattered in three locations. The administrators at each location want to control their own resources. However, the administrators at headquarters insist on creating all the user accounts. Which domain model is best for this situation?

    A. Single domain model

    B. Single master domain model

    C. Multiple master domain model

    D. Complete trust model

7. Disagree Corp. has seven locations. Administrators at each location refuse to allow others to manage their users or control access to their resources. The administrators will, however, allow other users to access their resources if the local administrators allow it. Which domain model is best for this situation?

    A. Single domain model

    B. Single master domain model

   C.   Multiple master domain model

   D.   Complete trust model

8.   The Getting Bigger By The Minute Company has 50,000 users. Each user has a Windows 95 workstation. Company management wants the corporate network administrators to administer all user accounts. Management also wants resources to be controlled by local administrators who understand who needs access to each resource. Which domain model is best for this situation?

   A.   Single domain model

   B.   Single master domain model

   C.   Multiple master domain model

   D.   Complete trust model

The following scenario applies to questions 9–12. A different solution to the scenario is proposed for each question.

Scenario: MCSEs-R-Us has three locations—Headquarters, R&D, and Manufacturing. Users in Manufacturing use files at Headquarters and R&D in addition to files on their own servers. Users at the other locations access files only on local servers.

9.   *Required results*: Centrally manage all user accounts; centrally manage access to all resources; users at Manufacturing must access resources at Headquarters and R&D. *Optional results*: Users at Headquarters can access resources at Manufacturing; users at R&D can access resources at Manufacturing.

   Solution: Implement a single master domain model with the master domain at Headquarters. Add the Domain Users group from Headquarters to the local Users group on each server to which users need access.

   A.   The proposed solution produces the required results and produces both optional results.

   B.   The proposed solution produces the required results and produces only one optional result.

   C.   The proposed solution produces the required results but does not produce any optional results.

   D.   The proposed solution does not produce the required results.

10.   *Required Results:* Headquarters manages all user accounts; manufacturing must access resources at Headquarters and R&D. *Optional Results*: R&D can access resources at Manufacturing; headquarters can access resources at R&D.

   Solution: Implement a single domain model. Add the Domain Users group to the local Users group on any server that needs to be accessed by users.

   A.   The proposed solution produces the required results and produces both optional results.

   B.   The proposed solution produces the required results and produces only one optional result.

   C.   The proposed solution produces the required results but does not produce any optional results.

   D.   The proposed solution does not produce the required results.

11.   The question is based on the scenario presented for question 9. *Required Result*: Users at Manufacturing need to access resources at Headquarters and R&D. *Optional Results*: Administrators at each location manage their own accounts; access to resources is managed from a central location.

Solution: Implement a complete trust domain model. Create accounts for each user in the domain for their location. Add the Domain Users groups from each domain to the local Users group on each server to which users need access.

A. The proposed solution produces the required result and produces both optional results.

B. The proposed solution produces the required result and produces only one optional result.

C. The proposed solution produces the required result but does not produce any optional results.

D. The proposed solution does not produce the required result.

12. *Required Result*: Users at Manufacturing must access resources at Headquarters and R&D. *Optional Results*: Users at Headquarters can access resources at Manufacturing; users at R&D can access resources at Manufacturing.

Solution: Create a domain for each location. Create trust relationships in which Manufacturing trusts R&D, and Manufacturing and Headquarters trust each other with a two-way trust. Assign domain users from each domain to the local Users group where users need to access resources.

A. The proposed solution produces the required result and produces both optional results.

B. The proposed solution produces the required result and produces only one optional result.

C. The proposed solution produces the required result but does not produce any optional results.

D. The proposed solution does not produce the required result.

13. How are the trusts configured in a single master domain model?

A. The master domain trusts all the resource domains in a one-way trust.

B. The resource domains trust the master domain with a one-way trust and trusts the other resource domains with two-way trusts.

C. The master domain is trusted by all the resource domains.

D. All the domains trust each other with two-way trusts.

14. What can be added to a local group in a resource domain in a multiple master domain model?

A. Members of the resource domain

B. Members of the resource domain and any master domain

C. Members of resource domain and global groups from the resource domain

D. Members of the resource domain and any master domain and global groups from any of these domains

15. An administrator in a resource domain is administering a local group on a server in his domain. The administrator adds members to the group by selecting a trusted domain. What can the administrator add to the local group from the trusted domain?

A. Local groups from the trusted domain

B. Global groups from the trusted domain

C. Global and local groups from the trusted domain

D. Users and global groups from the trusted domain

16. Which utility is used to create trust relationships?

    A. Server Manager

    B. User Manager for Domains

    C. Trust Manager

    D. DNS Manager

17. The Sales domain trusts the HR domain. The HR domain trusts the Accounting domain. How can users in the Accounting domain access resources in the Sales domain?

    A. Add a global group from the Accounting domain to a local group in the Sales domain.

    B. Add a global group from the Accounting domain to a global group in the HR domain, and then add the global group from the HR domain to a local group in the Sales domain.

    C. Add a global group from the Sales domain to a local group in the Accounting domain.

    D. Users in the Accounting domain cannot access resources in the Sales domain.

18. What best describes the trust relationships in a complete trust domain model?

    A. Each domain trusts every other domain.

    B. Each domain trusts the complete domain.

    C. All the resource domains and the master domain share a one-way trust.

    D. All the resource domains and the master domain share a two-way trust.

19. How should trust relationships be established?

    A. The trusting domain should specify the name of the trusted domain, and then the trusted domain should specify the name of the trusting domain.

    B. The trusting domain should specify the name of the trusted domain and the trusting domain along with a password; the trusted domain then enters the password.

    C. The trusted domain should specify the name of the trusting domain and the trusted domain along with a password; the trusting domain then enters the password.

    D. The trusted domain should specify the name of the trusting domain, and then the trusting domain should specify the name of the trusted domain.

20. What happens if the trust relationship is initiated by the trusting domain?

    A. A dialog box appears indicating that the trust relationship is established.

    B. The trust relationship is established without a dialog box confirming the trust.

    C. The trust relationship cannot be established.

    D. A two-way trust is established.

The following scenario applies to questions 21–24. A different solution to the scenario is proposed for each question.

Scenario: Contra Costa County has domains at each of their county offices in Concord, Martinez, and Richmond. The domains have member servers in addition to domain controllers. Each of the users has a Windows NT workstation.

1

21. *Required Result*: Server administrators in Concord need to configure domain controllers in all three domains. *Optional Results*: Server administrators in Concord need to configure member servers in all three domains; server administrators in Concord need to configure Windows NT workstations in all three domains.

Solution: The Martinez and Richmond domains are configured to trust the Concord domain. The Server Operators group from the Concord domain is added to the Server Operators group in the Martinez and Richmond domains.

A. The proposed solution produces the required result and produces both optional results.

B. The proposed solution produces the required result and produces only one optional result.

C. The proposed solution produces the required result but does not produce any optional results.

D. The proposed solution does not produce the required result.

22. *Required Result*: Administrators for the Concord domain need to administer the Richmond and Martinez domains. *Optional Results*: Administrators for the Concord domain need to administer the member servers of the Richmond and Martinez domains; administrators for the Concord domain need to administer the Windows NT workstations of the Richmond and Martinez domains.

Solution: The three domains are configured in a single master domain model with the Concord domain as the master domain. The Domain Admins group from the Concord domain is added to the Administrators group of the Martinez and Richmond domains.

A. The proposed solution produces the required result and produces both optional results.

B. The proposed solution produces the required result and produces only one optional result.

C. The proposed solution produces the required result but does not produce any optional results.

D. The proposed solution does not produce the required result.

23. *Required Result*: Administrators need to configure user accounts in any domain. *Optional Results*: Administrators need to back up any Windows NT machine in any domain; Administrators need to modify network settings on the member servers in any domain.

Solution: The three domains are configured in a complete trust model. The Domain Admins group from each domain is added to the administrators group in the other domains and the administrators group on each Windows NT member server in each domain.

A. The proposed solution produces the required results and produces both optional results.

B. The proposed solution produces the required results and produces only one optional result.

C. The proposed solution produces the required results but does not produce any optional results.

D. The proposed solution does not produce the required results.

24. *Required Result*: Administrators from the Concord domain need to administer member servers in the Richmond and Martinez domains. *Optional Results*: Administrators from the Concord domain need to manage domain accounts in the Richmond domain; administrators from the Concord domain need to back up domain controllers in the Martinez domain.

    Solution: The three domains are configured in a complete trust domain model. Domain Admins from the Concord domain is added to the Account Operators group in the Richmond domain. The default group assignments are used for the Concord to Martinez domain.

    A. The proposed solution produces the required result and produces both optional results.

    B. The proposed solution produces the required result and produces only one optional result.

    C. The proposed solution produces the required result but does not produce any optional results.

    D. The proposed solution does not produce the required result.

25. You are planning a complete trust domain model with four domains. How many trust relationships are required for this model?

    A. 4

    B. 6

    C. 10

    D. 12

1.1.1 Answers and Explanations: Exercise

For more information regarding directory services, see the section in this chapter titled "Selecting the Appropriate Directory Services Architecture." The following are the solutions to the exercise questions.

1. **B** Single master domain model; the key phrase that led to the answer was the centralized account administration, with distributed resource management.

2. **A** Single domain model; small network environment requiring centralized user and resource administration.

3. **C** Multiple master domain model; large organizations that require multiple account or master domains for user administration with distributed resource management.

4. **D** Complete trust domain model; each domain is completely independent of the other, allowing access into resources across the domains.

If you get into the habit of drawing out the domain models, or more importantly, the trust relationships in the scenario-based questions, you will find them easier to understand. Watch for key phrases in the questions; they generally lead you to the selection of the appropriate domain model. Some key phrases to watch for are the following:

- **Centralized user accounts:** When centralized user accounts are required, it narrows your selection to single domain, single master, or multiple master.

- **Distributed resource management:** This distribution of resources is available in single master domain model, multiple master domain model, and complete trust domain model.

- **Distributed users and resources:** The only model that offers both of these is the complete trust model.

- **Select domains to maintain user accounts with distributed resources:** The multiple master allows for numerous account (master) domains and distributed resource domains.

- **Large organization with 20,000 or more users:** This is restricted to multiple master or complete trust domain models.

- **Small organizations with less than 20,000 users:** Best models are single domain or single master domain.

By combining all these items, you should be able to select the appropriate domain model in any situation with which you are presented on the Enterprise exam.

1.1.2   Answers and Explanations: Exercise

This exercise taught you how to manually synchronize a Backup Domain Controller within your domain.

1.1.3   Answers and Explanations: Exercise

This exercise taught you how to establish a trust relationship between multiple domains.

1.1.4   Answers and Explanations: Exercise

1. Three domains would be required for this situation. One domain is needed for all user accounts in Los Angeles. Another domain is needed for the resource admin in San Franscisco. A third domain is necessary for the resource admin in San Diego. Only one account domain is needed to hold all the user accounts because the 1,500 accounts will easily fit in the 40 MB limit for the SAM database.

2. The Los Angeles domain would contain all the user accounts because the department is centrally located there.

3. See Figure 1.1.

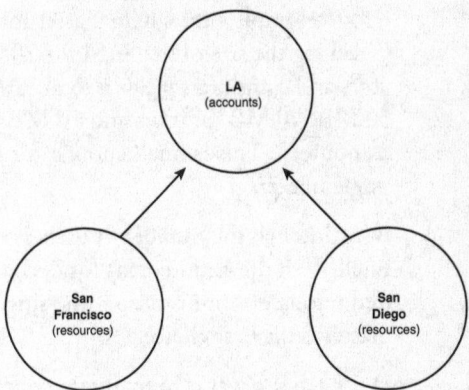

4. The resource administrator would be placed into a global group on the Los Angeles domain. That global group would then be placed into the Administrators group on each of the resource domains.

1.1   Answers and Explanations: Practice Problems

1. **A**   With a small number of users in one location and centralized administration of both accounts and resources, the single domain is the only possible answer.

2. **D**   Each domain controls both accounts and resource administration. The only way to give all these users access to resources in all the other domains is by using the complete trust model.

3. **B**   A small number of users with centralized account administration means a single accounts domain. With the demand for decentralized resource administration, separate resource domains must be created, thus necessitating the single master domain model.

4. **C**   Centralized control of users with decentralized administration suggests the single master domain model. However, with 30,000 users and 30,000 computer accounts, the SAM database would be 45 MB (30 MB for users and 15 MB for

computer accounts), which exceeds the recommended size for a single master. Therefore, multiple master is needed.

5. **B** Centralized administration of accounts and decentralized control of resources implies the single master model. Checking the size of the SAM for 20,000 users and computers yields a total SAM of 30 MB (20 MB for users and 10 MB for computers). This is small enough for a single master.

6. **B** Although the number of users is small, with the requirement for decentralized resource administration, the single master is the best choice.

7. **D** Each site wants to maintain control of both users and resources. The only way to enable all users to access all resources in all domains is to implement the complete trust model.

8. **C** Centralized account administration with distributed resource administration suggests the single master model. However, the size of the SAM is 50 MB with 50,000 users and no computer accounts, so the multiple master model must be used.

9. **D** Although the single master model enables centralized administration of accounts, it does not enable centralized administration of resources, which was one of the required results.

10. **A** With the single domain model, administration is centralized. In a single domain, the location of users is not important, so if the Domain Users group is added to all the servers where access is needed, all users can access all required resources regardless of location.

11. **B** The complete trust model lets all users access everything. It also allows decentralized account administration, but does not allow centralized resource administration.

12. **D** The trust between R&D and Manufacturing is in the wrong direction for the required result to be met.

13. **C** All the domains with resources trust the single domain with user accounts.

14. **D** Individual users and global groups from the local domain as well as any trusted domain can be added to local groups.

15. **D** Both users and global groups can be added.

16. **B** The Policies menu within User Manager for Domains is used to create trusts.

17. **D** No trust relationship exists between the Sales and Accounting domains. Users from one domain cannot access resources in another domain unless a trust relationship is explicitly created between them.

18. **A** Each domain has accounts and resources; therefore, every domain must trust every other domain.

19. **D** The trusted domain starts the process by naming its partner. The trusting domain then finishes the process by naming its partner.

20. **B** Although this is not the preferred method for creating a trust, the trust is still established. However, the user will not receive a dialog box with a positive confirmation that the trust has been created.

21. **D** The trust is correct, but Server Operators is the local group that cannot be copied across a trust and also cannot be assigned to another local group.

22. **C** The trust is correct, but Domain Admins is added only to the administrators group in the domain, which allows domain administration but not administration of member servers or Windows NT workstations.

23. **B** The complete trust model creates the proper trust relationships. Adding Domain Admins to the domain administrators group allows account administration. Adding Domain Admins to the member server administrators groups

allows server configuration. However, nothing is added to groups on the Windows NT workstations.

24. **D** The trusts will work but no group assignments are automatically made across a trust, so the required result is not produced.

25. **D** All four domains must trust the other three domains, 4×3=12.

1.1   Key Words

Complete trust domain model

Directory services

Directory synchronization

Domain

Multiple master domain model

Non-transitive trusts

One-way trust

Security Account Manager (SAM)

Single domain model

Single master domain model

Trust relationships

Two-way trust

Universal resource access

1.2   Planning the Fault-Tolerance Configurations for Windows NT Server 4.0

To prepare for this section of the exam, you must understand each of the fault-tolerant disk arrays supported by Windows NT Server and know which method should be used for a given scenario.

A.   RAID Systems in Windows NT Server 4.0

Windows NT Server supports fault-tolerant disk arrays that provide data recovery if a single physical disk fails. These fault-tolerant arrays are not supported on Windows NT Workstation. However, the disk arrays supported by Windows NT Workstation (striping and volume sets) are also supported by Windows NT Server.

Windows NT Server 4.0 supports RAID (Redundant Array of Inexpensive Disks)—Level 0 (Disk Striping), Level 1 (Disk Mirroring), and Level 5 (Disk Striping with parity). Disk duplexing is also supported, which is an extension to disk mirroring. RAID 0 is not a fault-tolerant disk array, but RAID 1 and RAID 5 are fault tolerant (the data is protected from the failure of a single disk).

1.   RAID Level 0: Stripe Sets

Stripe sets are not a fault-tolerant disk array. You can combine several disks into a single partition with a stripe set. The stripe set is similar to a RAID 5 array (striping with parity). RAID 0 is supported on both Windows NT Workstation and Server.

Disk striping divides the data into 64 KB blocks and writes the data across multiple physical disk drives. This process writes data to all the disks in the array at the same time, increasing write performance. Read performance is also improved because data can be read simultaneously from several disks at once. If one disk in the array fails, all the data on the stripe set is lost because the disks work together as a unit. A disk stripe set consists of multiple physical disks. A minimum of two disks is required to create a stripe set; a stripe set can include as many as 32 disks.

After a stripe set is created, no disks can be added to or removed from the array. When a stripe set is created, equal portions of disk space from each physical drive are used. The benefits of a disk stripe set are the following:

- Increased disk read performance
- Increased disk write performance

The limitations of a disk stripe set are the following:

- No data redundancy, or fault tolerance
- Cannot contain the system or boot partition in a stripe set

2. RAID Level 1: Disk Mirroring

Disk mirroring duplicates writes to the hard drive onto two physical disks. If each disk has a separate hard drive controller, a mirror is called disk duplexing, which provides redundancy for both hard drive failure and controller failure.

This method of fault tolerance is considered to be more expensive per megabyte of data due to the complete duplication of data. Every disk mirror requires two physical disks. Disk mirroring (and disk duplexing) are supported only on Windows NT Server. The benefits of disk mirroring are the following:

- All drives and partitions can be mirrored, including boot and system partitions.
- Complete data duplication is done, allowing a complete recovery of data.

The drawbacks to using disk mirroring are the following:

- Per megabyte cost is higher; 50 percent of total available disk space is utilized.
- Read and write performance is moderate.

3. RAID Level 5: Stripe Sets with Parity

Disk striping with parity is the more common of the fault-tolerant methods available through Windows NT Server 4.0. Disk striping with parity uses the same basic process of disk striping; it writes the data in 64 KB blocks across multiple physical disks.

A stripe set uses the stripes on disk to store redundant information, known as *parity*. The parity is basically a checksum that can be used to restore the rest of the data if a disk is lost. For example, consider a stripe set with parity with three disks.

If the data values 1 and 2 were written to the stripe set, the parity 3 (which is the sum of 1 and 2) would be written to the third disk. If one of the disks were lost, the data could still be recovered because an algebraic statement would exist. If disk 2 were lost, the equation 1+?=3 would exist. The value 2 could be computed as the missing data and Windows NT could recover from the missing drive.

To implement the disk striping with parity, a minimum of three physical disks is required and a maximum of 32 disks can be used. Note that an extra disk is required over striping without parity. This extra disk is devoted to parity information. If any one of the disks in the stripe set with parity fail, the data can be regenerated from the remaining disks. Striping with parity is supported only on Windows NT Server.

The cost for the fault tolerance is one disk in the array. For the smallest array (3 disks), the cost is the largest (1/3 or one disk of the three). For the largest array (32 disks), the cost is relatively small (1/32 or one disk of the 32). The benefits of a stripe set with parity include the following:

- Data can be regenerated from parity information.
- Read performance from stripe sets with parity is excellent.
- Cost per megabyte is lower with stripe sets than with disk mirroring.

The limitations and drawbacks of the stripe set with parity include the following:

- A minimum of three disks and a maximum of 32 disks is required.

- Write performance is moderate.

- More system memory is required to implement stripe set due to calculation of parity.

- System or boot partition cannot be included.

4. Hardware RAID

Hardware solutions for fault tolerance are by far the best solutions available. RAID 5 is commonly implemented in a hardware array of disks. For a hardware implementation, the disk controllers calculate the parity and control the striping of information on the disks. The operating system sees a hardware RAID 5 array as a single disk. Windows NT uses software emulation for its RAID 5 implementation. This is slower than the hardware method, but it allows you to use disks of different sizes and types. Hardware RAID is typically more expensive than buying individual drives and implementing software RAID.

Hardware RAID 5 does offer several advantages over the software implementation. First, you can install a system or boot partition on a hardware array. In fact, Windows NT recognizes an entire hardware array as a single disk; the operating system doesn't see the multiple drives because the disk controllers control the management of these drives as one physical unit. Also, many hardware arrays support *hot swapping*, which allows you to replace a bad drive while the computer is still running. When the new drive is added to the array, the information on the new disk is automatically written there.

B. Summary of Supported RAID Levels

Table 1.2.1 includes a summary of the RAID levels supported by Windows NT.

Table 1.2.1   Summary of Fault-Tolerance Options in Windows NT Server 4.0

Disk Striping	Disk Mirroring/ Disk Duplexing	Disk Striping w/Parity
No fault-tolerance	Complete disk duplication	Data regeneration from stored parity information
Minimum of two physical disks; maximum of 32 disks	Two physical disks	Minimum of three physical disks; maximum of 32 disks
100 percent available disk utilization	50 percent available disk utilization	Dedicates the equivalent of one disk's space in the set for parity information; the more disks, the higher the utilization
Cannot include system/boot partition	Includes all partition types	Cannot include system/boot partition
Excellent read/write performance	Moderate read/write performance	Excellent read; moderate write performance

C. Implementing RAID in Windows NT Server 4.0

The steps required to implement fault tolerance in Windows NT Server 4.0 are covered in detail in Chapter 2, "Installation and Configuration."

D. Sector Sparing

Sector sparing automatically fixes data on bad sectors of a hard drive. This is also known as *hot fixing*. Sector sparing is supported only on SCSI drives in RAID 1 or RAID 5 arrays that are formatted as NTFS partitions. Sector sparing is supported only on Windows NT Server. Sector sparing verifies each write of data onto the disk and, if it does not reread the data successfully, it will move the data to another sector of the drive. The operating system never receives a message about the bad write because the sector sparing automatically corrects the error. After a sector of the disk has been marked bad, the system will not use the bad sector until a disk defragmentation utility, or a disk tool utility, has been executed.

1.2.1 Exercise: Selecting the Proper Fault-Tolerance Method for Given Scenarios

1. Select all the disk fault-tolerance functions that are supported by Windows NT Server 4.0. Select all that apply.

   A. Disk mirroring

   B. Disk striping

   C. Disk striping with parity

   D. Sector sparing

2. List two differences between disk striping with parity and disk mirroring.

3. Your company wants to implement a fault-tolerance scheme. You have a Windows NT Server system with two hard disks. Which disk fault-tolerance method can be used?

4. Your organization has implemented a stripe set with parity; you have four physical disks: Disk 1 is a 1 GB disk that contains the system files and all Windows NT files. Disk 2 is a 2 GB disk to be used for data. Disk 3 is a 1.5 GB disk to be used for data. Disk 4 is a 2 GB drive also for data. What is the largest working disk space that can be used in a disk stripe set with parity?

1.2   Practice Problems

1. On which disk partitioning scheme can you place a system partition?

    A. Volume set

    B. Stripe set without parity

    C. Stripe set with parity

    D. Disk mirror

2. Which fault-tolerant disk scheme requires the least overhead in disk storage?

    A. Striping with parity

    B. Disk mirroring

    C. Disk duplexing

    D. Striping without parity

3. How many physical disks are required for a RAID 5 array?

    A. 2

    B. 3

    C. 4

    D. 32

4. How many physical disks can be included in a RAID 5 array?

    A. 2

    B. 3

    C. 4

    D. 32

5. Which file system can be used for a stripe set with parity? Select all that apply.

    A. HPFS

    B. FAT

    C. CDFS

    D. NTFS

6. Which file system supports sector sparing?

    A. HPFS

    B. FAT

    C. CDFS

    D. NTFS

7. What happens to data on a bad sector when sector sparing occurs?

    A. The data is copied to a good sector.

    B. The data is copied to a file called FILExxxx.chk.

    C. The data is copied to the sparing partition.

    D. The data can be recovered with the **SECTCHK** command.

The following scenario applies to questions 8–11. A different solution to the scenario is proposed for each question.

Scenario: Your SQL Server has four physical disks. The first disk is where the Windows NT files are located. SQL data is stored on the other three disks. You are asked to implement a fault-tolerant disk scheme for this SQL server.

8. *Required Result*: The boot partition must be protected from a single disk failure.
    Optional Results: The SQL data must have the fastest read and write access possible; the SQL data must be protected from a single disk failure.

    Solution: Mirror the first physical drive to the second physical drive. Make a stripe set without parity with the remaining two disks. Store the SQL data on the stripe set without parity.

    A. The proposed solution produces the required results and produces both optional results.

    B. The proposed solution produces the required results and produces only one optional result.

C. The proposed solution produces the required results but does not produce any optional results.

D. The proposed solution does not produce the required results.

9. *Required Result*: The SQL data is protected from a single disk failure. *Optional Results*: The system partition is protected from a disk crash; the disk space overhead used for fault tolerance is the least amount possible.

   Solution: Mirror the first physical disk to the second physical disk. Mirror the third physical disk to the fourth physical disk. Place the SQL data on the third physical disk.

   A. The proposed solution produces the required results and produces both optional results.

   B. The proposed solution produces the required results and produces only one optional result.

   C. The proposed solution produces the required results but does not produce any optional results.

   D. The proposed solution does not produce the required results.

10. *Required Result*: Access to the SQL data is maximized for read and write performance. *Optional Results*: Extra space from the first physical disk is used for SQL data; the SQL data can be accessed with one drive letter.

    Solution: Create a volume set with the second, third, and fourth physical disks. Add extra space from the first physical disk to the volume set. Place the SQL data on the volume set.

    A. The proposed solution produces the required results and produces both optional results.

B. The proposed solution produces the required results and produces only one optional result.

C. The proposed solution produces the required results but does not produce any optional results.

D. The proposed solution does not produce the required results.

11. *Required Result*: Provide the system partition with the maximum amount of failure for a hardware failure. *Optional Results*: Improve the read access for the SQL data; protect the SQL data from a single disk failure.

    Solution: Install an additional physical disk with a separate controller. Mirror the system partition to the new disk. Create a RAID 5 array with disks 2–4 and place the SQL data on this array.

    A. The proposed solution produces the required results and produces both optional results.

    B. The proposed solution produces the required results and produces only one optional result.

    C. The proposed solution produces the required results but does not produce any optional results.

    D. The proposed solution does not produce the required results.

12. What best describes a volume set?

    A. It allows a system partition to be duplicated.

    B. It combines disk space from several disks into one logical drive.

    C. It requires equal disk space from each drive included in the volume set.

    D. It provides faster read access to data.

13. What type of information can be put on a stripe set? Select all that apply.

    A. The boot sector

    B. Spool directory

    C. Data files

    D. Registry hives

14. What type of drives can be used to create a RAID 5 array? Select all that apply.

    A. Removable drives

    B. SCSI drives

    C. IDE drives

    D. EIDE drives

15. A server is currently used to store data on its single disk drive. How many disks must be added to protect the operating system from disk failure and also to protect the data?

    A. 0

    B. 1

    C. 2

    D. 3

16. A server currently has two EIDE controllers with a physical drive attached to each controller. What must be added to the server to enable sector sparing?

    A. Two SCSI hard drives with controller

    B. A tape device

    C. A PCI controller for the EIDE drives

    D. A Y-cable connecting the two EIDE drives

17. Which of the following best describes striping with parity?

    A. Provides fastest write access to the disk for any disk array

    B. Enables addition of new disks to an existing partition

C. Can be used only with NTFS

D. Requires at least three disks to implement

18. A Windows NT Server has four physical disks. The first disk, which contains the WINNT directory on a 400 MB FAT partition, has 200 MB of free space. The second disk has a 400 MB NTFS partition and 100 MB of free space. The third and fourth disks are unformatted with 500 MB of free space on each disk. Which fault-tolerant scheme would allow a 300 MB application to be installed on the disks? Select all that apply.

    A. Make a stripe set with parity using all the free space on disks 1, 3, and 4.

    B. Make a volume set using the remaining disk space on disk 2.

    C. Make a mirror using all the free space on disks 3 and 4.

    D. Make a mirror with the boot partition using free space on disk 4. Make a stripe set with parity using the remaining disk space on all four disks.

19. Which tool is used to create a RAID 5 array in Windows NT?

    A. RAID Configuration Wizard

    B. DNS Manager

    C. Disk Administrator

    D. Server Manager

20. Which platforms support disk mirroring? Select all that apply.

    A. Windows NT Workstation

    B. Windows NT Server

    C. Windows 95

    D. Windows for Workgroups

The following scenario applies to questions 21–24. A different solution to the scenario is proposed for each question.

Scenario: Your department manager wants you to create a web site to publish data to other departments within the company. Your manager wants to protect data, but also wants to do it at the lowest possible cost.

21. *Required Result*: Protect web server data from disk failure using the cheapest fault-tolerant disk scheme. *Optional Results*: Provide faster read access to web data; provide capability to expand storage for web data without moving existing data.

    Solution: Install Peer Web Services on a Windows NT machine. Create a stripe set with parity. Put the web data on this stripe set.

    A. The proposed solution produces the required results and produces both optional results.

    B. The proposed solution produces the required results and produces only one optional result.

    C. The proposed solution produces the required results but does not produce any optional results.

    D. The proposed solution does not produce the required results.

22. *Required Result*: Protect web server data from disk failure using the cheapest fault-tolerant disk scheme. *Optional Results*: Provide faster read access to the Web data; provide capability to expand storage for web data without moving existing data.

    Solution: Install IIS on a Windows NT machine. Create a volume set and place the web data on the volume set.

    A. The proposed solution produces the required results and produces both optional results.

B. The proposed solution produces the required results and produces only one optional result.

C. The proposed solution produces the required results but does not produce any optional results.

D. The proposed solution does not produce the required results.

23. *Required Result*: Protect the operating system and web data from a single disk failure. *Optional Result*: Provide faster read access for web data; enable file level permissions for the web data.

    Solution: Install Windows NT Server on a machine with three physical disks. Mirror the boot partition to another disk. Use the remaining disk space on the system disk and the other disks to create a stripe set with parity. Format the partition as NTFS. Place the web data on the stripe set.

    A. The proposed solution produces the required results and produces both optional results.

    B. The proposed solution produces the required results and produces only one optional result.

    C. The proposed solution produces the required results but does not produce any optional results.

    D. The proposed solution does not produce the required results.

24. *Required Result*: Protect the operating system and web data from a single disk failure. *Optional Results*: Provide faster read access for web data; enable file-level permissions for the web data.

    Solution: Install Windows NT Server on a machine with three physical disks. Create a stripe set with parity on the three physical disks. Format the stripe set with parity as NTFS. Install Windows NT and the web data on the stripe set with parity.

   A. The proposed solution produces the required results and produces both optional results.

   B. The proposed solution produces the required results and produces only one optional result.

   C. The proposed solution produces the required results but does not produce any optional results.

   D. The proposed solution does not produce the required results.

25. Which of the following is required for sector sparing?

   A. A disk controller for each disk

   B. An NTFS partition

   C. A PCI disk controller

   D. BIOS that supports hot swapping

1.2.1 Answers and Explanations: Exercise

1. The correct answer for this question is A and C. Disk mirroring and disk striping with parity are the supported disk fault-tolerance methods.

2. The differences between disk striping with parity and disk mirroring are the following:

   • System and Boot Partitions can be mirrored.

   • Mirroring uses two disks and striping with parity requires a minimum of three and a maximum of 32 disks.

3. The only fault-tolerance method that can be used is disk mirroring due to the two-disk limit.

4. Disk 1 cannot be used for the stripe set because it contains the boot and system

partition. Disks 2, 3, and 4 can be used to create the stripe set with parity. The stripe set would use equal amounts of disk space on each disk. With this restriction, the largest available disk space that could be used for the stripe set with parity is 4.5 GB with 3 GB of working disk space. To obtain this disk space, the system would use 1.5 GB from each of the three disks.

1.2 Answers and Explanations: Practice Problems

1. **D** Only a disk mirror allows a system partition.

2. **A** Although striping without parity requires no overhead, it's not a fault-tolerant scheme.

3. **B** At least three disks are required for a RAID 5 array; two disks are for data and one disk is for parity.

4. **D** Up to 32 disks can be part of a RAID 5 array.

5. **B, D** Any supported file system can be used for any of the disk arrays. HPFS is not supported for Windows NT 4.0. CDFS is the file system used to read data from CD-ROMs.

6. **D** Only NTFS supports sector sparing.

7. **A** The data is automatically copied to a new sector and the process is transparent to the user.

8. **B** Mirroring the first disk protects the boot partition. The stripe set without parity provides the fastest read and write access, but it isn't a fault-tolerant disk array.

9. **B** This method protects both the system partition and the SQL data. However, mirroring uses more disk overhead than striping with parity.

10. **D** A volume set can use all available space on different drives, but does not improve read or write performance.

11. **A** Disk duplexing was used for the system partition and RAID 5 for SQL, which gives SQL faster read access and fault tolerance.

12. **B** A volume set joins dissimilar disk space together in a single drive letter, but it does not improve access times, nor is it fault tolerant.

13. **B, C** Data can be placed on any partition. Although the spool directory is part of the boot partition by default, it can be moved to any partition.

14. **B, C, D** Any fixed type of hard drive can be used in a RAID 5 array.

15. **B** An additional drive would allow mirroring of both the operating system and data.

16. **A** Sector sparing is supported only on SCSI drives.

17. **D** Striping without parity is faster, and a stripe set cannot be modified after it's created. A stripe set can be formatted as FAT or NTFS.

18. **A, C, D** The mirror would be 1 GB, with 500 MB of usable space. A stripe set on three disks would yield 600 MB total, with 400 MB of usable space. A stripe set on four disks would yield 400 MB total, with 300 MB of usable space.

19. **C** Disk Administrator is the tool used to create any disk scheme.

20. **B** Only Windows NT Server supports fault-tolerant disk arrays.

21. **D** Peer Web Services is installed on a Windows NT Workstation. Windows NT Workstations do not support fault-tolerant disk arrays.

22. **D** IIS indicates this is a Windows NT Server, but a volume set is not a fault-tolerant disk array.

23. **A** Mirroring the boot partition protects the operating system. The stripe set with parity protects the web data and provides faster read access. The NTFS file system allows file-level permissions.

24. **D** Windows NT cannot be installed on a stripe set.

25. **B** NTFS on SCSI drives in a fault-tolerant array is required for sector sparing.

1.2 Key Words

Disk duplexing

Disk mirroring

Disk striping

Disk striping with parity

Fault tolerance

Parity

RAID (Redundant Array of Inexpensive Disks)

Sector sparing

Striping

Volume sets

1.3   Selecting the Proper Protocol

The interconnectivity of Windows NT with other operating systems and other Windows NT systems is critical to the proper functioning of your enterprise system. The protocols installed on a server determine the type of systems with which Windows NT can communicate. They include:

- NetBEUI
- TCP/IP
- NWLINK IPX/SPX Compatible
- DataLink Control (DLC)
- AppleTalk Protocol

A.   NetBEUI

The NetBEUI protocol is the easiest to implement. The *NetBEUI* protocol uses NetBIOS broadcasts to locate other computers on the network. This broadcasting generates extra traffic on the network, which increases to excessive amounts on larger networks. Also, the broadcasts that NetBEUI uses are not routable; in other words, you cannot access computers that are not on your physical network segment. For these reasons, NetBEUI is recommended only for small- to medium-sized networks that are on a single segment. NetBEUI does not provide connectivity to many other network types. This protocol is supported by most Microsoft clients as well as IBM OS/2 clients.

B.   TCP/IP

Transmission Control Protocol/Internet Protocol, or TCP/IP, is the most common protocol. *TCP/IP* is an industry standard protocol that is supported under most network operating systems. Because of this acceptance throughout the industry, TCP/IP allows a Windows NT system to connect to other systems running TCP/IP.

TCP/IP is a routable protocol that lends itself directly to enterprise or WAN communication. You can communicate with any number of physical network segments with TCP/IP. The advantages of using TCP/IP in a Windows NT environment include the following:

- Capability to connect dissimilar systems using numerous standard connectivity utilities; utilities include File Transfer Protocol, Telnet, and Ping.
- Internet access

Configuring TCP/IP is more difficult than configuring the other supported protocols.

1.   Heterogeneous Connectivity with TCP/IP

TCP/IP allows Windows NT to connect with many non-Microsoft systems. Some of the systems with which it can communicate include the following:

- Any Internet-connected system
- UNIX systems
- IBM Mainframe systems

- DEC Pathworks
- TCP/IP printers directly connected to the network

TCP/IP has increased in popularity and is now supported by virtually all the new operating systems being released today. Using TCP/IP gives you the widest possible choice of connectivity options.

2. WINS, DHCP, DNS, and IIS

TCP/IP is required for several Windows NT services. Because these services depend on TCP/IP, they cannot be installed if TCP/IP is not installed on the server. WINS, DHCP, DNS, and IIS all require TCP/IP.

DHCP (Dynamic Host Configuration Protocol) is a service that allocates TCP/IP addresses automatically to all the clients configured for DHCP. When clients use DHCP to obtain IP addresses and configuration information, the administrator does not have to manually configure these clients.

WINS (Windows Internet Name Service) Server is a dynamic database to resolve NetBIOS names to IP addresses. It is often used in conjunction with WINS because an administrator does not know which client will receive a particular IP address. WINS automatically registers a client's current IP address in the WINS database. In addition to the computer name, any networking services a computer provides are also registered with WINS.

DNS (Domain Name System) is used to resolve domain names, such as www.microsoft.com, to IP addresses. DNS is often used to resolve Internet names or to resolve names on a local intranet. *IIS* (Internet Information Server) provides World Wide Web publishing, FTP publishing, and Gopher server capabilities. You can use IIS to provide Web pages for Internet access or for local intranet use.

C. NWLink IPX/SPX Compatible Protocol

NWLink is Microsoft's version of IPX/SPX, the protocol suite that has been used within the NetWare environment for years. NWLINK is best suited for networks requiring communication with existing NetWare servers, and for existing NetWare clients.

1. NetWare Connectivity

A Windows NT Server running NWLink can serve as an application server for NetWare clients. However, the NetWare clients also need client software to communicate with the application; NWLink provides the common protocol. Other services can be installed on a Windows NT Server to enable additional NetWare connectivity. All these services depend on NWLink.

The NetWare clients also can use the Windows NT Server for file and print access if an additional service is installed (File and Print Services for NetWare [FPNW]). If the Gateway Service for NetWare (GSNW) is installed on the Windows NT Server, clients on the Windows NT network can communicate with NetWare servers without having NetWare client software installed.

If GSNW and NWLink are installed on a Windows NT Server, the Migration Tool for NetWare can be used to migrate NetWare users and files to the Windows NT Server. Microsoft also provides Client Services for NetWare (CSNW) to allow Windows NT Workstation computers to connect to NetWare servers.

Windows NT also can communicate with NetWare using TCP/IP if the NetWare servers have TCP/IP installed. However, NWLink (IPX/SPX) is usually thought of as the protocol used to connect to NetWare.

D. DLC (Data Link Control)

DLC is used to provide connectivity to IBM mainframes and AS400 servers. The BackOffice product SNA is used to connect to these IBM servers and requires DLC as its underlying protocol. DLC also can be used for HP network printers. However, if an HP printer has a JetDirect card installed, it can be assigned a TCP/IP address and thus use TCP/IP rather than DLC for its printing protocol. DLC is not used by any Microsoft clients—it is only used on a Windows NT Server to support IBM and HP connections.

E. AppleTalk Protocol

Apple Macintosh clients can connect to Windows NT servers running the AppleTalk protocol. This protocol is installed when Services for Macintosh is installed. This service (and the underlying AppleTalk protocol) allows Macintosh computers on your network to be able to access files and printers on the Windows NT Server. It also enables Windows NT clients to print to AppleTalk printers.

1.3.1 Exercise: Selecting the Proper Protocol for a Given Scenario

1. The production department needs to access a software product that can be installed only on a NetWare Server. They currently connect to the Windows NT system and would like be able to connect to both systems with one common protocol. Which of the following protocols can access both a NetWare system and a Windows NT system?

    A. NetWare Connect Protocol

    B. NetBEUI

    C. NWLink IPX/SPX Compatible

    D. GSNW

2. Users from your Windows NT system want to access your NetWare server, but you do not want to set up each one with the NetWare client. Which of the following is required to enable your Windows NT system to share a NetWare connection for the Windows NT users? Select all that apply.

    A. NWLink IPX/SPX Compatible

    B. NetBEUI

    C. GSNW

    D. Services for the Macintosh

1.3.2 Exercise: Selecting the Appropriate Protocol for Connectivity

Exercise 1.3.2 has you select the appropriate protocols to use for a specific scenario. Select the best protocols for each scenario.

1. Users need to access the Internet and to communicate with each other locally.

2. Users need to access a Novell server both running IPX and communicating with the Windows NT Server.

3. Users need to access resources on Novell servers, Windows NT systems, and UNIX systems.

4. A small number of users want to be able to share resources with no network configuration requirements. They do not need to access any computers outside their local network.

1.3 Practice Problems

1. You are installing Windows NT on a departmental LAN that will support 20 users. The network is wired on a single segment. Which of the following is the most efficient networking protocol you can use for this LAN configuration?

    A. NetBEUI

    B. NWLink

    C. TCP/IP

    D. AppleTalk

2. You are installing a Windows NT Server to support connections for Macintosh clients. This server will also have IIS installed to publish the company employee handbook. Which of the following protocols need to be installed on this server to support these functions? Select all that apply.

    A. NetBEUI

    B. NWLink

    C. TCP/IP

    D. AppleTalk

3. Your network includes Windows NT Servers and NetWare Servers running the IPX/SPX protocol. Which of the following protocols must be installed on the Windows NT Servers so that NetWare clients can connect to these servers?

    A. NetBEUI

    B. NWLink

    C. TCP/IP

    D. AppleTalk

4. You have several IBM AS400 servers in your environment that will communicate with a Windows NT server using SNA. You also have several HP network printers that will be managed by a Windows NT print server. Which of the following

protocols must be installed on the Windows NT Server to support connections to peripherals? Select all that apply.

    A. NWLink

    B. NetBEUI

    C. PrintTalk

    D. DLC

5. A Windows NT Server will be a RAS Server for incoming client calls. This server will provide file access to a NetWare Server and print support for a TCP/IP printer. Which of the following protocols must be installed on the RAS Server to provide client access to these resources and to enable the clients to connect over RAS using the most efficient protocol? Select all that apply.

    A. NetBEUI

    B. NWLink

    C. TCP/IP

    D. DLC

6. Which protocol uses broadcasts in attempts to communicate with other computers on the network?

    A. NetBEUI

    B. NWLink

    C. TCP/IP

    D. DLC

7. You want to configure a Windows NT Server to provide DHCP and WINS services. Which of the following protocols needs to be installed on the server to support these services?

    A. NetBEUI

    B. NWLink

    C. TCP/IP

    D. DLC

8. A Windows NT Primary Domain controller will be used to migrate accounts from several NetWare servers. This PDC will also provide domain-name resolution for web servers to the rest of the domain. Which of the following protocols need to be installed on this server? Select all that apply.

   A. NetBEUI

   B. NWLink

   C. TCP/IP

   D. DLC

9. Which of the following protocols can be used to support network printers? Select all that apply.

   A. NetBEUI

   B. NWLink

   C. TCP/IP

   D. DLC

The following scenario applies to questions 10–13. A different solution to the scenario is proposed for each question.

Scenario: Your company is adding two new servers to its network for applications, file serving, and print serving. The applications will be used by clients in the domain and also by NetWare clients.

10. *Required Result*: Allow both NetWare and Microsoft clients access to the file and print services. *Optional Results*: Minimize the number of protocols used on the network; allow UNIX hosts to access printers on the Windows NT network.

    Solution: Install File and Print Services for NetWare on the Windows NT servers. Install JetDirect cards into the network printers. Install the NetBEUI protocol on the servers.

    A. The proposed solution produces the required results and produces both optional results.

    B. The proposed solution produces the required results and produces only one optional result.

    C. The proposed solution produces the required results but does not produce any optional results.

    D. The proposed solution does not produce the required results.

11. *Required Result*: Allow Microsoft clients to access all the services on the new servers. *Optional Results*: Allow the NetWare clients to access file and print services on the new servers; allow Macintosh clients to access files on the new servers.

    Solution: Install NWLink on the servers.

    A. The proposed solution produces the required results and produces both optional results.

    B. The proposed solution produces the required results and produces only one optional result.

    C. The proposed solution produces the required results but does not produce any optional results.

    D. The proposed solution does not produce the required results.

12. *Required Result*: Allow both NetWare and Microsoft clients to access the client/ server application on the new servers. *Optional Results*: Minimize the protocols used on the network; allow NetWare clients to access the file and print services of the new servers.

    Solution: Install the client software needed for the application on the Microsoft and NetWare clients. Install NWLink on the servers.

    A. The proposed solution produces the required results and produces both optional results.

    B. The proposed solution produces the required results and produces only one optional result.

C. The proposed solution produces the required results but does not produce any optional results.

D. The proposed solution does not produce the required results.

13. *Required Result*: Allow access to the application for both Microsoft and NetWare clients. *Optional Results*: Minimize broadcast traffic on the network; minimize the number of protocols used on the network.

Solution: Install TCP/IP and the client software on the NetWare and Microsoft clients. Install TCP/IP on the new servers. Install a WINS Server and configure the Microsoft clients as WINS clients. Install WINS proxy agents on the network segments where the NetWare clients reside.

A. The proposed solution produces the required results and produces both optional results.

B. The proposed solution produces the required results and produces only one optional result.

C. The proposed solution produces the required results but does not produce any optional results.

D. The proposed solution does not produce the required results.

14. Which protocols can be used in a segmented network with routers separating the segments? Select all that apply.

A. NetBEUI

B. NWLink

C. NDIS

D. TCP/IP

15. Which of the following protocols must be installed before File and Print Services for NetWare can be installed?

A. NetBEUI

B. NWLink

C. DLC

D. TCP/IP

16. Which of the following protocols must be installed so that a server can be used as a DNS server?

A. NetBEUI

B. NWLink

C. DLC

D. TCP/IP

17. Windows NT supports printing to network printers that have a specific address assigned to the printer. Which of the following protocols supports this type of printing?

A. NetBEUI

B. NWLink

C. NDIS

D. TCP/IP

18. A RAS Server will allow a RAS client to connect by using only one protocol while routing information to other servers using several protocols. Which protocol is most efficient for the RAS client/server connection?

A. NetBEUI

B. NWLink

C. DLC

D. TCP/IP

19. Which protocol allows the greatest variety of non-Microsoft clients to connect to a Windows NT Server?

A. NetBEUI

B. NWLink

C. DLC

D. TCP/IP

20. Which protocols allow connections to both servers and network printers? Select all that apply.

    A. NetBEUI

    B. NWLink

    C. DLC

    D. TCP/IP

21. A friend runs a small warehouse. She wants to install a network to connect the warehouse parts workstations with the office server and the office workstations. The network will be used internally without outside access. Which of the following protocols would be the most efficient and easiest to configure for this environment?

    A. NetBEUI

    B. NWLink

    C. DLC

    D. TCP/IP

22. A friend runs a small warehouse. She wants to install a network to connect the warehouse parts workstations with the office server and the office workstations. She also wants to connect to parts suppliers through the Internet. Which of the following protocols is best for this environment?

    A. NetBEUI

    B. NWLink

    C. DLC

    D. TCP/IP

23. You want a server to provide WINS and DHCP services on the network. You also want this server to be a Gopher Server. How many protocols must be installed to support these services?

    A. 1

    B. 2

    C. 3

    D. 4

24. You want Macintosh clients to save data on a Windows NT Server. You also want Microsoft clients to have access to this data. How many protocols must be installed on the server to provide this access?

    A. 1

    B. 2

    C. 3

    D. 4

25. Which of the following protocols can be used by Microsoft clients to access file and print services on a Windows NT server? Select all that apply.

    A. NetBEUI

    B. NWLink

    C. DLC

    D. TCP/IP

    E. AppleTalk

1.3.1 Answers and Explanations: Exercise

1. **C** NWLink is the protocol that Microsoft provides to work with NetWare. NetBEUI is not supported on NetWare. GSNW is a service that allows Microsoft clients to access NetWare servers through a Windows NT Server without having NetWare client software installed.

2. **A, C** You need the protocol to let the Windows NT Server talk to NetWare (NWLink) and the service to let the Windows NT Server function as a gateway for Microsoft clients (Gateway Service for NetWare or GSNW).

1.3.2 Answers and Explanations: Exercise

1. TCP/IP. TCP/IP is the protocol required for Internet connections, but it also can be used for local network connections.

2. NWLink IPX/SPX Compatible. NWLink is the protocol used to connect with NetWare, but it also can be used by Microsoft clients.

3. TCP/IP, NWLink IPX/SPX Compatible. NWLink is required for NetWare connectivity. TCP/IP is required for UNIX connectivity. The Microsoft clients can use either of these protocols.

4. NetBEUI. All protocols would work; NetBEUI, however, is the easiest to configure and set up. It would also provide complete connectivity on the local network because no routers would be used in this environment.

1.3 Answers and Explanations: Practice Problems

1. **A** NetBEUI is the most efficient protocol for this small, single segment LAN.

2. **C, D** AppleTalk is needed for the Mac clients and IIS requires TCP/IP.

3. **B** NWLink is Microsoft's implementation of IPX/SPX.

4. **D** DLC provides support for IBM mainframes and AS400s in addition to HP network printer support.

5. **A, B, C** NWLink and TCP/IP must be installed so that the server can connect to these resources. NetBEUI is the most efficient protocol to use over a RAS link. The RAS Server functions as a NetBIOS gateway, converting the NetBEUI protocol to the protocols used by the servers with which the RAS client is trying to communicate.

6. **A** NetBEUI is broadcast-based.

7. **C** TCP/IP is needed for DHCP and WINS.

8. **B, C** NWLink supports the NetWare migration and TCP/IP supports DNS for domain-name resolution.

9. **C, D** DLC supports HP network printers and TCP/IP supports network printers, including HP network printers with JetDirect cards that can be assigned an IP address.

10. **C** Installing File and Print Services for NetWare forces the installation of NWLink. This allows both Microsoft and NetWare clients file and print access. Adding NetBEUI is not necessary. TCP/IP was not installed to allow UNIX printing support.

11. **C** NWLink allows Microsoft clients to connect to the server, but without additional services (FPNW). NetWare clients cannot access the file and print server. The Macintosh clients require the AppleTalk protocol on the server.

12. **B** The client software combined with the NWLink protocol allows both Microsoft and NetWare clients to access the application. However, the NetWare clients require FPNW on the server before they can connect for file and print access.

13. **A** NetWare clients can connect by using TCP/IP if they have the protocol installed. TCP/IP uses few broadcasts, and a single protocol can be used for these requirements.

14. **B, D** Both NWLink and TCP/IP can be used in this environment. NetBEUI is the only protocol limited to a single segment.

15. **B** FPNW depends on NWLink.

16. **D** DNS depends on TCP/IP.

17. **D** TCP/IP fits this description.

18. **A**   NetBEUI is the most efficient protocol for a RAS connection.

19. **D**   TCP/IP is the most common protocol.

20. **C, D**   DLC allows connections to IBM servers (AS400s) and HP network printers, whereas TCP/IP connects to a variety of servers and printers.

21. **A**   NetBEUI is most efficient for a small, single segment LAN.

22. **D**   With Internet connectivity as a requirement, TCP/IP is the only possible choice.

23. **A**   TCP/IP is the only protocol needed to support these services. A Gopher Server is part of IIS.

24. **B**   The Macintosh clients require the AppleTalk protocol. Because Microsoft clients cannot use this protocol, you must install one additional protocol to support these clients.

25. **A, B, D**   DLC is intended for specialized use, whereas AppleTalk is only for Mac clients.

1.3   Key Words

DHCP (Dynamic Host Configuration Protocol)

DLC (Data Link Control)

DNS (Domain Name System)

IIS (Internet Information Server)

TCP/IP

WINS (Windows Internet Name Service)

Practice Exam: Planning

Use this practice exam to test your mastery of the Planning objective. This practice exam is 15 questions long. The passing Microsoft score is 78.4 percent.

1. Where can computer accounts for a domain be created?

   A. Computer Manager for Domains

   B. User Manager for Domains

   C. Account Administrator

   D. Server Manager

2. How can you reestablish a broken trust?

   A. Enter the password used for the original trust.

   B. Remove the domains from the Trust Relationships dialog box and set up the trust again.

   C. Synchronize domain controllers in each domain in the trust.

   D. Choose the Reestablish Trust option in Trust Administrator.

3. You have created a stripe set with parity that uses five physical disks with 200 MB used on each disk. How much storage is available for data?

   A. 500 MB

   B. 600 MB

   C. 800 MB

   D. 1 GB

4. You have created a stripe set with parity that uses three physical disks. The stripe set is now filled and you want to expand it. How can you do this?

   A. Add a new volume to the stripe set.

   B. Regenerate the stripe set.

   C. Back up the data, create a new stripe set, and restore the data.

   D. Install the new drive and configure the stripe set to recognize the new drive.

5. Which disk arrays are supported by Windows NT Workstation?

   A. Striping

   B. Striping with parity

   C. Disk mirroring

   D. Volume sets

6. You are creating a stripe set with parity from five physical drives. One drive has 300 MB of free space left, another drive has 500 MB left, and the other three drives have 700 MB left. What is the maximum size of a stripe set with parity that can be created by using a combination of these disks, including both usable space and parity space?

   A. 1.5 GB

   B. 2.0 GB

   C. 2.1 GB

   D. 2.9 GB

7. What is the best way to protect the partition where the Windows NT files are stored from disk failure?

   A. Install the operating system on a stripe set with parity.

   B. Automate a backup of the Windows NT drive by using the interface in the Windows NT Backup utility.

   C. Use disk duplexing.

   D. Configure directory replication to copy the Windows NT directory to another server.

8. SNA is a BackOffice product that provides a connection from a Windows NT server to AS400s. Which of the

1

following protocols must be installed to support SNA?

    A. NetBEUI

    B. NWLink

    C. DLC

    D. TCP/IP

9. You want to install Gateway Services for NetWare to allow clients on your domain to access files on NetWare servers. You also want to provide file and print services to Microsoft clients on this server. How many protocols need to be installed on this server?

    A. 1

    B. 2

    C. 3

    D. 4

10. You want to provide Web services on a Windows NT Server. This server must also have NetBIOS support for a network application. How many protocols need to be installed on the server?

    A. 1

    B. 2

    C. 3

    D. 4

11. You want to have a single protocol on your network that can be routed and provides connectivity for the greatest variety of clients. Which protocol should you use?

    A. NetBEUI

    B. NWLink

    C. DLC

    D. TCP/IP

12. You want to use the Migration Tool for NetWare to copy files from a NetWare Server to a new Windows NT Server. Which of the following protocols must be installed on the Windows NT Server so that the Migration Tool can be used?

    A. NetBEUI

    B. NWLink

    C. DLC

    D. TCP/IP

13. You have established a trust relationship between two domains. Users in the trusted domain cannot log in to the trusting domain. What is the problem?

    A. Users in the trusted domain do not have access to accounts in the trusting domain.

    B. The trust is broken.

    C. The Domain Users group from the trusting domain has not been assigned to the Users group of the trusted domain.

    D. The pass-through authentication service must be started.

14. A trust is established between a master domain and two resource domains. Which of the following can be added to local groups in each of the resource domains? Select all that apply.

    A. Global groups from the other resource domain

    B. Global groups from the master domain

    C. Users from the master domain

    D. Global groups from the same resource domain

15. Your domain has 5,000 Windows 95 clients and 1,000 Windows NT Workstation clients. How much space in the SAM database is required for these clients?

    A. 500 KB

    B. 1 MB

    C. 3 MB

    D. 6 MB

Answers and Explanations: Practice Exam

1. **D** Server Manager is the tool used to create computer accounts.

2. **B** A trust must be manually broken and then reestablished.

3. **C** One disk is used for overhead; only 800 MB of the stripe set is usable space.

4. **C** You cannot expand a stripe set. You must remove it and create a larger one. To protect data, you should back it up first and then restore it to the larger stripe set.

5. **A, D** Fault-tolerant arrays are supported only on Windows NT Server.

6. **C** Stripe sets must use an equal amount of space from each disk. The largest possible combination is to use the three 700 MB disks, for a stripe set of 2.1 GB. Using four disks with 500 MB yields 2.0 GB while using all five disks with 300 MB results in a 1.5 GB stripe set.

7. **C** Disk mirroring or disk duplexing is the only way to provide instant backup of a system disk. By the way, Windows NT Backup does not have an automated backup utility. Disk replication wouldn't copy open files.

8. **C** DLC is required for this connection.

9. **A** NWLink can be used to provide access to NetWare and as the protocol for Microsoft clients.

10. **A** TCP/IP provides the Web support. TCP/IP (or any protocol on a Windows NT Server) also provides NetBIOS connectivity.

11. **D** TCP/IP is routable and provides the greatest connectivity options.

12. **B** NWLink is required for the Migration Tool.

13. **A** A trust allows accounts in the trusted domain to be visible to the trusting domain. Users in the trusted domain don't see anything from the trusting domain.

14. **B, C, D** You can always add users and global groups from the local domain. You also can add users and global groups from any trusted domain.

15. **A** Windows 95 computers do not require computer accounts. Each Windows NT computer account uses .5 KB of space; therefore, 1,000 computers would require 500 KB of disk space.

CHAPTER 2

Installation and Configuration

This chapter prepares you for the exam by covering the following objectives:

- Installing Windows NT Server in the various server roles of Primary Domain Controller, Backup Domain Controller, and member server.

- Configuring network protocols and protocol bindings (including TCP/IP with DHCP and WINS, NWLink IPX/SPX Compatible Transport Protocol, DLC, and AppleTalk).

- Configuring Windows NT Server core services, including Directory Replication and Computer Browser.

- Configuring hard disks to provide redundancy and to improve performance.

- Configuring printers, such as adding and configuring a printer, implementing a printer pool, and setting print priorities.

- Configuring NT Server for various types of clients, including Windows NT Workstation, Windows 95, and Macintosh.

This chapter focuses on the installation and configuration of your Windows NT Server computer in an enterprise environment. It also covers the additional components and services that can be used in an enterprise environment.

The Enterprise exam does not place a great deal of emphasis on the installation process. You need to have a strong knowledge of the configuration options, however, and an understanding of the reasons for selecting a specific configuration. As you go through the sections of this chapter, you will be introduced to the configuration options and the steps required to install and to configure each component.

2.1   Installing Windows NT Server 4 in Various Server Roles

This chapter begins with a quick overview of the entire installation process to provide you with a solid understanding of the steps involved in installing a Windows NT Server system.

A.   An Overview of the Installation Process

To install Windows NT Server, run the appropriate WINNT.EXE setup program. If you are installing from a 16-bit operating system, such as MS-DOS, Windows 3.x, or Windows 95, run WINNT.EXE. To install from a 32-bit operating system, use WINNT32.EXE.

1.   The first phase of Windows NT copies the source files into temporary directories held locally on your computer, and then restarts the system.

2.   After the setup program has copied all the files to your system and the computer has been restarted, you are presented with a screen welcoming you to the installation of Windows NT Server.

3.   If you are installing Windows NT, press Enter to continue with a new install, or select to repair a damaged NT installation or to upgrade your Windows NT system. You also can access help screens that give you additional information about the Windows NT Server installation process.

4.   The setup program then attempts to detect any mass storage devices in your system. To continue with this detection, press Enter.

5.   The detected mass storage devices are displayed. If you have any SCSI devices that are not recognized automatically by the setup program, you can press S to specify additional mass storage devices. When all mass storage devices have been recognized, press Enter to continue with the setup. Microsoft's End-User Licensing Agreement (EULA) is presented to you; read the agreement and continue with the installation.

6.   Next, system settings that the setup program has detected for your installation are displayed. Review the settings to ensure they are correct and continue with the installation. If any of the settings are incorrect, select the item to change and press Enter to view the options available.

7.   Next, select the disk partition in which to install Windows NT Server or to create a new partition by selecting the free space on your drive and pressing C. Partitions can be removed by selecting the partition and pressing D. The partition that holds the temporary files used by your NT installation cannot be removed by this method.

8.   After disk partition, you are prompted to select the file system for your installation partition. The default is to use the current file system; alternately, you can select to convert the partition to NTFS or to format the partition using FAT or NTFS.

9.   You then are prompted to enter the directory for Windows NT Server. The default directory is \WINNT. After you have entered the installation directory, press Enter to continue.

10. In the next screen, you are prompted to do an exhaustive check of the hard disk. Press Enter to do the search; press Esc to skip the search.

11. Press Enter to restart your system. When it restarts, you will be running the GUI portion of the installation.

12. The graphical portion of the Windows NT Server setup has been broken into three sections. Complete each section to properly configure your new Windows NT Server system.

13. Enter the registration information for your software and press Enter or click Next to continue.

14. Next, select the client licensing mode based on your licensing agreement with Microsoft. The two options available are Per Server and Per Seat.

15. Each computer in a Windows NT environment must have a unique NetBIOS computer name with a maximum length of 15 characters. Enter your computer name and press Enter or click Next to continue.

16. Next, select your server role. For more information about server roles, see the next section, "Defining Server Roles in Windows NT Server."

17. The first account created in Windows NT Server is Administrator. This account cannot be deleted, so assign a password that is secure. You can assign a password to this account during the installation.

18. The next option enables you to create an Emergency Repair Disk. It is recommended that you always have an up-to-date Emergency Repair Disk to help you recover from unforeseen accidents.

19. You now see the list of components available when installing your Windows NT Server system. Select any desired components, then press Enter or click Next to continue.

20. You are ready to install Windows NT Networking. Press Enter or click Next to continue.

21. The first option in this section is connectivity. You must clarify whether you are wired directly to the network or using a dial-up adapter for remote access, or using both for connectivity.

22. Internet Information Server (IIS) can be installed automatically at this point or installed later. You will learn more about installing IIS in a later section.

23. Next, the Windows NT Server 4 installation program attempts to automatically detect a network adapter on your computer. If you have multiple adapters, click Find Next to search for any additional adapters. If your adapter is not detected, you can click the Select from list button and manually select your network adapter. After all adapters have been selected, press Enter or click Next to continue.

24. Select the protocols you want to install. Three basic protocols are already listed. Select all required protocols and continue.

25. The default or core networking services are listed on the next screen. Additional network services can be added by clicking Select from the list. Add the additional networking services you want and continue the installation.

26. Each service, protocol, and adapter is then added to the binding list. You can configure the binding list for your networking needs.

27. If you previously elected to install a Primary Domain Controller from the Server Type screen, you are prompted to define the name of your domain. If you are installing a Backup Domain Controller or a Member Server, you have the option to join an existing domain.

28. Now you can add the final touches to your Windows NT Server installation. Press Enter or click Next to continue with the installation.

29. You can select the correct time zone and set the date and time. Enter the appropriate information and click Next.

30. Next, you select the proper video card driver and video settings.

> **Make sure you test all the video settings by clicking Test. This ensures that your selection works with Windows NT Server.**

31. Setup then saves your configuration and displays a message informing you that the installation was completed successfully.

32. After the installation has been successfully completed, you can restart your system to verify the Windows NT Server setup.

B. Defining Server Roles in Windows NT Server

The different server roles in which Windows NT Server can be installed are as follows:

- Primary Domain Controller
- Backup Domain Controller
- Member Servers

Each server role provides a specific function in your Windows NT system. The next three sections address each of the roles. You gain an understanding of both the function each role performs and the reasons for selecting a particular server role for your Windows NT Server system.

1. Primary Domain Controllers

The Primary Domain Controller (PDC) is the first domain controller installed into a domain. As the first computer in the domain, the PDC creates the domain. Each domain can contain only one PDC. All other domain controllers in the domain are installed as Backup Domain Controllers (BDCs). In addition to standard Windows NT Server functionality, the PDC contains the original copy of the Security Accounts Manager (SAM) database, which contains all user accounts and security permissions for your domain and handles user requests and logon validation. The PDC runs the Netlogon service.

> **The three main functions of the Netlogon service are covered in different sections of this chapter. The three main functions are as follows:**
> - **To handle logon requests from users**
> - **To control database synchronization between PDCs and all BDCs**
> - **To enable pass-through authentication of users across trust relationships**

2. Backup Domain Controllers

The Backup Domain Controller (BDC) is an additional domain controller used to handle logon requests by users in the network. To handle the logon requests, the BDC must have a complete copy of the domain database, or SAM. The BDC also runs the Netlogon service.

A PDC will announce that there have been changes to one of the three SAM databases. The BDCs then will connect to the PDC and will request the changes that they do not have in their copy of the database. The entire database is not present, only the changes to the database are. The BDC helps the PDC handle user requests and logon validation. It also acts as a Windows NT Server, offering all the available options and functionality.

3. Member Servers

A computer that handles the server functionality you require without the overhead of handling logon validation is called a *Member Server*. A Member Server either is a part of the domain or is simply a participant in the Workgroup environment, but it does not need a copy of the SAM database nor does it handle logon requests. The main function of a Member Server is to share resources.

C. Changing Server Roles

After you install your computer in a specific server role, you might decide to change the role of the server. This can be a relatively easy task if you are changing a PDC to a BDC, or vice versa. If you want to change a domain controller to a Member Server or Member Server to a domain controller, however, you must reinstall into the required server role.

1. BDC to PDC

To change the server role of a domain controller, use the Promote to Primary Domain Controller option in the Computer menu of the Server Manager. You can only access this option by high-lighting the appropriate BDC from the Server Manager list.

Selecting this option stops the Netlogon service of both the existing PDC and the BDC to be promoted. The Netlogon is then restarted with the role change in effect. The BDC starts as the PDC, and the old PDC restarts as a BDC. This is a relatively easy change and does not affect any of the other BDCs in the enterprise.

2. Member Server to Domain Controller

The only way to change the server role from a Member Server to a domain controller (or vice versa) is to do a reinstall, not an upgrade.

2.1.1 Exercise: Installing Windows NT Server 4 as a Primary Domain Controller

In this exercise, you step through the process of installing Windows NT Server 4 as a PDC. The setup also includes some additional services and protocols. This exercise should take approximately 45 minutes to complete. Your system should have at least 150 MB of free disk space to complete this exercise.

1. Access the Windows NT Server 4 source directory from a CD-ROM, or copy all of the source files for Windows NT Server onto the local hard drive. The I386 directory contains the files you use to install the Intel-based software.

> **Make sure SMARTDRV.EXE is loaded prior to starting the installation of Windows NT because it dramatically reduces the time required to complete the first stage of the setup.**

2. From the Windows NT Server directory, enter the command line **WINNT /B**. This starts Windows NT Setup and enables you to complete the setup without creating the three boot disks.

3. The setup program copies the Windows NT Server 4 software into temporary directories on your computer. When finished copying the files, it prompts you to restart the system.

4. After the system has been restarted, you should notice that the Windows NT boot menu is now configured to autostart Windows NT. At this time, you should prepare to start the DOS-based portion of the Windows NT setup. Read the Welcome to Windows NT Setup screen and press Enter to start the setup of Windows NT.

5. The program then attempts to detect all mass-storage devices in your system. Review the selection and, if correct, press Enter to continue.

6. The End User Licensing Agreement screen is displayed for you to review. Read the screen, pressing Page Down to view the entire document. When you reach the bottom, press F8 to accept the terms of the agreement.

7. You then are prompted for the type of installation to complete. If this is the first occurrence of Windows NT on this system, press Enter to install Windows NT. If an existing installation of Windows NT is still on this system, pressing Enter upgrades the installation. If you want a new installation of Windows NT, press N to cancel the upgrade.

8. The hardware and software found on your computer is displayed. Press Enter to continue with the installation.

9. Select the drive on which you want to install Windows NT Server. Make sure it has at least 120 MB of free disk space to complete the installation. You also want to make sure the current file system is left intact, so FAT is the file system for your Windows NT system.

If you want to use NTFS as the file system, this screen enables you to convert your file system to NTFS.

---

10. Press Enter to use the default directory, \WINNT.

11. Press Enter to have the setup program examine your hard disks.

12. The system then prompts you to restart. When the system is restarted, it is in the graphical portion of the setup.

13. When the Windows NT Server Setup Wizard appears, click Next to start using the Setup Wizard.

14. Enter your name and organization information; click Next.

15. Type your CD Key, located on the Windows NT Server CD-ROM, and click Next.

16. Select the licensing mode you want to use. For this exercise, select Per Server with 10 concurrent connections; click Next.

17. Enter the computer name for your Windows NT Server computer. For this exercise, enter **Comp1** as the computer name; click Next.

The computer name can be a maximum of 15 characters and must be unique on the network to which it is attached.

---

18. Select the Primary Domain Controller option and click Next.

19. Enter a password for the Administrator account. For this exercise, use **password** as the password. Make sure you confirm the password and then click Next.

20. You might get a prompt regarding a floating point workaround. Select Do Not Enable the Floating Point Workaround and click Next to continue.

21. Click Yes, create an Emergency Repair Disk, and then click Next.

22. Click Next to select the default components. You are then presented with Phase 2 of the setup, "Installing Windows NT Networking."

23. Click Next to begin Phase 2.

24. Make sure Wired to the network is selected and click Next.

25. Clear the Install Microsoft Internet Information Server check box and click Next.

26. Click Start Search to have the setup program automatically detect your network cards. If you have multiple cards, click Find Next until all have been located. If your card is not located automatically, click Select from list and choose your network card manually. When the proper network adapters have been selected, click Next to continue.

27. Select TCP/IP and NetBEUI as your protocols and click Next.

28. All of the default network services should be used, so click Next to continue.

29. Click Next to install the network components.

30. If you are prompted to confirm the settings for your network adapter, make sure they are displayed correctly and click Next to continue.

31. You are prompted to use DHCP. If you have a DHCP server, click Yes. If you do not have a DHCP server, click No.

32. Click Next to accept the default bindings for your system.

33. Click Next to start the network.

34. If you did not use DHCP, when you are prompted for your TCP/IP settings, use 131.107.2.100 for your IP Address and 255.255.255.0 for a subnet mask. No default gateway is required for this exercise.

35. When prompted for your domain name, enter **DomainA** and click Next.

36. Phase 3 of the setup starts. Click Finish to start the last phase of the setup.

37. When prompted, enter the date, time, and time zone information for your location; click Next.

38. You must then configure your video adapter. Click OK to confirm the detected video adapter.

39. Click Test to verify the settings for your video adapter.

40. If the settings appear correctly, click Yes. Click OK to continue the installation.

41. The system then prepares to create the Emergency Repair Disk. Get a blank high-density floppy disk and, when prompted, insert it into drive A: and click OK.

42. When the emergency repair information has been written to disk, the system removes the temporary files and prompts you to restart.

43. When the system restarts, Windows NT Server has been installed successfully.

2.1 Practice Problems

1. You need to install a new Member Server in the Pittsburgh Domain, but you are in St. Louis. What is the best method to install and configure a Member Server when it is not physically attached to the Domain?

   A. Install the new server as a PDC; then, convert it to a Member Server when it can be attached physically.

   B. Install it as a BDC of the St. Louis domain and change its domain when in the correct location.

   C. Install the machine as a computer in the workgroup. When it is in the correct location, add the computer to the Pittsburgh domain.

   D. None of the above.

2. You have correctly installed your NT server, but it has developed a problem that requires the Emergency Repair Disks. You do not have the three disks created during the original installation. How can you create them?

   A. SETUP32.EXE /B

   B. WINNT /OX

   C. WINNT /B

   D. WINNT32 /UDF

3. Your company has one server running Windows NT and has no plans to add additional servers. With 40 employees and 30 workstations, what kind of licensing do you choose?

   A. Purchase 30 CALs and configure them as Per Seat.

   B. Purchase 40 CALs and configure them as Per Seat.

   C. Purchase 30 CALs and configure them as Per Server.

   D. Purchase 40 CALs and configure them as Per Server.

4. You have installed four NT server machines in one domain (one PDC and three BDCs). Your company has grown and the following objectives have been set for the changing company network.

   Primary Objective: You want to add another domain to the network, but must use only the existing domain controllers.

   Secondary Objective: When the new domain has been created, you want to move several users and their machines to the new domain.

   Proposed Solution: To accomplish this, you want to promote one BDC to a PDC and rename it. You then plan to change another BDC to belong to the new domain by changing the domain name from the Network option in Control Panel.

   In addition, you want to migrate several NT Workstation computers by changing the domain name and by creating the computer account from the system option in the Control Panel.

   How well does this solution work?

   A. This solution fills the primary and the secondary objectives.

   B. This solution fills the primary but not the secondary objective.

   C. This solution does not fill the primary objective but does fill the secondary objective.

   D. This solution does not fill the primary or the secondary objectives.

5. What installation options are available when installing NT Server?

   A. Custom, Typical, Portable

   B. Typical, Custom

   C. Custom

   D. Typical

6. If an NT Workstation machine needs to migrate to another domain, what needs to happen? Select all that apply.

   A. From the Server Manager, use Add to Domain; then, from the workstation machine, change the workstation name from My Computer properties.

   B. From the Server Manager, use Add to Domain; then, from the workstation machine, change the workstation name from Network Neighborhood properties.

   C. Reinstall and create the computer account during the installation.

   D. On the local computer, add the computer account from the network applet in Control Panel.

7. Which of the following will create a server-based installation? Select all that apply.

   A. Copy the platform-specific folder to the server and share the folder.

   B. Share the platform-specific folder on the Windows NT Server compact disk.

   C. Copy the platform-specific files to the workstation.

   D. Connect the workstation to the shared files on the distribution server.

8. You already have created NT setup boot disks and do not want to create them again. How can you avoid creating the disks and use your original set?

   A. Start the installation with WINNT /X.

   B. Start the installation with WINNT /OX.

   C. Start the installation with WINNT /B.

   D. Start the installation with WINNT /disks:0.

9. You want to upgrade a Windows NT Workstation 3.51 to a Windows NT Server 4 domain controller. How do you do so?

   A. Run WINNT and choose yes to the upgrade question.

   B. Run WINNT32 and choose yes to the upgrade question.

   C. There is no direct upgrade path from NT Workstation 3.51 to an NT Server 4 domain controller.

   D. Run UPGRADE.EXE.

10. You want to upgrade a Windows NT Server 3.51 Member Server to a Windows NT Server 4 domain controller. How do you do this?

    A. Run WINNT and choose yes to the upgrade question.

    B. Run WINNT32 and choose yes to the upgrade question.

    C. There is no direct upgrade path from an NT Server 3.51 Member Server to an NT Server 4 domain controller.

    D. Run UPGRADE.EXE.

11. You want to upgrade a Windows NT Server 3.51 Member Server to a Windows NT Server 4 Member Server. How do you do this?

    A. Run WINNT and choose yes to the upgrade question.

    B. Run WINNT32 and choose yes to the upgrade question.

    C. There is no direct upgrade path from NT Workstation 3.51 to an NT Server 4 domain controller.

    D. Run UPGRADE.EXE.

12. You want to upgrade a Windows NT Server 3.51 domain controller to a Windows NT Server 4 domain controller. How do you do this?

    A. Run WINNT and choose yes to the upgrade question.

    B. Run WINNT32 and choose yes to the upgrade question.

    C. There is no direct upgrade path from an NT Workstation 3.51 to an NT Server 4 domain controller.

    D. Run UPGRADE.EXE.

13. You want multiple servers to contain the source files to increase the performance for installation of NT machines. How do you do this?

    A. Run WINNT /s

    B. Run WINNT32 /d

    C. Run WINNT32 /m

    D. Run WINNT /m

14. You have to remove NT from a logical partition formatted with NTFS and want to remove just the partition. How can you do this? Select all that apply.

    A. Use the NT Disk Administrator. Choose to remove the partition and it will do so the next time NT starts.

    B. Use the NT setup program and, when choosing a partition, highlight the NT partition and press D to delete.

    C. Use the OS/2 1.x installation disks.

    D. Use MS-DOS FDISK from versions 5.0 or earlier.

15. You want to automate the installation of 50 NT Workstations. You have created UNATTEND.TXT. How do you start your installations?

    A. WINNT /U:UNATTEND.TXT

    B. WINNT /A:UNATTEND.TXT

    C. WINNT /UDF:UNATTEND.TXT

    D. WINNT /I:UNATTEND.TXT

16. What is the name of the setup program for an upgrade installation of Windows NT Server 3.51 to 4?

    A. SETUP.EXE

    B. SETUP32.EXE

    C. WINNT.EXE

    D. WINNT32.EXE

17. What is the name of the setup program if you are not installing from a 32-bit operating system?

    A. SETUP.EXE

    B. SETUP32.EXE

    C. WINNT.EXE

    D. WINNT32.EXE

2.1.1 Answers and Explanations: Exercise

In this exercise, you reviewed the process of installing Windows NT Server 4 as a PDC. This setup also included some additional services and protocols. To perform this setup, you need 150 MB of free space, and SMARTDRV.EXE needs to be loaded prior to starting the installation of Windows NT. You can update your file system to NTFS at the time of installation as well.

2.1 Answers and Explanations: Practice Problems

1. **C** It is not possible to change a domain controller to a Member Server without reinstalling.

2. **B** Use WINNT /OX to create the three disks without performing a complete.

3. **C** Because there are only 30 workstations, only 30 connections would be used.

4. **D**   It is not possible to migrate domain controllers, and although computer accounts can be made from an NT Workstation, they are created through the Network icon in the Control Panel.

5. **C**   Custom is the only option under NT Server.

6. **B, D**   Reinstalling is not necessary.

7. **A, B, D**   Although it is possible to copy the files to the workstation and then install them, it isn't a server-based installation.

8. **B**   /OX will create the startup disks. /X will start an installation and use previously created disks.

9. **B**   When upgrading NT use WINN32.

10. **C**   Although 3.51 Member Servers are upgradable, they can be upgraded only to Member Servers.

11. **B**   Version 3.51 Member Servers are upgradable to 4 Member Servers.

12. **B**   Run Winnt32 to perform the upgrade from the Run line and keep your domain controller down time to a minimum.

13. **A**   WINNT /s and the source code paths.

14. **A, B, C**   FDISK will work if it is MS-DOS 6.0 or later and if the NTFS partition is a primary partition.

15. **A**   /UDF often accompanies an unattended installation, but it will provide information specific to each workstation.

16. **D**   WINNT32.EXE is used to upgrade 32-bit environments like NT 3.51.

17. **C**   WINNT.EXE is used for installing from DOS, Windows 3.1, or Windows 95.

2.1   Key Words

Primary Domain Controller

Backup Domain Controller

Member Server

WINNT

WINNT32

2

2.2   Configuring Networking Protocols and Protocol Bindings

In this section, you examine the configuration process for each protocol. You also learn the installation steps required to add any protocols.

Installing and configuring network protocols is controlled in the network properties of your Windows NT system. The installation of all the protocols is identical. The configuration of each protocol is different, however, so you must understand the process required for configuring each of the supported protocols.

A.   Installing Protocols

The installation of a new protocol in Windows NT Server is done through the Network dialog box. To open the Network dialog box, double-click the Network icon in the Control Panel.

To install a new protocol using the Network dialog box, select the Protocols tab. To see a list of the protocols available for you to install, click Add. Highlight the protocol you are installing; then click OK.

The system tries to locate the Windows NT installation files. If it cannot locate them, you are prompted to enter the directory path of the Windows NT Server 4 source files.

After the protocol has been installed, you cannot configure it until it has been bound to your network adapter. After the binding process is completed, you can configure the protocol. Click OK at the bottom of the Network dialog box when finished. When the binding process is completed, you will then be prompted to configure the protocol.

B.   Configuring Protocols

Each protocol is configured by changing its properties. The properties of each protocol can be accessed in the Protocols tab of the Network dialog box. On the Protocols tab, highlight the protocol you want to configure and then select the Properties button.

1.   TCP/IP

TCP/IP is the most common protocol because it is accepted across most platforms. It is the protocol that allows access to the Internet. The TCP/IP protocol also enables communication between various platforms, including UNIX systems.

> **Many of the questions on the Enterprise exam relate to the use of the TCP/IP protocol. Be sure you understand all the options available with the TCP/IP protocol.**

To access the properties of the TCP/IP protocol, highlight TCP/IP Protocol in the Network dialog box and click Properties. The tabs available for configuration in the Microsoft TCP/IP Properties dialog box are as follows:

- IP Address
- DNS

- WINS Address
- DHCP Relay
- Routing

You must configure each tab in the Microsoft TCP/IP Properties dialog box to complete the configuration of your TCP/IP settings. Note that on the IP Address tab, you have the option to select the network adapter you want to configure. Each network adapter card in your system can and should have different TCP/IP settings.

a. Configuring the IP Address

The IP Address tab allows configuring of the IP address, the subnet mask, and the default gateway. You also can enable the system to automatically obtain an IP address through the use of the DHCP server.

An IP address is a 32-bit address that is broken into four octets and is used to identify your network adapter card as a TCP/IP host. Each IP address must be unique. If users have IP address conflicts on the network, they cannot use the TCP/IP protocol until the conflict is resolved.

Your IP addresses then are grouped into a subnet. To subnet your network, assign a subnet mask. A *subnet mask* is used to identify the computers local to your network. Any address outside your subnet is accessed through the default gateway. The *default gateway* is the address of the router that passes your TCP/IP information to computers, or hosts, outside your subnet.

If your IP address was 131.107.2.100 and your subnet mask was 255.255.0.0, the first two octets would represent the network (131.107) and the last two octets would represent the unique host on the subnet (2.100).

b. Configuring DNS for TCP/IP

The *Domain Name System* (DNS) server translates TCP/IP host names of remote computers into IP addresses. The DNS server contains a database of all the computers you can access by hostname. This database is used when you access a web page on the Internet.

The DNS tab shows you the options available for configuring your TCP/IP protocol to use a DNS server. In configuring your DNS settings for the TCP/IP protocol, you must start by assigning a hostname to your computer. This *hostname* is part of the name other computers use to make TCP/IP connections to your computer system. The hostname is then combined with the TCP/IP domain name.

After your computer hostnames have been entered, enter the IP address of the DNS server containing your name database. Multiple DNS servers can be entered. The top DNS server is the first DNS searched by your system; other configured DNS servers will be used if the first server is unavailable. The Up and Down buttons directly beside your DNS servers can be used to modify your search order.

c. Assigning a WINS Address for TCP/IP

The WINS Address tab enables you to configure your primary and secondary *Windows Internet Names Services* (WINS) server addresses. WINS is used to reduce the number of NetBIOS broadcast messages sent across the network to locate a computer. By using a WINS server, the names of computers on your network are kept in a WINS database. Each computer or NetBIOS service registers its name into the database, enabling immediate lookup of computer names.

In configuring your WINS servers, you can enter a secondary WINS server. Your system first searches the primary WINS server database; your system searches the secondary database if the first server is unavailable.

Two other options are available on this tab. The first enables your system to search the DNS database if a computer name cannot be resolved to an IP address. The second option enables a local file, LMHOSTS, to be used as a local database of computer names. You then can configure the LMHOSTS file to enable named connections to your most common systems without using a DNS or WINS lookup.

d. Using a DHCP Relay Agent with TCP/IP

The DHCP relay agent is used to find your DHCP servers across routers. IP addresses are handed out by the DHCP servers. The client request, however, is made with local subnet broadcast messages. Broadcast messages do not normally cross routers. The solution is to use a DHCP relay agent to assist the clients in finding the DHCP server across a router.

After the DHCP Relay Agent Service is installed, you can configure your DHCP relay agent. Settings include the seconds threshold, the maximum number of hops to use in searching for the DHCP servers, and the IP addresses of the DHCP servers you want to use.

e. Routing

In an environment in which multiple subnets are used, you can configure your Windows NT Server as a multihomed system. By installing multiple network adapters, each connecting to a different subnet, you can enable the Enable IP Forwarding option: your computer acts as a router, forwarding the packets through the network cards in the multihomed system to the other subnet.

2. NWLink IPX/SPX Compatible

The NWLink IPX/SPX-compatible protocol was designed for NetWare connectivity, but it can be used for network connectivity between any systems running IPX-compatible protocols. The configuration of the NWLink protocol is simple in comparison to the TCP/IP protocol. To configure your NWLink protocol, highlight NWLink IPX/SPX Compatible Transport in the Network dialog box; then click Properties. The NWLink IPX/SPX Properties dialog box appears. The NWLink IPX/SPX Properties dialog box has two tabs: General and Routing.

On the General tab, you have the option to assign an internal network number. This eight-digit, hexadecimal number format is used by some programs with services that can be accessed by NetWare clients.

You also have the option to select a frame type for your NWLink protocol. The frame type you select must match the frame type of the remote computer with which you need to communicate. By default, Windows NT Server uses the Auto Frame Type Detection setting, which scans the network and loads the first frame type it encounters. If multiple frame types are detected, NT will default to using the 802.2 frame type. The topologies and frame types are listed in Table 2.2.1.

Table 2.2.1   Supported Frame Types

Topology	Supported Frame Types
Ethernet	802.2, 802.3, Ethernet II, SNAP
Token ring	802.5, SNAP
FDDI	802.2, SNAP

The default frame type is 802.2 in NetWare 3.12 and later. Earlier versions of NetWare used 802.3 as a default frame type.

The Routing tab of the NWLink IPX/SPX Properties dialog box is used to enable or disable the Routing Information Protocol (RIP). If you enable RIP routing over IPX, your Windows NT Server can act as an IPX router. This also requires the installation of the RIP for NWLink IPX/SPX Compatible Transport Service to be installed.

3. AppleTalk

To install the AppleTalk protocol, you must install Services for Macintosh. You will examine the requirements for that later in this chapter. Select the AppleTalk protocol; then, click Properties. The Microsoft AppleTalk Protocol Properties dialog box appears.

C. Configuring the Binding Order

The *binding order* is the sequence your computer uses to select which protocol to use for network communication. Each protocol is listed for each network-based service, protocol, and adapter available. Setting the binding order of your network services and protocols can optimize your network configuration. To modify the binding order, go to the Bindings tab in the Network dialog box.

The Bindings tab contains an option, Show bindings for, that can be used to select the service, adapter, or protocol that you want to modify in the binding order. By clicking the appropriate option, each binding can be enabled or disabled, or it can be moved up or down in the binding order.

2.2.1 Exercise: Configuring TCP/IP Protocol

In this exercise, you modify the TCP/IP protocol to use a DHCP server and to manually input an IP Address. This exercise should take about 15 minutes to complete.

1. Select Start, Settings, Control Panel, and double-click the Network icon.

2. Select the Protocols tab.

3. Highlight TCP/IP Protocol, then click Properties.

4. On the IP Address tab of the Microsoft TCP/IP Properties dialog box, enable Obtain an IP address from a DHCP server.

5. Click OK to close the Microsoft TCP/IP Properties dialog box; then click OK to close the Network dialog box.

6. The system prompts you to restart the system for the new settings to take effect. Restart the system.

7. When the system restarts, open a command prompt and enter **IPCONFIG /ALL** to view your current TCP/IP settings.

> If a DHCP server is not available when you run the IPCONFIG command, all of the addresses should be set to 0.0.0.0. If these are already the current settings, it is configured properly and you are only missing the DHCP server.

8. Next, you will reset the IP address back to a manual IP address. Right-click the Network Neighborhood icon and select Properties. The Network dialog box appears.

9. Select the Protocols tab.

10. Highlight TCP/IP Protocol and click Properties.

11. In the Specify an IP address section, enter **131.107.2.100** as the IP Address.

12. For the Subnet Mask, enter **255.255.255.0**.

13. For the Default Gateway, enter **131.107.2.1**.

14. Next, select the WINS Address tab.

15. Enter **131.107.2.2** for the Primary WINS Server.

16. Select the DNS tab.

17. Enter **131.107.2.2** in the list of DNS servers.

18. Click OK to save all settings.

19. Click OK in the Network properties dialog box. You are now using your new settings.

20. Start a command prompt and enter **IPCONFIG /ALL**.

21. Note that your current IP information has been changed to the settings you just entered.

2.2 Practice Problems

1. What is a subnet mask used for?

   A. It is the address of the router.

   B. It is used to determine whether a target host is on the same subnet or on a remote subnet.

   C. It is a unique 32-bit address that identifies your machine across a TCP/IP network.

   D. It passes addressing information to the Internet.

2. Your company is using TCP/IP as the primary network protocol. Users on the network randomly complain that they get messages about IP address conflicts. What could be a potential solution to this?

   A. Implement IIS

   B. Implement DNS

   C. Implement WINS

   D. Implement DHCP

3. Which service can be used to reduce the number of NetBIOS broadcast messages sent across the network to locate a computer?

   A. TCP/IP

   B. HOST files

   C. WINS

   D. DNS

4. By default, how are DHCP servers used to allocate an IP address to a client?

   A. Each client is configured to request an IP address from a specific DHCP server.

   B. Each client sends out a broadcast requesting a number from any DHCP server that can respond.

   C. Each client is configured to look for an LMHOSTS file with the IP address of the DHCP server.

   D. A DHCP server sends out broadcasts announcing itself across the network. Any client needing an address will respond to the broadcast.

5. Your multihomed system is connected to multiple TCP/IP subnets. What must be enabled to transfer packets between subnets?

   A. IP repeating

   B. IP forwarding

   C. Default Gateway

   D. DNS

6. What is the default frame type setting for Windows NT?

   A. 802.2

   B. 802.3

   C. Auto Frame

   D. SNAP

7. What needs to be installed to configure AppleTalk?

   A. Gateway Services for Macintosh

   B. NWLINK

   C. Services for Macintosh

   D. LocalTalk

8. To optimize your binding order, the protocols should be placed in what order?

   A. The protocols used most often should be at the top of the binding order.

   B. The least used protocols should be at the top of the binding order.

   C. Binding order will not affect speed.

   D. Stagger the protocols to keep a balanced load.

2.2.1 Answers and Explanations: Exercise

In this exercise, you modified the TCP/IP protocol to use a DHCP server and then manually inserted an IP address. You did this from the Settings, Control Panel, Network icon area. For more information on the TCP/IP protocol, review the section titled "Configuring Protocols."

2.2 Answers and Explanations: Practice Problems

1. **B** A subnet mask number will identify whether an address is local or needs to be passed on the default gateway.

2. **D** DHCP will assign IP addresses as needed. This will provide users with a unique address and will minimize the possibility of conflicts.

3. **C** WINS will keep a list of all NetBIOS names for machines.

4. **B** Machines broadcast a request for an address and will accept an address from any server that responds unless configured otherwise.

5. **B** A router works at the network layer of the OSI model and can filter protocol information.

6. **A** 802.2 is used in Windows NT as the preferred frame type.

7. **C** Services for Macintosh must be installed from the Service tab of the Network icon.

8. **A** To optimize the protocols, place the most used at the top of the list.

2.2 Key Words

Subnet mask

IP address

DNS

WINS

DHCP relay

Default gateway

2.3   Configuring Windows NT Server Core Services

Windows NT takes full advantage of its multithreaded, multitasking capabilities by running services in the background. In this section, you look at configuring some of the core services in Windows NT Server. These services are the following:

- Server service
- Workstation service
- Computer Browser service
- Directory Replication service

A. Server Service

The Server service answers network requests. By configuring Server service, you can change the way your server responds and, in a sense, the role it plays in your network environment. Servers in a network environment can be grouped into three different classes or roles:

- Logon server (domain controller)
- Application server
- File/print server

When configuring the Server service, the first step is to select the role your computer will play in your network environment. To configure Server service, you must open the Network dialog box. To do this, double-click the Network icon in Control Panel and select the Services tab.

To configure Server service, highlight Server and click Properties. You are then able to view the properties of your Server service. In the Server dialog box, you have four optimization settings. Each of these settings modifies memory management based on the role the server plays. These options are described in the following sections.

For the enterprise exam, you need to know when each optimization setting should be used and the differences between the four settings.

---

1.   Minimize Memory Used

The Minimize Memory Used setting is used when your Windows NT Server system is accessed by a small number of users (less than 10). This setting is used when the Windows NT Server computer is used as a user's desktop computer, not in a true server role. This setting allocates memory so a maximum of 10 network connections can be properly maintained. By restricting the memory for network connections, more memory is available at the local or desktop level.

2.   Balance

The Balance setting can be used for a maximum of 64 network connections. This setting is the default when using NetBEUI software. Like the Minimize setting, Balance is best used for a relatively low number of users connecting to a server that also can be used as a desktop computer.

3. Maximize Throughput for File Sharing

The Maximize Throughput for File Sharing setting allocates the maximum amount of memory available for network connections. It is the default on any Windows NT Member Server computer. This setting is excellent for large networks in which the server is accessed for file and print sharing.

4. Maximize Throughput for Network Applications

If you are running distributed applications, such as SQL Server or Exchange Server, the network applications do their own memory caching. Therefore, you want your system to enable the applications to manage the memory. This is accomplished using the Maximize Throughput for Network Applications setting. This setting also is used for very large networks and is suggested for domain controllers.

B. Workstation Service

The Workstation service is your redirector in Windows NT Server. The Workstation service handles all outgoing network communication. The Workstation service has no configuration options through the Control Panel, unlike the other services discussed. You can make some Registry changes. Registry modification is not recommended unless you have a strong understanding of the Registry and its entries.

> **To make Registry changes, run the REGEDT32.EXE program. The Registry in Windows NT is a complex database of configuration settings for your computer. If you want to configure the Workstation service, open the HKEY_LOCAL_MACHINE hive. The exact location to configure your Workstation service is:**
>
> `HKEY_Local_Machine\System\CurrentControlSet\Services\LanmanWorkstation\Parameters`

C. Computer Browser Service

The Computer Browser service is responsible for maintaining the list of computers on the network that are running the Server service or that have file and print sharing enabled. The browse list contains all the computers located on the physical network. As a Windows NT Server, your system plays a big role in the browsing of a network. The Windows NT Server acts as a master browser or backup browser.

The functions of a master or backup browser are to hold the list of computers in the domain and to share that list with other computers. In the Microsoft networking environment, all computers send broadcast messages across the network containing the domain/workgroup to which they belong as well as their computer names.

A master browser will gather all of these broadcasts for their subnets. The domain master browser will collect the lists from all master browsers to build a total domain browse list. Periodically, the master browsers will copy the browse list to backup browsers. When clients request a browse list, they receive it from a backup browser on their subnet.

Browsing happens automatically, so no configuration is required. You can, however, configure whether you want your server to be a master or backup browser. The configuration is done in the Registry. The settings are found in

`HKEY_Local_Machine\System\CurrentControlSet\Services\Browser\Parameters`

Two entries can be modified to select whether your server is a preferred master. The first entry is IsDomainMaster=True/False. You select True if you want your computer to be the master browser; select False if you do not want it to be the master browser.

The other entry is MaintainServerList=Auto. If this entry is set to Auto, your server is able to act in a browser role on the network.

The selection of browsers is through an election. The election is called by any client computer when it cannot connect to a master browser or when a preferred master browser computer starts up. The election is based on broadcast messages. Every computer has the opportunity to nominate itself, and the computer with the highest settings wins the election. The election criteria are based on three things:

- The operating system (Windows NT Server, Windows NT Workstation, Windows 95, Windows for Workgroups)

- The version of the operating system (NT 4, NT 3.51, NT 3.5)

- The current role of the computer (master browser, backup browser, potential browser)

This is a simplified breakdown of the election criteria. Look in the Windows NT Resource Kit for detailed information about the election criteria.

D. Directory Replication Service

In any network environment, it is a challenge to maintain consistent logon scripts and system policies across multiple servers. In Windows NT Server, this is handled through the use of the Directory Replication service. The Directory Replication service can be configured to synchronize an entire directory structure across multiple servers.

In configuring the directory replication service, you must select the export server and all the import servers. The export server is the computer with the original copy of the directory structure and files. Each import server receives a complete copy of the export server's directory structure, which is monitored by the Directory Replication service. If the contents of the directory change, the changes are copied to all the import servers. A special service account you create is needed by the service. You configure the Directory Replication service to use this service account.

The Directory Replication service can be used to maintain consistent logon scripts, system policies, or data files across the distributed network environment.

1. Directory Replication Service Account

The Directory Replication service account must have proper access on all the servers participating in the directory replication process. The following access is required for your Directory Replication service account:

- The account should be a member of the Backup Operators and Replicator groups.

- There should be no time or logon restrictions for the account.

- The Password Never Expires option should be selected.

- The User Must Change Password At Next Logon option should be turned off.

- This account also must be assigned the user right to log on as a service. This happens when replication is configured through the Services icon in Control Panel.

> **If you are not running the service packs for Windows NT Server, this replication account does not work properly. To fix this problem, apply the Windows NT service packs or assign the Administrators group membership to the service account. Another solution is to edit the Registry in the following area:**
>
> HKEY_LOCAL_MACHINE\System\CurrentControlSet\Control\SecurePipeServers\WinReg\AllowedPaths
>
> **You can modify the** Machine **value to include the entry System\CurrentControlSet\Services\Replicator.**

2. Installing Directory Replication Service

The Directory Replication service is installed during the installation of Windows NT Server. To get the Directory Replication service to work, you need to configure the service. Prior to configuring the service, be sure your Directory Replication service account has been created and assigned the appropriate permissions. Open the Control Panel and double-click the Services icon. You then are presented with a list of all the services installed on your Windows NT Server. Locate the Directory Replication service.

The Directory Replication service's start up option is set to manual. The service is not started at this time, and you should not start the system until all configuration has been completed. To change the properties for the Directory Replication service, make sure it is selected in the Service list and then click Startup.

To configure the service to work with the Directory Replication service account, you must change the Startup Type to Automatic. Fill in the Log On As This Account option with the name and password of your service account.

You have now configured the Directory Replication service, but you still need to configure replication. The export and import servers must be selected and prepared before starting the Directory Replication service.

a. Export Server

To configure the export server, start Server Manager and double-click the export server. Click Replication in the Server Properties dialog box. When configuring the export server, you have the option to specify the export directory. The default export directory is as follows:

```
%SystemRoot%\system32\repl\export\
```

All subdirectories and corresponding files are sent to all the computers listed as import computers in the Export Directories section of the Directory Replication dialog box. It is critical that you include all systems requiring the files. It is possible for your own computer to act as both an export and import computer.

b. Import Server

The import computer also is configured in the Server Manager, Properties dialog box. To configure the import computer, click Replication to open the Directory Replication dialog box. The import computer can be the same computer as the export server.

In the Import Directories section of the Directory Replication dialog box, you can select the import directory. The default import directory is as follows:

```
%SystemRoot%\system32\repl\import.
```

Remember that the default directory for executing logon scripts in a Windows NT system is as follows:

```
%SystemRoot%\system32\repl\import\scripts
```

The netlogon share points to the same directory. You must also select the export server from which the import computer should receive the information. Make sure your import computer does not receive updates from multiple export-servers, or you might have difficulty maintaining consistency across your servers.

3. Managing Directory Replication

You can control directory replication from both the export and import servers. You can place locks on certain directories to exclude them from the replication process. You also can designate a stabilization time to ensure that the files in your directories are not modified during a replication.

The import server has similar options. Directory locking can be managed from either the export server or the import server.

2.3.1   Exercise: Configuring Directory Replication on a Windows NT Server

In this exercise, you configure the Directory Replication service to automatically replicate logon scripts.

1. Before you can configure directory replication, you must create a Directory Replication service account. Start User Manager for Domains and create a new user named **replacct**. This account should be a member of the Replicator and Backup Operators groups. Make sure there are no password or time restrictions on this account. When the user has been created, click Add and close the User Manager.

2. Select Start, Settings, Control Panel, and double-click the Services icon.

3. Highlight Directory Replicator in the Services dialog box and click Startup.

4. In the Service dialog box, select Automatic in the Startup Type section.

5. In the Log on As section, click This Account and select **replacct**. Click Add to add the account. If you created a password for this account, make sure you enter it in the password fields. Click OK and the Services dialog box is displayed again.

6. Click Close to exit the Services dialog box.

7. Select Start, Programs, Administrative tools, Server Manager.

8. Locate your computer in the list and double-click to view the properties of your computer.

9. Click Replication.

10. The Directory Replication dialog box appears.

11. Enable the Export Directories radio button.

12. Click Add to add a new computer for exporting. Select your computer name in the list; then, click OK to add it to the list.

13. Enable the Import Directories radio button.

14. Click the Add button in this section and select your computer name; then, click OK.

15. Click OK to close the Directory Replication dialog box. The Directory Replication Service should start when you click OK to close the dialog box.

16. Start the Windows NT Explorer and locate the \WINNT\System32\Repl\Export\scripts directory.

17. Create a text file called LOGIN.TXT in this directory.

18. Open the \WINNT\System32\Repl\Import\Scripts directory. Watch this directory until the LOGIN.TXT file appears. This might take a few minutes, so be patient.

19. When you see the file in the directory, close Explorer.

20. Select Start, Programs, Administrative Tools, Server Manager.

21. Locate your computer and double-click to view its properties.

22. Click Replication.

23. In the Export Directories section of the Directory Replication dialog box, click Manage. You should see status information about your directory replication.

24. Click Manage in the Import Directories section to view the status from the import computer.

At the completion of this exercise, you might want to set the Directory Replication service back to a manual start.

2.3 Practice Problems

1. Where do you go to configure your server service?

    A. Double-click the System icon in Control Panel and select the Services tab.

    B. Double-click the Network icon in Control Panel and select the Services tab.

    C. Double-click the Services icon in Control Panel and select the Services tab.

    D. From the Run line, type **Net Start server /config**.

2. When an NT server is utilized as a desktop machine, which server configuration is appropriate?

    A. Minimize Memory Used

    B. Balance

    C. Maximize Throughput for File Sharing

    D. Maximize Throughput for Network Applications

3. If a server needs to run distributed applications, which server configuration is appropriate?

    A. Minimize Memory Used

    B. Balance

    C. Maximize Throughput for File Sharing

    D. Maximize Throughput for Network Applications

4. Which server configuration is appropriate if a server needs the most amount of memory available for network connections?

    A. Minimize Memory Used

    B. Balance

    C. Maximize Throughput for File Sharing

    D. Maximize Throughput for Network Applications

5. Which server configuration is appropriate when a machine will never have more than 64 network connections?

    A. Minimize Memory Used

    B. Balance

    C. Maximize Throughput for File Sharing

    D. Maximize Throughput for Network Applications

6. Where do you go to use a graphical interface to configure your workstation service?

    A. Double-click the System icon in Control Panel and select the Services tab.

    B. Double-click the Network icon in Control Panel and select the Services tab.

    C. There are no GUI interface configuration options for the Workstation service.

    D. From Run, type **Net service / workstation**.

7. What does the Workstation service provide?

    A. It maintains a list of computer resources available to the current user.

    B. When requests are made that are not local, the Workstation service forwards the request to the network.

    C. When requests are made to a computer, the Workstation service provides the information to the requesting client.

    D. It enables replication information broadcasts to be made.

8. Which service will initiate synchronizing the domain controllers?

    A. Server

    B. Replication

    C. Network DDE

    D. Netlogon

9. Which service maintains the dynamic list of computers on the network?

   A. DHCP

   B. Computer Browser service

   C. DNS

   D. Messenger service

10. How is a computer registered with the browser?

   A. Every computer with file and print sharing enabled sends a broadcast across the network with domain and computer name information that is picked up by the browser.

   B. Browsers send out broadcast requests across the network asking for domain and computer names.

   C. A machine is configured during installation to be the browser. All machines automatically send an identity packet to this machine on startup.

   D. The network administrator manually logs NetBIOS names into a file on the browser computer.

11. Where can you configure the role an NT Server plays in Browsing?

   A. Right-click Network Neighborhood and choose Properties.

   B. Run the Registry Editor and open the HKEY_Local_Machine hive.

   C. Browsing roles are automatic. Configuration is not possible.

   D. Open Control Panel Services and edit the Computer Browser Startup tab.

12. Which operating system is going to take precedence in a browser election?

   A. NT Server 3.51

   B. NT Server 4

   C. NT Workstation 4

   D. Either of the Server versions have equal criteria

13. When directory replication occurs, how much information is copied over to import servers?

   A. Initially, the whole directory structure is copied—subsequent imports copy only changes.

   B. The whole directory structure is copied each time.

   C. The directory structure is copied in stages. This prevents excessive traffic on the network.

   D. The entire directory structure is copied once a week. In between, full transfers of changed information are replicated.

14. Where must information be placed for replication to occur?

   A. Folders are placed in *Systemroot*\system32\repl\import.

   B. Folders are placed in *Systemroot*\system32\repl\import\scripts.

   C. Folders are placed in *Systemroot*\system32\repl\export\scripts.

   D. Folders are placed in *Systemroot*\system32\repl\export.

15. What can you use Directory Replication to maintain? Select all that apply.

   A. Directory database information

   B. System Policies

   C. Logon scripts

   D. User profiles

16. What groups should the Directory Replication service account be a member of? Select all that apply.

   A. Administrators

   B. Backup Operators

   C. Power Users

   D. Replicators

17. How do you change the properties of the Directory Replication service?

   A. Make sure it is selected in the Service list; then click Startup.

   B. From the Policy menu in User Manager for Domains.

   C. Run **replication /configure**.

   D. Replication is automatically configured when NT is first installed.

2.3.1 Answers and Explanations: Exercise

In this exercise, you configured the Directory Replication service to automatically replicate logon scripts. You did this from the Services icon in the Control Panel. Before you can configure directory replication, you must create a Directory Replication service account.

Consider setting the Directory Replication service back to a manual start after finishing this exercise. For more information on Directory Replication, review the section titled "Installing Directory Replication Service."

2.3 Answers and Explanations: Practice Problems

1. **B** Services are configured through the Network icon in Control Panel, or by right-clicking Network Neighborhood.

2. **A** Minimize Memory Used if no more than 10 users are going to connect to the machine.

3. **D** Applications running across the network are going to benefit from this if they do not perform memory management themselves.

4. **C** Maximize Throughput for File Sharing is the default selection.

5. **B** Balance is not recommended for more than 64 connections.

6. **C** Workstation is a service not generally configured. If needed, there are some settings in the Registry that can be modified.

7. **B** This service enables a client to request information from a server.

8. **D** The PDC announces changes and the BDCs will request them using the Netlogon service.

9. **B** Browse lists contain machines on the network. DNS servers do have computer names but are resolved to IP addresses and are static.

10. **A** Browse lists are gathered through broadcasts.

11. **B** Browse roles are configured in the Registry.

12. **B** Election criteria includes OS versions, time available, and others.

13. **A** When replication first occurs, the entire structure is copied only after the changed files are replicated out.

14. **D** Files must be placed in Folders under the export folder to replicate.

15. **B, D** Only information that will be applied to a number of users is practical to replicate. Policies and profiles will typically apply to many users on a network.

16. **B, D** The account must be a member of both.

17. **A** Replication is also configured in Server Manager.

2.3 Key Words

Browser election

Directory Replication service

Export server

Import server

Server service

2.4   Configuring Hard Disks to Improve Performance

In Windows NT Server, various hard disk options and fault tolerance options are available to help you improve disk performance. In this section, you look at configuring your system to use the disk options available in Windows NT Server. All hard disk configuring can be done using the Disk Administrator tool. The different disk configurations you need to understand for the enterprise exam are as follows:

- Stripe set
- Volume set
- Disk mirroring
- Stripe set with parity

To start the Disk Administrator, select Start, Programs, Administrative Tools (common), Disk Administrator. When the program is first started, you see a progress bar initializing your hard disk configuration.

A.   Configuring a Stripe Set

Implementing a stripe set improves disk performance. Information is written across multiple physical disks and can increase the speed of disk reads and writes.

A stripe set is created from free space on a non-boot or system partition of your hard disks. A stripe set is created using free disk space across multiple physical disks. A stripe set must use equal amounts of disk space on each physical disk. A stripe set requires a minimum of 2 disks and is limited to a maximum of 32 disks.

To create a stripe set, start the Disk Administrator and select the free space from each of the disks to be used in the stripe set. To select multiple disks, hold down Ctrl and click with the mouse on each section. When all the sections have been selected, select Partition, Create Stripe Set. The stripe set is created, and the space is treated as one drive letter.

B.   Configuring a Volume Set

A volume set enables you to extend a drive. The partitions can be on multiple physical disks or on the same physical disk. When setting up a volume set, select the free space from all the drives you want to include and then select Partition, Create Volume Set.

After the volume set has been created, you then must format the volume set. To format the drive, select Tools, Format in the Disk Administrator. If formatted with NTFS, you can extend the volume set if more space is required.

To extend a volume set, select the volume set and the free space to be added to it. Then select Partition, Extend Volume Set. The volume set can be extended across the entire disk space, or it can be spread across multiple physical disks and treated as one partition.

> Volume sets are discussed on the Windows NT Server exam. They also might be mentioned on the enterprise exam, especially as a question involving extending a volume set. Only an NTFS partition can be extended in a volume set. If the file system is FAT, it cannot be extended.

C. Configuring Disk Mirroring

To establish a disk mirror, you are required to have two physical disks in your NT system. With disk mirroring, you are able to use an existing disk partition—including the system and boot partitions. Disk mirroring provides a duplicate set of your data on a spare disk. To establish a disk mirror, select the drive to mirror, and then select the free space to use on a second physical disk. Select Establish Mirror from the Fault Tolerance menu. The mirror set begins to duplicate all existing information from the first drive onto the mirror copy. Any new data is written to both drives by FTDISK.SYS.

After the disk mirror has been created, you might need to break the mirror. As part of configuration, however, you should know how to break a mirror set. The mirror set is split across two physical disks. Both partitions, however, are labeled E:. To remove or break a mirror set, select the mirror set and then select Break Mirror from the Fault Tolerance menu.

Adding a second controller to the machine will provide extra redundancy. By placing each disk in a mirror set on a separate controller, there is a lesser chance of both disks being made unavailable. This is commonly referred to as *disk duplexing*.

D. Configuring a Stripe Set with Parity

A stripe set with parity writes data and parity information across a minimum of 3 and a maximum of 32 physical disks. If any one of the disks fails, the data can be regenerated from the remaining data and the parity. As with a stripe set, you cannot create a stripe set with parity from an existing partition. By holding down the Ctrl key, you can select multiple sections of free space. Only after the three sections have been selected can you select Create Stripe Set with Parity in the Fault Tolerance menu.

After you select Create Stripe Set with Parity, you are prompted to enter the size of the stripe set with parity. By default, the value shown is the maximum size available. The minimum size also is listed for your information. The stripe set is then configured. In the Disk Administrator, you can see the stripe set is written across multiple physical disks. The legend across the bottom of the Disk Administrator shows which partitions belong to the stripe set with parity.

After the creation of any new partition, you also must format your drive. To format, select the stripe set with parity and then select Format from the Tools menu.

2.4.1 Exercise: Planning for Fault Tolerance Scenarios

This exercise tests your knowledge of recovering from a disk failure with different fault-tolerant partitioning schemes.

The Scenario: The ABC Company wants to install a Windows NT Server that will have the following disks installed:

    DISK 0: IDE 2 GB

    DISK 1: IDE 2 GB

    DISK 2: SCSI 8 GB

    DISK 3: SCSI 8 GB

    DISK 4: SCSI 8 GB

The following disk partitions are created on the computer:

    DISK 0 and DISK 1 are mirrored and Windows NT is installed to the mirrored partitions.

    DISK 2, DISK 3, and DISK 4 are members of a stripe set with parity.

Answer the following questions based on disk failure:

1. How would you recover if DISK 1 were to crash?

2. How would you recover if DISK 0 were to crash?

3. How would you recover if DISK 3 were to crash?

4. Can you recover if both DISK 3 and DISK 4 were to crash?

5. How much disk space will be available on the mirror set for storage?

6. How much disk space will be available on the stripe set with parity for storage?

2.4 Practice Problems

1. You have several areas of free space on a hard disk. What is the best way to collect this area for use?

    A. Create a stripe set.

    B. Create a volume set.

    C. Create a new logical drive.

    D. Create a new primary partition.

2. You are running out of space on your NT boot partition and want to make it bigger. How do you do so?

    A. Select an empty section of the disk and extend the NT partition as a volume set.

    B. Select an empty section on another disk and create a stripe set.

    C. Choose a separate disk and mirror the NT partition.

    D. Back up the NT partition, create a larger partition, and restore the data.

3. You want to create a volume set. What is the minimum number of disks required to do so?

    A. 1

    B. 2

    C. 3

    D. 4

4. You want to create a stripe set. What is the minimum number of disks required?

    A. 1

    B. 2

    C. 3

    D. 4

5. You want to create a stripe set with parity. What is the minimum number of disks required?

    A. 1

B. 2

C. 3

D. 4

6. You created a volume set and now need to reclaim part of the space for another drive. What is the best way to do this?

    A. In the Disk Administrator, select the volume set. From the Partition menu, choose to break the volume.

    B. In the Disk Administrator, select the volume set. Right-click the area to be reclaimed and choose to remove it.

    C. Back up the data and delete the volume set; then, re-create the volume and restore the data.

    D. Run FDISK and delete the volume set.

7. How is data written to a volume set?

    A. Each new file is written to a different section.

    B. One volume is filled before the next one is used.

    C. Data is broken up into 64 KB chunks and is evenly spread across the volume.

    D. Data is broken up into 32 KB chunks and is evenly spread across the volume.

8. Disk striping is considered to be which RAID level?

    A. 0

    B. 1

    C. 2

    D. 5

9. Volume sets are which RAID level?

    A. 1

    B. 5

C. 0

D. Volume sets are not any RAID level

10. How many areas of unformatted free space can be combined into one volume set?

   A. 6

   B. 12

   C. 24

   D. 32

11. How many disks can be combined into one stripe set?

   A. 12

   B. 22

   C. 32

   D. 42

12. With what file systems can a volume set be formatted?

   A. FAT, HPFS, NTFS

   B. HPFS, NTFS

   C. FAT, NTFS

   D. FAT, HPFS

13. How many types of hard disks can be used in a stripe set?

   A. SCSI only

   B. IDE only

   C. ESDI or SCSI or IDE

   D. A combination of disk types can be used

14. What type of fault tolerance can contain a system or boot partition?

   A. RAID 0

   B. RAID 1

   C. RAID 5

   D. RAID cannot be used on a system or boot partition

15. With what file systems can a stripe set be formatted?

   A. FAT, HPFS, NTFS

   B. HPFS, NTFS

   C. FAT, NTFS

   D. FAT, HPFS

16. With what file system can a volume set be formatted to extend it?

   A. FAT

   B. NTFS

   C. FAT or NTFS

   D. HPFS

17. How many partitions can removable media contain?

   A. 2

   B. 3

   C. 4

   D. 1

18. What does an administrator need to do to add another hard disk to the system?

   A. Run WINNT and choose to update.

   B. Nothing; NT will automatically detect the new disk.

   C. Run the Disk Administrator and choose Update from the Disk menu.

   D. In the Control Panel, go to the System icon and then to the Hardware Profiles tab.

19. You have formatted your D: drive with NTFS and need it to be FAT without losing data. What is the best method to do this?

   A. From a command prompt, type **Convert d: /fs:NTFS**.

   B. From a command prompt, type **Format d: /fs:NTFS"**.

C. Back up the D: drive to tape. Format the drive with FAT and restore the data.

D. You cannot restore a drive to FAT after it is NTFS.

20. Your computer has two hard disks installed in a master/slave combination. On the first disk you have two primary partitions and one extended partition with three logical drives. On the second disk you have one primary partition and one extended partition with two logical drives. What arc name would appear in the BOOT.INI file if Windows NT were installed in the default directory on the second logical drive of the first disk?

A. multi(0)disk(0)rdisk(0)partition(4)\ WINNT

B. multi(1)disk(0)rdisk(0)partition(4)\ WINNT

C. multi(0)disk(0)rdisk(0)partition(3)\ WINNT

D. multi(1)disk(0)rdisk(0)partition(3)\ WINNT

21. Your computer has two hard disks installed in a master/slave combination. On the first disk you have two primary partitions and one extended partition with three logical drives. On the second disk you have one primary partition and one extended partition with two logical drives. What arc name would appear in the BOOT.INI file if Windows NT were installed in the default directory on the primary partition of the second disk?

A. multi(0)disk(0)rdisk(0)partition(0)\ WINNT

B. multi(1)disk(0)rdisk(0)partition(0)\ WINNT

C. multi(0)disk(0)rdisk(1)partition(1)\ WINNT

D. multi(1)disk(0)rdisk(1)partition(1)\ WINNT

22. Your computer has two hard disks installed in a master/slave combination. On the first disk you have two primary partitions and one extended partition with three logical drives. On the second disk you have one primary partition and one extended partition with two logical drives. What arc name would appear in the BOOT.INI file if Windows NT were installed in the default directory on the second logical drive on the second disk?

A. multi(0)disk(0)rdisk(1)partition(3)\ WINNT

B. multi(1)disk(0)rdisk(0)partition(2)\ WINNT

C. multi(1)disk(0)rdisk(0)partition(3)\ WINNT

D. multi(1)disk(0)rdisk(1)partition(7)\ WINNT

23. After adding a new partition, NT will no longer boot. What needs to be done to correct the problem?

A. Edit the BOOT.INI file to reflect the new partition numbering.

B. Run WINNT and change the partition information.

C. Select MS-DOS from the Boot menu. At the C:\ prompt, copy the NTOSKRNL file to the boot partition.

D. You must reinstall NT.

24. You have installed NT on a FAT partition (D:) and want the partition to be NTFS. How do you change it?

A. From the command prompt, type **Convert D: /FS:ntfs**. This will immediately start the conversion.

B. From the command prompt, type **Convert D: /FS:ntfs**. This will start the conversion the next time NT is started.

C. From the command prompt, type
    Format D: /FS:ntfs. This will
    immediately start the conversion.

D. Back up the data, and then reformat
    the drive to NTFS and restore the
    data.

25. You have three drives with extra space on
    them. One has 400 MB, another has 500
    MB, and a third has 300 MB. What is the
    largest stripe set that can be created?

    A. 1,200 MB

    B. 1,500 MB

    C. 900 MB

    D. 500 MB

26. You have three drives with extra space on
    them. One has 400 MB, another has 500
    MB, and a third has 300 MB. What is the
    largest volume set that can be created?

    A. 1,200 MB

    B. 1,500 MB

    C. 900 MB

    D. 600 MB

27. A user is complaining that he has lost all
    of his long filenames. He is currently
    running Office 97 and using Norton
    Utilities 5.0. What might have caused the
    problem?

    A. The user converted from FAT to
        NTFS and all LFNs are lost during
        a conversion.

    B. The use of the third-party disk
        utilities included with Norton
        Utilities 5.0 has destroyed the LFN
        entries.

    C. The user has been moving files
        from an NTFS to a FAT partition.

    D. Long filenames were supported only
        under Windows 3.1

28. Which RAID level provides the better
    I/O performance?

    A. Mirror sets.

    B. Stripe sets with parity.

    C. Mirror and stripe sets with parity
        offer equal I/O performance
        benefits.

    D. Mirror and stripe sets with parity
        offer no I/O performance increase.

29. Which RAID level provides the better
    read performance?

    A. Mirror sets.

    B. Stripe sets with parity.

    C. Mirror and stripe sets with parity
        offer equal read performance
        benefits.

    D. Mirror and stripe sets with parity
        offer no read performance increase.

30. Your computer has four hard disks with
    the following amounts of free disk space:
    250 MB, 400 MB, 450 MB, and 500
    MB. What is the largest usable space that
    can be created with a stripe set with parity
    using any combination of the four hard
    disks?

    A. 1,000 MB

    B. 750 MB

    C. 1,200 MB

    D. 800 MB

2.4.1 Answers and Explanations: Exercise

1. How would you recover if DISK 1 were
    to crash? If DISK 1 were to crash, you
    would probably still be able to boot the
    system as the primary hard disk will still
    be functioning. You would have to break
    the mirror set using the Disk Administra-
    tor program. After the mirror is broken,
    you could replace the defective drive and
    re-establish the mirror set.

2. How would you recover if DISK 0 were to crash? If DISK 0 were to crash, you would not be able to boot the computer as the primary boot disk has failed. You would need to create a fault-tolerant boot disk and have the BOOT.INI file on this disk point to the Windows NT installation on DISK 1. After you have booted the computer, you could use the Disk Administrator program to break the mirror partition, re-assign Disk 1 the original drive letter that the mirror set used, replace the defective drive, and re-establish the mirror.

3. How would you recover if DISK 3 were to crash? If DISK 3 were to crash, you would still be able to work with the data. A stripe set with parity will make use of its parity information to rebuild the data stored on the failed drive. After DISK 3 is diagnosed as being the failed drive, a new SCSI 8 GB disk will need to be installed. Using the Disk Administrator program, you can then regenerate the stripe set with parity using the Disk Administrator program

4. Could you recover if both DISK 3 and DISK 4 were to crash? If both DISK 3 and DISK 4 were to crash, you could only resort to restoring the data from a recent tape backup. Stripe sets with parity only protect against a single-disk failure.

5. How much disk space will be available on the mirror set for storage? The mirror set will have 2 GB of available disk space.

6. How much disk space will be available on the stripe set with parity for storage? The stripe set with parity will have 16 GB of usable disk space. 8 GB will be used to maintain parity information.

2.4 Answers and Explanations: Practice Problems

1. **B** Volume sets can take areas on the same disk and collect them into a larger drive.

2. **D** Volume sets and stripe sets are not supported on system or boot partitions.

3. **A** Because areas on the same disk can be used in a volume, only one disk is required.

4. **B** A striped set requires a minimum of two disks.

5. **C** Because parity information is written across all disks, a minimum of three disks is needed.

6. **C** The only way to retrieve space from a volume set is to delete and recreate the volume. Make sure to back up any needed data before reformatting.

7. **B** One area on the volume is filled before another one is used.

8. **A** Disk striping will not provide any fault tolerance and is considered to be RAID 0.

9. **D** Volumes are not part of RAID.

10. **D** Up to 32 areas can be used in one volume set.

11. **C** Up to 32 disks can be combined.

12. **C** A volume can be created and formatted with FAT or NTFS.

13. **D** A combination of disk types may be used.

14. **B** Only Disk Mirroring can be used on a system or boot partition.

15. **C** A stripe set can be created and formatted with FAT or NTFS.

16. **B** Only NTFS can be used on an extended volume.

17. **D** Only one partition on removable media is supported.

18. **B** NT will recognize the new drive when the computer is back on line.

19. **C** FAT can be converted to NTFS but not the other way around.

20. **A** The Arc Name that would appear in the BOOT.INI that would represent the second logical drive on the first disk would be multi(0)disk(0)rdisk(0)partition(4)\WINNT. Remember that all primary partitions are first assigned numbers and then the logical drives are assigned numbers. Partitions start numbering at 1.

21. **C** Remember that the second disk is a slave disk on the first controller. The Arc Name would be multi(0)disk(0)rdisk(1)partition(1)\WINNT.

22. **A** The slave disk would be represented as RDISK(1), and the second logical drive on this disk would be represented as partition(3) on the second disk.

23. **A** The BOOT.INI file uses ARC paths to locate NT.

24. **B** Because the Boot partition is in use, it can't be converted until the machine is restarted.

25. **C** Stripe sets require that each area is of similar size.

26. **A** A volume set can use various sized areas to create a new drive.

27. **B** Third-party disk programs will not recognize the secondary directory entries that store the LFNs and will attempt to "fix" them. This results in the loss of long filenames.

28. **B** Stripe sets with parity result in better I/O performance due to the use of additional disk controllers.

29. **B** With multiple disks read operations will be faster.

30. **D** The largest usable disk space that can be created is 800 MB. This is created by using 400 MB from the three disks with free space greater than 400 MB. Remember that 400 MB of the total 1,200 MB is used to store parity information in case of data loss.

2.4 Key Words

Stripe set

Volume set

Disk mirroring RAID level 1

Stripe set with parity RAID level 5

Disk Administrator

2.5 Configuring Printers

2

In this section, you examine the options available for configuring a printer. You also go through the installation steps required to configure a network printer.

All the settings for installing and configuring printers are found by clicking the Printer icon in My Computer or by selecting Start, Settings, Printers. The Printers dialog box contains all of your installed printers as well as an icon used for installing new printers. To configure an existing printer, right-click the printer and select Properties from the shortcut menu.

A. Adding a Printer

Add printers in Windows NT by accessing the Add Printer Wizard. When adding a printer, you must follow these steps:

1. Make sure the print device is on the Hardware Compatibility List (HCL) or have the driver for your printer available.

2. Log on to the system as a user with Print Operator, Administrator, or Server Operator access privileges.

3. Run the Add Printer Wizard and follow all prompts.

When installing a printer in a Windows NT system, you can connect to an existing network printer, or install your own printer and share it with other computers. To add a new printer to your computer, follow these steps:

1. Double-click the Add Printer icon to start the Add Printer Wizard.

2. Select whether you are installing a printer on your computer or connecting to a network printer server. For example, select the My Computer option and click Next.

3. Select the port on which you're installing your printer and click Next.

4. You are then prompted to select the manufacturer and model of your print device from the list boxes. You can click Have Disk if your print device is not listed and you have the printer driver for the computer. After your printer has been selected, click Next to continue.

5. Assign a name for your printer. The default is the printer model name, but you can assign any name to the actual printer. Then specify whether you want your Windows programs to use this printer as the default printer.

6. If you want to share your printer with other users on the network, assign a share name and select which client operating systems can access your shared printer. If you are not sharing the printer, select Not shared. After the screen has been completed, click Next to continue.

7. Finally, you get the option to print a test page to verify that your printer is communicating properly. Select the appropriate test option and click Finish.

The printer driver is now installed. If you are prompted for the location of the NT source files, enter the directory that contains the printer driver.

B. Connecting to an Existing Network Printer

If you are adding an existing network printer to your system, you can use the Add Printer Wizard to configure the printer with the following steps:

1. Start the Add Printer Wizard by double-clicking the Add Printer icon.

2. Select the Network printer server option and click Next.

3. Enter the network path to the network printer or select it from the Shared Printers list. When you have located the network printer, click OK to continue.

4. Select whether to use this printer as your default Windows printer, then click Next.

5. Click Finish and the printer driver is installed. You also can assign a name to this printer.

C. Implementing a Printer Pool

A printer pool enables one print driver to send documents to multiple print devices. Up to eight print devices can be combined to use the same printer driver and print spooler. This method can help to meet your organization's printing needs and to speed up the printing process. To implement a printer pool, follow these steps:

1. Double-click the Add Printer icon.

2. Select My Computer for the location or management of the printer pool and click Next.

3. When selecting the port for your printer pool, you must select all ports to be managed by this printer. The order the printer will use to send documents to the print device depends on which ports are selected first. Make sure you enable the printer pooling option in the lower-left corner of the dialog box first.

If you need to configure a jet-direct printer or other network-based printers not connected to your physical computer, click the Add Port option. Select the appropriate printer port to establish your connection. After all the ports have been configured and selected, click Next to continue with the installation. Continue by following these steps:

1. Select the printer driver to be used by all the printers in your printer pool and click Next.

2. Assign a printer name to the printer pool. Specify whether this printer pool should be your default Windows printer and click Next.

3. Share the printer with clients. Make sure all operating systems that can connect are selected. By selecting all the operating systems, your clients do not need to load the driver locally. When they first make a connection to the network printer, the printer driver is copied locally to their computer system.

4. After all the Wizard dialog boxes have been completed, click Finish. The printer driver is now loaded, and your printer is ready for use.

> **All of the printers in a printer pool must be able to use the same printer driver.**

2.5.1   Exercise: Adding a Printer in a Windows NT Server 4 Environment

In this exercise, you add a printer and share it so others in your domain can access it as a network printer.

1.   Select Start, Settings, Printers.

2.   Double-click the Add Printers icon.

3.   Enable the My Computer radio button and click Next.

4.   Under Available ports, select the LPT1 check box. Click Next to continue.

5.   Under Manufacturers, select HP (Hewlett Packard).

6.   Under Printers, select the HP LaserJet 4. Click Next to continue.

7.   In the Printer name box, enter **HP LaserJet 4** and click Next.

8.   Enable the Shared radio button.

9.   In the Share Name box, enter **Laser** and click Next.

10.   When asked if you want to print a test page, select No and click Finish.

11.   You should now see the HP LaserJet 4 icon in the Printers dialog box.

12.   To view the print queue for the HP LaserJet 4 printer, double-click the printer's icon.

13.   This dialog box is where all print jobs are transferred. The printer also can be paused from this screen.

14.   Close the Printers dialog box.

2.5.2   Exercise: Creating a Printer Pool in Windows NT Server 4

In this exercise, you install and configure a printer pool on your Windows NT Server.

1.   Select Start, Settings, Printers.

2.   Double-click the HP LaserJet 4 printer icon.

3.   Select Printer, Pause Printing.

4.   Close the HP LaserJet 4 dialog box.

5.   Right-click the HP LaserJet 4 printer icon and select Properties.

6.   Select the Ports tab.

7.   Turn on the Enable Printer Pooling option.

8.   Click LPT2, but make sure LPT1 is still selected.

9.   Click OK.

With printer pooling enabled, the print jobs can be redirected to any of the ports configured in the printer pool.

2.5 Practice Problems

1. What is the default permission granted to the Everyone group with Printer Permissions?

    A. Manage documents

    B. Print

    C. Full Control

    D. Creator Owner

2. Who can install a printer on a Domain Controller?

    A. Administrators, Power Users, and Print Operators

    B. Administrators, Power Users, and Server Operators

    C. Administrators, Server Operators, and Print Operators

    D. Administrators

3. After sharing a network printer for Windows NT and 95 clients, what else needs to be done to allow NT Workstation clients to use the printer?

    A. Users just connect to the printer.

    B. Users must right-click the printer under network neighborhood and choose to configure it to the appropriate port.

    C. Users must install a printer driver locally.

    D. Nothing else needs to be done. The printer will automatically be available for use.

4. For DOS-based clients using LAN Manager, what is the syntax to point LPT1 to the correct network location?

    A. `Capture quename`

    B. `lpr -Sserver_name -Pshare_name`

    C. `net use LPT1 = \\server_name\share_name`

    D. `net use LPT \\server_name\share_name`

5. When Joe prints, he needs his documents to be processed as soon as possible. Where should you set a printer priority and what should it be?

    A. In User Manager for Domains, edit Joe's account and set the priority to 99.

    B. In User Manager for Domains, edit Joe's account and set the priority to 1.

    C. Go to the Printer properties for each of the printers using the Print device and, on the Security tab, set Joe's account to use priority 99.

    D. Go to the Scheduling tab on the properties of the printer that Joe is using and set the priority to 99.

6. By default, who can take ownership of a printer?

    A. Only the Administrator

    B. Everyone

    C. Administrators, Print Operators, and Server Operators

    D. Creator Owner

7. What clients can access an NT printer? Select all that apply.

    A. Macintosh

    B. NetWare

    C. OS/2 (with LAN Manager 2.2C)

    D. Windows 3.1

8. When do you want to create a printer pool?

    A. When all of your print devices are identical and are located in the same general area. Some printers are used more heavily and you want to balance the load.

    B. When print devices are dissimilar and need to be grouped together.

    C. When employees are in different buildings, but all use the same kind of print devices.

D. When identical print devices are located in each wing of a building.

E. When some printers are used more heavily and you want to balance the load.

9. What permission is necessary for users to delete their own documents?

A. Assign each user the Print permission, and then they can delete their own documents.

B. Only Administrators with Full Control can delete a document.

C. Creator Owner with the Manage Document permission.

D. Creator Owner with Print permission.

10. To connect to a shared network printer, a user can do which of the following? Select all that apply.

A. Browse Network Neighborhood and right-click a printer to install it.

B. Use the Add Printer Wizard and choose Local Printer and install the printer.

C. Use the Add Printer Wizard and choose Network Printer and install the printer.

D. The administrator will need to install printers on workstations.

2.5.1 Answers and Explanations: Exercise

In this exercise, you added a printer and shared it so others in your domain could access it as a network printer. To do this, you chose Settings, Printers, and then selected the Add Printers icon. For more information on adding printers, review the section titled "Adding a Printer."

2.5.2 Answers and Explanations: Exercise

In this exercise, you installed and configured a printer pool on your Windows NT Server. The printer pool enables you to redirect the print jobs to any of the ports configured in the printer pool. For more information on adding printer pools, review the section titled "Implementing a Printer Pool."

2.5 Answers and Explanations: Practice Problems

1. **B** Unlike shared folder permissions, which give everyone Full Control, printer permissions allow Print.

2. **C** Administrators, Server Operators, and Print Operators may install printers.

3. **A** A user may connect to a printer to install the driver.

4. **D** `net use LPT \\server_name\share_name`.

5. **D** Priorities are set on the Print Properties.

6. **C** Anyone with Full Control can take ownership.

7. **A, B, C, D** NT will allow a variety of clients to connect.

8. **A** Printer pools are most effective with similar printers in close proximity.

9. **C** By default, the Creator Owners can delete their own documents.

10. **A, C** If users have permissions to use a printer, they just need to browse to it to gain access.

2.5 Key Words

Printer

Print device

Printer pool

Network printer

Local printer

2.6   Configuring Windows NT Server for Various Types of Clients

Your Windows NT Server is the selected server for various client operating systems. In this section, you look at the configuration requirements for the following:

- Windows NT Workstation clients
- Windows 95 clients
- Macintosh clients

Windows NT Server handles all the requests from each of these clients automatically. The Windows NT Workstation and Windows 95 clients use Windows NT logon security and provide complete functionality as a Windows NT client right out of the box. To enable connectivity with Apple Macintosh computers, the services for the Macintosh must be installed. The Network Client Administrator can be used to simplify the installation of your client computers.

The Network Client Administrator is found in the Administrative Tools group. You can use the Network Client Administrator program to do the following:

- **Make a network installation startup disk.** This option requires an MS-DOS boot disk. It will install the necessary files to connect to the network and start an installation of your client software.

- **Make an installation disk set.** This option enables the creation of installation disks for the DOS network client, LAN Manager 2.2c for DOS, or LAN Manager 2.2c for OS/2.

- **Copy client-based Network Administration Tools.** This option enables you to share the network administration tools with client computers. The client computers that can use the network administration tools are Windows NT Workstation and Windows 95 computers.

- **View remoteboot client information.** This option enables you to view the remoteboot client information. To install remoteboot, go to the Services tab of the Network dialog box.

A.   Windows NT Workstation Clients

Windows NT Workstation computers require a computer account to be created in order to join a domain. The computer account is then used by the Remote Procedure Call (RPC) service to make a secured communication. This verifies when the computer is started and can be used for monitoring services on your NT Workstation computer. Windows NT Workstation can be installed as a standalone system and then, in the Network dialog box, joined to the domain. You must, however, have Account Operator or Administrator access, or be assigned the User Right "Add Workstations to the Domain" to create this computer account. If you want to create the computer account in the Windows NT Server computer, you can use Server Manager.

After you have a Windows NT Workstation client configured, the users and the client computer can use the Windows NT security. You also can install the client-based Network Administration Tools. These tools enable you to manage your Windows NT Server from your Windows NT Workstation client computer.

The system requirements for installing the Windows NT Workstation server tools are as follows:

- Windows NT Workstation must be installed.

- It must have a 486DX/33 or higher processor.

- A minimum of 12 MB RAM is needed.

- There must be 2.5 MB of free disk space in the system partition.

- The Workstation and Server service must be installed on the NT Workstation computer.

The tools found in the Windows NT Workstation Server are listed in Table 2.6.1.

Table 2.6.1   Windows NT Workstation Server Tools

Tools	Use this Tool To...
Server Manager	Manage Windows NT-based computers and domain controllers.
User Manager	Manage users, groups, and user rights for Windows for Domains NT domains.
WINS Manager	Administer the WINS servers.
DHCP Manager	Administer the DHCP servers.
Remote Access Admin	Administer the remote access service on a computer running Windows NT.
Service for Macintosh	Share Windows NT resources with Macintosh clients.
System Policy Editor	Modify and maintain user and system policies.

B.   Windows 95 Clients

Using the Network Client Administrator program, you can create an automated installation from a floppy disk. Any installation of Windows 95 with a Microsoft Network client loaded, however, can be configured to log on to a Windows NT domain. This can be configured in the Network properties of a Windows 95 computer.

Windows 95 also has server tools available to enable Windows 95 computers to administer a Windows NT system. The system requirements for the Windows 95 computer to use the server tools are as follows:

- Windows 95 must be installed.

- A 486DX/33 or higher processor is required.

- A minimum of 8 MB of RAM is required.

- There must be 3 MB of free disk space available at the system partition.

- The client for Microsoft networks must be installed.

C.   Macintosh Clients

For Windows NT to integrate with Apple Macintosh clients, you must first install Services for Macintosh on your Windows NT Server. Services for Macintosh enable file and print sharing between the Macintosh clients and the Windows NT Server. The Windows NT Server also is able to share Macintosh printers with the other clients of Windows NT Server. When Services for Macintosh is installed, the AppleTalk protocol is installed as well.

1. Server and Client Requirements

A few requirements must be met prior to installing Services for Macintosh onto your network. The requirements for the Windows NT Server computer are as follows:

- 2 MB of free disk space
- An NTFS partition to be used as the Macintosh volume

Requirements for the Macintosh computer are as follows:

- Version 6.0.8 or later of the Macintosh operating system
- Version 2.0 of the AppleTalk Filing Protocol
- Network cards that enable connectivity into the same network as the Windows NT Server system

2. Installing Services for Macintosh

To install Services for Macintosh, open the Network dialog box of your Windows NT system. Change to the Services tab and click Add to add a new service. Services for Macintosh should be found in the list of available services. Select Services for Macintosh and click OK. Services for Macintosh is installed automatically, and you are prompted to restart your system.

2.6.1   Exercise: Setting Up a Central Network Share

This exercise reviews the steps necessary to set up a central network share for the installation of client software. This exercise will create the installation disks for the MS-DOS client.

1. Log in as the Administrator of your Windows NT Server.

2. Install the Windows NT Server CD-ROM.

2. Select Start, Programs, Administrative Tools, Network Client Administrator.

3. From the Network Client Administrator dialog box, select the option to Make Installation Disk Set. Click the Continue button.

4. In the Share Network Client Installation Files dialog box, you must configure where the Client directory is located. If your CD-ROM is drive letter Z:, this would be Z:\Clients. Click the Use Existing Path option and click OK to continue.

> You also can use this dialog box to create a network share for the client installation files. This process will copy the clients directory from the CD-ROM to a network share location. This directory will need about 64 MB of disk space.

5. From the Make Installation Disk Set dialog box, select the Network Client v3.0 for MS-DOS and Windows option. Select the format disks check box and click OK.

6. When prompted, insert each of the required disks. These can now be used to install the DOS client software on a system.

2.6 Practice Problems

1. The client Network Administration Tools are available for which operating systems on the Windows NT 4 Server CD-ROM? Select all that apply.

   A. Windows for Workgroups

   B. Windows 95

   C. Windows NT Workstation

   D. DOS

2. Which tools are available for network administration when the Network Administration Tools are installed on a Windows 95 client system? Select all that apply.

   A. Event Viewer

   B. DHCP Manager

   C. User Manager for Domains

   D. Server Manager

3. Which tools are installed when the Network Administration Tools are added to a Windows NT Workstation computer? Select all that apply.

   A. Event Viewer

   B. DHCP Manager

   C. User Manager for Domains

   D. Server Manager

4. How do you install the Windows 95 Network Administration Tools?

   A. Run SETUP.EXE from the CD:\Clients\srvtools\win95 directory.

   B. Right-click the SRVTOOLS.INF file in the CD:\clients\srvtools\win95 directory and choose install.

   C. Use the Add/Remove programs applet in Control Panel and run SETUP.EXE from there.

   D. Use the Add/Remove programs applet in Control Panel and use the Have Disk option to point to the CD:\clients\srvtools\win95 directory.

5. How do you install the Windows NT Workstation Network Administration Tools?

   A. Run SETUP.BAT from the CD:\Clients\srvtools\winnt directory.

   B. Right-click the SRVTOOLS.INF file in the CD:\clients\srvtools\winnt directory and choose install.

   C. Use the Add/Remove programs applet in Control Panel and run SETUP.BAT from there.

   D. Use the Add/Remove programs applet in Control Panel and use the Have Disk option to point to the CD:\clients\srvtools\winnt directory.

6. What manual configuration step must be performed on a Windows 95 client when the Network Administration Tools are installed?

   A. All icons must be created for the Network Administration Tools.

   B. Security must be set to use User level security on the Windows 95 system.

   C. C:\srvtools must be added to the path.

   D. No manual configuration must be performed.

7. What print data type is used when a Macintosh client sends a print job to a network-shared HP LaserJet II non-postscript printer?

   A. RAW

   B. EMF

   C. PSCRIPT1

   D. You cannot print to a PCL printer with a Macintosh client. Macintosh clients can print only to PostScript printers.

8. Which Network Client Administrator program option is used to install TCP/IP support for a Windows for Workgroups client?

    A. Make a network installation startup disk

    B. Make an installation disk set

    C. Copy client-based network administration tools

    D. View remoteboot client information

9 Which protocols can be used by an MS-DOS v3.0 network client? Select all that apply.

    A. NetBEUI

    B. IPX/SPX

    C. TCP/IP

    D. DLC

10. What file formats are supported for Macintosh Accessible Volumes?

    A. FAT

    B. NTFS

    C. HPFS

    D. FAT and NTFS

2.6.1 Answers and Explanations: Exercise

This exercise reviewed the steps necessary to set up a central network share for the installation of client software and created the installation disks for the MS-DOS client. For more information about setting up central network shares, review the section titled "Windows NT Workstation Clients."

2.6 Answers and Explanations: Practice Problems

1. **B, C** The Windows NT Server 4 CD-ROM ships with Network Administration Tools for Windows 95 and Windows NT Workstation. You also can administer Windows NT using Windows for Workgroups. The client software is available on the Windows NT Server 3.51 CD-ROM.

2. **A, C, D** You cannot perform DHCP administration from a Windows 95 system running the Network Administration Tools.

3. **B, C, D** The Event Viewer is already included with Windows NT Workstation administrative tools.

4. **D** The Network Administration Tools are added using the Add/Remove Programs applet in Windows 95.

5. **A** The Network Administration Tools are installed using SETUP.BAT on Windows NT Workstation. The batch file determines the platform that Windows NT Workstation is running on and then installs the correct version of the files.

6. **C** The directory where the Network Administration Tools are installed (C:\srvtools) must be added to the path to use the Explorer extensions.

7. **C** The job data type would be PSCRIPT1. The PostScript information is translated into bitmaps that are downloaded to the PCL printer.

8. **B** Using the Make an installation disk set option, you can create the TCP/IP 32B for Windows for Workgroups installation disks.

9. **A, B, C** All of the standard protocols can be used with the MS-DOS client software.

10. **B** MAC-accessible volumes must be formatted using NTFS.

2.6 Key Words

Network Client Administrator

Services for Macintosh

Network Administration Tools

Practice Exam: Installation and Configuration

Use this practice exam to test your mastery of Chapter 2, "Installation and Configuration." This practice exam is 37 questions long. The passing Microsoft score is 76.4 percent. Questions are in multiple-choice format.

1. Your company currently is running Windows NT Server in a single-domain model. You are finding that logon requests are very slow, and you want to install a new server into your network to help handle logon requests. What type of server should you install into your environment?

   A. File and Print server

   B. Primary Domain Controller

   C. Backup Domain Controller

   D. Member Server

2. What is the name of the setup program used for an upgrade installation of Windows NT Server 3.51 to 4?

   A. SETUP.EXE

   B. SETUP32.EXE

   C. WINNT.EXE

   D. WINNT32.EXE

3. What is the name of the setup program if you are not installing from a 32-bit operating system?

   A. SETUP.EXE

   B. SETUP32.EXE

   C. WINNT.EXE

   D. WINNT32.EXE

4. You can upgrade Windows NT Server when installed as a Member Server to a domain controller under what circumstances?

   A. The Member Server was installed with NT 3.51.

   B. The Member Server was installed with NT.

   C. It is not possible to upgrade NT servers from one server type to another.

   D. Reinstalling is the only way to upgrade Member Servers to domain controllers.

5. What action would you take if you needed to take your Primary Domain Controller down for repairs, and you wanted to set up one of your Backup Domain Controllers to act as the PDC?

   A. Demote the PDC, and then promote the BDC to take its place.

   B. Just turn off the PDC. The first BDC to detect the absence of a PDC will automatically be promoted to a PDC.

   C. Demote the PDC. This will automatically promote the BDC.

   D. Promote a BDC. This will automatically demote the PDC.

6. What service is used to send a copy of the SAM database from the PDC to the BDCs?

   A. Netlogon

   B. Redirector

   C. Replication

   D. Alert service

7. Which of the following network protocols are supported by Windows NT Server? Select all that apply.

   A. TCP/IP

   B. XNS

   C. AppleTalk

   D. DLC

8. What network protocol can be used to connect to the Internet?

    A. NWLink IPX/SPX

    B. AppleTalk

    C. DLC

    D. TCP/IP

9. What configuration options are mandatory when installing TCP/IP?

    A. DNS and IP address

    B. Default gateway and subnet mask

    C. IP address and subnet mask

    D. IP address and default gateway

10. What is the function of the default gateway?

    A. To translate IPX packets to TCP/IP.

    B. To route TCP/IP packets outside of your physical network to TCP/IP hosts on remote subnets.

    C. To allow for automatic assignment of TCP/IP addresses to clients.

    D. To identify the Host and Network portions of the IP address.

11. What service enables automatic configuration of IP addresses for client computers?

    A. DHCP

    B. WINS

    C. DNS

    D. Internet Explorer

12. What service must be installed to configure the AppleTalk protocol?

    A. Macintosh Gateway service

    B. LocalTalk

    C. Services for Apple

    D. Services for Macintosh

13. What is the function of the Server service?

    A. To route requests for information to local or network locations

    B. To handle incoming network communication

    C. To ensure information from the Security accounts database will be copied from the PDC to the BDC

    D. To register computer names

14. What is the default import directory for the Directory Replication Service?

    A. %*systemroot*%\system32\repl\export

    B. %*systemroot*%\system32\repl\import\scripts

    C. %*systemroot*%\repl\import

    D. %*systemroot*%\repl\import\scripts

15. You have three computers that you want to put into a printer pool. The printers are an HP LaserJet 4, an IBM Lexmark, and a Panasonic dot matrix. What will be the best way to do this?

    A. Install the dot matrix printer driver and configure the pool.

    B. Install an HP Series II printer driver and configure the pool.

    C. Install each printer driver appropriately and make all of them printer pools.

    D. You cannot configure these three printers to participate in a printer pool.

16. Mary is trying to add a new NT Workstation to her NT Domain. What is the maximum number of characters allowed?

    A. 14

    B. 20

    C. 15

    D. 10

17. Harry has installed a new NT Workstation computer. The next morning the machine starts up with the error "One or more services failed to start." Where should Harry go to try and troubleshoot the problem?

    A. Server Manager

    B. Event viewer

    C. NT diagnostics

    D. Disk Administrator

18. In the Directory Replication service, which types of computers can act as export computers? Select all that apply.

    A. Windows NT Server computers (domain controllers only)

    B. Windows NT Workstation computers

    C. Windows NT Server computers

    D. Windows 95 computers

19. To enable Macintosh users to store files on a Windows NT Server computer, what must be installed?

    A. GSNW

    B. Services for Macintosh

    C. WINS

    D. DNS

20. What is the disk-partitioning scheme that enables equal areas of disk space from 2 to 32 physical drives to be combined into one logical drive?

    A. Volume set

    B. Stripe set with parity

    C. Stripe set

    D. Mirror set

21. What type of disk system makes an exact copy of all data from one disk to another disk?

    A. Stripe set with parity

    B. Stripe set

    C. Volume set

    D. Mirror set

22. Select the types of disk systems that are fault tolerant.

    A. Volume sets

    B. Disk striping

    C. Disk striping with parity

    D. Disk mirroring

23. What is the name of the utility used to implement fault tolerance in Windows NT Server?

    A. User Manager for Domains

    B. Server Manager

    C. Disk Administrator

    D. Control Panel

24. You installed Windows NT Server 4, but during the installation process, you selected Server as the type of installation. You now want to make the server a Backup Domain Controller. What must you do to convert the server?

    A. Run the Convert command.

    B. Do nothing. The Member Server can act as a domain controller.

    C. Reinstall Windows NT Server as a domain controller.

    D. Under Control Panel, Network, change the server type to Backup Domain Controller.

25. What is the main difference between an NT Server installed as a domain controller and an NT Server not installed as a domain controller?

    A. A domain controller maintains a copy of the domain directory database; a non-domain controller does not.

    B. A non-domain controller validates user logons; a domain controller does not.

C.   A domain controller is best suited
to an application server role in the
network.

D.   There is no difference in the
domain controller and the non-
domain controller.

26.   To set up a printer pool, which of the
following criteria must be met? Select all
that apply.

A.   All printers should be in the same
general area.

B.   The printers should be able to use
the same printer driver.

C.   The printers must be managed by
the same print server.

D.   The printer must be connected to
the same type of port.

27.   How do you install a new printer? Select
all that apply.

A.   Select Start, Settings, Printers. Click
the Add Printers icon.

B.   Start Print Manager and add the
printer from the Printer menu.

C.   Open Control Panel and click the
Printer icon; then double-click the
Add Printer icon.

D.   Run the Windows NT Setup
program and install the printer
under the Configuration menu.

28.   How do you configure a network protocol in Windows NT Server? Select all that
apply.

A.   Select Start, Settings, Control Panel.
Double-click the Network icon.

B.   Right-click the Network Neighborhood icon and select the Properties.

C.   From Server Manager.

D.   From the Network Client Administrator.

29.   If you want to convert your C: drive from
FAT to NTFS as the file system, what is
the correct syntax?

A.   Format C: /FS:NTFS

B.   Convert /FAT:NTFS

C.   Convert C: /FS:NTFSD.

D.   You cannot convert FAT to NTFS

30.   What is the amount of usable space
provided by a stripe set with parity
consisting of four disks and the smallest
open space being 300 MB?

A.   600 MB

B.   1,200 MB

C.   900 MB

D.   1,500 MB

31.   When a drive that is part of a mirror fails,
how can you make the system available
again?

A.   Open the computer case and
physically swap out the drives, and
then from the Fault Tolerance menu
of the Disk Administrator, break
the mirror.

B.   Use a Fault Tolerance boot disk to
start the mirrored drive, and then
from the Fault Tolerance menu of
the Disk Administrator, break the
mirror.

C.   Use a Fault Tolerance boot disk to
start the mirrored driver, and then
from the Partition menu of the
Disk Administrator, break the
mirror.

D.   Boot to DOS and edit the
BOOT.INI.

32.   What files are required on a Fault
Tolerance boot disk?

A.   COMMAND.COM, IO.SYS,
MSDOS.SYS

B.   Ntldr, Ntoskrnl, BOOT.INI

C. Ntldr, NTDETECT.COM, BOOT.INI

D. COMMAND.COM, BOOTSECT.DOS

33. What file is required on a Fault Tolerance boot disk using a SCSI controller with the BIOS disabled?

A. OSLOADER.EXE

B. NTBOOTDD.SYS

C. Ntoskrnl

D. HAL.DLL

34. What happens if a stripe set with parity has a failed member?

A. Nothing; performance will continue unchanged.

B. The drive will continue to work; however, the system performance will slow.

C. The drive will not work until replaced.

D. An NT dialog box will let the administrator know of the problem.

35. If an ARC path reads `Multi (0)disk(0)rdisk(1)partition(3)`, it means which of the following?

A. NT is on the 1st controller, 1st disk, 4th partition.

B. NT is on the 1st controller, 1st disk, 3rd partition.

C. Would not be a possible ARC path.

D. NT is on the 1st controller, 2nd disk, 3rd partition.

36. If an ARC path reads `scsi (0)disk(0)rdisk(0)partition(3)`, it means which of the following?

A. NT is on the 1st controller, 1st disk, 4th partition.

B. NT is on the 1st controller, 1st disk, 3rd partition.

C. Would not be a possible ARC path.

D. NT is on the 1st controller, 2nd disk, 3rd partition.

37. What level of fault tolerance is available on NT Workstation?

A. 1

B. 5

C. 3

D. NT Workstation does not provide disk fault tolerance

Answers and Explanations: Practice Exam

1. **C** Because a domain is already in use, only a BDC would be able to assist.

2. **D** WINNT32 is designed to allow for the system to remain up for as long as possible.

3. **C** WINNT is for installing from DOS, Windows, or Windows 95.

4. **D** Reinstalling is the only way to upgrade Member Servers to domain controllers.

5. **D** By promoting a BDC, the PDC is automatically demoted to a BDC.

6. **A** Netlogon provides that service.

7. **A, C, D** These are all supported transport protocols.

8. **D** TCP/IP is the standard for the Internet.

9. **C** Every network device on a TCP/IP network must include IP address and subnet mask.

10. **B** If an address is not part of the local subnet, it is passed on to the gateway.

11. **A** DHCP uses a pool of addresses and assigns them to clients.

12. **D** Services for Macintosh must be installed.

13. **B**   The Server service enables remote computers to connect to resources on the local computer.

14. **B**   The default directory replication import directory is *%systemroot%*\system32\repl\import\scripts.

15. **D**   It is not possible to create a printer pool with printers that cannot use a single print driver between them.

16. **C**   Computer names must be 15 characters or less.

17. **B**   Event viewer will give information, errors, and warnings regarding services in the system log.

18. **A, C**   Any NT server machine may be a replication server.

19. **B**   Services for Macintosh enables Macintosh clients to access Windows NT network resources.

20. **C**   Stripe sets require a minimum of 2 and a maximum of 32 spaces to be combined.

21. **D**   Mirroring gives two identical drives.

22. **C, D**   These are fault tolerant.

23. **C**   The Disk Administrator is used for disk management.

24. **C**   NT cannot change a Member Server to a domain controller without reinstalling.

25. **A**   Domain controllers will validate users and maintain directory database information.

26. **A, B, C**   Printers in printing pools should be close together, part of the same print server, and able to use the same printer driver.

27. **A, C**   The printer folder is in several locations.

28. **A, B**   Network properties can be found in several locations.

29. **B**   From the command prompt, type the command to convert.

30. **C**   900 MB is correct because one fourth of the disk space will be used for parity if four disks are used.

31. **B**   With the Fault Tolerance disk, the system will start, and then use Disk Administrator to break the mirror.

32. **C**   You will require NTLDR, NTDETECT.COM, and the BOOT.INI file for your Fault Tolerant boot disk.

33. **B**   Also the ARC path on the BOOT.INI will read SCSI instead of Multi.

34. **B**   Because parity information is being generated, performance will slow.

35. **D**   NT is on the 1st controller, 2nd disk, 3rd partition.

36. **B**   NT is on the 1st controller, 1st disk, 3rd partition.

37. **D**   Disk fault tolerance is only provided in the Windows NT Server Disk Administrator program.

CHAPTER 3

Managing Resources

This chapter helps you prepare for the exam by covering the following objectives:

- Managing user accounts and rights
- Managing group accounts and rights
- Creating and managing policies and profiles for various situations
- Administering remote servers from various types of client computers
- Managing disk resources

3.1 Managing User and Group Accounts

Managing user and group accounts is best understood when divided into the following topics:

- Managing Windows NT user accounts
- Managing Windows NT user rights
- Managing Windows NT groups
- Administering account policies
- Auditing changes to the user account database

A. Managing Windows NT User Accounts

Windows NT user accounts, with their unique identifiers, enable users to log on to the Windows NT network. Their user account/password combinations are their tickets to all the resources on the NT network.

Create Windows NT user accounts in User Manager for Domains. To create a new account, the user running User Manager for Domains must be a member of either the Administrators local group or the Account Operators local group.

1. User Properties

Each user has several property pages. When creating a new user, the first screen contains individual settings. Each setting in the User Properties dialog box is described as follows:

- **Username:** The name that each user uses to log in to the network. The name must be unique, no longer than 20 characters, and cannot contain "/\[]:;|=,+*?<>" as characters. The goal of enterprise networking is for each user in the enterprise to have only *one* user account.

- **Full Name:** Enables the display of the user's full name. This can be used as a sort setting by choosing Sort by Full Name from the View menu.

- **Description:** Used to further describe a user, and if you use description as a template, you can copy the description from account to account.

- **Password/Confirm Password:** The password can be up to 14 characters. If the user is working at an NT class system, the password is also case-sensitive. If the user is at a Windows 95 or lower system, the password is case-insensitive.

Of the four properties at the top of the dialog box, only the description will be copied from account to account. All other settings must be re-entered for a copied user.

The lower settings in the User Properties dialog box relate to how passwords are handled. The settings are as follows:

- **User Must Change Password at Next Logon:** Forces users to change their password when they next log on to the network. This option should not be selected if the account policy Users Must Log On in Order to Change Password has been set.

- **User Cannot Change Password:** Used in higher security networks in which the users are assigned passwords for their accounts.

- **Password Never Expires:** Overrides the account policy of password expiration and should only be used for service accounts in Windows NT.

- **Account Disabled:** The Account Disabled setting prevents users from using the disabled account.

- **Account Locked Out:** Active only if a user's account has been locked out by the operating system by failing the Account Lockout settings. To reactivate an account, simply clear the check box for this setting.

2. Group Properties Tab

Use the Group Properties tab to assign the user whose account you are modifying to various groups. This dialog box enables you to assign users to global and local groups in only the same domain as the user (generally, you assign users to global groups). To assign a user to a group in a different domain, you must use that domain's local group properties.

The Primary Group option at the bottom of the dialog box is used by Services for Macintosh when it assigns permissions to Mac Shares. You can designate a primary Global Group for the account.

3. User Environment Profiles Page

The User Environment Profiles page is one of the main configuration pages used in an Enterprise Network. It enables the administrator to configure the following as centrally located:

- User Profile Path
- Login Script
- Home Directory

The main purpose in centrally locating these options is that you can have all these items stored on a central server. By having the users store their profiles and home directories in a central location, you make the process of backing up their data more manageable.

a. User Profile Path

The User Profile Path designates a specific location on a specified server where the user's profile is stored. As the directory structure reveals, the profile path contains the user portion of the Registry in the file NTUSER.DAT. The directory structure itself also contains a user's Start menu, desktop layout, and a recently used file listing. By using the profile path, the users can have their desktops and personal configuration settings follow them to each NT computer they use.

The most common path entered for the user profile path is \\SERVER\PROFILESHARE\%USERNAME%. You should note that this location is server-specific. To limit WAN traffic, consider locating the user's profile on a server in the same subnet as the client.

b. Login Script

The login script enables an administrator to configure common drive mappings, run central batch files, and configure the system. When configuring a login script, put the name of the *.bat or *.cmd file that you want to execute. The logon scripts are stored by default in the following directory:

```
\%systemroot%\system32\repl\import\scripts
```

This directory is shared as the netlogon share, and the logon script presents a common network layout to all clients on the network.

c. Home Directory

The home directory setting for the user's profile creates a personal directory where users can store their data on a network server. To create home directories, the most common entry is a common share called USERS. Assuming this share has been created, you enter that path for each home directory as `\\COMPUTER\USERS\%USERNAME%`.

4. Logon Hours Properties

The Logon Hours Properties tab enables the administrator to set the hours the user account is able to access to the network. If the user attempts to log on to the network during restricted hours, a dialog box appears that states that the user is not permitted to log on during the hours.

If users are currently logged on when their allotted logon hours end, they cannot connect to any more net shares. Likewise, they cannot use any of their current shares. If the users actually log out, they will not be able to log back on until the unrestricted hours begin.

5.   Logon to Properties

The Logon to Properties page restricts users to working at specific workstations. You can specify up to eight computer names. They are entered as the computer name, not UNC format. For example, you would type INSTRUCTOR, not \\INSTRUCTOR.

6.   Account Properties

An administrator uses the account properties page to define one of two options:

- **Setting an account expiration date:** Used for any short-term employees. The administrator sets when the account expires.

- **Setting whether the account is a global or local account:** Global is the default, as local accounts cannot cross trusts.

7.   Dial-In Properties

The Dial-In Properties page enables administrators to determine which users are granted dial-in access to the network and whether the administrators should implement call-back security.

If you choose No Call Back, the users will immediately be able to use network resources. No Call Back is commonly used in low-security networks and for users working out of hotel rooms.

If you choose Set by User, the users are prompted to enter their phone number, and the Remote Access Server calls them back at that number. If you choose Preset To, the users dial in to the office network. After connecting, the line is dropped, and the user will be called back at a predefined phone number.

B.   Managing Windows NT User Rights

User rights define security rights when the user's activity cannot be associated with one particular object. Several predefined user rights can grant these nondiscretionary levels of access to the system. The User Rights policy is implemented via the User Manager for Domain's User Rights option from the Policy menu.

1.   The Default User Rights

User rights are automatically implemented in Windows NT 4. The user rights are stored in the SAM Account Database. This is in the Security hive of the HKEY_LOCAL_MACHINE subtree in the Registry. Table 3.1.1 describes each of the basic and advanced user rights as defined in Windows NT Workstation and Windows NT Server.

Table 3.1.1 User Rights Assignments in Windows NT 4

User Right	This Right Enables:	Initially Assigned to:
Access This Computer from the Network	Enables users to connect to the computer via the network.	Administrators, Everyone, Power Users
Act as Part of the Operating System	Enables a process to perform as a secure, trusted part of the operating system. For example, the Microsoft Exchange 5.0 Server Service account requires this right to handle POP3 mail requests from clients.	None
Add Workstations to the Domain	Enables users to add workstations to the domain so that workstation can recognize the domain's user and global accounts.	None, but this is a pre-defined right for all members of the Administrators and Server Operators local groups, and the right cannot be revoked.
Backup Files and Directories	Enables users to back up files and directories on the computer, no matter what file and directory permissions they have.	Administrators, Backup Operators, and Server Operators
Bypass Traverse Checking	Enables users to change directories and traverse the directory structure, even if the user has no permissions for the traversed directory structures.	Everyone
Change System Time	Enables a user to set the time of the computer's internal clock.	Administrators, Server Operators, Power Users
Create a Pagefile	Determines which users can create a pagefile for the Virtual Memory Manager to use.	Administrators

continues

Table 3.1.1   Continued

User Right	This Right Enables:	Initially Assigned to:
Create a Token Object	Gives the right to create access tokens.	None; this is a predefined right of the Local Security Authority.
Create Permanent Shared Objects	Enables a user to create shared objects, such as \\Device, used within Windows NT. The right has nothing to do with creating file or printer shares.	None
Debug Programs	Enables a user to debug various low-level objects such as threads.	Administrators
Force Shutdown from a Remote System	This right is not currently implemented in Windows NT 4, but it has been reserved for future use.	Administrators, Server Operators, Power Users
Generate Security Audits	Enables a process to generate security audit logs.	None
Increase Quotas	This right is not currently implemented in Windows NT 4, but it has been reserved for future use. Products such as Disk Quota Manager might use this right.	Administrators
Increase Scheduling Priority	Enables a user to boost the execution priority of a process by using the Task Manager.	Administrators, Power Users
Load and Unload Device Drivers	Enables a user to install and remove device drivers.	Administrators
Lock Pages in Memory	Enables a user to lock pages into memory so that the pages cannot be paged out to the paging file.	None

User Right	This Right Enables:	Initially Assigned to:
Log On as a Batch Job	This right is not currently implemented in Windows NT 4, but it has been reserved for future use.	None
Log On as a Service	Enables users to register with the systems as a Service. This right is automatically granted to any account set up as a service account.	None
Log On Locally	Enables users to log on to the system by typing their usernames and passwords into the User Authentication dialog box.	Account Operators, Administrators, Backup Operators, Everyone, Print Operators, Server Operators, Power Users, Guests, Users
Manage Auditing and Security Log	Enables users to specify which files to audit, which groups to audit, and which printers to audit. The right does not enable the user to change the audit policy, but to work only within the framework defined by a member of the Administrators group. This right also enables the user to view and clear the security log in the event viewer.	Administrators
Modify Firmware Environment Variables	Enables a user to modify system environment variables stored in non-volatile RAM on RISC-based systems.	Administrators
Profile Single Process	Enables a user to perform performance sampling on a process.	Administrators, Power Users

continues

Table 3.1.1   Continued

User Right	This Right Enables:	Initially Assigned to:
Profile System Performance	Enables a user to perform performance sampling on a computer.	Administrators
Replace a Process Level Token	The system uses this right to modify a process's security access token. The right is used by the process of impersonation.	None
Restore Files and Directories	Enables users to restore backed-up files and directories regardless of their personal permissions on these files and directories.	Administrators, Backup Operators, Server Operators
Shut Down the System	Enables a user to shut down the Windows NT computer system.	Account Operators, Administrators, Backup Operators, Print Operators, Server Operators, Everyone Users, Power Users
Take Ownership of Files or Other Objects	Enables users to take ownership of any object on the computer, even if they do not have sufficient permissions to access the object.	Administrators

2. Modifying User Rights

Generally, you do not want to adjust the default user rights. If you do change the user rights, a possibility exists that the server might be rendered unusable. The following are some suggested guidelines to further secure your system's user rights. Two of the rights that have been granted default *excess* rights are as follows:

- **Log on Locally:** The default membership includes the Everyone and Guest groups on Windows NT Workstation. Remove these two groups and replace them with the Users local group from the local account database. Be sure that the Domain's Domain Users global group is a member of the Users local group.

- **Shut Down the System:** The default membership in Windows NT Workstation includes the Everyone group. This group should not be assigned the shut-down privilege. You may also want to consider revoking this right from the Everyone group if you want all systems to run during the night.

C. Managing Windows NT Groups

Using the global and local groups in an enterprise Windows NT environment is one of the key concepts tested in the exam. This section looks into the following areas:

- Differences between global and local groups

- Creation of global groups

- Built-In global groups

- Creation of local groups

- Built-In local groups

- Special groups

- Management of global and local groups in a multidomain environment

1. Differences Between Global and Local Groups

One of the most difficult enterprise concepts to get a handle on is the difference between global and local groups. In an Enterprise network, the acronym AGLP helps to define the use of global and local groups.

AGLP stands for Accounts/Global Groups/Local Groups/Permissions. This means that when you want to assign permissions to any resource, the following steps must be performed.

1. Make sure that user accounts exist for each user that needs access to the resource.

2. Assign all user accounts to a common global group. If the users are spread across multiple domains, you have to create a global group in each domain because global groups can contain only users from the domain in which they are located.

3. Assign the global groups from each domain to a local group in the domain where the resource exists. If the resource is on a Windows NT domain controller, create the local group on a domain controller. If the resource is on a Windows NT Workstation or Windows NT Member Server, create the local group on that system's local account database.

4. Assign necessary permissions to the local group.

Local groups are the only groups that you should assign permissions. When assigning local group permissions, the administrator should always determine whether there is an existing local group with the appropriate permissions. For example, if you want to grant a user the capability to create new users or change group memberships, the Account Operators local group already has these permissions. You have no reason to create a new local group to perform this task. Instead, make the user a member of the Account Operators local group.

> **Think of it this way: Global groups exist across the domain, whereas local groups are local to the machine in question.**

2. Creation of Global Groups

You create global groups by using the User Manager for Domains utility. When you create a global group, it is initially written to the SAM database on the Primary Domain Controller. Then the global group is synchronized with the Backup Domain Controllers during the synchronization process. The global groups are accessible from any domain controller.

To create a new global group, choose User, New Global Group from the menus of User Manager for Domains.

The New Global Group dialog box enables you to add and remove users as members of the global group in the current domain. After you have added all users, click the OK button to complete the creation of the global group.

3. Built-in Global Groups

When you first install an NT domain, three global groups are predefined. They are described in Table 3.1.2.

Table 3.1.2   Initial Global Group Memberships

Global Group	Initial Membership
Domain Admins	Administrator
Domain Guests	Guest
Domain Users	All user accounts except for Guest

4. Creation of Local Groups

To create a new local group, choose User, New Local Group from the menus of User Manager for Domains.

To add a global group to the local group, click the Add button in the New Local Group dialog box. A list of global groups and global accounts appears that you can make members of the local group. Note that the drop list at the top enables you to add global accounts and global groups from trusted domains to the local group.

5. Built-In Local Groups

The built-in groups that you have depends on the version of Windows NT you are running. They vary depending on whether you are on Windows NT Workstation, Windows NT Member Servers, or Windows NT domain controllers. The local groups found only on domain controllers include:

- Account Operators
- Print Operators
- Server Operators

The local group found only on Windows NT Workstations or member servers is Power Users. The local groups found on all Windows NT systems include:

- Administrators
- Backup Operators
- Guests
- Replicator
- Users

a. Account Operators Local Group

Members of the Account Operators local group have the capability to create and manage users and groups within the domain. They cannot modify membership in the following groups:

- Administrators
- Account Operators
- Backup Operators
- Print Operators
- Server Operators
- Domain Admins

If they were able to modify the membership of these groups, they ultimately could increase their own rights. Only administrators can change the membership of these groups. Account operators cannot modify users who are members of the operator groups, either.

b. Print Operators Local Group

The Print Operators local group can create new printers and maintain existing printers in the domain. The maintenance activities include sharing printers and managing all jobs in a printer queue.

c. Server Operators Local Group

Members of the Server Operators local group can create shared directories on a domain controller. Other capabilities include:

- Locking or unlocking the server console
- Formatting disks on a server
- Backing up and restoring files to a server
- Managing all facets of printing
- Shutting down servers

d. Administrators Local Group

The Administrators local group is found on all Windows NT class computers. This group can manage any and all aspects of the Windows NT domain. The initial membership in the Administrators group is the pre-created Administrator account and the Domain Admins global group.

e. Backup Operators Local Group

The members of the Backup Operators local group can back up and restore any files on the system. This right supersedes any permissions assigned to these files and directories. Backup Operators can also shut down a server.

f. Guests Local Group

The Guests local group can grant access to specific resources to guests of the domain. The initial membership in the Guests local group is the Domain Guests global group from the domain.

g. Replicator Local Group

The Replicator local group is used by the Directory Replicator service. Membership in this group enables a member to be involved in the process of maintaining a directory structure and its contents on multiple domain controllers.

h. Users Local Group

The Users Local group contains the global group Domain Users. This group is most often used when increasing the security on a Windows NT domain. Rather than keeping the default share and NTFS permissions, use the local group users instead of everyone.

6. Special Groups

In addition to the predefined local and global groups in Windows NT 4, there are special groups. The membership in these groups is not based as much on usernames as on how the user is functioning on the network. The special groups implemented in Windows NT 4 are as follows:

- **Everyone:** The Everyone group membership includes absolutely everyone that can connect to your network. The everyone group includes users that are not defined in the Account database.

- **Creator/Owner:** The Creator/Owner group membership is applied to every object created in Windows NT. If you take ownership of a file or directory, you automatically become a member of the Creator/Owner group.

- **Network:** The Network group membership is based on whether the user is connecting remotely to a resource.

- **Interactive:** The Interactive group membership is based on whether the user is sitting locally at the server where the data is stored. If the data is stored on a local drive, assigned permissions to the Interactive group affect any users working with that data.

- **System:** This special group never includes users. The System group refers to the Windows NT operating system itself when it must access resources on the network.

7. Management of Global and Local Groups in a Multidomain Environment

The real art of using global and local groups emerges in a multidomain environment. When working with groups across trust relationships, the following guidelines are useful:

- Always gather users into global groups. Remember that global groups can contain user accounts only from the same domain. You may have to create global groups with the same name in multiple domains.

- If you have multiple account domains, use the same name for a global group that has the same types of members as another global group in a separate domain. Remember that when multiple domains are involved, the group name is referred to as DOMAIN\GROUP.

- Before you create the global groups, determine whether an existing local group meets your needs. There is no sense in creating duplicate local groups.

- Remember that you must create the local group where the resource is located. If the resource is on a domain controller, create the local group in the Domain Account database. If the resource is on a Windows NT Workstation or Member Server, create the group in that system's local account database.

- Be sure to set the permissions for a resource before you make the global groups members of the local group assigned to the resource so that security has been set for the resource.

D.   Administering Account Policies

Before you start implementing user accounts, one of the most important policies to set is your account policy. These policies affect every account in the domain—you cannot pick and choose which ones are affected. The account policies define how password changes and improper passwords are handled.

The password portion of account policy determines your rules for password security. Options within the account policy include:

- Maximum password age
- Minimum password age
- Minimum password length
- Password uniqueness
- Account lockout
- Account lockout duration
- Handling remote users whose logon hours have expired
- Changing passwords

Template Accounts

As an administrator, consider creating template user accounts for the various types of users that you plan to create. The template enables you to quickly create new user accounts when required. You should disable these template accounts to prevent their use for network access.

To use the template account to your advantage, just choose the template account in User Manager for Domains and create a copy of the account by choosing Copy from the User menu (or press F8). Doing so copies all properties of the template account except:

- **Username**
- **Full Name**
- **Password**
- **Confirm Password**

Template accounts also work best when you make use of the %USERNAME% environment variable for both the User Profile Path and the Home Directory. The environment enables the option User Must Change Password at Next Logon while it disables the Account Disabled box.

E. Auditing Changes to the User Account Database

When an organization implements decentralized administration of the Windows NT Account database, you may want to audit all changes to the Accounts database. Remember, only members of the local groups Administrators and Account Operators can add, modify, and delete users in User Manager for Domains.

To enable auditing of changes to the Account database, a member of the Administrators group must enable Auditing User and Group Management. If you want to know exactly what files are being updated, enable File and Object Access.

The addition of File and Object Access helps you determine when Account Operators attempt to add a member to the Operators or Administrators local groups. When this attempt is made, they see a dialog box that states that their attempt was unsuccessful. Auditing User and Group Management will not catch this error. You must enable File and Object access so that you see the unsuccessful attempt to write to the SAM database.

3.1.1 Exercise: Viewing the SAM and SECURITY Hives

The following steps enable you to view the SAM and SECURITY hives of the HKEY_LOCAL_MACHINE subtree:

1. Start a Command prompt.

2. Start the schedule service by typing **NET START SCHEDULE** at the command prompt. This also can be done from the Services applet of the Control Panel.

3. Type the following AT command. The time portion should be set to a minute or two later than the current time. Remember that you must be logged on as a member of the Administrators group to do this.

   AT [time] /interactive "regedt32.exe"

4. When [time] arrives, the Registry Editor will launch and then give you access to the SAM and SECURITY hives.

3.1.2 Exercise: Application of User Rights When Implementing the Directory Replication Service

The Directory Replication service requires a service account that it uses to perform its tasks of maintaining a consistent NETLOGON share on all domain controllers. You must complete the following steps to set up the service:

1. Create an account in the User Manager for Domains that will be used as the service account.

2. Set the account properties as shown in Figure 3.1.1. Be sure to deselect User Must Change Password at Next Logon and to select Password Never Expires. All service accounts should be set this way so that the accounts will never be prompted to change their passwords.

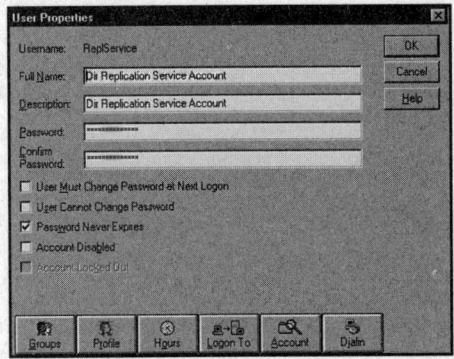

Figure 3.1.1 Setting up the Directory Replication Service Account in User Manager for Domains.

3. Make the user a member of the Replicator local group and the Backup Operators group. These groups grant the service account the necessary rights to perform its predetermined tasks. The Replicator local group enables the account to perform the directory replication task. The Backup Operators group enables the account to read all files in the REPL$\scripts directory of the export server regardless of the permissions on the share. The Backup Operators group also enables the account to write these files to the NETLOGON share of all import servers no matter what permissions exist on these directories.

4. From the Policies menu, choose User Rights. Grant the newly created account to the user right Log On as a Service. This right displays only when you select the advanced check box.

5. Open the Control Panel.

6. Open the Service applet.

7. From the list of services, choose the Directory Replicator Service and click the Startup Button.

8. Fill in the dialog box as shown in Figure 3.1.2. Change the startup type to Automatic. Also be sure to change Log On As option to Use the Account that You Have Set Up. Use the ... button to select the account name from the list as it must be the full domain\username. Finally, enter the password you set for the account.

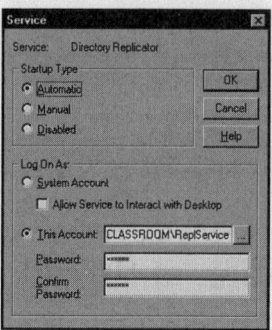

Figure 3.1.2   Configuring the Directory Replicator Service to use your pre-created service account.

9. Click the Start button to start the service. The next time you restart the system, the service will start automatically because of your Automatic Start setting.

3.1 Practice Problems

1. Which option enables Windows NT users to access accounts and log on to a network?

   A. Unique identifiers

   B. Bindery entries

   C. NDS entries

   D. Policies

2. Accessing resources and identifying yourself to a network requires which two items?

   A. Policies

   B. User ID

   C. Password

   D. Group accounts

3. Windows NT user accounts are created in:

   A. User Manager

   B. Server Manager

   C. Network Administrator

   D. User Manager for Domains

4. To create a new account, the user running the utility must be a member of either of which two groups?

   A. Administrators

   B. Account Operators

   C. Domain Users

   D. Guest

5. Which portion of account policy determines your rules for password security?

   A. User

   B. Group

   C. Logon

   D. Password

6. Options within the account policy include all the following except?

   A. Maximum Password Age

   B. Minimum Password Age

   C. Maximum Password Length

   D. Minimum Password Length

7. Template accounts work best when you make use of which environment variable for both the User Profile Path and the Home Directory?

   A. %root%

   B. %Winnt%

   C. %username%

   D. %path%

8. Which setting does not normally appear in the User Properties dialog box unless there is a problem?

   A. User Must Change Password at Next Logon

   B. User Cannot Change Password

   C. Password Never Expires

   D. Account Locked Out

9. Which two statements are true of the Password Never Expires setting in the User Properties dialog box?

   A. This setting overrides the account policy of password expiration.

   B. This setting forces users to change their password when they next log on to the network.

   C. This setting is used in higher security networks in which the users are assigned passwords for their accounts.

   D. This setting should be used only for service accounts in Windows NT.

10. The %username% variable must be unique in the domain, and no longer than how many characters?

   A. 14

   B. 20

   C. 26

   D. 256

11. The password for each username must be no longer than how many characters?

   A. 14

   B. 20

   C. 26

   D. 256

12. The goal of enterprise networking is for each user in the enterprise to have how many user accounts?

   A. 1

   B. 2

   C. 14

   D. 256

13. If the user is working at an NT class system, the password is:

   A. Lowercase

   B. Uppercase

   C. Case-sensitive

   D. Case-insensitive

14. Which feature enables an administrator to configure common drive mappings, run central batch files, and configure the system?

   A. User Manager for Domains

   B. Server Manager

   C. Login scripts

   D. User Manager

15. When configuring a login script, the recommended extensions are? Select two.

   A. *.bat

   B. *.cmd

   C. file

   D. *.txt

16. The logon scripts are stored by default in which directory?

   A. \%systemroot%

   B. \%systemroot%\system32

   C. \%systemroot%\system32\scripts

   D. \%systemroot%\system32\repl\import\scripts

17. The netlogon directory is which directory?

   A. \%systemroot%

   B. \%systemroot%\system32

   C. \%systemroot%\system32\scripts

   D. \%systemroot%\system32\repl\import\scripts

18. Which properties page enables the administrator to determine whether call-back security is to be implemented?

   A. RAS

   B. Dial-in properties

   C. System

   D. Modem

19. This call-back option is commonly used in low-security networks and for users working out of hotel rooms.

   A. No Call Back

   B. Set by User

   C. Preset to

   D. Permanent Connection

20. Which key should you press in User Manager for Domains to create a copy of the template account?

    A. F3

    B. F5

    C. F8

    D. F10

21. A security risk—the user right to shut down the system in Windows NT Workstation—is granted by default to whom?

    A. Everyone group

    B. Backup group

    C. NT Users group

    D. PPP group

22. Global groups, as a general rule, contain:

    A. Resources

    B. Users

    C. Domains

    D. Text files

23. Local groups, as a general rule, are related to:

    A. Resources

    B. Users

    C. Domains

    D. Text files

24. Global groups can contain what? Select all correct answers.

    A. Local groups

    B. Global groups from the same domain

    C. Users from the same domain

    D. Users from a trusted domain

25. Local groups can contain what? Select all correct answers.

    A. Local groups

    B. Global groups from the same domain

    C. Global groups from a trusted domain

    D. Users from the same domain

    E. Users from a trusted domain

3.1.1 Answers and Explanations: Exercise

In Exercise 3.1.1 you learned that when viewing the hives, you must start the Registry Editor in system mode. You viewed the values of the SAM and SECURITY hives of the HKEY_LOCAL_MACHINE subtree.

3.1.2 Answers and Explanations: Exercise

In Exercise 3.1.2, you saw the interaction between user rights and the directory replication service. It is important to note that after established, the service will automatically start for all future sessions.

3.1 Answers and Explanations: Practice Problems

1. **A**   Unique identifiers enable a user to log on to the Windows NT network.

2. **B, C**   User ID and password combinations are the access tickets to all resources on the NT network.

3. **D**   You create Windows NT user accounts in User Manager for Domains.

4. **A, B**   To create a new account, the user running User Manager for Domains must be a member of either the Administrators local group or the Account Operators local group.

5. **D**   The password portion of account policy determines your rules for password security.

6. **C** Options within the account policy include Maximum Password Age, Minimum Password Age, and Minimum Password Length.

7. **C** Template accounts work best when you make use of the %username% environment variable for both the User Profile Path and the Home Directory.

8. **D** The Account Locked Out setting is only active if a user's account has been locked out by the operating system for failing the Account Lockout settings.

9. **A, D** The Password Never Expires setting will override the account policy of password expiration and should be used for service accounts in Windows NT.

10. **B** The %username% variable must be no longer than 20 characters.

11. **A** The password for the user can be up to 14 characters long.

12. **A** The goal of enterprise networking is for each user in the enterprise to have only *one* user account.

13. **C** When the user is working at an NT class system, the password is case-sensitive.

14. **C** The login scripts enable an administrator to configure common drive mappings, run central batch files, and configure the system.

15. **A, B** When configuring a login script, recommended extensions are *.bat or *.cmd.

16. **D** The logon scripts are stored by default in the directory:

    ```
    \%systemroot%\system32\repl\
    import\scripts
    ```

17. **D** The \%systemroot%\system32 \repl\import\scripts directory is shared as the netlogon share.

18. **B** The dial-in properties page enables the administrator to determine which users are granted dial-in access to the network and whether call-back security should be implemented.

19. **A** If No Call Back is selected, the user immediately is able to use network resources.

20. **C** F8 in User Manager for Domains will create a copy of the template account.

21. **A** The default membership in Windows NT Workstation includes the Everyone group.

22. **B** As a general rule, global groups contain users and local groups contain resources. The local groups are then related to resources and assigned the appropriate permissions.

23. **A** Local groups contain resources and global groups contain users. The local groups are then related to resources and assigned the appropriate permissions.

24. **A, B** Global groups can contain local groups and other global groups.

25. **A** Local groups cannot contain global groups, but can contain other local groups.

3.1   Key Words

Global group

Local group

Replication

Replication service

User Manager

User Manager for Domains

3.2   Creating and Managing System Policies and User Profiles

System policies and user profiles assist in the centralization of management in a Windows NT Enterprise network. System policies help an administrator implement common Registry settings across the enterprise. User Profiles store the user portion of the Registry, and you can implement the user profiles as either local profiles or roaming profiles. A roaming profile enables users to have the user portion of their configuration follow them wherever they log in on the Windows NT network.

A.   Local Profiles Versus Roaming Profiles

When users log in at a system, they create a local profile on that system. The local profile is implemented as a set of directory structures. This directory structure includes the desktop folder and the Start menu folder. The user portion of the Registry is stored in the file NTUSER.DAT.

When a user logs in to the network, their desktop and Start menu are also based on the local system that they are logging in to. The desktop is based on the user's profile directory and the ALL USERS directory. The same is true for the Start menu directory.

The problem with local profiles is that every workstation that you log in to will have its own version of the local profile. User configuration settings will have to be set at each workstation that they log in to.

To overcome this problem, you must implement Roaming profiles. Roaming profiles include the user portion of the Registry, which is downloaded from a designated system to the system that the users are currently logged on to. Any changes to their settings will be stored in the central location so that the next workstation can retrieve the settings.

1.   Configuring Roaming Profiles in Windows NT

To configure a roaming profile for a user account, first set the profile path in the User Manager for Domains for that account. If you are configuring a block of users, the best method is to do a group property change by choosing all users you want to have roaming profiles, and then choosing Properties from the User menu.

The most common setting is to have a directory shared with a share name such as profiles. It should enable the local group USERS the permission FULL CONTROL. With this share, you can now set the user's profile path to \\server\share\%username%. The next time the users log on, their profile information is saved to this central profile directory.

2.   Tuning Roaming Profiles

An administrator can determine whether the User Profiles stored on the local system are roaming or local profiles by viewing the User Profiles tab in the System applet in Control Panel.

The dialog box shows all the profiles currently stored on the system and whether they are roaming or local profiles. You can change the profile between a roaming and local profile by clicking the Change To button. A dialog box appears.

3

You also use this dialog box to configure how to handle roaming profiles when the user logs in to the network over a slow WAN link. This is an extremely useful setting for laptop users that may log in to the enterprise network from various locations. Remember that the roaming profile is stored on a specific server even though the user can be authenticated on any domain controller within the domain.

3. Implementing Roaming Profiles in Windows 95

Windows 95 users can also have roaming profiles configured so that their user-based configurations can follow them from workstation to workstation. Implementing roaming profiles in Windows 95 differs from Windows NT in the following ways:

- Separate user profiles are not implemented automatically in Windows 95 as they are in Windows NT.

- The user portion of the Registry is saved in the file USER.DAT in Windows 95, whereas it is stored in NTUSER.DAT in Windows NT.

- The user profile path setting in the user's properties has no effect on Windows 95 clients. The roaming profile information is stored in their Windows NT Home Directory.

B. Understanding System Policies

System policies help the network administrator restrict the configuration changes users can perform to their profiles. By combining roaming profiles and system policies, the administrators cannot provide the users a consistent desktop, but they can control what the users can do to that desktop. Likewise, the administrator can ensure that the users cannot modify certain settings.

System policies work like a merge operation. Think of system policies as a copy of your Registry. When you log in to the network and the NTCONFIG.POL file exists on the domain controller, it merges its settings into your Registry, changing your Registry settings as indicated in the system policy.

You implement system policies by using the System Policy Editor. The System Policy Editor is automatically installed with any Windows NT domain controller.

You can configure system policies to do the following:

- Implement defaults for hardware configuration for all computers or for a specific machine using the profile.

- Restrict the capability to change specific parameters that affect the hardware configuration of the participating system.

- Set defaults for all users on the areas of their personal settings that they can configure.

- Restrict the users from changing specific areas of their configurations to prevent them from tampering with the system. An example is disabling all Registry editing tools for a specific user.

- Apply all defaults and restrictions on a group level rather than just a user level.

You can also use the System Policy Editor to change settings in the Registry of the system on which the System Policy Editor is executed. Many times it is easier to use the System Policy Editor because it has a better interface for finding common restrictions.

1. Implementing System Policies

To create Computer, User, and Group policies, you must use the System Policy Editor. The System Policy Editor is automatically installed on all domain controllers, and you can find the editor in the Administrative Tools Group of the Start menu.

When you create a new policy file, you see two default icons within the policy:

- **Default Computer:** Used to configure all machine-specific settings. All property changes within this section affect the HKEY_LOCAL_MACHINE subtree of the Registry.

- **Default User:** Used for any client that uses the policy and does not have a specific machine entry created for itself in the policy file. Used to specify default policy settings for all users that use the policy. It affects the HKEY_CURRENT_USER subtree of the Registry. If the users are configured to use a roaming profile, this information is stored in their centralized version of NTUSER.DAT in their profile directories.

2. Configuring Computer Policies

You can configure computer policies to lock down common machine settings that affect all users of a Windows NT system. Common settings that are configured include:

- Programs to automatically run at startup of the computer system. These can include virus scans. Opening the System/Run option in the Default Computer Properties sets this.

- Ensuring that all Windows NT clients will have the administrative shares automatically created on startup of these systems. This enhances the capability of the administrator to centrally manage the network. Opening the Windows NT Network/Sharing option in the Default Computer Properties sets this option.

- Implementing customized shared folders. These include the Desktop folder, Start menu folder, Startup folder, and Programs folder. These can be set to point to an actual network share location so that multiple machines have common desktops or Start menus. Opening the Windows NT Shell/ Custom Shared Folders option in the Default Computer Properties sets this.

- Presenting a customized dialog box called the Logon Banner that you can use to inform users of upcoming maintenance to the network or for other network information. Opening the Windows NT System/Logon option in the Default Computer Properties sets this option.

- Removing the last logged on user from the Authentication dialog box. Many users have predictable passwords, and knowing the user's login name can help lead to guessing their passwords. This is also set in the Windows NT System/Logon option in the Default Computer Properties.

You also can implement computer policies on a computer-by-computer basis by choosing Add Computer from the Edit Menu. This adds a new icon to the policy with that computer's name.

3. Configuring User Policies

Implement user policies through the System Policy Editor. These policies affect the HKEY_CURRENT_USER Registry subtree. Each user is affected individually by these settings.

You can also implement user policies on a user-by-user basis. To create an individual user policy, choose Add User from the Edit menu. When a user logs in, NTCONFIG.POL will be checked to see whether there is a policy for the specific user. If there is not, the default user policy is used for the login process.

Some of the common implementations of user profiles are the following:

- Locking down display properties to prevent users from changing the resolution of their monitors. You can lock down display properties as a whole or on each individual property page of display properties. Adjust this setting in the Control Panel/Display/Restrict Display option of the Default User Properties sheet.

- Setting a default color scheme or wallpaper. You can set the default in the Desktop option of the Default User Properties sheet.

- If you want to restrict access to portions of the Start menu or Desktop, you can do this via the Shell/Restrictions option of the Default User Properties sheet.

- If you need to limit the applications run at a workstation, set this in the System/Restrictions option of the Default User Properties sheet. You can use the System/Restrictions option to prevent the users from modifying the Registry.

- You can prevent users from mapping or disconnecting network drives by setting the options in the Windows NT Shell/Restrictions option of the Default User Properties sheet.

4. Implementing Group Policies

If you need to have user settings affect multiple users, you can implement group policies. Group policies add another level of complexity to the processing of the policies. Some of the additional considerations include:

- The System Policy Editor uses global groups for group membership. Appropriate trust relationships must be implemented to see the necessary global groups.

- Because a user can belong to multiple global groups, the order in which the groups are processed is very important. One group's settings could be the opposite of another group's. Set group order in the Group Priority option of the Options menu.

5. Processing Order for System Policies

When a user logs on to a network in which system policies have been implemented, the following steps occur:

1. The user successfully logs in to the network.

2. The user profile is read from the NETLOGON share of the authenticating domain controller.

3. If a predefined policy exists for a user, that policy is merged into the HKEY_CURRENT_USER Registry subtree. Then the processing moves to step 6.

4. If no predefined user policy exists, the default user policy is processed.

5. The group priority list is examined. If the user is a member of any of the global groups for which policy exists, the account is processed according to the group priority order. The priority is ordered from bottom to top of the group priority list. Each of the group policies is applied to the HKEY_CURRENT_USER Registry subtree.

6. After the user and group policies have been processed, the machine policies are determined. If there is a predefined machine policy, that policy is merged with the HKEY_LOCAL_MACHINE Registry subtree. If there is no predefined machine policy for the system from which the user is logging in, the default machine policy is merged with the HKEY_LOCAL_MACHINE subtree.

6. Differences Between Windows NT and Windows 95 Profiles

Although Windows NT automatically implements system policies in its clients, there is more configuration required for Windows 95 if you want Windows 95 to recognize group policies. First, you must individually configure the Windows 95 clients to recognize group policies, as follows:

1. Open the Windows 95 Control Panel.

2. In the Control Panel, open the Add/Remove Programs applet.

3. Change to the Windows Setup tab and click the Have Disk button.

4. The System Policy installation files are located on the Windows 95 CD in the directory \ADMIN\APPTOOLS\POLEDIT. Choose this directory by using the Browse button.

5. When the options to install appear, choose Group Policies.

Following these steps installs the necessary files. After you configure the client to use system policies, one more change is recommended in a Windows NT network environment. By default, the Windows 95 client only looks for the file CONFIG.POL on the Primary Domain Controller's NETLOGON share. If you want the Windows 95 client to be able to process the system policy from any domain controller as in Windows NT, you must enable the Load Balancing option under the Network/System Policies Update/Remote Update option.

3.2.1 Exercise: Changing Windows 95 from Shared to Separate Profiles

To change Windows 95 from using shared user profiles to separate profiles, perform the following steps:

1. Open the Control Panel.

2. Open the Password applet in the Control Panel.

3. Choose the User Profile Tab. You must change the setting to Users Can Customize Their Preferences and Desktop Settings. Be sure to also enable the options to Include Desktop Icons and Network Neighborhood Contents in User Settings and Include Start Menu and Program Groups in User Settings.

4. Then you must restart the computer for the change to take effect.

3.2.2 Exercise: Creating a New System Policy

Creating a system policy is outlined in the following steps:

1. From the Start menu, choose Programs, Administrative Tools (Common), System Policy Editor.

2. Verify that the proper template files are loaded by choosing Policy Template from the Options menu. The default templates that should be loaded are:

   - `c:\%winntroot%\INF\COMMON.ADM`

   - `c:\%winntroot%\INF\WINNT.ADM`

3. From the File menu, choose New Policy.

4. To adjust settings affecting the HKEY_LOCAL_MACHINE subtree, double-click the Default Computer icon. To adjust settings affecting each user's HKEY_CURRENT_USER subtree in the Registry, double-click the Default User icon. The following settings are available:

   - **Clear:** Changes the client's Registry to not implement the Registry setting. If it has been previously enabled in the client's Registry, it will be disabled after the policy is implemented.

   - **Shaded:** Leaves the client's Registry exactly as it is before the policy is implemented. If the option was enabled in the client's Registry, it remains enabled. If the option was disabled, it remains disabled.

   - **Checked:** Changes the client's registry to match exactly what the system policy has configured. There is no choice on the part of the client.

5. After you make all your desired setting changes, you must save the file. The location that all Windows NT clients will look for the file is in the NETLOGON share of the domain controller that authenticates the user. The best place to save this file is in the following location:

```
\\CENTRAL SERVER\REPL$\SCRIPTS\NTCONFIG.POL
```

where *NTCONFIG.POL* is the name of your policy. This file is available only if you set up directory replication among your domain controllers.

3.2 Practice Problems

1. What two items are used to assist in the centralization of management in a Windows NT Enterprise network?

    A. System policies

    B. Local groups

    C. User profiles

    D. Global groups

2. Which of the following help an administrator implement common Registry settings across the enterprise?

    A. System policies

    B. User profiles

    C. Regedt32

    D. Login scripts

3. Which of the following store the user portion of the Registry?

    A. System policies

    B. User profiles

    C. Regedt32

    D. Login scripts

4. User profiles can be implemented in which two ways?

    A. Local

    B. Global

    C. Roaming

    D. Group

5. Which user profile type enables users to have the user portion of their configurations follow them wherever they log on to the Windows NT network?

    A. Local

    B. Global

    C. Roaming

    D. Group

6. The user portion of the Windows NT Registry is stored in which file?

    A. USER.DAT

    B. USER.MAN

    C. NTUSER.DAT

    D. NTUSER.MAN

7. If you want to configure a user account to use a roaming profile, the first thing to do is:

    A. Set the profile path in the User Manager for Domains for that account.

    B. Rename USER.DAT to USER.MAN.

    C. Move USER.DAT to the NETLOGON directory.

    D. Enable TTS.

8. An administrator can determine whether the User Profiles stored on the local system are roaming or local profiles by viewing the User Profiles tab in which Control Panel applet?

    A. Network Neighborhood

    B. Passwords

    C. System

    D. Users

9. If a roaming profile is only stored on one specific server, the user can be authenticated:

    A. Only on that server

    B. On any domain controller within the domain

    C. Only on the local workstation

    D. At any workstation within the domain

10. Implementing roaming profiles in Windows 95 differs from Windows NT in which of the following ways? Select all correct answers.

    A. Separate user profiles are not implemented automatically in Windows 95 as they are in Windows NT.

    B. The user portion of the Registry is saved in the file USER.DAT in Windows 95, whereas it is stored in NTUSER.DAT in Windows NT.

    C. The user profile path setting in the user's properties has no effect on Windows 95 clients.

    D. Windows NT roaming profile information is stored in the Windows NT Home Directory.

11. Which of the following help the network administrator restrict what configuration changes users can perform to their profiles:

    A. Roaming profiles

    B. System policies

    C. Group assignments

    D. Login scripts

12. The System Policy file on NT is, by default, named:

    A. CONFIG.POL

    B. NTCONFIG.POL

    C. SYSTEM.DAT

    D. SYSTEM.POL

13. Implement system policies by using:

    A. System Policy Editor

    B. User Manager for Domains

    C. Server Manager

    D. Regedit

14. The System Policy Editor is installed by default:

    A. From the Resource Kit

    B. On any Windows 95 workstation

    C. On any NT Workstation

    D. On any Windows NT domain controller

15. You can configure system policies to do all the following except:

    A. Implement defaults for hardware configuration for all computers.

    B. Restrict the capability to change specific parameters that affect the hardware configuration of the participating system.

    C. Eliminate the need for backups of user-specific information.

    D. Set defaults for all users on the areas of their personal settings that they can configure.

16. Using the System Policy Editor, you can create policies for which of the following? Select all correct answers.

    A. Domain

    B. Computer

    C. User

    D. Group

17. The System Policy Editor can be found in what group of the Start menu?

    A. System

    B. User Manager

    C. Administrative Tools

    D. Programs

18. When you create a new policy file, what two default icons appear within the policy?

    A. Default Computer

    B. Default User

C. Default Domain

D. Default Group

19. Which item is used to configure all machine-specific settings?

   A. Default Computer

   B. Default User

   C. Default Domain

   D. Default Group

20. All property changes within the Default Computer section affect which subtree of the Registry:

   A. HKEY_USER

   B. HKEY_SYSTEM

   C. HKEY_CURRENT_USER

   D. HKEY_LOCAL_MACHINE

21. Which item is used to specify default policy settings for all users that use the policy:

   A. Default Computer

   B. Default User

   C. Default Domain

   D. Default Group

22. The default user settings affect which subtree of the Registry:

   A. HKEY_USER

   B. HKEY_SYSTEM

   C. HKEY_CURRENT_USER

   D. HKEY_LOCAL_MACHINE

23. Which of the following do you use to lock down common machine settings that affect all users of a Windows NT system:

   A. System policies

   B. User policies

   C. Computer policies

   D. Domain policies

24. Which type of policies should you use to prevent users from changing the resolution of their individual monitors:

   A. System policies

   B. User policies

   C. Computer policies

   D. Domain policies

25. Which type of policies should you use to set a default color scheme or wallpaper for individual users:

   A. System policies

   B. User policies

   C. Computer policies

   D. Domain policies

3.2.1 Answers and Explanations: Exercise

Any user that logs on for the first time is informed that they have not logged on to this network. Then they are asked if they want to have this user's settings maintained in their own personal profile.

3.2.2 Answers and Explanations: Exercise

A new system policy is created by systematically following the steps outlined earlier in the chapter. It is important to load the template files first, and enable the directory replication service at the conclusion—to ensure that an up-to-date version of the policy is stored in each domain controller to which the export server has been configured to replicate.

3.2 Answers and Explanations: Practice Problems

1. **A, C** The use of system policies and user profiles assists in the centralization of management in a Windows NT Enterprise network.

2. **A** System policies help an administrator implement common Registry settings across the enterprise.

3. **B** User Profiles store the user portion of the Registry.

4. **A, C** You can implement user profiles as either local profiles or roaming profiles.

5. **C** A roaming profile enables users to have the user portion of their configurations follow them wherever they log on to the Windows NT network.

6. **C** The user portion of the Registry is stored in the file NTUSER.DAT.

7. **A** If you want to configure a user account to use a roaming profile, the first thing to do is set the profile path in the User Manager for Domains for that account.

8. **C** An administrator can determine whether the user profiles stored on the local system are roaming or local profiles by viewing the User Profiles tab in the System applet in Control Panel.

9. **B** Although the roaming profile is stored on a specific server, the user can be authenticated on any domain controller within the domain.

10. **A, B, C** Implementing roaming profiles in Windows 95 differs from Windows NT in the following ways: Separate User profiles are not implemented automatically in Windows 95 as they are in Windows NT; the user portion of the Registry is saved in the file USER.DAT in Windows 95, whereas it is stored in NTUSER.DAT in Windows NT; and the user profile path setting in the user's properties has no effect on Windows 95 clients.

11. **B** System policies help the network administrator restrict the configuration changes the users can perform to their profiles.

12. **B** NTCONFIG.POL is the default system policy filename on NT networks.

13. **A** System policies are implemented by using the System Policy Editor.

14. **D** The System Policy Editor is automatically installed with any Windows NT domain controller.

15. **C** System policies do not eliminate the need for backups of user-specific information.

16. **B, C, D** To create Computer, User, and Group policies, you must use the System Policy Editor.

17. **C** The System Policy Editor is automatically installed on all Domain Controllers, and you can find the editor in the Administrative Tools Group of the Start menu.

18. **A, B** When you create a new policy file, it presents you with two default icons within the policy: Default Computer and Default User.

19. **A** Use the Default Computer item to configure all machine-specific settings.

20. **D** All property changes within this section affects the HKEY_LOCAL_MACHINE subtree of the Registry.

21. **B** Use the Default User item to specify default policy settings for all users that use the policy.

22. **A, C** The default user setting affects the HKEY_CURRENT_USER subtree of the Registry and the HKEY_USER subtree.

23. **C** You can configure computer policies to lock down common machine settings that affect all users of a Windows NT system.

24. **B** User policies can be used to prevent users from changing the resolution of their monitors.

25. **B** User policies can be used to set a default color scheme or wallpaper.

3.2   Key Words

Domain controller

Primary Domain Controller

Backup Domain Controller

System Policy Editor

System policies

User policies

User profiles

Local profiles

Roaming profiles

3

3.3　Administering Remote Servers from Various Client Computers

A common initial misconception is that you must be located at a Windows NT domain controller to manage a Windows NT Domain. On the contrary, you can choose from several versions of the Remote Administration Tools for Windows NT that enable you to administer Windows NT Domains from Windows 95 and from Windows NT Workstation.

A.　Remote Administration Tools for Windows 95

The Windows 95 Remote Administration Tools allow a client running Windows 95 to manage the following aspects of a Windows NT Server domain:

- You can manage users in a domain with User Manager for Domains.

- Manage servers in the domain using Server Manager.

- Troubleshoot servers using the Event Viewer to view System, Application, and Audit Logs.

- Extensions to the Windows 95 Explorer enable you to manage NTFS permissions, auditing, and print permissions through the Network Neighborhood.

- Manage servers running File and Print Services for NetWare from the Windows 95 system through the FPNW tab of any drive on that server.

B.　Remote Administration Tools for Windows NT

The Windows NT Server Tools for Windows NT Workstation enable you to manage a Windows NT domain from either a Windows NT Workstation or a Windows NT Member Server. The Windows NT Server Tools for Windows NT Workstation include the following utilities:

- **DHCP Manager:** Covered in Chapter 4, "Connectivity."

- **System Policy Editor:** As discussed in the previous section, you implement system policies by using the System Policy Editor.

- **Remote Access Admin:** Covered in Chapter 4.

- **Remote Boot Manager:** Covered in Chapter 2, "Installation and Configuration."

- **Server Manager:** Covered in Chapter 2.

- **User Manager for Domains:** As discussed in Section 3.1, you create Windows NT user accounts in the User Manager for Domains.

- **WINS Manager:** Covered in Chapter 4.

- **Extensions for Managing Services for Macintosh:** Covered in Chapter 2.

C.　Web-Based Administration Tools

The Windows NT Server Resource Kit includes a new utility that enables you to remotely administer Windows NT Servers from Windows, Macintosh, and UNIX hosts running web browser software. This utility is also available for download from the Microsoft web site. Implement Web Administration tools as an Internet Information Server extension. The only caveat is that the person connecting to the NT Administration page must be a member of the Domain's Administrators local group.

To install the Web Administration tools on a Domain Controller, use the following steps:

1. Insert the Windows NT Server Resource Kit CD into the CD Drive of the domain controller to be managed.

2. From the autorun screen presented, choose the Web Administration link.

3. On the next screen, choose the Install Now link.

4. To continue the installation, you must agree to the End User License Agreement by clicking the Yes button.

5. To start the installation, click the Continue button.

6. To complete the installation, click the Exit to Windows button. The Readme file for the Web Administration tools is displayed to finalize the installation.

7. To access the web-based administration tools, start your web browser and go to the address `http://<your_server_name>/ntadmin/ntadmin.htm`.

The Web Administration tools are intended for an experienced NT administrator. These tools allow limited administration of a Windows NT domain controller using HTML forms. Management tasks that can be performed from Web Administration tools include:

- Managing user accounts.

- Managing global and local accounts.

- Adding and removing Windows NT computer accounts to/from a domain.

- Stopping and starting devices on the system.

- Viewing the System, Audit, and Application.

- Managing shared directories and their permissions.

- Managing NTFS file and directory permissions.

- Sending a broadcast message to all users with open sessions to the server.

- Setting up the server to run the Windows NT Resource Kit Remote Console Utility.

- Rebooting the server using the web page.

- Setting the preferences for the Web Administration Tools.

- Managing printers hosted by the server.

- Stopping, starting, and configuring services running on the server.

- Managing all active sessions. This includes disconnecting all or specific sessions.

- Viewing the server configuration. This makes use of the WINMSDP utility from the resource kit. This utility provides the same information as the graphical WINMSD utility, but in text-only format.

- Viewing a report format on selected performance counters.

- Viewing server statistics.

3.3.1 Exercise: Installing Remote Administration for Windows NT Server on Windows 95

To install the Remote Administration for Windows NT Server, perform the following steps:

1. Open the Windows 95 Control Panel.

2. Open the Add/Remove Programs applet in Control Panel.

3. On the Windows Setup tab, click the Have Disk button.

4. Insert the Windows NT Server CD and on the CD select the \CLIENTS\SRVTOOLS\WIN95 directory where the SRVTOOLS.INF file is located using the Browse button.

5. In the dialog box that appears after clicking the OK button, select the Windows NT Server Tools option and click the Install button. This installs the Server Tools into the c:\srvtools directory by default using about 3 MB of disk space.

6. You must manually adjust the path statement in AUTOEXEC.BAT to include the directory c:\srvtools.

7. After the path has been adjusted in AUTOEXEC.BAT, you must reboot the system for all changes to take place.

3.3.2 Exercise: Installing Server Tools for Windows NT Workstation

To install the Server Tools for Windows NT Workstation, perform the following steps:

1. Insert the Windows NT 4 Server CD.

2. Run SETUP.BAT from the \clients\srvtools\winnt folder. This copies all the necessary files to the NT Workstation and makes the necessary Registry setting changes to enable you to manage Windows NT domains.

3. The installation program does not automatically create the Windows NT Server Tools icons in the Start menu. You must create the server tool icons manually in the Start menu.

3.3 Practice Problems

1. Versions of the Remote Administration Tools for Windows NT that shipped on the Windows NT 4.0 Server CD enable you to administer Windows NT domains from which two of the following operating systems?

    A. Windows 95

    B. Windows for Workgroups

    C. Windows NT Workstation

    D. LAN Manager

2. The Windows 95 Remote Administration Tools enable a client running Windows 95 to manage all but which of the following aspects of a Windows NT Server domain?

    A. You can manage users in a domain with User Manager.

    B. Servers in the domain.

    C. Troubleshooting of servers.

    D. Extensions to the Windows 95 Explorer enable you to manage NTFS permissions.

3. When using the Windows 95 Remote Administration Tools, which of the following can you manage on a Windows NT Server Domain? Select all correct answers.

    A. Auditing

    B. Print permission management

    C. NTFS permissions

    D. Dial-up connections

4. Which tool do you use from Windows 95 Remote Administration to manage servers in a domain?

    A. Event Viewer

    B. User Manager

    C. Server Manager

    D. Network Neighborhood

5. Which tool do you use from Windows 95 Remote Administration to manage users in a domain?

    A. Event Viewer

    B. User Manager

    C. Server Manager

    D. Network Neighborhood

6. Which tool do you use from Windows 95 Remote Administration to troubleshoot servers in a domain?

    A. Event Viewer

    B. User Manager

    C. Server Manager

    D. Network Neighborhood

7. You can manage servers running File and Print Services for NetWare from the Windows 95 system through:

    A. Network Neighborhood

    B. User Manager

    C. Event Viewer

    D. The FPNW tab of any drive on that server

8. The Windows NT Server Tools for Windows NT Workstation include which of the following utilities? Select all correct answers.

    A. DHCP Manager

    B. System Policy Editor

    C. Remote Access Admin

    D. User Manager

9. The Windows NT Server Tools for Windows NT Workstation include which of the following utilities? Select all correct answers.

    A. Remote Boot Manager

    B. Server Manager

C. WINS Manager

D. Extensions for Managing Services for Macintosh

10. The Web Administration tools are available from what two sources:

A. The Microsoft web site.

B. The NT Server Resource Kit.

C. Through mail-order houses.

D. A subdirectory on the original distribution CDs.

11. The Web Administration tools enable you to remotely administer Windows NT Servers from what platforms? Select all correct answers.

A. OS/2 Workstations

B. Macintosh

C. UNIX hosts

D. CP/M

12. The Web Administration tools are implemented as:

A. A CMD script

B. An ActiveX plug-in

C. A DirectX extension

D. An Internet Information Server extension

13. When using the Web Administration tools, the person connecting to the NT Administration page must be a member of:

A. The domain's Administrators local group

B. Any domain's Administrators local group

C. The domain's Administrators global group

D. Any domain's Administrators global group

3.3.1 Answers and Explanations: Exercise

In this exercise, you installed Remote Administration for Windows NT Server on a Windows 95 client. Whenever a user tries to administer an NT domain using the Windows NT Remote Administration tools, users are asked to enter their passwords before running the utility. This ensures that the users have sufficient privileges to run the Administration Tools.

3.3.2 Answers and Explanations: Exercise

In this exercise, you installed the Server Tools for Windows NT Workstation. The Windows NT Server Tools for Windows NT Workstation enable you to manage a Windows NT domain from either a Windows NT Workstation or a Windows NT Member Server.

3.3 Answers and Explanations: Practice Problems

1. **A, C** You can choose among several versions of the Remote Administration Tools for Windows NT that enable you to administer Windows NT domains from Windows 95 and from Windows NT Workstation.

2. **A** You can use User Manager for domains, but not User Manager.

3. **A, B, C** The Windows 95 Remote Administration Tools enable a client running Windows 95 to manage NTFS permissions, auditing, and print permissions through the Network Neighborhood.

4. **C** Manage servers in the domain by using Server Manager.

5. **B** You can manage users in the domain by using User Manager.

6. **A** You can troubleshoot servers by using the Event Viewer to view System, Application, and Audit Logs.

7. **D** You can manage servers running File and Print Services for NetWare from the Windows 95 system through the FPNW tab of any drive on that server.

8. **D** The Windows NT Server Tools for Windows NT Workstation include User Manager for Domains and not User Manager (a Workstation utility).

9. **A, B, C, D** The Windows NT Server Tools for Windows NT Workstation include all four utilities listed.

10. **A, B** The Web Administration tools are available from the Microsoft web site or on the Server Resource Kit.

11. **B, C** The Web Administration tools enable you to remotely administer Windows NT from Windows, Macintosh, and UNIX hosts running web browser software.

12. **D** The Web Administration tools are implemented as an Internet Information Server extension.

13. **A** The person connecting to the NT Administration page must be a member of the domain's Administrators local group.

3.3 Key Words

Remote server

Web Administration tools

3.4   Managing Disk Resources

After you create your groups in Windows NT, the next step in securing your system is to protect your disk resources. Windows NT has two levels of security for protecting disk resources:

- Share permissions
- NTFS permissions

The management of both sets of permissions protects your Windows NT system from inappropriate access.

A.   Creating and Sharing Resources

Share-level security enables a Windows NT administrator to protect resources from Network users. Shares have a level of security, and they are also used as the entry point into the system for Windows NT users.

There are four explicit share permissions that you can implement, as follows:

- **Read:** Enables users to connect to the resource and run programs. They also can view any documents that are stored in the share, but they cannot make any changes to the documents.

- **Change:** Enables users to connect to a resource and run programs. It also enables them to create new documents and subfolders, to modify existing documents, and to delete documents.

- **Full Control:** Enables users to do anything they want in the share. It also enables them to change the share permissions to affect all users. The full control permission generally is not required for most users. Change is sufficient for most day-to-day business needs.

- **No Access:** The most powerful permission. When it is implemented, the user assigned this permission has no access to the specified resource. It does not matter what other permissions are assigned. The No Access permission overrides any other assigned permissions.

1.   Determining Effective Share Permissions

When users, through group membership, have been assigned varying levels of share permissions, the users' effective shared permissions are the accumulation of their individual shared permissions.

The only time that this is not the case is when you assign the user or a group to which the user belongs the explicit permission of No Access. The No Access permission always takes precedence over any other permissions you assign.

Remember you must create the local groups in the accounts database where the resource is located. If the resource is located on a domain controller, you can create the local group in the domain's accounts database. If the resource is located on a Windows NT Workstation or a Windows NT Member Server, you must create the local group in that system's accounts database.

B.   Implementing Permissions and Security

NTFS permissions enable you to assign more comprehensive security to your computer system. NTFS permissions can protect you at the file level. Share permissions, on the other hand, can apply only to the directory level. NTFS permissions can affect users logged on locally or across the network to the system where you apply the NTFS permissions. Share permissions are in effect only when the user connects to the resource via the network.

You can apply NTFS permissions, when applied at the directory level, as one of the following default assignments shown in Table 3.4.1.

Table 3.4.1   NTFS Directory Permissions

NTFS Permission	Meaning
No Access (none)(none)	The No Access NTFS permission means that the user will have absolutely No Access to the directory or its files. This will override any other NTFS permissions they may have been assigned to them through other group memberships.
List (RX) (Not Specified)	The List NTFS permission enables the user to view the contents of a directory and to navigate to its subdirectories. It does not grant them access to the files in these directories unless specified in file permissions.
Read (RX) (RX)	The Read NTFS permission enables the user to navigate the entire directory structure, view the contents of the directory, view the contents of any files in the directory, and to execute programs.
Add (WX) (Not Specified)	The Add NTFS permission enables the user to add new subdirectories and files to the directory. It does not give the user access to the files within the directory unless specified in other NTFS permissions.
Add & Read (RWX) (RX)	The Add & Read NTFS permission enables a user to add new files to the directory structure. After the file has been added, the user has read only access to the files. This permission also enables the user to run programs.
Change (RWXD) (RWXD)	The Change NTFS permission enables the user to do the most data manipulation. They can view the contents of directories and files, run programs, modify the contents of data files, and delete files.
Full Control (All) (All)	The Full Control permission gives the user all the capabilities of the Change Permission. In addition, the user can change the permissions on that directory or any of its contents. They also can take ownership of the directory or any of its contents.
Special Directory	You can set the NTFS permissions as desired to any combination of (R)ead, (W)rite, E(X)ecute, (D)elete, Change (P)ermissions, and Take (O)wnership.

You can apply NTFS permissions to individual files in directories. The NTFS file permissions are shown in Table 3.4.2.

Table 3.4.2   NTFS File Permissions

NTFS Permission	Meaning
No Access (none)	The No Access NTFS file permission means that the users have absolutely No Access to that file. This overrides any other NTFS directory and file permissions they may have assigned to the users through other group memberships.
Read (RX)	The Read NTFS file permission enables the users to view the contents of files but make no changes to the contents. The users can also execute the file if it is a program.
Change (RWXD)	The Change NTFS file permission enables the users to make any editing changes they want to a data file, including deleting the file.
Full Control (All)	The Full Control file permission gives the users all the capabilities of the Change permission. The users can also change the permissions on that file and take ownership of that file, if they are not the present owner.
Special File	You can set the NTFS file permissions as desired to any combination of (R)ead, (W)rite, E(X)ecute, (D)elete, Change (P)ermissions, and Take (O)wnership.

1.   Determining Effective NTFS Permissions

The determination of NTFS permissions is based on the cumulative NTFS permissions based on group membership. As with share permissions, the only wildcard is the No Access permission. If you assign users or a local group to which users belong the No Access permission, the other assigned permissions do not matter. Users have no access.

2.   The Effects of Moving and Copying on NTFS Permissions

If a file is moved or copied to a new directory, this could change the permissions on an NTFS file. The permissions depend on whether the target directory is on the same NTFS volume as the current directory.

If a file is copied from one directory to another on a single NTFS volume, the file inherits the directory permissions for new files of the target directory. If a file is moved from one directory to another directory on the same NTFS volume, it retains the same NTFS permissions it had from the original directory.

The permissions get confusing when files are moved or copied from one NTFS volume to another NTFS volume. When you copy a file from an NTFS volume to another NTFS volume, the file always inherits the permissions of the target directory. This is also the case when you move a file between NTFS volumes because the file is not actually moved between NTFS volumes. The process is as follows:

- The file is copied to the target directory. This causes the file to inherit the permissions of the target directory.

- The file in the target directory is compared to the original file to verify that it is identical.

- The original file is deleted from the original directory.

3. Setting NTFS Permissions

You set NTFS permissions from the Security page of an NTFS file or directory object. To set NTFS permissions, users must meet one of the following criteria:

- Be a member of the Administrators local group.

- Be a member of the Server Operators local group.

- Be a member of the Power Users local group in a Windows NT Workstation or Windows NT Member Server environment.

- Be assigned the NTFS Permission of Change Permission (P) for a directory or file resource.

- Be the owner of a file or directory object. The owner of any object can change the permissions of that object at any time.

- Have the permission to Take Ownership so that they can become the owner of the file or directory object and change the permissions of that object.

When combining NTFS and share permissions, remember the following tips:

- You can assign users only to global groups in the same domain.

- Only global groups from trusted domains can become members of local groups in trusting domains.

- You assign NTFS permissions only to local groups in all correct test answers.

- Only NTFS permissions give you file-level security.

C. The Windows NT Security Model

In the Windows NT security model, users are associated with resources. Each resource has an Access Control List (ACL) that contains Access Control Entries (ACEs). When you determine whether you should grant users access to resources, the users' access tokens are compared to the ACL for the resources they are trying to access.

When users log in to the system, they receive access tokens that are attached to any processes that they run during the logon session. The access tokens contain their security IDs (SID) and all their group memberships. The access tokens serve as the credentials for the logon session. Whenever users try to access an object, they present the access tokens as their credentials. Because the access token is built during the logon process, group membership is not modified until the next user logon.

When the user attempts to open a resource, the user's access token is compared to the Access Control List for the resource. The Access Control Entries within the Access Control List are, by default, sorted with all No Access permissions at the top of the list. The evaluation of whether the user should be granted access to the resource is as follows:

1. If the users or any group that they belong to is explicitly denied access (assigned the No Access permission), the access to the resource is denied.

2. The ACEs are next checked to see whether any of the entries explicitly assigns the users or a group to which the users belong the type of access that they are attempting. If there is such an entry, access is granted to the resource.

3. Each entry in the ACL is investigated to determine whether the accumulated permissions enable the users to have the access that they attempt.

4. If the necessary rights cannot be accumulated from the ACL, the users are denied the access that they have attempted.

When a user opens the object successfully, the user's process is given a handle to the object. The handle is used to identify the user accessing the object. The system also creates a list of granted access rights to the object. This way, if the user attempts different transactions with the object, only the list of granted rights needs to be evaluated. The entire process of checking the object's ACL does not have to be performed on every transaction attempt.

Not checking the object's ACL is both good and bad. It is good because subsequent actions on a resource do not require a check against the ACL every time that the user attempts to manipulate the data. This reduces network traffic, because the Windows NT Challenge/Response transaction does not have to perform over and over again. It is bad because the users have the same access to the object as they did when they opened the object, even if the ACL is modified for the object after access occurs. The list of granted rights to the object stored in the users' process tables for that handle is not modified. They have the same level of access until they close the object and ultimately close the handle to the object.

D. Implementing File-Level Auditing

File-level auditing enables an administrator to review the security log to determine who may have created, deleted, or modified a specified file or directory. This can help identify problems in the security model implemented in a domain. To set up file-level auditing, two separate steps are required:

- Enable File and Object Access Auditing in the domain's Audit policy.

- Enable the detail of file level auditing you want to employ on specific file and directory objects on an NTFS volume.

A member of the Administrators local group must enable the File and Object Access auditing. After this has been enabled, administrators and any users or groups that you assign the User Right Manage Auditing and Security Log can set auditing on specific directories and review the security log for audit successes and failures.

To set up auditing on a specific directory or file on an NTFS volume, the person you assign the task of setting up auditing must bring up the properties for that directory or file object. By choosing the Security tab of the object, they can click the Auditing button to set the auditing levels for that object.

1. Setting the Permissions to Audit

Figure 3.4.1 provides an example of the Auditing property sheet of an object's Security properties.

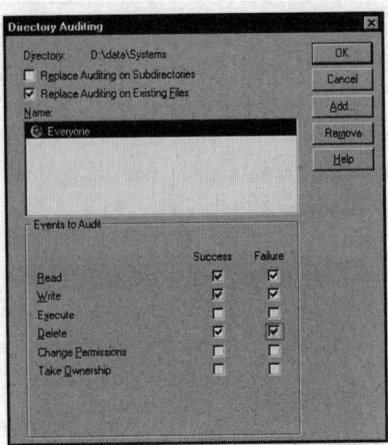

Figure 3.4.1 Setting auditing on a folder.

The administrator has to answer the following questions:

- Who are you going to audit?
- What actions are you going to audit?
- Do you want to apply this auditing to files and subfolders?

When determining the users to audit, remember that you are more likely to determine who performed a task by auditing the Everyone group rather than a smaller local group. The Everyone group is preferred when auditing because it includes all users that connect to the network (whether they are a known user is not important). If you know that only members of the local group Accounting_Users have access to a folder and its subfolders, it is fine to audit just this group.

After you select the users to audit, you now must select the actions to audit. Auditing is always based on either successes or failures. Be careful what you choose here. The actions that you can audit for a file or folder directly match the six different NTFS permissions. You must choose the correct combination of permissions that are being used to determine who is performing the task that causes the need for an audit. For example, if you are trying to determine who has been deleting the General Ledger, you must audit delete successes (as they have been very successful in deleting the file). The actions that you can audit include

- By enabling the Read event, you can determine whether an attempt was made to open a file.
- By enabling the Write event, you can determine when a user attempted to modify the contents of a file.
- By enabling the Execute event, you can determine when a user attempted to run a program.
- By enabling the Delete event, you can determine when a user attempted to delete a file object.
- By enabling the Change Permissions event, you can determine when a user tried to change the permissions on a file or directory.
- By enabling the Take Ownership event, you can determine when a user attempted to take ownership of a file or directory object.

After you set the auditing, you can check the Event Viewer's Security Log to determine the access done to the file or directory on which auditing was enabled. Figure 3.4.2 shows an event where bkomar attempted to delete the file named SECRET.DOC. It records as a failure event in the event viewer. The event shows that bkomar from the classroom domain was denied when attempting to delete the file d:\data\systems\secret.doc. If you scrolled down in the dialog box, it reveals that the access tried was DELETE.

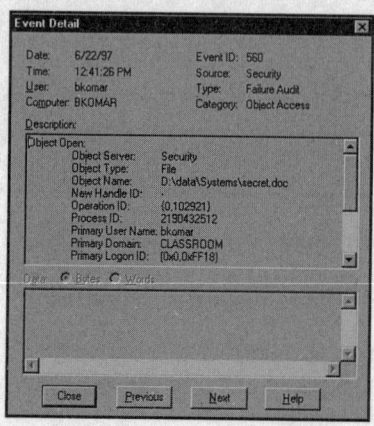

Figure 3.4.2   Security Failure Event for an attempt to delete a file.

2.   The Effects of Moving and Copying Files on Auditing

As with NTFS permissions, the task of copying and moving files directly affects the auditing on files. If you copy a file from one NTFS directory to another NTFS directory, the new copy of the file inherits the auditing set on the target directory.

If you move a file from one NTFS directory to another NTFS directory on the same logical volume, the file maintains the same auditing settings that it had in the first directory.

If you move a file from one NTFS directory to another NTFS directory but they reside on different NTFS logical volumes, the file inherits the audit settings of the new folder. Anytime a file is moved between volumes on Windows NT, the actual chain of events is a copy, verify, and delete. That is, a copy of the original file is placed in the new directory. This copy is verified against the original copy of the file. Finally, if they match, the original file is deleted.

E.   Auditing Logons and Logoffs

If you feel that your network has been compromised and unwanted users are accessing the network, the auditing of logons and logoffs can help determine what account they are using to access the network and what computer they are accessing the network from.

By auditing the successes and failures of the Logon and Logoff audit category, you can determine the location of the access point to your network. It is recommended that you monitor both successes and failures, because you want to know where the attempts to access the network are taking place and whether the attempts are successful.

3.4.1   Exercise: Creating a Shared Folder

To create a shared folder, complete the following:

1. Right-click the folder that you want to share in either My Computer or the Windows NT Explorer. Remember that this folder is an artificial root directory for all users who access the share.

2. From the pop-up menu, choose the Sharing option.

3. The Sharing property sheet enables you to give a name to the share and set limits to the number of users who can access the share simultaneously.

4. Click the Permissions button.

5. You should first determine whether you can use an existing local group to grant access to the resource. If you can, grant access to the share by clicking the Add button and choosing the local group from the list of groups. If no local group exists, you may need to switch briefly into User Manager for Domains and add the local group to the appropriate accounts database. To remove a group from the list, choose the group you want to remove and click the Remove button.

6. Click the OK button to finalize the permissions for the share.

7. Click the OK button to close the Sharing Properties page.

3.4.2   Exercise: Setting NTFS Permissions

To set the NTFS permissions on a directory or file object, complete the following steps:

1. Right-click the NTFS Resource.

2. Choose Properties from the pop-up menu for the object.

3. Switch to the Security Page of the object. This appears only if the resource is on an NTFS volume.

4. Click the Permissions button.

5. Click the Add button to add new groups and users to assign NTFS permissions to the resource.

6. Click the local group or user to which you want to assign permissions and choose the NTFS permission you want to assign from the bottom drop list.

7. Click the OK button to return to the Directory Permissions dialog box. From the top of the dialog box, choose whether you want to replace the permissions on all existing files in the directory and whether you want the changes to propagate to all subdirectories.

8. Click OK to make effective your changes to NTFS permissions.

9. Answer Yes to the dialog box that asks whether you want the change in security information to replace the existing security information on all files in all subdirectories.

10. Click OK to exit the Directory's Properties dialog box.

3.4 Practice Problems

1. Which two of the following are the two levels of security for protecting your disk resources in Windows NT?

   A. Share permissions

   B. NTFS permissions

   C. User permissions

   D. Attributes

2. Which of the following enables Windows NT administrators to protect their resources from Network users?

   A. Share-level security

   B. User-level security

   C. Resource security

   D. Attributes

3. Which of the following is used as the entry point into the system for Windows NT users?

   A. Share-level security

   B. User-level security

   C. Resource security

   D. Attributes

4. Which of the following explicit share permissions can you implement? Select all correct answers.

   A. Modify

   B. Read

   C. Full Control

   D. No Access

5. Which is the minimum permission that enables users to connect to a resource and run programs?

   A. Full Control

   B. Read

   C. No Access

   D. Change

6. Which permission enables users to view documents that are stored in the share, but does not enable them to make changes to the documents?

   A. Full Control

   B. Read

   C. No Access

   D. Change

7. Which minimum share permission enables users to connect and to create new documents and subfolders?

   A. Full Control

   B. Read

   C. No Access

   D. Change

8. Which minimum permission enables users to modify existing documents and delete documents?

   A. Full Control

   B. Read

   C. No Access

   D. Change

9. Which permission enables users to do anything they want in the share?

   A. Full Control

   B. Read

   C. No Access

   D. Change

10. Which permission is sufficient for most day-to-day business needs?

    A. Full Control

    B. Read

    C. No Access

    D. Change

11. As a general rule, which permission is considered the most powerful?

    A. Full Control

    B. Read

    C. No Access

    D. Change

12. Users whom you assign varying levels of permissions through group memberships have effective shared permissions of:

    A. The accumulation of their individual shared permissions.

    B. The lowest possible permissions.

    C. Those permissions assigned the highest priority.

    D. The permissions assigned to the highest priority group of which they belong.

13. The only time the situation in question 12 differs is when the user or a group to which the user belongs has been assigned the explicit permission of:

    A. Full Control

    B. No Access

    C. Change

    D. Read

14. To what level of depth can share permissions go?

    A. Root level

    B. Directory level

    C. Subdirectory level

    D. File level

15. To what level of depth can NTFS permissions go?

    A. Root level

    B. Directory level

    C. Subdirectory level

    D. File level

16. At what levels do share permissions affect users? Select all correct answers.

    A. Locally.

    B. When logged across the network.

    C. When running other operating systems locally.

    D. They do not affect them.

17. At what levels do NTFS permissions affect users? Select all correct answers.

    A. Locally.

    B. When logged across the network.

    C. When running other operating systems locally.

    D. They do not affect them.

18. Which of the following NTFS directory permissions enables users to view the contents of a directory and to navigate to its subdirectories?

    A. No Access

    B. List

    C. Read

    D. Add

19. Which of the following NTFS directory permissions overrides all other permissions?

    A. No Access

    B. List

    C. Read

    D. Add

20. Which of the following NTFS directory permissions enables users to do the most data manipulation?

    A. No Access

    B. List

    C. Read

    D. Change

3

21. Which of the following NTFS directory permissions enables users to navigate the entire directory structure, view the contents of the directory, view the contents of any files in the directory, and execute programs?

   A. No Access

   B. List

   C. Read

   D. Add

22. Which of the following NTFS directory permissions enables users to add new subdirectories and files to the directory, but does not enable them to access files within the directory?

   A. No Access

   B. List

   C. Read

   D. Add

23. Which set of NTFS directory permissions enables users to add new files to the directory structure, and after the files have been added, users have read-only access to the files?

   A. No Access

   B. List

   C. Read

   D. Add

24. If an NTFS file is moved to a new directory on the same volume, what will become of the permissions?

   A. The file will maintain its existing permissions.

   B. The file will assume permissions from the source.

   C. The file will assume permissions from the target.

   D. The file will abandon permissions.

25. If an NTFS file is copied to a new directory on the same volume, what will become of the permissions?

   A. The file will maintain its existing permissions.

   B. The file will assume permissions from the source.

   C. The file will assume permissions from the target.

   D. The file will abandon permissions.

3.4.1　Answers and Explanations: Exercise

The exercise illustrated how to create a shared folder and share it in Windows NT. You should be very familiar with this operation.

3.4.2　Answers and Explanations: Exercise

In this exercise, you created and changed NTFS permissions and saw the effects it created through the Directory's Properties dialog box.

3.4　Answers and Explanations: Practice Problems

1. **A, B**　Windows NT has two levels of security for protecting disk resources: Share permissions and NTFS permissions.

2. **A**　Share-level security enables Windows NT administrators to protect their resources from Network users.

3. **A**　Shares have a level of security, and they are also used as the entry point into the system for Windows NT users.

4. **B, C, D**　There are four explicit share permissions that can be implemented. They are: Read, Change, Full Control, and No Access.

5. **B**　The Read permission enables a user to connect to the resource and run programs.

6. **B** With the Read permission, users can view any documents that are stored in the share, but they cannot make any changes to the documents.

7. **D** The Change permissions setting enables users to connect to a resource and run programs. It also enables them to create new documents and subfolders, modify existing documents, and delete documents.

8. **D** See answer to 7.

9. **A** The Full Control permission enables users to do anything they want in the share.

10. **D** Change permission is sufficient for most day-to-day business needs.

11. **C** The No Access permission is the most powerful permission. When it is implemented, the user that you assign this permission has no access to that resource.

12. **A** When users, through group membership, have been assigned varying levels of share permissions, their effective shared permissions are the accumulation of their individual shared permissions.

13. **B** The No Access permission always takes precedence over any other assigned permissions.

14. **C** Share permissions can be applied only to the subdirectory level.

15. **D** NTFS permissions protect you at the file level.

16. **B** Share permissions are in effect only when the user connects to the resource via the network.

17. **A, B** NTFS permissions can affect users logged on locally or across the network to the system where the NTFS permissions apply.

18. **B** List enables the user to view the contents of a directory and to navigate to its subdirectories.

19. **A** No Access overrides all other permissions.

20. **D** Change enables the user to do the most data manipulation.

21. **C** Read enables the user to navigate the entire directory structure, view the contents of the directory, view the contents of any files in the directory, and execute programs.

22. **D** Add enables the user to add new subdirectories and files to the directory, but Add does not enable the user to access files within the directory.

23. **C, D** Add enables a user to add new files to the directory structure, and after the files have been added, the users have read-only access to the files.

24. **A** If a file is moved from one directory to another directory on the same NTFS volume, it retains the same NTFS permissions it had.

25. **C** If a file is copied from one directory to another on a single NTFS volume, the file inherits the directory permissions for new files of the target directory.

3.4 Key Words

Access Control List

Access Control Entries

Security log

3

Practice Exam: Managing Resources

Use this practice exam to test your mastery of "Managing Resources." This practice exam is 17 questions long. The passing Microsoft score is 78.4 percent (13 right on this practice test). Questions are in multiple-choice format.

1. If you take ownership of a file or directory, you are automatically a member of which group?

   A. Domain Local

   B. Domain User

   C. Creator/Owner

   D. Admin

2. To enable auditing of changes to the account database, a member of which group must enable auditing User and Group Management?

   A. Creator/Owner

   B. Administrators

   C. Local

   D. Global

3. To know exactly what files are being updated, what component of auditing must you enable?

   A. File and Object Access

   B. Account Operator

   C. TTS

   D. SAM

4. This is the Security hive of the HKEY_LOCAL_MACHINE subtree in the Registry:

   A. File and Object Access

   B. The SAM Account Database

   C. Audit records

   D. TTS

5. Built-in global groups include all the following except:

   A. Everyone

   B. Domain Admins

   C. Domain Guests

   D. Domain Users

6. The System Policy Editor uses which types of groups for group membership?

   A. Local

   B. Global

   C. Domain

   D. Admin

7. If you use group policies, and a user belongs to more than one group, the order in which the group settings are processed becomes critical. What setting can you use to change the processing order?

   A. Group Priority

   B. Group Process

   C. Group Order

   D. Group Rank

8. When Kristin logs in to the network, her login script executes only some of the time. What would be a likely reason for this?

   A. She is not using the correct password.

   B. She is not logging out of one session before beginning the next.

   C. Group policies are overriding user policies.

   D. Directory Replication is not functioning properly.

9. System policy files are stored where on a NetWare 4.x network?

   A. SYS:PUBLIC

   B. In individual users' mail directories

   C. NETLOGON share

   D. Locally

10. System policy files are stored where on a NetWare 3.x network?

    A. SYS:PUBLIC

    B. In individual users' mail directories

    C. NETLOGON share

    D. Locally

11. The Web Administration tools enable limited administration of a Windows NT domain controller using:

    A. HTTP protocols

    B. HTML forms

    C. RPC calls

    D. UDP sessions

12. Management tasks that you can perform from the Web Administration tools include which of the following?

    A. Manage user accounts

    B. Manage global and local groups

    C. Reboot connected workstations

    D. Add and remove Windows NT computer accounts to/from domains

13. If an NTFS file is moved to a new directory on a different NTFS volume, what will become of the permissions?

    A. The file will maintain its existing permissions.

    B. The file will assume permissions from the source.

C. The file will assume permissions from the target.

D. The file will abandon permissions.

14. Where are NTFS permissions set?

    A. From the Security page of an NTFS object

    B. From the NET USE command line

    C. From User Manager

    D. From DiskPerf

15. To set NTFS permissions, a user must meet one of which two of the following criteria?

    A. Be a member of the Administrators local group

    B. Be a member of the Administrators global group

    C. Be a member of the Server Operators local group

    D. Be a member of the Server Operators global group

16. To enable the File and Object Access auditing, a member of which group must enable this auditing feature:

    A. Administrators global

    B. Administrators local

    C. Domain Users global

    D. Domain Users local

17. Susan has been told to enable auditing for a specific NTFS file. What must she do, assuming that auditing is already turned on?

    A. Select the Security tab of the object from Properties and click the Auditing button.

    B. Issue the appropriate NET USE command.

    C. Place the Audit attribute on the file.

    D. Turn Auditing on from User Manager.

Answers and Explanations: Practice Exam

1. **C** If you take ownership of a file or directory, you are automatically a member of the Creator/Owner group.

2. **B** To enable auditing of changes to the account database, a member of the Administrators group must enable auditing User and Group Management.

3. **A** To know exactly what files are being updated, you should enable File and Object Access.

4. **B** The SAM Account Database is the Security hive of the HKEY_LOCAL_MACHINE subtree in the Registry.

5. **A** Built-in global groups are: Domain Admins, Domain Guests, and Domain Users.

6. **B** The System Policy Editor uses global groups for group membership.

7. **A** Group order is set in the Group Priority option of the Options menu.

8. **D** Directory Replication ensures that each domain controller in the domain contains the same files and versions of the files in their NETLOGON share. If there is a problem with replication, login scripts can execute only some of the time when a user accesses the network.

9. **A** System policy files are stored in the SYS:PUBLIC directory in Novell NetWare 4.x networks.

10. **B** System policy files are stored in individual users' mail directories in Novell NetWare 3.x networks.

11. **B** The Web Administration tools enable limited administration of a Windows NT domain controller using HTML forms.

12. **A, B, D** With Web Administration tools, you have the capability to Manage User Accounts, Manage Global and Local Accounts, and Add and Remove Windows NT Computer accounts to a domain, among others.

13. **C** When you move a file from an NTFS volume to another NTFS volume, the file always inherits the permissions of the target directory.

14. **A** NTFS permissions are set from the Security page of an NTFS file or directory object.

15. **A, C** To set NTFS Permissions, a user must meet be a member of one of the two local groups.

16. **B** To enable the File and Object Access auditing, a member of the Administrators local group must enable this auditing feature.

17. **A** To set up auditing on a specific directory or file on an NTFS volume, the person assigned the task of setting up auditing must bring up the properties for that directory or file object. By choosing the Security tab of the object, they can click the Auditing button to set the auditing levels for that object.

CHAPTER 4

Connectivity

This chapter helps you prepare for the exam by covering the following objectives:

- Configure Windows NT Server for interoperability with NetWare servers using Gateway Services for NetWare and Migration Tool for NetWare.

- Install and configure multiprotocol routing to serve various functions including Internet Router, BOOTP/DHCP Relay Agent, and IPX Router.

- Install and configure Internet Information Server (IIS).

- Install and configure Internet services including World Wide Web and DNS.

- Install and Configure Remote Access Service (RAS) including communications, protocols, and security.

4.1 Interoperability with NetWare

Although organizations continue to rapidly deploy Windows NT in the enterprise, many organizations still have legacy NetWare systems that must be able to interoperate with Windows NT. Microsoft ensured compatibility with NetWare servers by including the NWLINK IPX/SPX compatible protocol, but they did not end there. Microsoft bundles in the Gateway Services for NetWare (GSNW) and also includes a utility to help smooth the conversion from NetWare into Windows NT Server. In the following sections you learn about:

- Gateway Services for NetWare (GSNW)

- Installing and configuring GSNW

- NWCONV: Migration Tool for NetWare

A. Gateway Services for NetWare

Gateway Services for NetWare performs the following functions:

- Enables Windows NT Servers to access NetWare file and print resources.

- Enables the Windows NT Servers to act as a gateway to the NetWare file and print resources. The Windows NT Server can share off the connection to the NetWare server.

GSNW can provide Windows NT networks with convenient access to NetWare resources. GSNW enables one single connection to be shared by multiple Windows NT clients. This sharing of a connection is very convenient. However, it also causes a significant performance loss for the NetWare resource. GSNW is ideal for occasional NetWare resource access, but it is not recommended for large-scale routing.

1. Installing GSNW

GSNW is a network service, and you install it using the Services tab of the Control Panel Network icon. Click the Add button to view a list of available services, and in the list, find the Gateway Services for NetWare option, and then click OK. You may be prompted for the location of your Windows NT source files—give the location, and then you will be prompted to restart your system.

2. Configuring GSNW

After the system restarts, you can configure GSNW to act as a gateway to the NetWare resources. To enable GSNW to act as a gateway for your Windows NT clients, you must perform the following steps:

1. On the NetWare server, create a group called NTGATEWAY.

2. Create a user account on the NetWare server for the gateway to use and add the account to the NTGATEWAY group.

3. From the Control Panel, double-click the GSNW icon to start the Gateway Services for NetWare dialog box.

4. To configure the gateway options, click the Gateway button located on the right corner of the dialog box.

5. The Configure Gateway dialog box appears.

6. Click the Enable Gateway check box. In the account box, enter the name of the gateway account and password matching the account you created on the NetWare server.

7. You can then create shares to the NetWare resources in the bottom section of the Configure Gateway dialog box. Click the Add button to create a share to the NetWare resources.

8. After you create the share, you can apply the standard Windows NT share permissions to the NetWare share. Click the Permissions button to assign specific permissions to your Windows NT users.

9. After you complete the Configure Gateway screen, click OK to close the dialog box. You can then select your preferred NetWare server, default tree and context, and print options for your Windows NT Server to connect to the NetWare server.

10. After you establish all configuration settings, click OK to close the Gateway Services for NetWare dialog box.

Gateway Services for NetWare is now available to the users of the Windows NT Server. A user can use GSNW by making a network connection to the NetWare share created on the Windows NT Server computer.

B. NWCONV: Migration Tool for NetWare

The Migration Tool for NetWare transfers file and directory information and user and group account information from a NetWare server to a Windows NT domain controller. The Migration Tool can preserve the directory and file permissions if it is being transferred to an NTFS partition. Table 4.1.1 displays the corresponding NetWare and Windows NT NTFS rights that are being converted.

Table 4.1.1 Conversion of Rights

Novell NetWare Permission	Windows NT Permission
Supervisor (S)	Full Control (All)
Read (R)	Read (RX)
Write (W)	Change (RWXD)
Erase (E)	Change (RWXD)
Modify (M)	Change (RWXD)
Create (C)	Add (WX) Custom right
File Scan (F)	List (RX) Custom right
Access Control (A)	Change Permission (P)

If the partition to which you are migrating is a FAT partition, no rights or permissions are maintained.

To start the Migration Tool for NetWare, run the NWCONV.EXE file. For test purposes, it must be executed from a command prompt or from the Start, Run command.

1. Steps for Migrating from NetWare

When the Migration Tool for NetWare is first started, a dialog box displays that enables you to select the NetWare and Windows NT Server domain controller with which you will be working.

> **To be able to accomplish the migration from the NetWare server onto your Windows NT Server computer, you must have supervisor access to the NetWare system, and you must be an administrator in the Windows NT domain to which you will be migrating.**

To complete the migration from a NetWare server to a Windows NT Server, follow these steps:

1. From the Start menu choose the Run command, type **NWCONV**, and press Enter.

2. Click the Add button and select your NetWare server and Windows NT domain controller, and then click OK.

3. You then have the option to configure the User Options or the File Options. After you configure each of these sections, you can either click the Start Migration button, or you can do a trial migration first to verify your settings (which is highly recommended).

2.   User and Group Options

All the user accounts from your NetWare server are migrated by default to the Windows NT domain controller. To disable the transfer of users and groups, click the Transfer Users and Groups check box located at the top of the User and Group Options dialog box.

The User and Group Options dialog box holds all the options available on four pages: Passwords, User Names, Group Names, and Defaults.

3.   Passwords

The passwords from the NetWare server cannot be migrated across for security reasons; however, the Migration Tool can be used to specify how the passwords for the migrated users should be handled:

- **No Password:** The migrated users have no passwords assigned to them.

- **Password is Username:** The migrated users have passwords the same as their usernames.

- **Password is:** Assigns a single password to all migrated users.

- **User must Change Password:** Forces the migrated users to change their passwords the first time they log on to the Windows NT Server.

4.   User Names and Group Names

You need to configure the Migration Tool in case it runs into a duplicate username or group name during the migration. The User Names page enables you to select how the Migration Tool should react to the duplicates.

- **Log Error:** Adds an error to the ERROR.LOG file.

- **Ignore:** Causes the account to be skipped with no error messages or warnings. This is the default option.

- **Overwrite with New Information:** The existing account would be overwritten with the new NetWare user information.

- **Add Prefix:** Includes a prefix with the user account to enable you to distinguish between the existing account and the migrated account.

5.   Defaults Page Tab

The Defaults page tab contains two options:

- **Use Supervisor Defaults:** You can use the supervisor account restrictions for the migrated users instead of using the account policies in the Windows NT Server.

- **Add Supervisors to the Administrators Group:** The migrated users that have supervisor equivalent access are added into the Windows NT domains Administrators group. By default, the supervisors from the NetWare system are not added into this group.

4.1.1   Exercise: Installing Gateway Services for NetWare

This exercise assumes several things:

- The NetWare server is version 3.x.

- The NTGATEWAY groups has been created on the NetWare server.

- The gateway account has been created on the NetWare server and is a member of the NTGATEWAY group.

This exercise steps you through the process of installing Gateway Services for NetWare, and setting up a gateway from the Windows NT Server into the NetWare Server.

1. Click the right mouse button on the Network Neighborhood, and choose the Properties option.

2. Click the Services page tab.

3. Click the Add button, and then select the Gateway (and Client) Services for NetWare.

4. Click OK.

5. Windows NT prompts you for the location of your Windows NT Server source directory. Enter the location of the source files, and then click Continue.

6. Click Close to close the Network Properties dialog box. The network is reconfigured.

7. The system prompts you to restart your computer. Click OK to enable the restart.

8. When the system restarts, log on to the Windows NT domain, and the system prompts you for the NetWare server to which you want to log on. Select the NetWare server available, and then click OK to log on to the NetWare server.

9. After the system completes the logons, click the Start menu, Settings, Control Panel option.

10. After the Control Panel opens, locate the GSNW icon and double-click it to launch the GSNW dialog box.

11. In the Select Preferred Server dialog box, choose your NetWare server.

12. Click the Gateway button. The Configure Gateway dialog box opens.

13. Click Enable Gateway.

14. Enter the Gateway account name and password information. Remember that the Gateway account must be a valid account on the NetWare server, and it must be a member of the NetWare NTGATEWAY group.

15. Click the Add button to create a NetWare share to the NetWare server.

16. Enter the share name. For this example, enter NetWare as the share name.

17. In the network path, enter the UNC path to the NetWare server SYS volume. Type **\\NWSERVER\SYS**.

18. In the Use Drive box, click Z:, and then click OK.

19. Click OK to close the Configure Gateway dialog box.

20. Click OK to close the Gateway Services for NetWare dialog box.

4.1.2   Exercise: Running a Trial Migration from a NetWare Server to a Windows NT Domain Controller

This exercise steps you through the configuration settings for the migration process, and then through a trial migration.

1. To start a NetWare migration, click the Start menu and choose the Run command.

2. In the Run command box, type **NWCONV.EXE** and press Enter.

3. When the NWCONV utility starts, the system prompts you to select the NetWare and Windows NT servers to use for the migration. After you select the servers, click OK.

4. Click the User Options button.

5. Select the Transfer Users and Groups check box.

6. In the Passwords page tab, select the No Password option.

7. Click on the User Names page tab, and select the Add Prefix command and enter **NW** for the prefix.

8. Click on the Group Names page tab, and select the Add Prefix command and enter **NW** for the prefix.

9. Click OK on the User and Group Options dialog box.

10. Click the File Options Button, and select the files and directories to transfer.

11. After you select the files and directories, click OK to close the File Options dialog box.

12. After you configure the User and File Options, click the Trial Migration button.

13. After the Trial Migration completes, view the log files to see whether there are any potential problems in your migration, which are signified by error messages.

14. After the Trial Migration completes and you have reviewed the log files, click Exit to close the Migration Tool for NetWare.

4.1   Practice Problems

1. Microsoft ensured compatibility with NetWare servers by including what protocol with NT Server?

   A. NWLINK

   B. IPX/SPX

   C. TCP/IP

   D. NetBEUI

2. What utility has Microsoft bundled with NT to help smooth the conversion from NetWare into Windows NT Server?

   A. Migration Tool for NetWare

   B. NetBEUI

   C. Gateway Services for NetWare

   D. IIS

3. Which of the following two functions does Gateway Services for NetWare perform? Choose all that apply.

   A. Enables Windows NT Servers to access NetWare file and print resources.

   B. Provides additional security for NetWare servers.

   C. Enables login scripts to be processed.

   D. Enables the Windows NT Servers to act as a gateway to the NetWare file and print resources.

4. How many connections to the NetWare server does GSNW require?

   A. 1

   B. 2

   C. 4

   D. 8

5. What utility transfers file and directory information and user and group account information from a NetWare server to a Windows NT domain controller?

   A. Gateway Services for NetWare

   B. Migration Tool for NetWare

   C. NTFS

   D. NetBEUI

6. For the Migration Tool for NetWare to maintain directory and file permissions, what type of partition must the target be?

   A. FAT

   B. VFAT

   C. NTFS

   D. CDFS

7. For the Migration Tool for NetWare to maintain directory and file permissions, what type of partition must the source be?

   A. FAT

   B. VFAT

   C. NTFS

   D. CDFS

8. To what NetWare permission does the NT Full Control permission map?

   A. Read

   B. Write

   C. Modify

   D. Supervisor

9. To what NetWare permission does the NT Read permission map?

   A. Read

   B. Write

   C. Modify

   D. Supervisor

10. To what NetWare permission does the NT Change permission map? Choose all that apply.

    A. Read

    B. Write

    C. Modify

    D. Supervisor

11. To what NT permission does NetWare's Create permission map?

    A. Change Permission

    B. List

    C. Add

    D. Change

12. To what NT permission does NetWare's File Scan permission map?

    A. Change Permission

    B. List

    C. Add

    D. Change

13. To what NT permission does NetWare's Access Control permission map?

    A. Change Permission

    B. List

    C. Add

    D. Change

14. What rights and permissions are maintained when migrating from NetWare to an NT FAT partition?

    A. All rights and permissions.

    B. All rights but no permissions.

    C. No rights but all permissions.

    D. No rights and no permissions.

15. What utility is used to start the Migration Tool for NetWare?

    A. NWCONV.EXE

    B. MIGRATE.COM

    C. MIGRATE.EXE

    D. MGTOOL.EXE

16. What becomes of passwords from the NetWare server during migration?

    A. Duplicate ones are discarded.

    B. Duplicate ones are written to an error file.

    C. All passwords are maintained.

    D. All passwords are discarded.

17. What is the result of selecting "Password Is:" in the Migration Tool?

    A. Migrated users have no passwords assigned to them.

    B. Migrated users' passwords are the same as their usernames.

    C. A single password is assigned to all migrated users.

    D. Migrated users are forced to change their passwords the first time they log on to the Windows NT Server.

18. What is the result of selecting "User Must Change Password:" in the Migration Tool?

    A. Migrated users have no passwords assigned to them.

    B. Migrated users' passwords are the same as their usernames.

    C. A single password is assigned to all migrated users.

    D. Migrated users are forced to change their passwords the first time they log on to the Windows NT Server.

19. What is the result of selecting "Password is Username:" in the Migration Tool?

  A. Migrated users have no passwords assigned to them.

  B. Migrated users' passwords are the same as their usernames.

  C. A single password is assigned to all migrated users.

  D. Migrated users are forced to change their passwords the first time they log on to the Windows NT Server.

4.1.1 Answers and Explanations: Exercise

In this exercise, you walked through the process of installing Gateway Services for NetWare. After the installation, you set up a gateway from the Windows NT Server into the NetWare server.

4.1.2 Answers and Explanations: Exercise

In this exercise, you walked through the configuration settings for the migration process, and then attempted a trial migration. You should also examine the log files for errors that occurred.

4.1 Answers and Explanations: Practice Problems

1. **A** Microsoft ensures compatibility with NetWare servers by including the NWLINK IPX/SPX-compatible protocol.

2. **C** Microsoft also bundles Gateway Services for NetWare (GSNW) to help smooth the conversion from NetWare to Windows NT Server.

3. **A, D** Gateway Services for NetWare performs the following functions: enables Windows NT Servers to access NetWare file and print resources, and enables the Windows NT Servers to act as a gateway to the NetWare file and print resources.

4. **A** GSNW enables multiple Windows NT clients to share a single connection.

5. **B** The Migration Tool for NetWare transfers file and directory information and user and group account information from a NetWare server to a Windows NT domain controller.

6. **C** The Migration Tool for NetWare can preserve the directory and file permissions if it is being transferred to an NTFS partition.

7. **A** NetWare partitions are always FAT.

8. **D** Full Control equates to NetWare's Supervisor permission.

9. **A** The Read permission is identical on both NetWare and NT.

10. **B, C** Change equates to NetWare's Write, Erase, and Modify permissions.

11. **C** NetWare's Create permission equates to NT's Add permission.

12. **B** NetWare's File Scan permission equates to NT's List permission.

13. **A** NetWare's Access Control permission equates to NT's Change Permission (P) permission.

14. **D** If the partition to which you are migrating is a FAT partition, no rights and permissions are maintained.

15. **A** To start the Migration Tool for NetWare, you must run the NWCONV.EXE file from the command prompt.

16. **D**   For security reasons you cannot migrate across the passwords from the NetWare server.

17. **C**   "Password Is:" assigns a single password to all migrated users.

18. **D**   "User Must Change Password:" forces the migrated users to change their passwords the first time they log on to the Windows NT Server.

19. **B**   "Password is Username:" means that the migrated users' passwords are the same as their usernames.

4.1   Key Words

File and Print Sharing

IPX/SPX

NetWare

NWLink

4.2   Installing and Configuring Multiprotocol Routing

This section discusses installing and configuring multiprotocol routing, including Internet router and IPX router. Multiprotocol routing enables you to send more than one protocol across the router.

A.   Internet Router

Windows NT can act as a router between the Internet and the internal network. With a router, all incoming packets from the Internet are forwarded into the network.

Setting Windows NT up as an Internet router is as simple as installing two network adapters in the system, and then enabling IP routing via Control Panel, Networks, the TCP/IP protocol configuration. This option enables Windows NT to act as a static router. Take note that Windows NT cannot exchange Routing Information Protocol (RIP) routing packets with other IP RIP routers unless the RIP routing software is installed.

To enable IP RIP routing, you must install the RIP routing software from Control Panel, Networks. This enables Windows NT to send out RIP packets once every 60 seconds, to exchange routing information with other dynamic RIP routing routers.

> **NT supports RIP I routing. Steelhead (RRAS) supports RIP II routing.**

Without the RIP protocol, you must manually set up router tables using the ROUTE ADD command.

B.   DHCP Server Service

DHCP is a service available on NT that dynamically assigns IP addresses to clients. Instead of manually assigning an IP address to each new computer you purchase, DHCP can assign an IP address to the computer each time it boots. This simplifies administration tremendously.

Setting up the DHCP Server Service requires Windows NT Server, with DHCP installed as a service. To install the DHCP Server Service, add the service under Control Panel, Networks.

After you install the DHCP Server Service, you can configure the service using the Administrative Tools, DHCP Manager option.

The local machine always appears on the list, but you can remotely administrate other servers by adding a server using the Servers menu option. After clicking on the local machine (or any other server that might appear in the list), you set up the DHCP scope—the range of available IP addresses.

The DHCP database is created in JET format and stored in the `\%systemroot%\system32\dhcp` subdirectory. You should back up the database occasionally using the JETPACK command, which also clears out deleted records.

1. DHCP Relay

The DHCP Relay tab enables a Windows NT system to relay DHCP messages for clients across an IP router. Normally, you configure IP routers not to forward broadcasts, so a client asking (broadcasting) for an IP address on a local segment when the DHCP server is located on a remote segment does not receive an answer. You also can specify optional timeout parameters in the DHCP Relay tab.

Add the addresses of any DHCP servers on the DHCP Relay tab so that DHCP requests (IP packets) can be directed appropriately.

> **The DHCP protocol originated as an expansion of the BOOTP protocol that enables diskless workstations to get their boot information from a server.**

C. IPX Router

IPX is another protocol common to networks interacting with NetWare's IPX/SPX protocol. You enable the IPX router by installing the IPX RIP router software via Control Panel, Networks, Services.

After installing the IPX RIP router, Windows NT can route IPX packets over the installed network adapters. It uses the RIP to exchange its routing table information with other RIP routers. The default sending interval is once every 60 seconds, so you must be careful in deploying hundreds of RIP routers in an enterprise environment; these packets can consume a big chunk of network bandwidth (especially on WANs, where the bandwidth commonly is limited to 64 Kbps).

The configuration screen for the IPX Rip router is straightforward, and only prompts for whether the administrator wants to propagate NetBIOS broadcasts (type 20) packets over the router.

You have to propagate NetBIOS broadcasts over the router only if both sides of the Windows NT router contain Microsoft Clients (such as Windows 95 or Windows for Workgroups) that need to communicate browsing information over the router.

Although RIP does offer a number of benefits—including a reduction in administrative overhead associated with updating router tables—it does have a drawback in that RIP can increase network traffic in large networks as it routes table updates.

4.2.1 Exercise: Setting Up a DHCP Scope

In this exercise, you are working in the DHCP Manager to set up the DHCP scope. To do so, use the following steps:

1. Click on the Scope option and select Create Scope. The Create Scope dialog box appears.

2. Fill in the start and end address of the pool of addresses that will be distributed. For example, you might enter 177.22.34.100 for the Start Address field and 177.22.34.200 in the End Address field.

3. You also can exclude a set of addresses. You normally do this when the network consists of machines that aren't DHCP-aware, such as printers or legacy operating systems.

4. You should give the scope a name to identify the batch of systems to which this pool of addresses will be distributed.

5. Specifying the lease duration, which indicates how long a client machine may keep an address before it must reapply, is an important step. Keep the lease period short (a few days) when users are highly mobile. Lengthen the lease period to several months or years if you want the workstation to keep the IP addresses for a long time. You also can set the period to unlimited, in which case the workstations keep their assigned addresses forever.

4.2.2 Exercise: Backing Up the DHCP Database

In this exercise, you learn to back up the DHCP database and compress it with two simple steps:

1. Stop the DHCP Server Service via Control Panel, Services, because this service holds the files open, preventing the files to close for backup.

2. To check database consistency and back up the database in the C:\backup.dir directory, execute the following command from the DHCP subdirectory:

```
JETPACK DHCP.mdb C:\backup.dir\dhcp.mdb
```

4.2 Practice Problems

1. To set up Windows NT as an Internet router, what two steps should you follow?

    A. Install two network adapters in the system.

    B. Enable IP routing.

    C. Start GSNW.

    D. Enable the NetBEUI protocol.

2. An NT router cannot exchange Routing Information Protocol (RIP) routing packets with other IP RIP routers unless

    A. GSNW is running.

    B. The RIP routing software is installed.

    C. NetBEUI is enabled.

    D. The Default Gateway has been defined.

3. After you enable RIP, how often are RIP packets sent?

    A. Every 5 seconds

    B. Every 30 seconds

    C. Every minute

    D. Every 5 minutes

4. What is the purpose of the RIP packets?

    A. To exchange queued messages

    B. To exchange e-mail

    C. To exchange routing information

    D. To verify host existence

5. To whom are the RIP packets sent?

    A. Hosts

    B. Clients

    C. Other routers

    D. Domain controllers

6. Without the RIP protocol, router tables are maintained _____.

    A. By OSPF

    B. Manually

    C. Automatically

    D. At startup

7. If administrators decide to manually add an entry to the routing table, what command must they use?

    A. ROUTE ADD

    B. TRACERT

    C. NBSTAT

    D. NETSTAT

8. After the DHCP Server Service has been installed, you can configure the service using which tool?

    A. Server Manager

    B. DHCP Manager

    C. DHCP Administrator

    D. DHCP Client Configuration

9. The DHCP database is created in which format?

    A. Access

    B. JET

    C. DNS

    D. IP

10. Where is the DHCP database stored?

    A. \%systemroot%\system32\dhcp

    B. \%systemroot%\system32\jet

    C. \%systemroot%\dhcp

    D. \%systemroot%\jet

11. Spencer, the new administrator, is complaining about the size of the DHCP database. Which command should Spencer use to clear deleted records from the DHCP database?

    A. COMPRESS

    B. DELETE

    C. JETPACK

    D. CLEAR

12. What is the primary purpose for the DHCP Relay tab?

    A. To allow an NT system to relay DHCP broadcasts for clients across an IP router.

    B. To block broadcast messages from foreign networks.

    C. To relay alerts regarding the DHCP database to the administrator.

    D. To relay inventory messages to a central JET database.

13. Under normal conditions, IP routers are configured to do what with broadcasts?

    A. Forward them

    B. Ignore them

    C. Answer them

    D. Send them continuously

14. Given the situation in question 13, if a client asks for an IP address on a local segment when the DHCP server is located on another network segment, what becomes of the request?

    A. It goes unanswered.

    B. It is answered immediately.

    C. It is routed for answer.

    D. It is continuously sent until an answer is received.

15. When the IPX RIP router is installed, Windows NT can route IPX packets over the installed network adapters, and it uses what to exchange routing table information?

    A. IP

    B. RIP

    C. TCP/IP

    D. UDP

4.2.1 Answers and Explanations: Exercise

In this exercise, you learned to establish a scope for a DHCP server, and looked at the values used to do so.

4.2.2 Answers and Explanations: Exercise

In this short exercise, you learned to back up and pack the DHCP database.

4.2 Answers and Explanations: Practice Problems

1. **A, B**   To set up Windows NT as an Internet router, install two network adapters in the system, and then enable IP routing.

2. **B**   An NT router cannot exchange Routing Information Protocol (RIP) routing packets with other IP RIP routers unless the RIP routing software is installed.

3. **C**   RIP packets are sent out once every 60 seconds.

4. **C**   RIP packets are used to exchange routing information.

5. **C**   RIP packets are sent to other dynamic RIP routing routers.

6. **B** Without the RIP protocol, router tables must be set up manually when using Windows NT to route information.

7. **A** Without the RIP protocol, router tables must be set up manually using the ROUTE ADD command.

8. **B** After you install the DHCP Server Service, you can configure the service using the DHCP Manager option.

9. **B** The DHCP database is created in JET format.

10. **A** The DHCP database is stored in the `\%systemroot%\system32\dhcp` subdirectory.

11. **C** You should back up the database occasionally using the JETPACK command, which also clears out deleted records.

12. **A** The DHCP Relay tab enables a Windows NT system to relay DHCP broadcasts for clients across an IP router.

13. **B** Normally, you configure IP routers not to forward broadcasts.

14. **A** A client asking (broadcasting) for an IP address on a local segment when the DHCP server is located on a different network segment does not receive an answer.

15. **B** It uses the RIP to exchange its routing table information with other RIP routers.

4.2　Key Words

Gateway Services for NetWare

Migration Tool for NetWare

DHCP Scope

RIP for IP

RIP Packets

Multiprotocol Routing

DHCP Server Service

4.3   Installing and Configuring Internet Information Server

Internet Information Server is bundled into Windows NT 4, and you can automatically install it during the initial installation of your Windows NT Server system.

Internet Information Server, or IIS, serves primarily as a World Wide Web (WWW), server, but it also offers FTP and Gopher support. Because this software is included with the Windows NT Server software, it makes perfect sense to learn about what IIS can do for you. The enterprise exam has a few questions relating to installation and configuration of IIS. Before you can look into the installation and configuration of IIS, though, you must understand the different components and functions of IIS.

A.   Overview of IIS

Internet Information Server uses Hypertext Transfer Protocol (HTTP), File Transfer Protocol (FTP), and the Gopher services to provide Internet publishing services to your Windows NT Server computer.

1.   HTTP: Hypertext Transfer Protocol

HTTP is a client/server protocol used on the World Wide Web. HTTP web pages allow the client and server machines to interact and be updated very quickly using Windows Sockets. HTTP is, of course, pervasive on the Internet and more information on this standard can be found at `http://www.ics.uci.edu/pub/ietf/http/`.

2.   FTP: File Transfer Protocol

FTP is the protocol used to transfer files from one computer to another using the TCP/IP protocol. In any FTP file transfer, the two computers must each play a role in the connection. One system must be designated the FTP server and the other the FTP client. The FTP client does all the work in the transfer; the FTP server is a depository only. This protocol is very handy for quick transfer of files across the Internet.

3.   Gopher Service

The Gopher service provides a means to create a set of hierarchical links to other computers or to annotate files or directories. This service is not as common as FTP or HTTP, but is included with IIS for backward compatibility with the older Gopher Internet technology.

B.   Installation Steps for IIS

Installing IIS is very simple. During the initial install of your Windows NT Server software, you were prompted about whether you wanted to install IIS at that time. However, if you said no, you still have the opportunity to install it at anytime from a working installation of Windows NT Server.

Exercise 4.3.1, "Installing Internet Information Server," walks you through the steps to installing IIS.

When the installation steps are complete, your Windows NT Server is ready to host your Internet publications. If you want to test your IIS installation, from a Web browser enter http:// your_computername and verify that you can see the default web page installed with IIS. If you can see this web page, your installation and all the Internet services are functional. If you do not see the default web page, begin the process anew and look for errors along the way.

Getting the Internet Information Service installed is the easy part. You may need to configure the system based on your specific needs. Each of the services can be configured, and in the following sections you learn about the configuration options for each of the IIS services.

C.   Overview of Internet Service Manager

Internet Information Server provides a graphical administration tool called the *Internet Service Manager*. With this tool, you can centrally manage, control, and monitor the Internet services in your Windows NT network. The Internet Service Manager uses the built-in Windows NT security model so it offers a secure method of remotely administering your web sites and other Internet services. To start the Internet Service Manager from the Start Menu, click Programs, Microsoft Internet Information Server, and then select the Internet Service Manager icon. When the Internet Service Manager has started, you can view the status of your Internet services.

The Internet Service Manager has three views that you can select to more easily monitor the information that you need. The three main views are as follows:

- **Report view:** This is the default view. The report view lists each computer alphabetically with each Internet service shown on a separate line in the screen.

- **Servers view:** This view groups all the services on each server and lists only computers with an Internet service loaded on them. The servers can then be expanded to display the loaded services.

- **Services view:** Each Internet service is listed with the corresponding servers grouped by service.

In each of the views, you can double-click on an entry to view the Properties dialog box for the selected item. You can make the configuration of the servers and services in these dialog boxes.

4.3.1   Exercise: Installing Internet Information Server

This exercise steps you through the installation of IIS, with the services for WWW, FTP, and Gopher enabled.

1.   Click the right mouse button on the Network Neighborhood, and choose the Properties command.

2.   Click the Services page tab.

3.   Click the Add button, and then click the Microsoft Internet Information Server 2.0 option. Click OK.

4.   The Internet Information Server Welcome dialog box displays. Click OK to continue.

5.   Review the installation options to ensure that all are selected, and then click OK .

6.   You may be prompted to create the installation directory for IIS; click Yes to create the directory.

7. The Publishing Directories dialog box appears. Click OK to select the default publishing directories.

8. Again, you may be prompted to create the directories. Click Yes to create them.

9. When the Internet Domain Name Warning dialog box appears, click OK.

10. Select the SQL Server entry on the ODBC Drivers dialog box, and click OK.

11. When the setup is complete, click OK.

4

4.3   Practice Problems

1. Internet Information Server, or IIS, serves primarily as a server of what?

   A. World Wide Web (WWW)

   B. FTP

   C. Gopher

   D. Archie

2. What three servers is Internet Information Server capable of being or supporting?

   A. World Wide Web (WWW)

   B. FTP

   C. Gopher

   D. Archie

3. What version of IIS ships with NT Server 4?

   A. 2.0

   B. 3.0

   C. 4.0

   D. 5.0

4. What three publishing services does Internet Information Server use?

   A. WWW

   B. HTTP

   C. HTML

   D. FTP

   E. Gopher

5. Which of the following is a client/server protocol used on the World Wide Web?

   A. WWW

   B. HTTP

   C. HTML

   D. FTP

   E. Gopher

6. Which of the following is a protocol used to transfer files from one computer to another over TCP/IP?

   A. WWW

   B. HTTP

   C. HTML

   D. FTP

   E. Gopher

7. Which of the following is a means to create a set of hierarchical links to other computers?

   A. WWW

   B. HTTP

   C. HTML

   D. FTP

   E. Gopher

8. In any FTP file transfer, what two roles must the computers play?

   A. Client

   B. Server

   C. Router

   D. Bridge

9. Internet Information Server provides a graphical administration tool called:

   A. Internet Tool

   B. Server Manager

   C. User Manager

   D. Internet Service Manager

10. Using the tool mentioned in question 9, you can centrally perform what three functions?

   A. Manage

   B. Add and Delete

   C. Control

   D. Monitor

11. The Internet Service Manager has three views that you can select to enable you easily to monitor the information that you need. What are the three main views?

    A. Report view

    B. Log view

    C. Servers view

    D. Services view

12. In reference to question 11, which is the default view?

    A. Report view

    B. Log view

    C. Servers view

    D. Services view

13. What does the Report view do?

    A. Groups all the services on each server and only lists each computer with an Internet service loaded on it.

    B. Reports each computer's load and capacity.

    C. Lists each Internet service, with the corresponding servers grouped by service.

    D. Lists each computer alphabetically with each Internet service shown on a separate line on the screen.

4.3.1 Answers and Explanations: Exercise

In this exercise, you installed Internet Information Server (IIS) on your Windows NT machine. Version 2.0 is the IIS version shipping with all current versions of Windows NT.

4.3 Answers and Explanations: Practice Problems

1. **A** Internet Information Server, or IIS, serves primarily as a World Wide Web (WWW) server.

2. **A, B, C** Internet Information Server serves primarily as a World Wide Web (WWW) server, but it also offers FTP and Gopher support.

3. **A** IIS 2.0 ships with NT Server 4.

4. **B, D, E** Internet Information Server uses Hypertext Transfer Protocol (HTTP), File Transfer Protocol (FTP), and the Gopher services to provide Internet publishing services to your Windows NT Server computer.

5. **B** HTTP is a client/server protocol used on the World Wide Web.

6. **D** FTP is the protocol used to transfer files from one computer to another using the TCP/IP protocol.

7. **E** The Gopher service provides a means to create a set of hierarchical links to other computers or to annotate files or directories.

8. **A, B** One system must be designated the FTP server and the other the FTP client.

9. **D** Internet Information Server provides a graphical administration tool called the Internet Service Manager.

10. **A, C, D** Using Internet Service Manager, you can centrally manage, control, and monitor the Internet services in your Windows NT network.

11. **A, C, D** The three main views are Report view, Servers view, and Services view.

12. **A** Report view is the default view.

13. **D** The Report view lists each computer alphabetically with each Internet service shown on a separate line on the screen.

4

4.3   Key Words

FTP

Gopher

HTML

HTTP

Internet Information Server (IIS)

Internet Service Manager

4.4   Installing and Configuring Internet Services

Installing and configuring Internet services can be broken into a number of components: installing the service World Wide Web, FTP, or Gopher (WWW is used for all the examples here, as it is the most popular) and configuring DNS services. Intranet services are identical to Internet with the exception of the clients accessing them, and thus only Internet is examined.

A.   Configuring WWW Services

To view the configuration for your WWW service, double-click on the WWW service in the Internet Service Manager application.

After you are in the properties dialog box for the WWW service, you notice the page tabs across the top of the dialog box. Each of these pages contains the configuration options available, as described in the following sections.

1.   The Services Property Page

The Services Property page tab enables you to set user logon and authentication requirements, as well as port and connection information for the service.

2.   The Directories Property Page

The Directories Property page shows you the location of your home directories and the location in which to place all your Internet publications. This page also sets the name of the default document to be used and whether or not directory browsing is enabled.

3.   The Logging Property Page

The Logging Property page enables you to select logging of the activity of the services. You can select a log filename and the log format, and you can also specify how often you should start a new log file. A nice feature of this page is the option to log to a SQL/ODBC database. This option is available only if the ODBC drivers are installed on your system.

4.   The Advanced Property Page

The Advanced Property page enables you to prevent access to the service based on IP addresses. This enables you to secure an intranet very easily by selecting an IP address range and then limiting the access allowed to the site. You can also use this page to limit the network bandwidth available for outbound traffic from the server.

B.   The DNS Service

You use the Domain Name Server Service on the Internet and UNIX-based systems primarily to resolve Fully Qualified Domain Names (FQDN) to IP addresses. You install the service via Control Panel, Networks. This installs the service into the service database, and after rebooting, starts the service automatically. The service is configured using the DNS Manager application in the Administrative Tools menu. After you install it, you must set up the records in the DNS database.

You set up information concerning DNS (Domain Name System) servers on the DNS tab. The first two optional entries are the Host Name and Domain fields. You can use the Domain field to identify your computer on a smaller, local network, such as the one in your company. By default, this is your Windows NT computer name, but the network administrator can assign a different name. The host name is combined with a domain name or suffix to create your Internet address.

> **Take note that a DHCP server can supply the DNS Service information as well. If a DHCP server supplies the DNS server information, you can leave these fields empty.**

The next entries are more important, especially if your machine is connected to the Internet. The DNS Service Search Order section lists the Domain Name System (DNS) servers. These servers contain a database that Windows NT searches to find the name assigned to your computer or other hosts on the internetwork. Servers are searched in the order listed.

> **The servers are searched in the order listed until the first server is contacted. If you always contact the first DNS server in the list, the second server will never be used for Internet name resolution. It only checks the second DNS server listed when a connection cannot be made to the first server in the list.**

4.4.1   Exercise: Installing and Configuring the DNS Service in Windows NT Server 4

This exercise steps you through the installation and configuration of the DNS service under Windows NT Server 4.

1. Get the IP address of your computer by typing **IPCONFIG** at the command line. You need the IP address for the upcoming steps.

2. Right-click the Network Neighborhood, and choose the Properties option.

3. Click the Services page tab.

4. Click Add.

5. In the Network Service list, select Microsoft DNS Server and click OK.

6. Enter the path to the Windows NT Server source directory and click Continue.

7. Click Close in the Network Properties dialog box.

8. Click Yes to restart the computer.

9. After the system restarts, log on.

10. Click the Start menu, Programs, Administrative Tools, and then click the DNS Manager.

11. Click the DNS menu, and then click the New Server option.

12. In the DNS Server box, type your computer name and click OK.

13. Highlight your computer name in the DNS Manager window.

14. Click the DNS menu, and click the New Zone command.

15. Click the Primary check box, and then click Next.

16. In the Zone Name type **xyz.com**, and then press the tab key to move to the Zone file box. The Zone file is automatically filled in as **xyz.com.dns**.

17. Click Next to finish.

18. To add a computer into your DNS Server, right click the Zone name, and then click the New Host option.

19. In the Host name, enter the computer name.

20. In the Host IP address, enter the IP address for the new computer.

21. Click the Add Host button.

22. Click Done.

4.4.2 Exercise: Configuring the DNS Manager

After you install DNS, you must configure the DNS Manager. This exercise walks you through the configuration process using two imaginary systems.

In this example, the two systems are located in the `imaginary.com` domain. The two hostnames are referred to as `www.imaginary.com` and `ftp.imaginary.com`, and the relevant IP addresses are provided. To set up the example in the DNS Manager, follow these steps:

1. Create the top domain structure first. In this case, it is COM. Choose the DNS menu and add the server. Enter the IP address of the DNS Server. You can use the loopback address of 127.0.0.1 for the current system.

2. Select the server, and then from the DNS menu, choose New Zone. Select Primary, and type **com** for the zone name. A tab automatically fills in the zone filename. Then click Finish.

3. Create the subdomain, imaginary, using the same approach as you used for the previous domain; that is, choose New Zone from the DNS menu and step through the wizard.

4. Create the two hosts, ftp and www, in the domain by selecting New Host and entering the hostname (for example, ftp or www) and the IP address for the host. Be sure to enable the Create PTR Record option to ensure that reverse lookups can also work.

5. Enable the Update Server Data Files option to refresh the server records and you're finished. To test the DNS setup, open a command prompt and try the following command:

   ```
   ping ftp.imaginary.com
   ```

   The command should return the proper IP address for the server if the DNS entries are complete.

4.4 Practice Problems

1. Internet services can be broken into what three components?

   A. Reverse lookup

   B. WWW

   C. Gopher

   D. FTP

2. In the Internet Service Manager application, which page enables you to set user logon and authentication requirements?

   A. The Services Property page

   B. The Directories Property page

   C. The Logging Property page

   D. The Advanced Property page

3. In the Internet Service Manager application, which page enables you to select logging of the activity of the services?

   A. The Services Property page

   B. The Directories Property page

   C. The Logging Property page

   D. The Advanced Property page

4. In the Internet Service Manager application, which page shows you the location of your home directories and the location in which to place all your Internet publications?

   A. The Services Property page

   B. The Directories Property page

   C. The Logging Property page

   D. The Advanced Property page

5. In the Internet Service Manager application, on which page do you set the name of the default document to be used and whether to enable directory browsing?

   A. The Services Property page

   B. The Directories Property page

C. The Logging Property page

D. The Advanced Property page

6. In the Internet Service Manager application, which page enables you to prevent access to the service based on IP addresses?

   A. The Services Property page

   B. The Directories Property page

   C. The Logging Property page

   D. The Advanced Property page

7. In the Internet Service Manager application, which page can you use to limit the network bandwidth available for outbound traffic from the server?

   A. The Services Property page

   B. The Directories Property page

   C. The Logging Property page

   D. The Advanced Property page

8. What is the primary use of the DNS Service on the Internet and UNIX-based systems?

   A. Page delivery

   B. FQDN Name resolution to IP addresses

   C. Management statistics

   D. Monitoring and optimization of existing resources

9. DNS is the abbreviation for:

   A. Domain Name System

   B. Domain Name Service

   C. Dynamic Name System

   D. Dynamic Name Service

10. The DNS Service Search Order section lists the DNS servers. These servers contain a database that Windows NT searches to find the name assigned to

your computer or other hosts on the internetwork. Servers are searched in what order?

A. Alphabetically

B. By region

C. Order listed

D. Frequency

4.4.1 Answers and Explanations: Exercise

In this exercise, you walked through the installation and configuration of the DNS service under Windows NT Server 4.

4.4.2 Answers and Explanations: Exercise

This exercise stepped you through the process of configuring DNS to provide Internet name resolution for two imaginary hosts in an Internet domain.

4.4 Answers and Explanations: Practice Problems

1. **B, C, D** Internet services can be broken into three components: World Wide Web services, FTP services, and Gopher services.

2. **A** The Services Property page enables you to set user logon and authentication requirements.

3. **C** The Logging Property page enables you to enable logging of the activity of the services.

4. **B** The Directories Property page shows you the location of your home directories and the location in which to place all your Internet publications.

5. **B** The Directories Property page enables you to set the name of the default document to use and whether to enable directory browsing.

6. **D** The Advanced Property page enables you to prevent access to the service based on IP addresses.

7. **D** You can use the Advanced Property page to limit the network bandwidth available for outbound traffic from the server.

8. **B** You use the Domain Name Server Service on the Internet and UNIX-based systems primarily to resolve Fully Qualified Domain Names (FQDN) to IP addresses.

9. **A** DNS is the abbreviation for Domain Name System.

10. **C** Servers are searched in the order listed in the file.

4.4 Key Words

DNS

FQDN

4

4.5   Installing and Configuring Remote Access Service (RAS)

The enterprise exam contains a few questions on the use of RAS. To be successful with these questions, you must have a solid understanding of RAS, including the installation and configuration of RAS.

Windows NT Remote Access Service extends the power of Windows NT networking to anywhere you can find a phone line. Using RAS, a Windows NT computer can connect to a remote network via a dial-up connection and fully participate in the network as a network client. RAS also enables your Windows NT computer to receive dial-up connections from remote computers.

RAS supports SLIP and PPP line protocols, and NetBEUI, TCP/IP, and IPX network protocols. NT supports SLIP only as a client. PPP, on the other hand, is supported as both a server and client protocol. Because so many Internet users access their service providers using a phone line, RAS often serves as an Internet interface.

The Dial-Up Networking application (in the Accessories program group) enables you to create phonebook entries. A phonebook entry is a pre-configured dial-up connection to a specific site. The Control Panel Telephony application enables the remote user to preconfigure dialing properties for different dialing locations.

RAS can connect to a remote computer using any of the following media:

- **Public Switched Telephone Network (PSTN):** (Also known as the phone company.) RAS can connect using a modem through an ordinary phone line.

- **X.25:** A packet-switched network. Computers access the network via a Packet Assembler Disassembler device (PAD). X.25 supports dial-up or direct connections.

- **Null modem cable:** A cable that connects two computers directly. The computers then communicate using their modems (rather than network adapter cards).

- **ISDN:** A digital line that provides faster communication and more bandwidth than a normal phone line. (It also costs more, which is why not everybody has it.) A computer must have a special ISDN card to access an ISDN line.

Windows NT also includes a new feature called Multilink. Using Multilink, a Windows NT computer can form a RAS connection using more than one physical pathway. One Multilink connection, for example, can use two modems at once (or one modem line and one ISDN line) to form a single logical link. By using multiple pathways for one connection, Multilink can greatly increase bandwidth. Of course, the computer has to have access to more than one pathway (that is, it must have two modems installed). Multilink, however, is not supported for callback features; you can configure only one number for callback.

A.   RAS Security

Like everything else in Windows NT, RAS is designed for security. As standard practice, all events are written to the system log, and you can view them with Event Viewer (which is used to view event logs). The following are some of RAS's other security features:

- **Auditing:** RAS can leave an audit trail, enabling you to see when users logged in and what authentication they provided.

- **Callback security:** You can enable RAS server to use callback (hang up all incoming calls and call the caller back), and you can limit callback numbers to prearranged sites that you know are safe.

- **Encryption:** RAS can encrypt logon information, or it can encrypt all data crossing the connection.

- **Security hosts:** In case Windows NT isn't safe enough, you can add an extra dose of security by using a third-party intermediary security host—a computer that stands between the RAS client and the RAS server and requires an extra round of authentication.

- **PPTP filtering:** You can tell Windows NT to filter out all packets except ultra-safe PPTP packets (described later in this chapter).

B. RAS Line Protocols

RAS (Remote Access Service) supports the SLIP, PPP, and PPTP line protocols. The following sections define these protocols in more detail.

1. SLIP

Serial Line Interface Protocol (SLIP) is a standard protocol for serial line connections over TCP/IP networks. SLIP is relatively old for the computer age—it was developed in 1984—and, although it is not yet completely obsolete, it does lack some of the features that are available in PPP. Each node in a SLIP connection must have a static IP address; that is, you can't use Windows NT features such as DHCP and WINS. Unlike PPP, SLIP does not support NetBEUI or IPX. You must use TCP/IP with SLIP. Also, SLIP cannot encrypt logon information.

2. PPP

Point-to-Point Protocol (PPP) was originally conceived as a deluxe version of SLIP. Like SLIP, PPP is an industry standard for point-to-point communications, but PPP offers several advantages over SLIP. Most notably, PPP isn't limited to TCP/IP. PPP also supports IPX, NetBEUI, and several other network protocols, such as AppleTalk and DECnet. Because PPP supports so many protocols, it enables you to have much more flexibility in configuring network communications, and also provides secure authentication.

3. PPTP

PPTP is a protocol that enables you to securely transmit PPP packets over a TCP/IP network. Because the Internet is a TCP/IP network, PPTP enables highly private network links over the otherwise highly public Internet. PPTP connections are encrypted, making them nearly impenetrable to virtual voyeurs.

In fact, PPTP is part of an emerging technology called Virtual Private Networks (VPNs). The point of VPN is to provide corporate networks with the same (or close to the same) security over the Internet that they would have over a direct connection.

Another exciting advantage of PPTP (and another reason that it fits nicely into the scheme of the VPN) is that PPTP doesn't discriminate among protocols. Because PPP supports NetBEUI, IPX, and other network protocols, and because PPTP operates on PPP packets, PPTP actually lets you transmit non-TCP/IP protocols over the Internet.

Because PPTP provides intranet privacy over the open Internet, it can significantly reduce costs in some situations. Networks that once would have depended on extravagant direct connections now can hook up via a local Internet service provider.

C. Installing a RAS Server

Remote Access Service is installed using the Services tab of the Network Properties dialog box. Prior to the installation, you should gather some basic information that you use during the installation of RAS:

- The type of modem to be used by RAS.

- Whether the device will be used for outgoing RAS communication, incoming RAS communication, or both.

- The protocols to be used by RAS.

- Whether the callback security feature needs to be configured.

After you have all the required information, you are ready to begin the installation of RAS. To complete the RAS installation, follow these steps:

1. In Control Panel, double-click on the Network Application icon.

2. In the Network dialog box, choose the Services tab. Click on the Add button, invoking the Select Network Service dialog box.

3. In the Select Network Service dialog box, choose Remote Access Service from the service list and click OK. Windows NT prompts you for the path to the Windows NT Installation CD-ROM.

4. Windows NT prompts you for name of a RAS-capable device and an associated communications port. A modem installed on your system typically appears as a default value. Click OK to accept the modem, or click on the down arrow to choose another RAS-capable device on your system. You also can install a new modem or an X.25 Pad using the Install Modem and Install X25 Pad buttons.

5. The Remote Access Setup dialog box appears. Click on the Configure button to specify whether to use the port for dial-out connections, dial-in connections, or both. The Port Usage options apply only to the port. In other words, you could configure COM1 for dial out only and COM2 for receive only. In the Remote Access Setup dialog box, you also can add or remove a port entry from the list. The Clone button enables you to copy a port configuration.

6. Click on the Network button to specify the network protocols for your Remote Access Service to support. The Server Settings options in the lower portion of the Network Configuration dialog box only appear if you configure the port to receive calls. Select one or more dial-out protocols. If you want RAS to take care of receiving calls, select one or more server protocols, and choose an encryption setting for incoming connections. You also can select Multilink, which enables one logical connection to use several physical pathways.

   A Configure button follows each of the Server Settings protocol options. Each Configure button opens a dialog box that enables you to specify configuration options for the protocol, as follows:

   - The RAS Server NetBEUI dialog box enables you to specify whether the incoming caller will have access to the entire network or to only the RAS server.

By confining a caller's access to the RAS server, you improve security (because the caller can access only one PC), but you reduce functionality because the caller can't access information on other machines.

- The RAS Server TCP/IP Configuration dialog box enables you to define how the RAS server assigns IP addresses to dial-up clients. You can use DHCP to assign client addresses, or you can configure RAS to assign IP addresses from a static address pool. If you choose to use a static address pool, input the beginning and ending addresses in the range. To exclude a range of addresses within the address pool, enter the beginning and ending addresses in the range you're excluding in the From and To boxes. Then click on the Add button. The excluded range appears in the Excluded Ranges list box.

  The RAS Server TCP/IP Configuration dialog box enables you to specify whether a client can access the entire network or only the RAS server. By confining a caller's access to the RAS server, you improve security (because the caller can only access one PC), but you reduce functionality because the caller cannot access information on other machines.

- The RAS Server IPX Configuration dialog box enables you to specify how the RAS server assigns IPX network numbers.

  You also can specify whether a client can access the entire network or only the RAS server. By confining a caller's access to the RAS server, you improve security (because the caller can only access one PC), but you reduce functionality because the caller can't access information on other machines.

7. After you define the RAS settings to your satisfaction, click OK.

8. The Network Services tab appears in the foreground. You should see Remote Access Service in the list of services. Click the Close button.

9. Windows NT asks whether you want to restart your computer. Choose Yes.

D. Configuring RAS

When configuring Remote Access Service, you need to configure the communication ports, network protocols, and encryption settings required for remote users when they dial into your Windows NT Server using the RAS as a server.

1. The Remote Access Setup Dialog Box

The RAS server is configured using the Control Panel Network icon located on the Services page tab. Locate the Remote Access Service and click the Properties button. The Remote Access Setup dialog box opens. A number of configuration options are available from this dialog box:

- **Add:** Add a port to be used by RAS. May be accessed by a modem or X.25 pad.
- **Remove:** Remove a port being used by RAS.
- **Configure:** Change the settings for a port being used by RAS.
- **Clone:** Copy the settings being used from one port to another.
- **Network:** Configure the network protocols and encryption to be used by RAS.

To make configuration changes to an existing port being used by RAS, click the Configure button. The following list describes each of the options:

- **Dial Out Only:** Port only used for outgoing RAS connections.
- **Receive Calls Only**: Port only used for receiving calls from RAS clients.
- **Dial Out and Receive:** Port used for both outgoing and incoming RAS connections.

You can configure each port that is listed in the RAS Setup dialog box for different roles. Com1 can be configured for dial-out only, whereas Com2 is used for Receive Calls Only. By allowing each port to be configured separately, you have a great deal of flexibility in the Remote Access Service.

2. The Network Configuration Dialog Box

After you configure the ports, you must configure the network settings. Start from the Remote Access Setup dialog box. Click the Network Button to view the Network Configuration dialog box.

The Network Configuration settings apply to all the ports that are enabled in RAS. Notice in the top section of the screen that you can select which protocols to use for dial-out calls. By clicking the check box next to the required protocols, you can enable or disable each of the protocols.

For the RAS server settings, you must configure the middle section of the screen. As a RAS server, you can control how far each of the selected protocols can go, or whether RAS clients accept the protocols at all. Again the check box directly next to each of the protocols enables or disables the protocols.

Clicking the Configure button located to the right of the listed protocols can also restrict each of the protocols. You can configure each protocol slightly differently.

E.   Dial-Up Networking

The Dial-Up Networking application lets you establish remote connections with other computers. The most common uses for Dial-Up Networking are as follows:

- Accessing an Internet service provider
- Accessing a remote Windows NT computer or domain

You can reach the Dial-Up Networking application as follows:

1. Choose Programs from the Start menu.
2. Choose Accessories from the Programs list.
3. Click the Dial-Up Networking icon.

Dial-Up Networking maintains a list of phonebook entries. A phonebook entry is a bundle of information that Windows NT needs to establish a specific connection. You can use the Dial-Up Networking application to create a phonebook entry for your access provider, your Windows NT domain, or any other dial-up connection. When it's time to connect, select a phonebook entry from the drop-down menu at the top of the screen and click the Dial button. If you access the phonebook entry often, you can create a desktop shortcut that enables you to access the phonebook entry directly by following these steps:

1. Click on the New button in the Dial-Up Networking main screen to open the New Phonebook Entry dialog box.

2. In the New Phonebook Entry Basic tab, specify a name for the entry, an optional comment, and the phone number you want Windows NT to dial to make the connection. The Alternates button beside the phone number box enables you to specify a prioritized list of alternative phone numbers. You also can specify a different modem or configure a modem from the Basic tab.

3. In the New Phonebook Entry Server tab, specify the communications protocol for the dial-up server (in the drop-down menu at the top of the screen) and the network protocol.

   If you select the TCP/IP network protocol, click the TCP/IP button to configure TCP/IP settings.

4. The New Phonebook Entry Script dialog box defines some of the connection's logon properties. You can tell Windows NT to pop up a terminal window before or after dialing or to run a logon script after dialing. A terminal window enables you to interactively log on to the remote server in terminal mode. The Run This Script option option automates the logon process. For more information on dial-up logon scripts, click the Edit Script button. The Edit Script button places you in a file called SWITCH.INF that provides instructions and sample logon scripts. The Before Dialing button enables you to specify a terminal window or a logon script to execute before you dial.

5. The New Phonebook Entry Security tab offers some encryption options. You can require encrypted authentication, or you can accept any authentication including clear text. You also can specify data encryption.

6. The New Phonebook Entry X.25 tab serves only for X.25 service (described earlier in this chapter). Select an X.25 access provider from the drop-down menu and enter the requested information.

7. After you make changes to the New Phonebook Entry tab, click OK. The new phonebook entry appears in the drop-down menu at the top of the Dial-Up Networking screen.

F. Troubleshooting RAS

If you have problems with PPP, you can log PPP debugging information to a file called PPP.LOG in the `\<winnt_root>\System32\Ras` directory. To log PPP debugging information to PPP.LOG, change the Registry value for `\HKEY_LOCAL_MACHINE\System\CurrentControlSet\Services\Rasman\PPP\Logging` to 1.

RAS authentication problems often stem from incompatible encryption methods. If you can connect using clear text and you can't connect using encryption, you know the client and server encryption methods are incompatible. You should try to connect using the Allow any Authentication Including Clear Text option.

4.5.1   Exercise: Installation of Remote Access Service on a Windows NT Server

This exercise helps you install the RAS service and configure it only to receive calls.

1. Right-click the Network Neighborhood Icon, and click the Services page tab.

2. Click the Add Button.

3. Select the Remote Access Service, and then click OK.

4. Enter the location of the source files for your Windows NT Server software.

5. The Remote Access Setup dialog box opens, prompting you to allow the Setup Wizard to detect your modem. Click Yes. If your modem is not found, start the wizard again and click the Don't Detect my Modem, I Will Select it from the List option, and then click Next.

6. Select the Dial-Up Networking Serial Cable Between Two PCs, and then click next.

7. Select COM1 as the selected port and click Next.

8. In the Location Information dialog box, enter the appropriate country.

9. Enter your area code in the What Area (or City) Code Are You in Now box.

10. Click Next.

11. Click Finish.

12. Click OK to add the Modem into your Remote Access Setup dialog box.

13. Click the Configure button.

14. Click to select the Receive Calls Only option.

15. Click OK to close the Port Configuration dialog box.

16. Click OK to close the Remote Access Setup dialog box.

4.5.2   Exercise: Configuring RAS for Dial Out and Receiving Communication

This exercise enables you to configure your RAS settings to allow your RAS server to dial out and receive RAS calls.

1. In the Control Panel, double-click the Network icon.

2. Click the Services page tab.

3. Locate the Remote Access Service, and then click the Properties button.

4. In the Remote Access Setup dialog box, click the Configure button.

5. Click the Dial Out and Receive Calls option, and then click OK.

6. Click the Network button.

7. In the dial out protocols, disable all protocols except for TCP/IP.

8. In the Server Settings, go to the Allow Remote Clients section and disable all protocols except TCP/IP.

9. Click the TCP/IP configure button.

10. Ensure that the remote clients can access the entire network through TCP/IP.

11. Click to enable the Remote clients to use the DHCP server.

12. Click OK to close the TCP/IP settings.

13. Click OK to close the Network Configuration dialog box.

14. Click OK to close the Remote Access Server Setup dialog box.

4

4.5   Practice Problems

1. Karen, a remote administrator, complains that RAS is not working properly, and that it keeps failing. What should be one of the first tools used to look for problems?

   A. Performance Monitor

   B. Event Viewer

   C. Server Manager

   D. User Manager for Domains

2. To justify additional expenses, you need to gather statistics on RAS. Which of the following tools displays statistics on current conditions of RAS?

   A. Performance Monitor

   B. The Status tab of the Dial-Up Networking Monitor in Control Panel

   C. Event Viewer

   D. User Manager for Domains

3. A sure way to find problems with RAS is to check the PPP.LOG. Which of the following statements are true of PPP logging? Choose two.

   A. It is enabled by default.

   B. Information is written to the PPP.LOG.

   C. You must edit the Registry to turn it on.

   D. It also contains logging information on modems.

4. Madonna, in customer service, must gather statistics about RAS. She needs to view the PPP.LOG, but she cannot find it. The PPP.LOG is stored, by default, where?

   A. `\<winnt_root>\System32\Ras`

   B. `\<winnt_root>\System32`

   C. `\<winnt_root>`

   D. `c:\`

5. Susan, a remote user, can connect using clear text, but cannot connect using encryption. What is the most likely problem?

   A. Connection speeds are too low to support verification.

   B. Encryption is not enabled at both client and server.

   C. The client and server encryption methods are incompatible.

   D. The server requires additional resources.

6. If you, as the RAS administrator, suspect that the client and server encryption methods are incompatible and cause problems, what should you do?

   A. Try to connect using the Allow Any Authentication Including Clear Text option.

   B. Try to avoid using any form of encryption.

   C. Try to discourage users from seeking dial-in functionality.

   D. Try to connect using the Incompatible Encryption Methods option.

7. Which of the following statements is true in regards to Callback with MultiLink?

   A. RAS can use multiple phone numbers for callback.

   B. RAS can use only one phone number for callback by default, but can use multiple phone numbers with the MultiLink function enabled.

   C. RAS can utilize callback only over ISDN lines.

   D. RAS can use only one phone number for callback.

8. If a non-ISDN client makes a connection using Multilink over multiple phone lines with Callback enabled, the server will call back using:

   A. Only a single phone line.

   B. Multiple phone lines.

   C. An ISDN line.

   D. One phone line unless, the default has been changed to Utilize Multiple.

9. Which three of the following are RAS problem areas, as identified by Microsoft?

   A. AutoDial at logon

   B. Authentication

   C. Heterogeneous connectivity

   D. Callback with MultiLink

10. Jerry complains that AutoDial spontaneously attempts to dial a remote connection during his logon. How should an administrator address this problem?

    A. Move Jerry to another machine.

    B. Disable AutoDial.

    C. Restrict Jerry's profiles and groups.

    D. Reinstall Windows NT.

11. RAS can use which protocols for dial-in connections? Choose all correct answers.

    A. TCP/IP

    B. NWLink

    C. NetBEUI

    D. SMTP

12. RAS can use which protocols for dial-out connections? Choose all correct answers.

    A. TCP/IP

    B. NWLink

    C. NetBEUI

    D. SMTP

13. Of the protocols RAS supports for dial-in and dial-out, which one benefits from being available on a number of different platforms and being easily routable?

    A. TCP/IP

    B. NWLink

    C. NetBEUI

    D. SMTP

14. Each node in a SLIP connection must:

    A. Have its own phone number

    B. Have a static IP address

    C. Be PPP enabled

    D. Be DHCP configured

15. Which of the following protocols cannot be used on DHCP and WINS?

    A. PPP

    B. TCP/IP

    C. SLIP

    D. PPTP

16. Which of the following protocols does PPP support?

    A. TCP/IP

    B. NetBEUI

    C. IPX

    D. Appleshare

17. Which of the following protocols does SLIP support?

    A. TCP/IP

    B. NetBEUI

    C. IPX

    D. Appleshare

4

18. Which protocol enables you to securely transmit PPP packets over a TCP/IP network?

    A. SLIP

    B. PPP

    C. PPTP

    D. UDP

19. Which protocol is part of an emerging technology called Virtual Private Networks?

    A. SLIP

    B. PPP

    C. PPTP

    D. UDP

20. What is the purpose of Virtual Private Networks (VPNs)?

    A. To provide corporate networks with the same security over the Internet that they would have over a direct connection.

    B. To provide corporate networks with the same support over the Internet that they would have over a direct connection.

    C. To provide corporate networks with the same speed over the Internet that they would have over a direct connection.

    D. To provide corporate networks with the same access over the Internet that they would have over a direct connection.

21. Which configuration option is used to copy the settings being used from one RAS port to another?

    A. Copy

    B. Clone

    C. Add

    D. Duplicate

4.5.1 Answers and Explanations: Exercise

In this exercise, you installed the RAS service and configured it to only receive calls.

4.5.2 Answers and Explanations: Exercise

In this exercise, you configured your RAS settings to enable your RAS server to dial out and receive RAS calls.

4.5 Answers and Explanations: Practice Problems

1. **B** If RAS isn't working, check the Event Viewer. Several RAS events appear in the system log.

2. **B** In Control Panel, the Status tab of Dial-Up Networking Monitor displays statistics on current conditions, including connection statistics and device errors.

3. **B, C** If you have problems with PPP, you can log PPP debugging information to a file called PPP.LOG in the \<winnt_root>\System32\Ras directory. To log PPP debugging information to PPP.LOG, change the Registry value for \HKEY_LOCAL_MACHINE\System\CurrentControlSet \Services\Rasman\PPP\Logging to 1.

4. **A** The PPP.LOG is stored, by default, in the \<winnt_root>\System32\Ras directory.

5. **C** RAS authentication problems often stem from incompatible encryption methods.

6. **A** If you can connect using clear text, and you can't connect using encryption, you know the client and server encryption methods are incompatible. You should try to connect using the Allow Any Authentication Including Clear Text option.

7. **D** RAS can use only one phone number for callback.

8. **A** If a client makes a connection using MultiLink over multiple phone lines with Callback enabled, the server calls back using only a single phone line—in other words, MultiLink functionality is lost.

9. **A, B, D** AutoDial at logon, authentication, and callback with MultiLink have all been identified as potential RAS problem areas by Microsoft.

10. **B** At logon, when Explorer initializes, it might reference a shortcut or some other target that requires an AutoDial connection, causing AutoDial to spontaneously dial a remote connection during logon. The only way to prevent the AutoDial is to disable AutoDial, or to eliminate the shortcut or other targets causing the AutoDial to occur.

11. **A, B, C** RAS supports TCP/IP, NWLink, and NetBEUI protocols for both dial-in and dial-out connections.

12. **A, B, C** RAS supports TCP/IP, NWLink, and NetBEUI protocols for both dial-in and dial-out connections.

13. **A** TCP/IP benefits from being available on a number of different platforms and being easily routable (as well as having the compatibility choice of the Internet).

14. **B** Each node in a SLIP connection must have a static IP address.

15. **C** SLIP cannot be used with DHCP and WINS.

16. **A, B, C** PPP supports TCP/IP, NetBEUI, and IPX.

17. **A** Unlike PPP, SLIP does not support NetBEUI or IPX. You must use TCP/IP with SLIP.

18. **C** PPTP is a protocol that enables you to securely transmit PPP packets over a TCP/IP network.

19. **C** PPTP is part of an emerging technology called Virtual Private Networks (VPNs).

20. **A** The point of VPNs is to provide corporate networks with the same (or close to the same) security over the Internet that they would have over a direct connection.

21. **B** The Clone option copies the settings being used from one port to another.

4.5   Key Words

Dial-Up Networking

Event Viewer

ISDN

Phonebook Entry

RAS

Virtual Private Networks

4

Practice Exam: Connectivity

Use this practice exam to test your mastery of "Connectivity." This practice exam is 17 questions long. The passing Microsoft score is 78.4 percent (13 right on this practice test). Questions are in multiple-choice format.

1. Which of the four configuration options is the default for how the Migration Tool is to react in the event that duplicate usernames are found on the NetWare server and the NT server?

   A. Add an error to the ERROR.LOG file.

   B. Skip the account with no error messages or warnings.

   C. Overwrite the existing account with new information.

   D. Include a prefix with the user account to distinguish between the existing account and the migrated account.

2. To migrate files from NetWare to NT using the Migration Tool for NetWare, what must be running on the NT Server?

   A. TCP/IP

   B. Client Services for NetWare

   C. File and Print Sharing

   D. NWLink

3. What would be a reason for NetBIOS broadcasts to be propagated over RIP routers?

   A. Routing tables need to be automatically updated.

   B. NetBIOS is the default protocol of the network.

   C. Windows 95 clients on both sides of the router need to communicate browsing information over the router.

   D. The Default Gateway is not configured.

4. The Migration Tool for NetWare can specify which of the following options for migrated passwords?

   A. No Password: The migrated users have no passwords assigned to them.

   B. Exact Password: The migrated users will have the same passwords as before.

   C. Password is: Assigns a single password to all migrated users.

   D. User must change password: Forces the migrated users to change their passwords the first time they log on to the Windows NT Server.

5. Kristin is trying to convince management that RIP for IP should be installed on every router. One justification she can use is that it reduces?

   A. Administrative overhead

   B. DNS usage

   C. Dependence on automatic router updates

   D. Network traffic

6. Evan works for the same company as Kristin, and is trying to convince management that RIP for IP should not be installed on every router. One justification he has is that it increases:

   A. Administrative overhead

   B. DNS usage

   C. Dependence on automatic router updates

   D. Network traffic

7. What does the Server view do?

   A. Groups all the services on each server and only lists each computer with an Internet service loaded on it.

   B. Reports each computers load and capacity.

C.   Lists each Internet service, with the corresponding servers grouped by service.

D.   Lists each computer alphabetically with each Internet service shown on a separate line in the screen.

8.   What does the Services view do?

A.   Groups all the services on each server and only lists each computer with an Internet service loaded on it.

B.   Reports each computers load and capacity.

C.   Lists each Internet service, with the corresponding servers grouped by service.

D.   Lists each computer alphabetically with each Internet service shown on a separate line in the screen.

9.   DNS is the abbreviation for:

A.   Domain Name System

B.   Domain Name Service

C.   Dynamic Name System

D.   Dynamic Name Service

10. Which configuration option do you use to configure the protocols and encryption used by RAS?

A.   Add

B.   Configure

C.   Clone

D.   Network

11. The Network Configuration settings apply to?

A.   Individual ports

B.   All the ports that are enabled in RAS

C.   Dial-in ports only

D.   Dial-out ports only

12. What is a collection of information that Windows NT needs to establish a specific connection?

A.   A phonebook entry

B.   A property

C.   A configuration

D.   A setting

13. To what NetWare permission does the NT Full Control permission map?

A.   Read

B.   Write

C.   Modify

D.   Supervisor

14. Which of the following statements is false about the Domain Name Server Service?

A.   You can use it on the Internet and UNIX-based systems primarily to resolve Fully Qualified Domain Names (FQDN) to IP addresses.

B.   You install the service via Control Panel, Networks.

C.   DNS Service information can be supplied via a DHCP server as well.

D.   You set up information concerning DNS (Domain Name System) servers on the Networks tab.

15. Which of the following statements is false?

A.   Gateway Services for NetWare transfers file and directory information and user and group account information from a NetWare server to a Windows NT domain controller.

B.   Gateway Services for NetWare enables Windows NT Servers to access NetWare file and print resources.

C. The passwords from the NetWare
server can be migrated across to NT
by setting the right option.

D. RIP packets are sent out once every
60 seconds.

16. Which of the following statements is not
true about Gateway Services for NetWare?

A. GSNW enables Windows NT
Servers to access NetWare file and
print resources.

B. GSNW is ideal for large-scale
routing.

C. GSNW enables the Windows NT
Servers to act as a gateway to the
NetWare file and print resources.

D. GSNW enables multiple Windows
NT clients to share a single connection.

17. RAS can connect to a remote computer
using which of the following media?

A. The phone company

B. X.25

C. Null modem cable

D. ISDN

Answers and Explanations: Practice Exam

1. **B** The Migration Tool for NetWare
default is Ignore, which causes the
account to be skipped with no error
messages or warnings.

2. **D** NWLink must be running on the
NT Server to use the Migration Tool.

3. **C** You only propagate NetBIOS
broadcasts over RIP routers if both sides
of the Windows NT router contain
Microsoft clients that need to communicate browsing information over the
router.

4. **A, C, D** The passwords from the
NetWare server cannot be migrated to
NT for security reasons, but other options
are available.

5. **A** RIP for IP reduces administrative
overhead.

6. **D** RIP for IP can increase network
traffic.

7. **A** Server view groups all the services on
each server and only lists computers with
an Internet service loaded on them.

8. **C** With Services view, each Internet
service is listed with the corresponding
servers grouped by service.

9. **A** DNS is the abbreviation for Domain
Name System.

10. **B** You use the Network configuration
option to configure the network protocols, and encryption to be used by RAS.

11. **B** The Network Configuration settings
apply to all the ports that are enabled in
RAS.

12. **A** A phonebook entry is a bundle of
information that Windows NT needs to
establish a specific connection.

13. **D** Full Control equates to NetWare's
Supervisor permission.

14. **D** You set up information concerning
DNS (Domain Name System) servers on
the DNS tab, not the Networks tab.

15. **C** For security reasons, the passwords
from the NetWare server cannot be
migrated to NT.

16. **B** GSNW enables multiple Windows
NT clients to share a single connection.
This sharing causes a significant performance loss for the NetWare resource. For
this reason, it is not recommended for
large-scale routing.

17. **A, B, C, D** RAS can connect to a
remote computer using all mentioned
methods.

CHAPTER 5

Monitoring and Optimization

This chapter covers the following Microsoft exam objectives:

- Establishing a baseline for measuring system performance. Tasks include creating a database of measurement data.

- Monitoring performance of various functions by using Performance Monitor. Functions include Processor, Memory, Disk, and Network.

- Monitoring network traffic by using Network Monitor. Tasks include collecting, presenting, and filtering data.

- Identifying performance bottlenecks.

- Optimizing performance for various results. Results include controlling network traffic and controlling server load.

Some of the tools that Microsoft provides for monitoring system performance are as follows:

- **Server Manager:** Monitors the number of users connected, open files, idle time, shared resources, and so on.

- **Windows NT Diagnostics:** Displays the current configuration for the processor, memory, disk, and network.

- **Response Probe:** A utility used to apply a controlled stress on a system and monitor the response.

- **Performance Monitor:** An administrative tool for monitoring NT workstations and servers. Performance Monitor helps you to better plan for future use and, at the same time, to optimize its current performance.

- **Task Manager:** Enables the viewing, stopping, and starting of applications and processes. It also contains the Performance Monitor capabilities that enable the viewing of memory and CPU utilization.

- **Network Monitor:** Captures and views the network traffic going in and out of the system on which Network Monitor is running.

All these tools come with Windows NT 4 (Network Monitor must be installed) except Response Probe, which comes with the Resource Kit.

5.1   Analysis Using Performance Monitor

To conduct analysis and optimization, do the following:

- Create a baseline of current use.

- Monitor the use over a period of time.

- Analyze data to determine non-optimum system use.

- Determine how the system should be used.

- Determine whether additional resources should be added to the system or whether the system needs to be upgraded.

Performance Monitor helps you to better plan for future use and, at the same time, to optimize its current performance.

A.   An Overview of Performance Monitor

This section identifies some of the options available in Performance Monitor for monitoring, analyzing server performance, and gathering specific data. Some of the options include:

- Viewing data from multiple computers simultaneously

- Seeing how changes affect the computer

- Changing charts of current activity while viewing them

- Starting a program or procedure automatically, or sending a notice when a threshold is exceeded

- Exporting Performance Monitor data to spreadsheets or database programs, or using it as raw input for programs

- Saving different combinations of counter and option settings for quick starts and changes

- Logging data about various objects from multiple computers over time

- Creating reports about current activity or trends over time

A number of other factors can adversely affect the data gathered by using Performance Monitor:

- If the sample interval is too short, the log file becomes very large.

- If sampled too often, the processor has additional burden.

- If the interval is too long, significant changes in data may be missed.

- Monitoring too soon after startup records all the processes and services being initiated.

- Take the computer off the network to stop the burden of network resources skewing the performance of other resources.

B.   What Resources Should You Monitor?

The throughput of each resource should be monitored both individually during installation and after installation is complete with all resources in use. The following four resources have the greatest impact on the performance of the server:

- Memory
- Processor
- Disk
- Network

Monitoring the four resources—memory, processor, disk, and network—simultaneously shows the effects the resource combinations have on each other and the server system.

1.   Memory

Two main types of memory need to be considered when analyzing server performance:

- Physical random access memory (RAM)
- Virtual memory (pagefile)

The more physical memory the better because the disk drive does not have to be accessed as often for the pagefile. The pagefile can be moved to another partition to reduce access to the boot partition, but it prevents debugging system problems if the system tends to crash often. The best option is to leave the pagefile in its default location with its size set to be the same as physical memory and to create a large secondary pagefile on another physical drive.

2.   Processor

The type and number of processors greatly affects the performance of the system. Windows NT Server 4 can scale up to 32 processors.

3.   Disk

A number of factors affect disk performance, and all of them should be taken into account when analyzing and optimizing the system. The factors include:

- **Type and number of controllers:** Whether they are IDE, EIDE, SCSI, fast SCSI, and so on, can make a big difference.
- **Types of drives implemented:** Disk drives come with varying specs as far as access speed and rotation speed.
- **Controllers that support RAID:** RAID can provide fault tolerance.
- **Disk striping with parity:** If you are using Microsoft's disk striping with parity, write performance can improve greatly.
- **Busmaster controllers:** Have a processor on board to handle requests and reduce the load on the system processor.
- **Caching:** Read and write performance can improve due to requests being held in onboard memory until free time is available.

- **Type of work being performed:** Application server, file and print server, network protocol(s) being used, number of users, type of network adapter(s), services being run (DHCP, WINS, IIS, and so on).

- **Matching disk controllers to disk types:** Ensure that disk controllers are matched to the disk types. A fast-wide SCSI disk should be used with a fast-wide SCSI controller.

4. Network

A number of different topologies as well as network architecture standards are available. The two main architectures in use today are Ethernet and Token Ring:

- Ethernet is the most commonly implemented type of network that operates anywhere from 10 MHz to 100 MHz and more.

- Token Ring is a standard that was developed by IBM and operates anywhere from 4 MHz to 16 MHz and more.

In each case, whether Ethernet or Token Ring is used, it is always advisable to use the fastest network card with the largest bus. Both Ethernet and Token Ring are available in 32-bit formats, and 64-bit cards should be available soon if they are not already.

C.   Objects in Performance Monitor

When monitoring a computer system, what is really being monitored is the behavior of its objects. An *object* is a standard mechanism for identifying and using a system resource. Objects are created to represent individual threads, processes, physical devices, and sections of shared memory. Performance Monitor groups counters by their object type. Each object has a unique set of counters assigned to it. Certain objects and their respective counters are available on all systems; others are available only when the computer is running the associated software or service.

Each object type can have more than one component installed in the computer. These components are referred to as *instances* and are displayed in the Instance box of any Add to dialog box. The Instance box also can contain the Total instance. This instance represents the total of all instances. Some objects are dependent on or a part of another object. This type of object also can be referred to as a *child object*. An object that has one or more dependent objects can be referred to as a *parent object*.

A *thread* is an object with a process that executes program instructions. By having multiple threads, a process can carry out different parts of its program on different processes concurrently. Threads dependent on a process or parent object are indicated by an arrow from parent object to child object.

Microsoft designed Performance Monitor to cause as little impact on Windows NT as possible. It still, however, has an effect on the system. Therefore, when monitoring anything other than network performance, it is recommended that you monitor the server system from a different computer. When monitoring for network performance, it is best to do so in Log mode.

The core objects that can be monitored on any Windows NT 4 system are described in Table 5.1.1.

Table 5.1.1   Core Objects Capable of Being Monitored

Core Object Name	Description of Object
Cache	An area of physical memory that holds recently used data
LogicalDisk	Partitions and other logical views of disk space
Memory	Physical random access memory used to store code and data
Objects	Certain system software objects
Paging File	File used to back up virtual memory locations to increase memory
PhysicalDisk	A single spindle-disk unit or RAID device
Process	Software object that represents a running program
Processor	Hardware unit (CPU) that executes program instructions
Redirector	File system that diverts file requests to the network servers; also referred to as the Workstation service
System	Contains counters that apply to all system hardware and software
Thread	The part of a process that uses the processor

D.   Counters in Performance Monitor

A *counter* defines the type of data available from a type of object. Performance Monitor can display, collect, and average data from counters by using the Windows NT Registry and the Performance Library DLLs. Counters can be divided into three types:

- **Instantaneous:** Instantaneous counters always display the most recent measurement. In the case of the Process:Thread Count, the number of threads found in the last measurement is displayed.

- **Averaging:** Averaging counters measure a value over a period of time and display the average of the last two measurements.

- **Difference:** Difference counters subtract the last measurement from the preceding measurement and display the difference if it is a positive value. A negative value is shown as zero.

Other performance monitoring applications can read the data gathered from Performance Monitor and can display and use the negative values.

Data is broken down into either absolute or relative information, with the difference being that an *absolute* value is exactly the duration taken or the amount reached, whereas a *relative* value is one measurement compared to another. (See Table 5.1.2 for an example of absolute values.)

Table 5.1.2   Absolute Transfer Rates

Counter	5-Second Interval	5-Minute Interval
Disk time	4.652 seconds	263.89 seconds
Bytes transferred	82,524 bytes	4,978,335 bytes

It is difficult to tell which measurement is showing a faster rate of transfer. If you look at the same information in Table 5.1.3 that uses relative counters, however, it is easier to compare the results.

Table 5.1.3   Relative Transfer Rates

Counter	5-Second Interval	5-Minute Interval
Disk time	93.04%	87.96%
Bytes transferred	16504.8 bytes/sec	16594.45 bytes/sec

A brief description displays at the bottom of the dialog box if the Explain button is selected. This is useful if you are unsure to what a counter refers.

E.   Views in Performance Monitor

You can view data in Performance Monitor in various ways. The Chart, Report, Log, and Alert views are described in Table 5.1.4.

Table 5.1.4   Various Ways to View Data in Performance Monitor

View	Description
Chart	A chart is a graphical display of the value of a counter over a period of time.
Report	A report shows the value of the counter. A report of all the counters can be created.
Log	The selected data is stored in a file on a disk for future analysis.
Alert	An alert can be set on an individual counter. This causes an event to display if the counter attains the specified value.

The four views are always available, but only one can be viewed at a time. The default view is the Chart view. To highlight an individual chart line, select the desired line in the legend and press Ctrl+H. This turns the corresponding line white and makes it much wider than the other lines. After the highlight is enabled, it can be moved from one chart line to another by using either the up/down arrow keys or the mouse. To disable the highlight, press Ctrl+H again.

If you want to view the contents of the log while it is still collecting data, open a second instance of Performance Monitor. Switch to the desired view (Chart or Report) and set the Data values displayed from option to the name of the running log file.

F.   Performance Analysis

Now that the process for creating a baseline has been established, analysis of the system and resource requirement forecasting can start. Analysis on a system takes four steps:

- Determine what is normal for the system and how to deal with the abnormal.

- Set expectations of how the system or resource should respond under specific conditions.

- Help plan for upgrades and additions.

- Provide better input into system budgeting requirements.

When a system is to be analyzed, you should first determine what functions the server performs. Three types of Windows NT Servers exist, as described in Table 5.1.5.

Table 5.1.5 Windows NT Servers

Server Type	Description
File and print server	Used for data storage and retrieval. It also can be used for loading application software over the network.
Application server	The server runs the application engine that users access by using a local version of the application front end.
Domain server	A domain server validates user account logons. Domain controllers synchronize the account database among themselves.

To set expectations, you must know what is to be expected of a system. This is referred to as *workload characterization*. A *workload unit* is a list of requests made on the system or a resource. An example of a workload unit might be the number of bytes transferred per second.

To determine workload characterization, you must understand what is taking place in each environment.

> **Many Windows NT installations have the servers acting in one, two, or all three server roles. In these situations, the administrator might have to sacrifice or reduce the performance of one server role to bring the performance of another role up to a satisfactory level to get the best overall performance.**

A resource that restricts the workflow is referred to as a *bottleneck*. Sometimes the performance of one resource makes another resource appear to be the bottleneck.

Because Windows NT is self-tuning to a certain degree, a good percentage of optimization involves upgrading hardware, not changing Registry settings. It is important, however, to know what needs to be upgraded and what doesn't.

1. Analysis of a File and Print Server

File and print servers generally are accessed for data storage and retrieval and sometimes for loading applications across the network. Therefore, the largest load applied is from users who access the server at the same time and demand resource requirements. Events that need to be monitored for this type of server are listed in Table 5.1.6.

Table 5.1.6   File and Print Server Monitoring

Workload Unit	Performance Monitor Counter
Concurrent user sessions	Server: Server Sessions
The number of open files	Server: Files Open
Average transaction size	PhysicalDisk: Avg. Disk Bytes/Transfer
Amount of disk activity	PhysicalDisk: %Disk Time
Type of disk activity	PhysicalDisk: %Disk Read Time PhysicalDisk: %Write Time
Network use	Network Segment: %Network Utilization

In addition to the preceding, you might find that additional resources (such as memory) are being consumed and should also be monitored. All four of the main system components are important in any server; however, some resources are more important than others, depending on the type of server being analyzed. For a file and print server, the order of importance is explained in Table 5.1.7.

Table 5.1.7   Order of Importance in a File and Print Server

Priority	Resource	Implications
1	Memory	Memory is used for caching opened files; if RAM is insufficient for caching, performance takes a big hit.
2	Processor	The processor is used for each network connection. This means all network traffic must pass through the processor.
3	Disk	The disk drive is the primary resource that users are going to access. The speed of the disk drives affects the general perception of how the server operates.
4	Network	A number of factors affect the network system (adapter type, number of adapters, protocols used, and so on). It does not matter, however, how fast the disk drive is, how much RAM exists, or how many processors exist if the network adapter is slow.

When forecasting resource requirements, keep the following in mind:

- Monitor the number of user sessions and the effect each session has on the four main system resources.

- If the server is used to retrieve and update data files, monitor the disk and network resources.

- If the server is used for data files and to load applications, monitor memory, disk, and network resources.

- Make sure Maximize Throughput for File Sharing is selected in the Server dialog box. This is found in the Network Applet of the Control Panel on the Services tab.

2. Analysis of an Application Server

Workload units are key when analyzing an application server. (Workload units that need to be monitored are shown in Table 5.1.8.)

Table 5.1.8   Monitoring Workload

Workload Unit	Performance Monitor Counter
Concurrent user sessions	Server: Server Sessions
Processor usage	Processor: %Processor Time
Average disk transaction size	PhysicalDisk: Avg. Disk Bytes/Transfer
Amount of disk activity	PhysicalDisk: %Disk Time
Network use	Network Segment: %Network Utilization
Average network transaction	NetBEUI: Frame Bytes/sec (similar size counter for each protocol)
Available memory	Memory: Available Bytes
Amount of paging	Memory: Pages/sec
Usage of cache	Cache: Copy Read Hits %

In addition to the counters that Performance Monitor provides, certain applications (such as Microsoft Exchange Server) provide additional counters and predefined charts. If application-specific counters are available, be sure to utilize them when analyzing the server.

Table 5.1.9 lists the four main resources in order of importance and briefly describes their role in an application server.

Table 5.1.9   Resources and Their Roles in an Application Server

Priority	Resource	Roles
1	Processor	Applications run on the server instead of the client side of the network.
2	Memory	Memory is needed at the server to support both the server needs and the application needs.
3	Disk	Client/server applications typically access large amounts of data; therefore, they demand more of the disk drives.
4	Network	Client/server applications transfer many requests across the network. These requests often are queries or commands that are small in size.

5.1.1 Exercise: Monitoring Memory Performance

The purpose of this exercise is to illustrate the monitoring of the memory resource in a server. To this exercise, edit the BOOT.INI file and add the switch /MAXMEM:16 so that the available memory is limited to 16 MB. Then follow these steps and note the Average, Minimum, and Maximum measurements.

1. Start Performance Monitor.

2. Click Add to Chart to open the dialog box.

3. Add the counters of Pages/sec and Page Faults/sec for the Memory object.

4. Open the Chart Options dialog box and change the time interval to one second.

5. Open Disk Administrator, and then open Server Manager.

6. Return to Performance Monitor and view the results.

5.1.2 Exercise: Monitoring the Network Performance

The purpose of this exercise is to illustrate the monitoring of the network services using one or multiple protocols.

1. Ensure that all three protocols are installed (TCP/IP, NetBEUI, IPX/SPX) on your server.

2. Ensure that SNMP Service is installed to activate the TCP/IP network counters.

3. Ensure that Network Monitor Agent Service is installed to activate the network segment object.

4. Open Performance Monitor if it is not already open and ensure that no counters have been added.

5. Add all the counters for the Workstation object.

6. Open Server Manager.

7. Open Explorer to the *WindowsNtroot*\System32 directory.

8. Map a drive to a computer share on the network.

9. Copy the files from the current directory on your computer to the mapped drive.

10. Although the files are being copied, switch to Server Manager and open the properties of a computer on the network.

11. Return to Performance Monitor to view the results and make note of the Average, Minimum, and Maximum values during file transfer.

5.1   Practice Problems

1. How is Performance Monitor installed on a Primary Domain Controller?

    A. It is installed from the Windows NT 4.0 Resource Kit.

    B. Performance Monitor is automatically installed as part of Windows NT 4.

    C. Performance Monitor is purchased as an add-on package.

    D. Performance Monitor is a separate service that must be installed after Windows NT has been installed.

2. Performance Monitor can be used to monitor the activity of the disk. To activate the disk counters, diskperf -y must first be run. What must be run if you want to monitor a disk system that is a RAID?

    A. diskperf -yr

    B. diskperf -y stripe

    C. diskperf -ye

    D. diskperf -raid

3. Which is the default window in Performance Monitor?

    A. Report

    B. Chart

    C. Objects, Counters, Instances

    D. Sessions, Real Time, Transfer Statistics

4. What does a Counter represent in Performance Monitor?

    A. A process that executes a set of program instructions

    B. A mechanism for identifying system resources

    C. The type of data available from an object

    D. The type of data available from a thread

5. What does an Object represent in Performance Monitor?

    A. A process that executes a set of program instructions

    B. A mechanism for identifying system resources

    C. The type of data available from a type of object

    D. The type of data available from a thread

6. What does an Instance represent in Performance Monitor?

    A. The type of data available from a thread

    B. The type of data available from an object

    C. One of multiple installed objects

    D. One of multiple installed counters

7. What command is used to enable the disk monitoring counters in Performance Monitor?

    A. perfdisk -y

    B. perfdisk /y

    C. diskperf /yes

    D. diskperf -y

8. What is used to enable the TCP/IP network counters in Performance Monitor?

    A. perfnet -y

    B. perfnet /yes

    C. netperf -y

    D. SNMP service

9. How often do you have to enable the disk counters for Performance Monitor?

    A. Each time Performance Monitor is restarted.

    B. Each time the computer is restarted.

    C. It never has to be re-enabled.

    D. Each time an administrator logs onto the server.

5

10. Jack has added the 15 counters that his supervisor recommended to monitor for his file and print server. Now when he views the chart he has a hard time distinguishing which line corresponds with which counter. How can Jack make it simpler to distinguish one line from the other? Choose the best answer.

   A. Start three separate Performance Monitor sessions and add just five of the counters to each of the sessions.

   B. Press Ctrl+C to highlight the selected counter.

   C. Press Ctrl+H to highlight the selected counter.

   D. Modify the color selections to make each line more obvious.

11. Susan wants to get the most accurate reading on the network counters on her file and print server. What should she do? Choose the best answer.

   A. Run Performance Monitor on the file and print server while running multiple applications on the server.

   B. Run Performance Monitor on a different server while running multiple applications on the server.

   C. Run Performance Monitor on the file and print server while transferring files to another computer.

   D. Run Performance Monitor on a different server while transferring files to another computer.

12. What is Response Probe used for, and how is it enabled?

   A. Like Performance Monitor, it is automatically installed as part of Microsoft Windows NT 4.

   B. Like Performance Monitor, it is a service that can be installed from the Microsoft Windows NT 4 CD.

   C. Response Probe doesn't exists.

   D. Response Probe is an application for creating a workload that is available on the Resource Kit.

13. Select the three types of counters available in Performance Monitor.

   A. Averaging

   B. Maximum

   C. Difference

   D. Instantaneous

14. What are the two types of data that are gained from Performance Monitor?

   A. Average and Maximum

   B. Absolute and Refined

   C. Relative and Accrued

   D. Relative and Absolute

15. Mike needs to compare disk transfer rates between two computers. What counter should he select in Performance Monitor? Choose the best answer.

   A. Bytes Transferred

   B. %Disk Time

   C. Bytes Transferred/sec

   D. Disk Time

5.1.1 Answers and Explanations: Exercise

The purpose of this exercise was to illustrate the monitoring of the memory resource in a server. You edited the BOOT.INI file and added the switch /MAXMEM:16 so that the available memory was limited to 16 MB. Be sure to note the Average, Minimum, and Maximum measurements.

5.1.2 Answers and Explanations: Exercise

The purpose of this exercise was to illustrate the monitoring of the network services using one or multiple protocols. (For more information, see the section "Performance Analysis.")

5.1 Answers and Explanations: Practice Problems

1. **B**   Performance Monitor is a built-in utility of Windows NT 4.

2. **C**   The -*y* enables the disk counters and the *e* indicates that every drive should be monitored.

3. **B**   The chart is the default view in Performance Monitor.

4. **C**   A counter represents the type of data that is available from an object.

5. **B**   An object represents a mechanism for identifying system resources.

6. **C**   An instance represents one of multiple installed objects. For example, if two disk drives exist, two instances for the object Physical Disk exist.

7. **D**   diskperf -y enables the disk counters the next time the system is restarted.

8. **D**   The SNMP service enables the TCP/IP network counters in Performance Monitor.

9. **C**   The disk counters remain enabled until an administrator disables them by running diskperf -n.

10. **C**   The best answer is to press Ctrl+H while viewing Performance Monitor to highlight the selected counter.

11. **C**   Run Performance Monitor on the file and print server while transferring files so that additional network traffic is not generated by monitoring.

12. **D**   Response Probe is an application that is available on the Resource Kit that is used to create a workload on the server.

13. **A, C, D**   Maximum is not one of the types of counters that are available in Performance Monitor.

14. **D**   Relative and Absolute are the two types of data that is generated in Performance Monitor.

15. **C**   Bytes Transferred/sec is the best selection because it gives relative information. Mike can see how many bytes are transferred in one second. Bytes Transferred provides the number of bytes transferred but no indication of how long it took.

5.1   Key Words

Pagefile

Object

Counter

Thread

RAID

Striping

Cache

Logical disk

5

5.2　Establishing a Baseline

Whenever you analyze a system's performance, you must first create a baseline from which to measure. After you have an established baseline, you can always compare system performance to that baseline whenever changes are made to the system, whether they are good or bad.

The method in which data is collected can provide a wide variety of information. Taking a measurement, for example, adding all the components, and then measuring again displays the effect of having all the components working together. Another way of measuring is to take a separate measure as each component is added. This provides data about how each individual component affects the performance of the system. Yet another way is to add components one at a time, but in different combinations. This provides a better understanding of how each component affects the performance of the others.

A.　Creating a Baseline Using Performance Monitor

You should always include memory, processor, disk, and network objects in the baseline. After the initial set of data is captured, use the same settings and capture data on a regular basis. Place this information in a database and analyze the performance of the system.

You must use the Log view to create a baseline measurement; this is the only way to create a log of activity. While measuring, you log, relog, and append logs to get a complete set of information. Objects that should be included are as follows:

- Cache
- Logical disk
- Memory
- Network adapter
- Network segment activity on at least one server in the subnet
- Physical disk (if using a RAID system)
- Processor
- Server
- System

Measurements should be taken for a full week at different times of the day so that information can be recorded at both peak and slack times. Ideally, you should have enough data to know whether the different counters experience significant change during different times of the day.

To automate the collection of data, a utility is available on the Resource Kit that enables Performance Monitor to be started as a service.

Performance Monitor log files can grow to be quite large. Set up monitoring to be done on a system that is not being monitored and that has a large amount of free disk space. Practice taking logs that use different time intervals to get a feel for the size of the created file.

B.   Establishing a Database

The second step in preparing for analysis is to take the collected data and put it into a database so that it can be analyzed. This involves collecting the information over a period of time and adding it to a database. After it's in a database, the information can be used to identify bottlenecks and trends.

5.2.1   Exercise: Establishing a Baseline

This exercise reinforces the concept of establishing a baseline regardless of the tool(s) used. Scenario: You are assigned the task of being the network administrator for the new office that your company is opening. Two logon servers exist, as well as a file and print server controlling four printers.

The network protocol is TCP/IP, with 150 users. Because the office is smaller, they only work one shift—8:00 a.m. to 4:30 p.m. weekdays. From the information you have, what kind of schedule would you set up for creating the baseline?

5.2.2   Exercise: Using a Baseline

This exercise reinforces the use of a baseline to qualify assumptions. Scenario: You have inherited the role of administering a network. When the network was first set up, a baseline was created. Now that six months have passed and a few new users have been added, you want to see whether performance has improved, deteriorated, or stayed the same.

Explain what steps should be taken to judge how performance has faired over the last six months.

5.2 Practice Problems

1. Which is the primary tool used for creating a baseline in Windows NT Server? Choose the best answer.

   A. Server Manager

   B. User Manager

   C. Network Monitor

   D. Performance Monitor

2. Which monitoring tool that Microsoft provides does not come on the Microsoft Windows NT Server CD?

   A. Task Manager

   B. Response Probe

   C. Network Monitor

   D. Performance Monitor

3. What is a baseline?

   A. The performance specifications for all hardware components.

   B. The performance specifications for all software components.

   C. A collection of performance information to which all future measurements can be compared.

   D. A baseline in Microsoft Windows NT is like "Safe Mode" in Windows 95. It is the minimum standard configuration for the system.

4. How many baselines should be created? Choose the best answer.

   A. One for each server, even if they have "identical" configurations

   B. One for each Primary Domain Controller

   C. One for each domain controller (Primary and Backup)

   D. One for each computer on the network

5. Which components should be included in the creation of the baseline? Choose all that apply.

   A. Memory

   B. Processor

   C. Disk

   D. Network

6. Which component is the most important when creating a baseline? Choose all that apply.

   A. Memory

   B. Processor

   C. Disk

   D. Network

7. When should a baseline be created?

   A. When the server is first configured.

   B. After two months, so that the system has stabilized.

   C. At the first sign of problems on the network.

   D. At the first sign of problems on the server.

8. What time of day should data for the baseline be recorded? Choose the best answer.

   A. 7:00 a.m. to 10:00 a.m.

   B. 2:30 p.m. to 6:30 p.m.

   C. All day

   D. 10:00 a.m. to 2:00 p.m.

9. How often should the baseline be upgraded? Choose the best answer.

   A. Every two weeks.

   B. Whenever changes have been made to the server or the network.

   C. Once a year.

   D. The baseline does not need to be upgraded.

10. Your server has to be shut down during business hours. What is the first thing that should be done? Choose the best answer.

   A. Notify the users that the server will be shut down so that they can close any files that may be open on the server.

B. Go to the server that is to be shut down and stop the Server Service.

C. Disconnect the network cable from the server so that it cannot be accessed.

D. Just turn off the server. Windows NT automatically saves and closes files before it shuts down.

11. Bill is planning to shut down his file and print server but wants to make sure that no one has files open. How can Bill check for open files?

A. Open User Manager for Domains to see who is logged onto the network.

B. Start Windows NT Diagnostics to see which resources are being used.

C. Open the Services dialog box to see who is using the Server Service.

D. Open Server Manager to see which files are open and who has them open.

12. Jane has inherited the role of network administrator and finds that a baseline has never been created on any of the five servers. Two of the servers are logon servers and the other three are file and print servers. What should she do?

A. Create a baseline for each of the five servers.

B. Because the hardware is the same on all servers, create a baseline on one of the logon servers and one of the file and print servers.

C. Because the hardware is the same on all servers, create a baseline on only one of the servers.

D. Because the network has been up and running for eight months, it is too late to create a baseline.

13. When Sean creates a baseline for his application server by using Performance Monitor, which view should he use?

A. Chart

B. Report

C. Log

D. Alert

The following scenario applies to questions 14 and 15.

Scenario: Alice has taken over as administrator of a small network. The network consists of 150 users with two domains that fully trust each other. Three file servers are in DomainA of which the Primary Domain Controller is one. In DomainB, the Primary Domain Controller is a print server, and an application server also exists. No baseline has been created for the domain controllers of either domain also exists.

Required Result: A baseline must be created for each of the domain controllers. *Optional Result 1:* A baseline must be created for the application server. *Optional Result 2:* A baseline must be created for the print server.

14. *Proposed Solution:* Alice uses Performance Monitor on each domain controller and file server each day, throughout the day, for two weeks. She uses the Log view so that a log file can be created and referenced at a later date. Ratings:

A. The required result is met, and both optional results are also met.

B. The required result and one optional result is met.

C. The required result is met, and neither optional result is met.

D. The required result is not met, and one optional result is met.

E. None of the results is met.

15. *Proposed Solution:* Alice uses Performance Monitor on each file server, print server, and application server each day, throughout the day, for two weeks. She uses the Log view so that a log file can be created and referenced at a later date. Ratings:

A. The required result is met, and both optional result are also met.

B. The required result and one optional result is met.

C. The required result is met, and neither optional result is met.

D. The required result is not met, and one optional result is met.

E. None of the results is met.

5.2.1 Answers and Explanations: Exercise

To establish a baseline for any network, it is important to take a sampling of data for all parts of the day. The peak periods for the logon servers will be shortly after the working day starts, lunch time, and again at the end of the day. For the file and print server, peak times could be spread throughout the day depending on a number of factors. Because the office is only operational during the day, sample data for evening or night is not necessary, except maybe to compare with a non-loaded network.

5.2.2 Answers and Explanations: Exercise

First review the baseline to see which objects were selected when it was created. Collect data into a log file with the same objects selected, being sure to run the log at the same times of day with the same polling interval. Take the log files and compare them with the baseline and use whatever application you want to draw your conclusions.

5.2 Answers and Explanations: Practice Problems

1. **D** Performance Monitor can capture data for all aspects of the computer performance.

2. **B** Response Probe is available on the Resource Kit for Windows NT 4.

3. **C** A baseline is a collection of performance information to which all future measurements can be compared.

4. **A** One baseline should be created for each server, even if hardware and software seems to be "identical," because nothing is ever really "identical."

5. **A, B, C, D** Memory, Processor, Disk, and Network should all be included when creating a baseline.

6. **A, B, C, D** All components are important because any one of them could cause a computer to perform poorly.

7. **A** A baseline should be created when a server is first configured so that configuration changes can be evaluated for performance.

8. **C** The performance should be monitored at all times during the day to compare "load" to "no load" times.

9. **B** The baseline should be upgraded each time the configuration has been changed.

10. **A** Notify the users so that any files that are open can be saved and closed.

11. **D** Open Server Manager to view the users who have files open.

12. **A** Create a baseline for each of the servers.

13. **C** The Log view creates a file that can be referenced at a later date.

14. **B** Both domain controllers and the print server had a baseline created. The application server did not get a baseline created.

15. **A** Both domain controllers as well as both the print server and the application server had a baseline created.

5.2 Key Words

Baseline

Log

Subnet

5.3 Identifying and Resolving Performance Bottlenecks

Bottlenecks are the problem areas that need to be addressed to improve the performance of the system. Trends are useful for capacity planning and preparing for future needs.

Any spreadsheet or database application can be used to analyze the data collected.

A. Finding Memory Bottlenecks

The reason memory has the greatest impact on the system is that a shortage of memory causes the system to read and write from the disk more often. The RAM in Windows NT is broken down into two categories:

- **Nonpaged:** Data placed directly into a specific memory location that cannot be written to or retrieved from disk.

- **Paged:** Virtual memory, in which all applications believe they have a full range of memory addresses available.

The best indicator that memory is the bottleneck is when a sustained, high rate of hard page faults is present. Table 5.3.1 shows some of the memory counters to watch and the range that is acceptable.

Table 5.3.1 Page Fault Counters

Counter	Description
Pages/sec	This is the number of requests that had to access the disk because the requested pages were not available in RAM.
Available Bytes	This is the amount of available physical memory.
Committed Bytes	This is the amount of virtual memory allocated either to physical RAM for storage or to the pagefile.
Pool Nonpaged Bytes	This is the amount of RAM in the pool nonpaged memory area, where space is used by operating system components as they carry out their tasks.

B. Finding Processor Bottlenecks

The two most common problems when the processor is a bottleneck are CPU-bound applications and drivers and excessive interrupts generated by inadequate disk or network components. Table 5.3.2 shows the counters to watch and the type of values for which to look.

Table 5.3.2   Bottleneck Indicators

Counter	Description
Processor: %Processor Time	This is the amount of time the processor is busy. It is the %Privileged Time plus the %User Time. When the processor is consistently above 75%–80%, it has become a bottleneck.
Processor:% Privileged Time	This is the amount of time the processor spends performing operating system services. Like %Processor Time, this value should average below 75%.
Processor: %User Time	This is the amount of time the processor spends running user services such as desktop applications. Again, this value should average below 75%.
Processor: Interrupts/sec	This is the number of interrupts the processor is handling from applications and hardware devices.
System: Processor Queue Length	This is the number of requests the processor has in its queue. Each of these requests is a thread waiting to be processed. Normally, this value is at zero, but if the queue length is consistently two or greater, the queue has a problem.
Server Work Queues: Queue Length	This is the number of requests in the queue for a particular processor. Again, if the queue length is two or greater, the queue has a problem.

C.   Finding Disk Bottlenecks

Performance Monitor has counters for both the PhysicalDisk and LogicalDisk objects. The LogicalDisk monitors the logical partitions of physical drives that indicate when a service or application is making excessive requests. The PhysicalDisk is used to monitor the physical disk drive as a whole.

Remember to activate Performance Monitor disk counters before trying to monitor the disk drives. By default, the counters are not enabled and do not show activity when added in Performance Monitor.

Type **diskperf -y** at a command prompt to enable the counters on the local computer.

Type **diskperf -y \\servername** at a command prompt to enable the counters on a remote computer.

Type **diskperf -ye** at a command prompt to enable the counters on the local computer with a RAID implementation.

Type **diskperf -n** at a command prompt to disable the counters on the local computer.

Table 5.3.3 shows some of the counters to use and the values to watch for when monitoring the physical disk—logical disks also have similar counters.

Table 5.3.3   Disk Monitoring

Counter	Description
%Disk Time	This is the amount of time the disk is busy with reads and writes. An acceptable value is around 50%.
Disk Queue Length	This is the number of waiting disk I/O requests. If this value is consistently two or higher, upgrade the disk.
Avg. Disk Bytes/ Transfer	This is the average number of bytes transferred to or from the system during read and write operations.
Disk Bytes/ sec	This is the rate at which bytes are transferred to or from the disk during read and write operations.

D.   Finding Network Bottlenecks

Table 5.3.4 shows some counters to monitor and some values to watch for when a lot of activity from the network is at the server.

Table 5.3.4   Finding Bottlenecks

Counter	Description
Server: Bytes Total/sec	This is the number of bytes the server has sent and received over the network. If this value is low, try adding an adapter.
Server: Logon /sec	This is the number of logon attempts for local, across-the-network, and service-account authentication in the last second. Add domain controllers if the value is low.
Server: Logon Total	This is the number of logon attempts for local, across-the-network, and service-account authentication since the server was started.
Network Segment: % Network utilization	This is the percentage of bandwidth in use for the local network segment. This is used to monitor the effects of different network operations, such as account synchronization and logon validation. Limit the number of protocols used if this number is high.
Network Interface: Bytes Sent/sec	This is the number of bytes sent by using the selected adapter. Upgrade the network adapter if a problem exists.
Network Interface: Bytes Total/sec	This is the number of bytes sent and received by using the selected adapter. Upgrade the network adapter if a problem exists.

5

> To have the network segment available in Performance Monitor, the Network Monitor Agent service must first be installed.

5.3.1   Exercise: False Bottlenecks

This exercise illustrates how the poor performance of one resource can make another resource appear to be a bottleneck.

1. From a Command prompt enter **diskperf -y** on the server and reboot the system.

2. Open Performance Monitor on the server and select Physical Disk: Bytes Read/sec and Bytes Written/sec.

3. Go to a client system and try copying about 20 MB of data to the server and then about 20 MB from the server. Take note of the results in Performance Monitor.

4. Restore the memory in your server to its original amount prior to the Performance Monitor exercise by removing the /MAXMEM switch that was added in the previous exercise.

5. Carry out the procedure in step 3 again and compare the transfer rates. The rate should have improved.

5.3.2   Exercise: Memory as a Bottleneck

This exercise illustrates how memory can be a bottleneck for running applications and transferring files by comparing results with the Pages/sec and Page Faults/sec results from Exercise 5.1.1.

1. Recall the notes you made during the Performance Monitor exercise. In that exercise you reduced the amount of memory that was available to your server and started some applications.

2. Start Performance Monitor.

3. Click Add to Chart to open the dialog box.

4. Add the counters of Pages/sec and Page Faults/sec for the Memory object.

5. Open the Chart Options dialog box and change the time interval to one second.

6. Open Disk Administrator, and then open Server Manager.

7. Return to Performance Monitor and view the results.

5.3 Practice Problems

1. What is a bottleneck? Choose the best answer.

    A. A slow network card

    B. A faulty memory simm

    C. A crashed disk drive

    D. A resource that restricts workflow

2. Jackie wants to check to see whether the disk drive in the server is a bottleneck. What should she do?

    A. Use Performance Monitor to compare byte transfer rates to the baseline.

    B. Use Task Manager to view the amount of memory that is being used.

    C. Use Windows NT Diagnostics to verify the size, speed, and type of disk drive that is installed.

    D. Open Disk Administrator to adjust the cluster size being used on the disk drive.

3. What is the meaning of Nonpaged RAM?

    A. Data that is placed on disk before it gets moved into physical memory.

    B. Data that is placed directly physical memory.

    C. Data that is stored to a text file prior to being moved into memory.

    D. Windows NT has no such thing as Nonpaged RAM.

4. What is the meaning of Paged RAM?

    A. Data that is placed on disk before it gets moved into physical memory.

    B. Data that is placed directly into physical memory.

    C. Data that is stored to a text file prior to being moved into memory.

    D. Windows NT has no such thing as Nonpaged RAM.

5. Chuck has been running some tests on one of his file and print servers and has come to the conclusion that the disk drives are the bottleneck. What is the best solution for Chuck's network?

    A. Add another disk to his server.

    B. Add a faster disk to his server.

    C. Redistribute the load across all the file and print servers.

    D. Reinstall Windows NT Server 4, making sure to choose the disk optimization option during installation.

6. John discovered that the processor was the bottleneck on his application server but found that when he added another processor to the system, the server's performance did not improve. What could be the problem?

    A. John forgot to activate the new processor in the System dialog box.

    B. The application is not written to be multithreaded.

    C. More memory has to be added to enable the new processor.

    D. Windows NT cannot work with multiple processors unless it is an OEM version.

7. Sharon found that the processor in her server was a bottleneck and upgraded to a faster one. Although the processor was rated much faster, the performance did not improve as expected. What other option did Sharon have?

    A. Install the latest Service Pack.

    B. Upgrade to Windows NT 4 b-release.

    C. Add a second processor instead of upgrading the existing processor.

    D. The application needs to be rewritten.

5

8. What two counters make up the %Processor Time?

   A. %Privileged Time

   B. Bytes Processed/sec

   C. %Free Time

   D. %User Time

9. When monitoring memory, to what does Available Bytes refer?

   A. The amount of space available in the pagefile that has not been committed to an application

   B. The amount of space available on the disk drive that has not been committed to the pagefile

   C. The amount of cache that has not been written back to the disk

   D. The amount of physical memory that has not been used

10. When monitoring memory, to what does Committed Bytes refer?

    A. The amount of physical memory being used

    B. The difference between the amount of physical memory and virtual memory

    C. The amount of virtual memory that has been allocated to either physical RAM for storage or to the pagefile

    D. The total amount of both physical and virtual memory that is being used

11. Silvia has been monitoring her application server for a few days and has found that the processor has exceeded 95% for %Processor Time quite frequently. What should she do to rectify the situation?

    A. Nothing.

    B. Stop the Server service to see if the %Processor Time is reduced.

    C. Have the application rewritten to make better use of the resources.

    D. Upgrade the processor.

12. To ensure that no one can see what applications are being run on the server, Sam has set up a screen saver. Whenever the screen saver comes on, however, people complain about poor server performance. What should Sam do?

    A. Change the screen resolution.

    B. Disable the screen saver.

    C. Turn the monitor off when not sitting at the server.

    D. Upgrade the processor.

13. What other counter, besides %Processor Time, indicates that the processor is not fast enough?

    A. %Free Time.

    B. System: Processor Queue Length.

    C. Processor: Bytes/sec.

    D. No other counters exist.

14. Which bottleneck makes the access time to a disk seem slow to a locally logged on user? Choose all that apply.

    A. Memory

    B. Processor

    C. Disk

    D. Network

15. You suspect your processor to be the bottleneck of your system. What two counters should you check?

    A. %DPC Time, %User Time

    B. %Processor Time, Avg. Disk Queue Length

    C. Interrupts/sec, Processor Queue Length

    D. Processor Queue Length, %Processor Time

16. A file server is being used by 65 users for storing files, as well as for installation source files. The server has 64 MB of RAM, a 9.2 GB fast SCSI drive, a 16-bit network card, and enabled shadow RAM. The users complain that access to the server is slow at different times of the day.

    Required Result: Determine whether memory is the bottleneck. *Optional Result 1:* Determine whether the disk is the bottleneck. *Optional Result 2:* Improve the performance of the server.

    Proposed Solution: Run Performance Monitor at different times throughout the day for a number of days, watching the counters of %Processor Time, Page Faults/sec, and Processor Queue Length. Ratings:

    A. The required result is met, and both optional results are also met.

    B. The required result and one optional result is met.

    C. The required result is met, and neither optional result is met.

    D. The required result is not met, and one optional result is met.

    E. None of the results is met.

17. A file server is being used by 65 users for storing files, as well as for installation source files. The server has 64 MB of RAM, a 9.2 GB fast SCSI drive, a 16-bit network card, and enabled shadow RAM. The users complain that access to the server is slow at different times of the day.

    Required Result: Determine whether memory is the bottleneck. *Optional Result 1:* Determine whether the processor is the bottleneck. *Optional Result 2:* Improve the performance of the server.

    Proposed Solution: Run Performance Monitor at different times throughout the day for a number of days watching the counters of %Processor Time, Page

Faults/sec, and Processor Queue Length. Ratings:

    A. The required result is met, and both optional result are also met.

    B. The required result and one optional result is met.

    C. The required result is met, and neither optional result is met.

    D. The required result is not met, and one optional result is met.

    E. None of the results is met.

5.3.1 Answers and Explanations: Exercise

By looking only at the transfer rates, it appeared as though the disk drives were the bottleneck. When the memory was increased, however, the performance improved, indicating that memory was the bottleneck. For this reason, it is important to look at counters for all objects when analyzing a server.

5.3.2 Answers and Explanations: Exercise

By increasing the amount of memory, the number of page faults was reduced. As indicated, memory was the bottleneck; without ample memory, the virtual memory manager performs excessive page swapping.

5.3 Answers and Explanations: Practice Problems

1. **D** A bottleneck is a resource that restricts workflow.

2. **A** Use Performance Monitor to compare byte transfer rates to the baseline.

3. **B** Nonpaged RAM is data that is placed directly into physical memory without being written to or retrieved from disk.

4. **A** Paged Ram is data that has been written to or read from disk prior to being moved to physical memory.

5. **C** Redistribute the load across multiple file and print servers so that they have more equal usage.

6. **B** If the application is not written to be multithreaded, all requests must go through the one processor.

7. **C** If the application is written to be multithreaded, it is more beneficial to have multiple processors than to have one processor that is fast.

8. **A, D** %Privileged Time and %User Time together make up %Processor Time.

9. **D** Available Bytes refers to the amount of physical memory that is not being used.

10. **C** The amount of virtual memory that has been allocated to either physical RAM for storage or to the pagefile.

11. **A** It is normal for the %Processor Time to go over 95% on numerous occasions.

12. **B** Disable the screen saver. No one should be logged onto the server except for administrative tasks.

13. **B** System: Processor Queue Length indicates how many requests are waiting to be processed.

14. **A, B, C, D** All resources could have an affect on a locally logged on user.

15. **D** Processor Queue Length and %Processor Time should be checked.

16. **C** Monitoring Page Faults/sec can help determine whether memory is a bottleneck.

17. **B** Monitoring Page Faults/sec can help determine whether memory is a bottleneck and monitoring %Processor Time and Processor Queue Length can help determine whether the processor is a bottleneck.

5.3   Key Words

Bottleneck
Nonpaged Memory
Paged Memory

5.4   Analysis Using Network Monitor

Network Monitor is a tool that enables monitoring of the network traffic going in and out of the system running the monitor. A second format that comes with Systems Management Server permits traffic to be monitored anywhere on the network.

Windows NT 4 provides a number of network services that enable users to carry out specific requirements on their network. Table 5.4.1 lists some of the more commonly installed network components. Some are installed by default; others are not.

Table 5.4.1   Network Components

Component	Description
Computer Browser	Enables users to find or browse resources on the network without having to remember specific paths or the correct syntax
DHCP	The automatic distribution and administration of TCP/IP addresses and related parameters to DHCP clients
Directory Replicator	The automatic duplication of directories among Windows NT computers
Domain Name System (DNS)	The resolution of TCP/IP host names to IP addresses
Internet Explorer	An Internet browser that provides access to the World Wide Web (WWW) to view and download files
Netlogon	Service that performs user account logon validation and synchronization of user accounts in a domain
Server	Enables network clients to access shared resources
WINS	A centralized database that resolves NetBIOS names to TCP/IP addresses
Workstation	Provides network access to shared resources

A.   Traffic Analysis

To optimize or capacity plan your network, as with the optimization of a server, the administrator must know what traffic is currently being generated. Analysis involves determining what effect each Windows NT Server service has on the network. This is done with a network analyzer. You can optimize network traffic in two ways:

- Provide users with better response time by implementing network services that can increase network traffic.

- Provide users with more bandwidth on the network by reducing network traffic generated by services.

Each method is valid and deserves consideration, but a properly optimized network is going to strike a compromise between the two. *Capacity planning* is the method of analyzing the network as one or more factors are increased. As the network grows, different services are added.

1. Classifying Services

Classifying services enables an administrator to better predict the effects on a network as changes are made. Each of the Windows NT Server services can be classified with three simple questions:

- What kind of traffic does this service generate?
- How often is this traffic generated?
- What impact does this traffic have on the network?

Following are some basic guidelines for classifying services on the server:

1. Isolate a network segment. This helps to prevent other network traffic from skewing the results of monitoring.
2. Use Network Monitor or some third-party program to monitor the network traffic.
3. Capture the appropriate traffic by initiating the service to be classified.
4. Identify each captured frame to ensure that all the traffic is generated by the service and not by some other function.

2. Frame Types

Frames are divided into three types: broadcast, multicast, and directed. Table 5.4.2 provides a description of each frame type.

Table 5.4.2   Frame Types

Frame Type	Description
Broadcast	Broadcasts are sent with the destination of FFFFFFFFFFFF. No host can be configured with this address, but all hosts on the network (subnet) accept this frame and process it. The frame is passed up the stack until it is determined whether the frame is meant for that computer or not.
Multicast	Multicasts are sent to a portion of the computers on the network. Like broadcast frames, multicast frames are not sent to a specific Media Access Control (MAC) address, but to a select few addresses on the network. Each host on the network must register its multicast address to become a member of a multicast set. NetBEUI and some TCP/IP applications utilize multicasting.
Directed	Directed frames are the most common type of frame. Each of these frames has a specific address for a host on the network. All other hosts disregard this frame because it does not contain the host's MAC address.

3. Contents of a Frame

All frames are broken down into different pieces, or fields, that can be analyzed. Some contain addressing information, others contain data, and so on. By analyzing the addressing portion of the frame, you can determine whether the frame was a broadcast type. This helps administrators determine which service created the frame and whether it can be optimized.

4. Network Protocols and Frames

The type of network traffic generated often depends on the protocol used to send the frames. As more companies want connectivity over WANs and more people want access to the Internet, TCP/IP has become the protocol of choice.

B. Installing Network Monitor

Network Monitor is a network packet analyzer that comes with Windows NT Server 4. The advantage of the version that comes with Systems Management Server is that any system can be monitored on the network.

1. Hardware

Network Monitor does not require special hardware other than a network adapter supported by the system on which it is installed; Windows NT 4 supports NDIS 4 and allows the viewing of local traffic only or full network traffic. In Windows NT 3.51, a special adapter (which is available with Microsoft Systems Management Server) was needed to support the promiscuous mode of Network Monitor.

2. Software

Network Monitor is made up of two components:

- **Network Monitor application:** Enables a system to capture and display network data, to display network statistics, and to save the captured data for future analysis

- **Network Monitor Agent:** Enables a computer to capture all network traffic and to send it over the network to the computer running the Network Monitor application

3. Network Monitor Window

The Capture Window is the default view of Network Monitor. (Table 5.4.3 describes each area of the Network Monitor window.)

Table 5.4.3   Network Monitor Window Areas

Window Area	Description
Graph	A horizontal bar chart that displays the current activity as a percentage of network utilization
Session Statistics	A summary of the transactions between two hosts and a display of which host initiated the broadcasts or multicasts
Total Statistics	Statistics for the traffic on the network as a whole, the frames captured, the per second statistics, and the network adapter statistics
Station Statistics	A summary of the number of frames and bytes sent and received, the number of frames initiated by a host, and the number of broadcasts and multicasts

C.   Capturing and Displaying Data

Capturing data by using Network Monitor is quite simple and can be initiated in one of three ways:

- Select Capture, Start from the menu bar.
- Click the Start Capture button in the toolbar.
- Press F10, the function key.

Stopping the capture of data is just as simple as starting it. It can been done in one of four ways:

- Select Capture, Stop from the menu bar.
- Click the Stop Capture button in the toolbar.
- Press F11, the function key.
- Click the Stop and View button in the toolbar.

To control the amount of data captured, the user can set a capture filter. A *filter* describes what type of data should be captured and displayed. The most common items to filter are either the protocol (NetBEUI, IPX, TCP/IP, and so on) or the destination or source address (MAC address, IP address, and so on).

Captured data can be displayed for analysis, or it can be saved to a capture file (*.CAP) for analysis later. After the data is captured, it needs to be analyzed. To analyze the data, it must be displayed. Displaying the data can be done in one of three ways:

- Select Capture, Display Captured Data from the menu bar.
- Click the Display Captured Data button in the toolbar.
- Press F12, the function key.

As with capturing data, filters can be applied while viewing the data. This enables the capture of numerous types of information, but it also permits the user to filter for frames of particular interest during analysis. The following three areas make up the display window for Network Monitor:

- **The Summary pane:** Shows a list of all the frames that were captured and information about each of them.
- **The Detail pane:** Shows protocol information for the frame selected in the Summary pane.
- **The Hexadecimal pane:** Displays the contents of the frame in hexadecimal format. The actual contents of data sent can be viewed in this area.

D.   Analyzing Data

As with any kind of monitoring and analysis, the analysis is the difficult part.

1.   Client Traffic

One of the first provisions to a user is the capability to log on to the network and to be validated by a server. Other considerations for the network administrator follow:

- When do people log on? Are they all logging on at 8 a.m. or randomly over an hour during the morning from 7:30 a.m. to 8:30 a.m.?

- Are all the users logging on from a local network computer, or are some users logging on from remote sites?

a.   Locate a Logon Server

The first action that must take place is finding the logon server. In a Windows NT network, that can be done in two ways, depending on what has been implemented:

- Send a broadcast message across the network to the NETLOGON mail slot (only located on domain controllers).

- Send a query to the WINS server for all registered domain controllers in the selected domain (appears as a domain [1C] entry in WINS). If found, send a request through directed frames.

b.   Logon Validation

After the requests have all been sent out, the client computer then accepts the first server response to that request. It does not matter whether the request was generated from a broadcast or from a directed message. Four factors are involved in validating the logon:

- The amount of traffic generated by establishing the session

- The amount of traffic generated if the client is at a Windows 95 computer

- The amount of traffic generated if the client is at a Windows NT computer

- The termination of the session

c.   File Session Traffic

Almost all communication between computers requires the establishment of a session before the communication actually takes place. DHCP, WINS, and DNS are a few of the communications in a Windows NT network that do not require an established session before communication starts. Establishing a session occurs in five steps:

1. Resolve the NetBIOS name (computer name) to an IP address.

2. Resolve the IP address to the MAC address (hardware address) of the computer.

3. Establish a TCP session.

4. Establish a NetBIOS session.

5. Negotiate the computer's SMB protocols.

2.   Client-to-Server Browser Traffic

Client-to-server traffic is the communication a client has with a server. Browser traffic is all the traffic generated during the browser process, both in announcing available resources and in retrieving lists of available resources. The entire process is as follows:

1. Servers (any computer with sharing enabled) are added to the browse list by announcing themselves to the master browser.

2. The master browser shares the list of servers with the backup browsers and the master browsers of other domains.

3. The client computer retrieves a list of backup browsers from the master browser.

4. The client retrieves a list of servers from a backup browser.

5. The client retrieves a list of shared resources from the server.

3. Server to Server Traffic

A large amount of traffic is generated between servers. The basics of server browsing are as follows:

1. At startup, the PDC assumes the role of domain master browser for its domain.

2. At startup, each BDC becomes either a backup browser or the master browser of its subnet, if no PDC is on the subnet.

3. Each master browser announces itself every 12 minutes to the master browsers of other domains on the local subnet.

4. Every 12 minutes, each domain master browser contacts the WINS server for a listing of all domains.

5. Every 12 minutes, each master browser contacts the domain master browser for an update of the browse list.

6. Each backup browser contacts its local master browser to retrieve an updated list every 15 minutes.

Along with the announcement traffic a server generates, it also can create additional traffic by taking part in other browser traffic.

- Browser elections take place if a client cannot find a master browser, if the master browser announces it is being shut down, or if a domain controller is being initialized.

- Master browsers in different domains share their browse lists to permit servers and resources to be accessed throughout the network.

- Backup browsers retrieve updated browse lists from their local master browser.

The three areas that Trust Relationships generate traffic are as follows:

- Creating the trust creates a lot of traffic (about 16,000 bytes), but it only takes place at the time the trust is created.

- Using trusted accounts creates traffic. When the administrator of the trusting domain assigns permissions to an account from the trusted domain, much traffic is generated.

- Pass-through authentication creates additional traffic.

5.4.1 Exercise: Browser Traffic

This exercise illustrates the amount of traffic that can be generated by browsing the network to find a resource.

1. Open the Network dialog box from the Control Panel and ensure that NetBEUI, IPX/SPX, and TCP/IP are all installed.

2. Open Explorer.

3. Open Network Monitor and start capturing traffic data.

4. Return to Explorer and click Network Neighborhood.

5. Double-click a domain or workgroup name.

6. Select one of the computers within the selection.

7. Return to Network Monitor and stop capturing.

8. Open the Details window in Network Monitor to see how much traffic was generated by browsing the network.

5.4.2 Exercise: Client to Server Traffic

This exercise illustrates the amount of network traffic generated by a client logging onto a domain.

1. Open Network Monitor on your Primary Domain Controller.

2. Start capturing data.

3. Log on to the domain from another computer (any computer that is a part of the domain).

4. After you are logged onto the network, log off again.

5. Switch to Network Monitor and stop capturing data.

6. Open the Details window to view the traffic generated by a user logging on and off of the network.

7. Close Network Monitor.

5

5.4   Practice Problems

1. Nancy is trying to verify that logon requests are reaching the server with the correct user name because a number of users are not getting validated. How can she verify that particular user names are being forwarded to the logon server?

   A. Have each user go to the server and logon locally.

   B. Have Nancy watch them enter their name and password to ensure that they are not making typos.

   C. Run Network Monitor on the logon server and check the Hexadecimal pane to see whether the names are getting to the server.

   D. It's not possible to verify that the information is reaching the server.

2. What are the areas of the Network Monitor window when it is capturing data?

   A. Network Statistics, Session Statistics, Counters

   B. Graph, Session Statistics, Total Statistics, Station Statistics

   C. Objects, Counters, Instances

   D. Sessions, Real Time, Transfer Statistics

3. What areas can be displayed while viewing the captured data in Network Monitor?

   A. Resource pane, Data pane

   B. Summary pane, Detail pane, Hexadecimal pane

   C. Report pane, Alert pane, Detail pane

   D. None of the above

4. What are the two versions of the Network Monitor?

   A. Real mode and Protected mode

   B. Local traffic only and full network traffic

   C. Promiscuous mode and Server mode

   D. LAN mode and WAN mode

5. A network has a large number of Windows 95 and Windows NT Workstation 4 systems. Select all that could help reduce network traffic.

   A. Reduce the number of protocols being used at the workstations and servers.

   B. Increase the number of network cards in the servers.

   C. Turn off file and print sharing on the desktop systems.

   D. Install SNMP.

6. Which of the following services helps to reduce network traffic?

   A. WINS

   B. DHCP

   C. Remote Access Service

   D. SNMP

7. A user says that he cannot connect to a resource displayed for a remote system in Explorer. Why would a resource be displayed if it is not available?

   A. The Browser service has been disabled.

   B. The WINS server is providing an old list of resources.

   C. The system is down or has removed the share, but the browse list has not been updated.

   D. Browsing was enabled before the browse list was updated.

8. Jack is administering a network that has three distinct groups. Approximately 200 users share the network, and most of them complain that network response time is slow. What can be done to increase performance?

   A. Subnet the network and put each of the groups onto its own subnet.

B. Move the pagefile to a different directory.

C. Remove file and print sharing from the workstations and have all access go through a server.

D. Add another network card to the server.

9. How can logon validation be speeded up over a slow link?

A. Add another WINS server.

B. Install a Proxy server.

C. Add more resource domains.

D. Put a Backup Domain Controller at each of the remote sites.

10. Why is TCP/IP the default protocol for Windows NT?

A. TCP/IP was designed for use on LANs and WANs.

B. It reduces the number of bytes sent across the network.

C. TCP/IP is the fastest protocol.

D. It is the simplest to set up.

5.4.1 Answers and Explanations: Exercise

You can see that a great deal of traffic is generated just to find out what resources are available on the network. First, broadcasts are sent to discover which computer is the master browser. From the master browser, the client receives a list of backup browsers. The client must then find the addresses of the servers on the network so that it can "talk" to them. Finally, the selected server must provide the client with a list of the available resources.

5.4.2 Answers and Explanations: Exercise

You can see the traffic generated by a client logging onto the domain. First, the client computer broadcasts to find an available domain controller. Then it sends the logon

request to the server for validation. At this time, it checks the username and password in the SAM to determine whether it is a valid name and then to see what group memberships exist. After all this information is gathered, a token is generated and passed back to the client. When the client logs back off again, similar traffic is generated to inform the domain controller that the user is no longer active on the network.

5.4 Answers and Explanations: Practice Problems

1. **C** Run Network Monitor at the logon server and view the Hexadecimal pane to see whether the names are getting to the server correctly.

2. **B** Graph, Session Statistics, Total Statistics, Station Statistics.

3. **B** Summary pane, Detail pane, Hexadecimal pane.

4. **B** Local traffic only and full network traffic.

5. **A, C** Reduce the protocols being used and disable file and print sharing from the workstations.

6. **A** WINS helps to reduce network traffic.

7. **C** The browse list has not been updated as of yet.

8. **A, C, D** Subnet the network, remove all sharing and have all access go through the server, and add an additional network card(s) to the server.

9. **D** Put a Backup Domain Controller at each remote location.

10. **A** TCP/IP was designed for use on LANs and WANs.

5.4 Key Words

Promiscuous

Global group

Local group

5.5   Performance Optimization

The most common and now the least expensive method of optimizing memory is to add more physical memory (RAM). Adding more memory to a server, whatever function that server serves, helps performance.

A.   Processor Optimization

When the processor becomes a bottleneck, you have two options depending on the situation:

- Upgrade the processor.
- Add a processor(s).

If the server hardware is not capable of handling additional processors, then the processor can be upgraded to a faster, more robust one.

If the server is capable of handling multiple processors, then the decision has to be made depending on what type of server it is and what kind of requests it is handling. In the case of an application server where the application is written to be multithreaded, multiple processors may be the best choice. In the case of a server that is controlling a single printer and files, for example, it might be more realistic to just upgrade the processor.

B.   Disk Optimization

If the disk is the bottleneck, you have a number of possible solutions:

- Offload some of the processes to another system.
- Add a faster controller or an on-board caching controller.
- Add more memory to permit more caching by Windows NT.
- Add more disk drives in a RAID environment. This spreads the data across multiple physical disks and improves performance.

C.   Network Optimization

If the network is found to be the bottleneck, a number of things can be done:

- On the server, add an adapter, upgrade to a better adapter, or upgrade to better routers/bridges.
- Add more servers to the network to distribute the load.
- Segment the network to isolate traffic to appropriate segments.

1. Optimizing Logon Traffic

To have the optimum response time for logon validation, the proper number and configuration of domain controllers must be set up. This creates four things to consider when optimizing the logon validation:

- Determine the hardware required for better performance.
- Configure the domain controllers to increase the number of logon validations.
- Determine the number of domain controllers needed.
- Determine the best location for each of the domain controllers.

2. Optimizing File Session Traffic

Although file session traffic is minimal when compared to the amount of traffic generated during the transfer of a file, a few things can still be done to reduce traffic.

- Remove excess protocols, or at least disable them for functions or services where they are not needed. To change the binding configurations, open the Network applet in Control Panel and select the Bindings tab.
- Try to make sure the servers are in a location close to the people that use them most, especially if they can be kept on the same subnet.

3. Optimizing Browser Traffic

Browsing is provided to enable efficient use of network resources by a typical end user. By making it easy for users to access resources on the network, the efficiency of the network has been sacrificed due to the increase in network traffic.

A few things can be done to help reduce the network traffic generated by browsing:

- Disable the Server component on all computers that do not need to share resources.
- Configure which systems can be browsers.
- Reduce the number of protocols used.
- Create internal web sites.
- Limit the size of the intranet web pages.
- Increase the cache at the client computers.

4. Optimize Server Browser

Most of the traffic generated by browsing takes place automatically and at intervals that cannot be configured. However, server browser traffic can be reduced in three ways:

- Reduce the number of protocols.
- Reduce the number of entries in the list.
- Increase the amount of time between browser updates.

5. Optimize Trust Relationship Traffic

Normally, trust relationships do not create a lot of network traffic. However, traffic from a trust relationship can be reduced in two ways:

- Create fewer trust relationships.
- Assign global groups from the trusted domain to local groups and then assign permissions to the local group.

5.5.1   Exercise: Virtual Memory Optimization

This exercise illustrates the performance degradation when virtual memory is minimal.

1. Right-click My Computer on the Desktop and select Properties.
2. Select the Performance tab and then select Virtual Memory.
3. Change the pagefile size to be the minimum size of 2 MB and select Set.
4. Close the dialog boxes and select Yes to restart the system.
5. Open Explorer, Disk Manager, Performance Monitor, and Network Monitor.
6. Return to Explorer and copy 20 MB of data to another computer.
7. Take note of how long it takes to copy the data.
8. Change the pagefile size to what it was originally.
9. Delete the files that were copied to the other computer.
10. Ensure that Explorer, Disk Manager, Performance Monitor, and Network Monitor are all open.
11. Transfer the same files to the other computer again and take note of how long it takes.

5.5.2   Exercise: Broadcast Traffic

This exercise illustrates the amount of traffic generated by broadcasts with multiple protocols installed.

1. Ensure that NetBEUI, IPX/SPX, and TCP/IP protocols are installed.
2. Open Network Monitor and start capturing data.
3. Select Start, Run.
4. Enter **net view** and select OK. Net view may be run from a command prompt if you want to see the results of the command.

5. Return to Network Monitor after you have received the results of the `net view` command.

6. Stop capturing data and open the Details window.

7. Notice the number of broadcasts that were generated by all three protocols.

8. Open the Network dialog box and remove the NetBEUI and IPX/SPX protocols.

9. Repeat steps 2 through 7.

10. Close Network Monitor.

5

5.5   Practice Problems

1. Jane wants to optimize the network components on her server. What should she do?

    A. Remove unused adapter cards and protocols.

    B. Disable the Server service.

    C. Make sure that TCP/IP, IPX/SPX, and NetBEUI are all installed to create the maximum number of network paths possible.

    D. Nothing needs to be done because Windows NT is self-optimizing.

2. Which of the following items can make the system use virtual memory more efficiently? Choose all that apply.

    A. Move the pagefile to the partition where the Windows NT system files are located.

    B. Move the pagefile from the partition where the Windows NT system files are located.

    C. Spread the pagefile over multiple drives.

    D. Set the minimum pagefile size to that which it reaches during peak system load.

3. Optimum performance in Windows NT 4 depends on which two components?

    A. Pagefile location

    B. Software

    C. Hardware

    D. Processor type (RISC, Intel, MIPS, and so on)

4. What is the definition of optimal performance?

    A. To make threads process at a greater speed

    B. To make processors work at a higher percentage capacity

    C. To have the maximum number of services running possible

    D. To get the best performance result with the available hardware and software

5. Although the Backup Domain Controller is used to validate logons, what other functions does it perform if it is also a file and print server?

    A. Account database updates from the Primary Domain Controller

    B. Service resource requests from users

    C. Act as Master Browser in the domain

    D. Directory replication updates

6. What are the advantages of using a stripe set? Select all that apply.

    A. They are more efficient for I/O management.

    B. Stripe sets are not advantageous.

    C. Less overhead is required.

    D. Simultaneous writes may be accomplished if multiple controllers exist.

7. How many disk drives are needed to implement a stripe set with parity?

    A. 2

    B. 3

    C. 8

    D. 32

8. What can be done with device drivers to optimize Windows NT?

    A. You don't need to do anything because Windows NT is self-tuning.

    B. Remove unneeded drivers.

    C. Create separate hardware drivers that use only specific drivers.

    D. Pause all unnecessary devices in the Network dialog box from the Control Panel.

9. Which of the following components are automatically optimized by Windows NT?

   A. Pagefile

   B. Mouse

   C. Disk cache

   D. Bindings

10. To optimize your network cards, what should you consider? Choose all that apply.

    A. Never use NetBEUI.

    B. Always use NetBEUI.

    C. Use a card with the widest available bus.

    D. Split your network into multiple subnets, with each subnet attaching to a separate network card in the server.

11. Why is hardware fault tolerance considered to be better than software fault tolerance?

    A. Hardware fault tolerance does not work with the HAL of Windows NT.

    B. Windows NT's version of fault tolerance only works with NTFS.

    C. Software fault tolerance works only with FAT.

    D. Hardware fault tolerance removes the parity calculation from the processor.

12. When tuning a file server for optimum performance, what question must you first ask?

    A. For what type of tasks is the file server going to be used?

    B. How large is the budget for upgrading hardware?

    C. For what type of business is this unit being used? Companies that do business for the government or military, have a restriction on tuning.

    D. Is the fastest hardware installed?

13. When choosing disk drives for a server, what should be considered? Choose all that apply.

    A. Use the FAT file system.

    B. Use the fastest drives.

    C. Use stripe sets with parity when possible.

    D. Use SCSI over IDE.

14. A user tells you that his Windows NT 4 Workstation system is running slowly. Which is the best way you can monitor the performance of the system?

    A. Connect to the administrative share C$, and then run Performance Monitor.

    B. Go to the workstation and run Performance Monitor.

    C. You cannot monitor a Windows NT 4 Workstation system.

    D. Use Performance Monitor to connect to the workstation and monitor it across the network.

15. Where is the best place to modify the virtual memory settings in Windows NT 4?

    A. Through the Registry

    B. Through Control Panel, Services, Virtual Memory

    C. Through Control Panel, System, Virtual Memory

    D. Through WinMSD

16. The Server Service Properties dialog box has a number of options, of which

Balance is one. When would the Balance option be selected?

  A. When the number of users is between 10 and 64

  B. When the number of users is 10 or less

  C. When the number of users is greater than 64

  D. When setting up an application server or when a domain has only the Primary Domain Controller

17. The Server Service Properties dialog box offers a number of options, of which Minimize is one. When would the Minimize option be selected?

  A. When the number of users is between 10 and 64

  B. When the number of users is 10 or less

  C. When the number of users is greater than 64

  D. When setting up an application server or when a domain has only the Primary Domain Controller

18. Jane has been monitoring the Total Bytes/sec on each of the servers on her network. When she adds up the total, she finds that it is nearly as much as the maximum capacity for her network. What should she do to improve general network performance?

  A. Upgrade her NIC drivers.

  B. Subnet her network.

  C. Upgrade the network cards.

  D. Increase the amount of memory on each server.

19. The Server Service Properties dialog box offers a number of options, of which Maximize Throughput for Network Applications is one. When would the Maximize Throughput for Network Applications option be selected?

  A. When the number of users is between 10 and 64.

  B. When the number of users is 10 or less.

  C. When the number of users is greater than 64.

  D. When setting up an application server or when a domain has only the domain controller.

20. What may occur on the network if the Server service becomes a bottleneck on a server? Choose all that apply.

  A. Response times become longer.

  B. Client requests are denied.

  C. Logon requests may be denied.

  D. Database synchronization may not occur between domain controllers.

21. What is the most common hardware upgrade that generally provides the greatest performance increase?

  A. Install a faster processor.

  B. Install a faster disk controller.

  C. Install more memory.

  D. Install a faster network card.

22. Fred's network has a number of machines that are using different protocols (NetBEUI and IPX/SPX) because of specific needs. The server is also used to access different web sites to download the drivers. What can Fred do to improve performance?

  A. Remove all except one protocol from all systems.

  B. Unbind TCP/IP from the Workstation service and unbind NetBEUI and IPX/SPX from the Server service.

C. Unbind NetBEUI and IPX/SPX from the Workstation service and unbind TCP/IP from the Server service.

D. Bindings can be rearranged, but they cannot be disabled.

23. The Server Service Properties dialog box offers a number of options, of which Maximize Throughput for File Sharing is one. When would the Maximize Throughput for File Sharing option be selected?

A. When the number of users is between 10 and 64

B. When the number of users is 10 or less

C. When the number of users is greater than 64

D. When setting up an application server or when a domain has only the domain controller

24. What is one reason why the NetBEUI protocol causes the most broadcast messages on a network?

A. NetBEUI does not cache broadcast results.

B. NetBEUI cannot perform directed messaging.

C. NetBEUI cannot use multicasts.

D. NetBEUI does not use broadcasts.

25. Joe has decided that the amount of traffic on his network has become too great, so he is going to split it into three subnets with his NT Server as the router. This enables each user to have the server available on his subnet. Since this implementation, the network performance has not changed or has become worse. What could be the problem?

A. Windows NT Server cannot act as router.

B. Because of the subnetting, additional cable had to be added, which caused resistance problems.

C. The system that is acting as a router doesn't have enough memory.

D. The server was configured to forward broadcast messages, so traffic was not reduced.

26. Albert has organized his subnets so that the people who need access to certain servers are on the same subnet, but network traffic is still bad. What could be the problem with Albert's network?

A. The network cards must have specific IP addresses for optimum performance.

B. The disk controllers on the servers all need to be synchronized.

C. The server that is acting as the router is configured to forward broadcast packages.

D. WINS is only enabled on one subnet.

27. While monitoring the Disk Queue length, it is determined that the disk is the bottleneck. What could be done to improve this? Choose all that apply.

A. Implement RAID.

B. Use asynchronous disk drives.

C. Add more memory.

D. Use a faster disk interface.

28. While monitoring the Disk Queue Length, John was trying to remember which value indicated that the disk was a bottleneck. Which number indicates that the disk is a bottleneck?

A. A value of less than 2

B. A value of greater than 2

C. A value of less than 4

D. A value of greater than 4

5

5.5.1 Answers and Explanations: Exercise

This exercise illustrates that not only physical memory but also virtual memory is important to the operation of Windows NT 4. The operation of Windows NT 4 was definitely hampered by the lack of ample virtual memory.

5.5.2 Answers and Explanations: Exercise

This exercise illustrates that having more protocols can cause unnecessary traffic on the network. By removing protocols or stripping unnecessary bindings, network traffic can be reduced.

5.5 Answers and Explanations: Practice Problems

1. **A** Always remove unused hardware and software when trying to optimize a server.

2. **B, C, D** Spread the pagefile across multiple drives. Move the pagefile from the boot partition. Set the minimum pagefile size to the size it needs to be during peak load.

3. **B, C** Performance depends on both hardware and software because the hardware can restrict performance, and if the software is written to use the full potential of the hardware, it becomes a bottleneck (16-bit as opposed to 32-bit applications).

4. **D** To get the best performance possible by using the available hardware and software.

5. **A, B, D** Backup Domain Controllers receive database updates from the Primary Domain Controller. A file and print server responds to requests for access to files. Most Backup Domain Controllers participate in Directory Replication.

6. **D** If more than one controller is installed, disks may be written to simultaneously.

7. **B** Three drives are needed to implement a fault-tolerant stripe set.

8. **B** Remove unneeded drivers.

9. **A, C** The pagefile and Disk cache are automatically optimized by Windows NT.

10. **C, D** Use a card with the largest possible bus. Subnet the network to reduce the amount of traffic on each subnet.

11. **D** Hardware fault tolerance removes the parity calculation from the processor.

12. **A** You must ask what type of tasks the server is expected to perform.

13. **B, C, D** Use the fastest drives. Use stripe sets with parity. Use SCSI instead of IDE. The use of faster drives and SCSI improves disk access time and the use of stripe sets with parity adds fault tolerance.

14. **D** Systems may be monitored from across the network.

15. **C** The settings are in Control Panel, System, Performance tab.

16. **A** Balance is chosen when the number of users is between 10 and 64.

17. **B** Minimize is selected when the number of users is 10 or less.

18. **B** Subnet the network to decrease the amount of traffic on each segment.

19. **D** Maximize Throughput for Network Applications is chosen when setting up an application server or when a domain has only one domain controller.

20. **A, B, C** The Server service is set to start automatically on all servers to share resources.

21. **C** Install more memory.

22. **C** The Server must act as a Workstation on the Internet and act as a Server to the local network.

23. **C** Maximize Throughput for File Sharing is chosen when the number of users is greater than 64.

24. **A** NetBEUI does not cache the results of broadcast messages.

25. **D** If the client computers are all creating their own shares and they are accessing each other's resources across the three, traffic is slowed by having to go through the router.

26. **C** If broadcast packages are being forwarded across the router, then the purpose of subnetting has been defeated.

27. **A, B, D** RAID helps reduce degradation; asynchronous drives boost performance; and faster controllers reduce disk access time.

28. **B** If the Disk Queue Length becomes greater than 2, the disk is a bottleneck.

5.5 Key Words

Trust

Optimize

Practice Exam: Monitoring and Optimization

Use this practice exam to test your mastery of "Monitoring and Optimization." The passing Microsoft score is 76.4 percent.

1. Which of the following protocols utilize broadcast messages? Choose all that apply.

    A. NetBEUI

    B. IPX/SPX

    C. TCP/IP

    D. None of the above

2. What type of counter should an Alert be assigned to? Choose all that apply.

    A. Low disk space

    B. Byte transfer rate over 80%

    C. %Processor time over 80%

    D. High number of page faults

3. What Registry settings should be monitored and modified on a regular basis to optimize the server?

    A. Nothing. Windows NT Server 4 is self-tuning.

    B. DiskRotationSpeed

    C. FileTransferRate

    D. NetworkBindings

4. What is a workload unit when referring to Performance Monitor?

    A. Workload units are the counters that are added in Performance Monitor to monitor the server.

    B. A workload unit is any service that is installed and running on the server.

    C. A workload unit is a list of requests made on a server.

    D. No such thing as a workload unit exists when referring to Performance Monitor.

5. Which resource seems to have the greatest impact on a file and print server? Choose the best answer.

    A. Processor

    B. Disk

    C. Network

    D. Memory

6. Which resource seems to have the greatest impact on an application server? Choose the best answer.

    A. Processor

    B. Disk

    C. Network

    D. Memory

7. Which resource seems to have the greatest impact on a domain controller (logon server)? Choose the best answer.

    A. Processor

    B. Disk

    C. Network

    D. Memory

8. Sara has a server that is both a file and print server and a domain controller. The server doesn't seem to be performing as well as it should. What is the best way to monitor the system to get the most accurate results? Choose all that apply.

    A. Use Performance Monitor on another system to gather data from the server.

    B. Monitor all possible counters from the server at the same time.

    C. Stop certain services to isolate the resource usage by the different server roles.

    D. Monitor the power supply to ensure that it is supplying the proper voltage.

9. Performance Monitor has a counter named Memory: Pages/sec. What does this counter indicate?

    A. The number of pages that can be swapped in one second from RAM to pagefile.sys by the Virtual Memory Manager

    B. The general activity of the pages being swapped

    C. The number of pages that can be swapped in one nanosecond from RAM to PAGEFILE.SYS by the virtual memory manager

    D. The number of RAM pages that can be read in one second

10. Which Performance Monitor object and counter measures the amount of time that the CPU is busy?

    A. System: TotalProcessorUsage

    B. System: % Total Processor Time

    C. Processor: % Processor Time

    D. Processor: % Busy Time

11. What answer best explains what the System:Processor Queue Length counter's purpose in Performance Monitor?

    A. A measure of the amount of activity at the CPU

    B. The total CPU usage across the entire network for all CPUs

    C. The number of threads waiting for a response to their request for CPU time

    D. The number of users waiting for a response to their request for CPU time

12. Cathy is just learning how to use Performance Monitor and wants to know whether and how she can be notified when the server is becoming low on disk space. Can it be done, and if so, how would she set it up?

    A. It cannot be done with Performance Monitor.

    B. When a counter is added while in the Alert view, threshold values can be set and computer or user names may be specified to receive the alert.

    C. When a counter is added while in the Report view, threshold values can be set, and computer or user names may be specified to receive the report.

    D. The Chart view automatically notifies all Administrators on the network.

13. Janice wants to analyze the data generated from Performance Monitor with a database program. What view does she have to use to generate the proper information?

    A. Chart

    B. Report

    C. Log

    D. Alert

14. Alice is creating a baseline for network traffic on her logon server using the Log view in Performance Monitor. What must she do to view the data as it is being recorded?

    A. Open a second instance of Performance Monitor and select the Chart view.

B. Start Performance Monitor on another server on the network to monitor the logon server.

C. Nothing has to be done because the Log view enables you to view the data as it is being recorded.

D. The Log view is not the correct view for creating a baseline.

15. To which hardware items do changes make a difference to performance? Choose all that apply.

A. Memory

B. Keyboard

C. Disk Controller

D. Video Resolution

16. What is the name of the virtual memory file that is used in Windows NT 4?

A. SWAPFILE.386

B. PAGEFILE.386

C. SWAPFILE.SYS

D. PAGEFILE.SYS

17. Alice has taken over as administrator of a small network. It consists of 150 users with two domains that fully trust each other. There are three file servers in DomainA of which the Primary Domain Controller is one. In DomainB, the Primary Domain Controller is a print server and there is also an application server. No baseline has been created for the domain controllers of either domain.

Required Result: A baseline must be created for each of the domain controllers. *Optional Result 1*: A baseline must be created for the application server. *Optional Result 2:* A baseline must be created for the print server.

Proposed Solution: Alice uses Performance Monitor on each of the file servers and the application server each day, throughout the day, for two weeks. She uses the Log view so that a log file can be created and referenced at a later date. Ratings:

A. The required result is met, and both optional results are also met.

B. The required result and one optional result is met.

C. The required result is met, and neither optional result is met.

D. The required result is not met, and one optional result is met.

E. No result is met.

18. A file server is being used by 65 users for storing files, as well as for installation source files. The server has 64 MB of RAM, a 9.2 GB fast SCSI drive, a 16-bit network card, and shadow RAM is enabled. The users complain that access to the server is slow at different times of the day.

Required Result: Determine whether memory is the bottleneck. *Optional Result 1:* Determine if the disk is the bottleneck. *Optional Result 2:* Improve the performance of the server.

Proposed Solution: Run Performance Monitor at different times throughout the day for a number of days, watching the counters of %Processor Time, and Processor Queue Length. Off-load the application source files onto a different server. Ratings:

A. The required result is met, and both optional results are also met.

B. The required result and one optional result is met.

C. The required result is met, and neither optional result is met.

D. The required result is not met, and one optional result is met.

E. No result is met.

19. How should users and groups be arranged when assigning permissions across domain trusts?

A. Assign the users to local groups, and then assign the local groups to global groups in the appropriate domain.

B. Create a global group in the resource domain and add the users from the account domain to the global group. Assign the global group to the local group and then assign the permissions to the local group.

5

C. Users from an account domain do not have access to resources in a resource domain.

D. Assign users to a global group in their domain and add that global group to a local group in the resource domain. Assign permissions to the local group.

20. A server has two hard drives and one partition for each drive. What can be done to make the pagefile more efficient?

A. Keep a pagefile in the default location that is a little more than the size of the physical memory, and place a large pagefile on the other partition.

B. Remove the pagefile from the default location and place the pagefile on the other partition.

C. Move the pagefile to a different directory on the same partition.

D. Remove the pagefile because it is not needed as long as there is 32 MB or more of RAM.

Answers and Explanations: Practice Exam

1. **A, B, C**   All three protocols utilize broadcast messages. The difference is how they implement broadcasts.

2. **A, C, D**   These three items are something with which any network administrator would be concerned.

3. **A**   For the most part, Windows NT 4 is self-tuning; therefore, the administrator should not have to make many changes to the Registry.

4. **B**   A workload unit is any service that is installed and running on the server.

5. **D**   Memory seems to have the greatest impact on a file and print server because of the amount of caching used while files are being written and read from the disk.

6. **A**   Because the application is being run on the server for multiple users, the processor plays a large role in an application server.

7. **C**   During logon, very little processor time or memory is needed; therefore, the speed at which the requests are transferred has the greatest impact.

8. **A, C**   Monitoring from a different system does not skew readings on the server, except for the network counters. By stopping different services, the resource usage can be isolated.

9. **B**   The Memory: Pages/sec indicates the general activity of the pages being swapped.

10. **B, C**   Both System: % Total Processor Time and Processor : % Processor Time are valid answers. If only one processor exists, these readings are the same. If multiple processors exist, then the System counter provides an average of all the processors.

11. **C**   The number of threads waiting for CPU time.

12. **B**   When a counter is added in the Alert view, a threshold value may be entered and a computer or user name may be entered that receives the alert.

13. **C**   The log view creates a file that may be used in other applications.

14. **A**   Open a second instance on the server that is to be monitored. If you monitored the server from another machine, additional network traffic would be generated.

15. **A, C**   Changes to memory and the disk controller can alter the performance of a server.

16. **D**   PAGEFILE.SYS is the name of the virtual memory file in Windows NT 4.

17. **D**   The application server had a baseline created. Neither of the other results was achieved.

18. **D**   The processor is the only resource being monitored and by off-loading the application source files, more resources should be available for performing as a file server.

19. **D**   Assign users to a global group in their domain and add that global group to a local group in the resource domain. Assign permissions to the local group.

20. **A**   Leave a pagefile in its original location (boot partition) that is the same as the physical memory and place a larger pagefile on another physical disk.

CHAPTER 6

Troubleshooting

This chapter covers the following Microsoft exam objectives:

- Installation failures

- Boot failures

- Configuration failures (including backing up and editing the Registry)

- Printer problems

- RAS problems

- Connectivity problems

- Resource access and permission problems

- Fault-tolerance failures: mirroring, striping with parity, and tape backup

- Advanced problem resolution, including diagnosing and interpreting a blue screen, configuring a memory dump, and using the event log service

6.1 Solving Installation Failures

This section discusses choosing the appropriate course of action to solve installation failures. These failures occur for two basic reasons: hardware-related problems and configuration-related problems. This section also discusses some of the methods available for automating the installation process.

A. Hardware-Related Problems

Windows NT supports a wide variety of hardware. As such, a variety of problems can occur with these hardware devices. Windows NT has very specific minimum hardware requirements, as you can see in the following list:

- **CPU:** For Intel-based systems, any 486 or higher processor is sufficient. For RISC-based systems, any supported RISC processor (MIPS 4×00, Alpha, PreP-compliant PPC) is sufficient.

- **Video adapter:** A VGA or better is required.

- **Hard disk drive:** A minimum of 110 MB of free space is required.

- **Floppy disk drive:** A 3.5 or 5.25 floppy drive for Intel systems (used for setup boot disks) is required.

- **CD-ROM drive:** A supported CD-ROM drive is necessary. It can be located on the system on which NT Server is being installed or on another computer connected by a network.

- **Memory:** At least 16 MB is recommended for Intel- or RISC-based systems (although 12 MB is sufficient for installation of NT Workstation on an Intel platform). The price of memory has decreased dramatically and it significantly improves system performance. Therefore, a larger quantity is advisable (32 MB being a reasonable minimum).

- **Network adapter:** Although a network adapter is not absolutely necessary, networking is not available unless a network adapter is installed.

- **Pointing device:** A mouse or other pointing device is not absolutely necessary, but it is highly recommended.

In addition to the minimum hardware requirements, it is essential to consider the Windows NT Hardware Compatibility List (HCL). If your system and all its installed components are on the HCL, many potential difficulties can be avoided. Before installing Windows NT, make a list of all the components on your system and the resources they use. Having this information available can greatly simplify the installation process.

> If you are unsure whether your computer's hardware is on the Windows NT HCL, you can use the Hardware Quantifier tool. This tool itemizes and identifies all hardware on your system necessary for Windows NT. The program runs from a floppy disk created by running the MAKEDISK.BAT batch file in the \SUPPORT\HQTOOL directory on the Windows NT Server CD-ROM.

---

1. Hard Disk Errors and Unsupported Hardware Errors

Installation failure most commonly occurs due to media errors or hardware problems, including hard disk errors. Problems also can arise from unsupported CD-ROMs and network adapters. Boot sector viruses affect the master boot record and can cause problems with Windows NT. Therefore, you might want to scan each of your hard drives for viruses.

The actual boot error you receive when a boot sector virus is encountered during installation is reported as 0×4,0,0,0. This error message occurs after the first reboot during an installation. To fix this error, you can boot with a write-protected disk with anti-virus software loaded. Another method is to run the command fdisk /mbr after booting into DOS. This command rewrites the master boot record for the hard disk.

If you are using small computer system interface (SCSI) drives, make sure your SCSI chain is properly terminated. The BIOS on the boot SCSI adapter should be enabled, and the BIOS on all other SCSI adapters should be disabled. All SCSI devices should have unique SCSI IDs.

For enhanced integrated drive electronics (EIDE) drives, make sure the system drive is on the first controller on the motherboard. In addition, the file I/O and disk access should be set to standard.

For IDE/EIDE or EDSI drives, the controller should be functional before installing Windows NT. If the disk lights come on briefly upon starting the computer, you know the controller is working. You also will hear the disk start up. If drives are larger than 1024 cylinders, make sure Windows NT supports the disk configuration utility you are using. Finally, the jumpers should be set correctly for master or slave drives.

Even if Windows NT does not support your CD-ROM drive, it still is possible to perform the installation. Assuming you have DOS or Windows 95 drivers for your CD-ROM, you can copy the \i386 directory from the CD-ROM to the local hard disk. You then can run the command winnt_ /b from the newly created directory. The /b parameter installs the Windows NT boot files to the local hard disk in the directory c:\WIN_NT.~bt instead of generating the three boot disks. Windows NT also can be installed from a network share of the target computer that is participating in a network.

> **The three startup disks are still necessary to perform an Emergency Repair Process. To create the three startup disks for Windows NT, run the command WINNT /OX from DOS or Windows 95 and the command WINNT32 /OX from Windows NT.**

2. Adapter Card Problems

Network adapters and their associated hardware also can cause problems during installation. Prior to starting Windows NT installation, you should obtain a list of which resources are used by your network adapter cards and make sure there are no conflicts within your system. Typically, a network adapter requires an interrupt (IRQ) and an I/O port, and might require other resources such as a DMA channel. These resources should not be in use by other components of your system before starting the Windows NT installation. Cabling, adapter settings, and terminators are the most likely problem areas.

Other adapter cards in the machine also can create problems. This generally is observed in the area of conflicting settings for IRQ and I/O ports:

- **Sound adapters:** Make sure you have the correct values for interrupts, I/O ports, and DMA channels prior to installing Windows NT. The default installation process does not install sound adapter cards. Sound cards are installed using the Multimedia applet in the Control Panel.

> **Windows NT provides minimal support for Plug and Play ISA drivers by installing the PNPISA drivers, located in the** \Drvlib\PNPISA\%platform% **directory on the Windows NT CD-ROM. They are installed by right-clicking the INF file in this directory and choosing INSTALL. When the system is restarted, all Plug and Play ISA cards are detected and installation routines run automatically.**

- **SCSI devices:** Each device on your SCSI chain should have a unique SCSI ID, and your host adapter should be configured to operate with each device. Also make sure your SCSI bus is terminated correctly.

- **PCMCIA cards:** If your system supports PCMCIA cards and you want to use them with Windows NT, make sure they are present in your system during installation.

You should check the following networking connections:

- **10Base2 (or thinwire) Ethernet networks:** Make sure both ends of the segment are terminated properly. Also make sure your cabling does not run next to (or over) electrical conduits.

- **10Base-T (twisted pair) Ethernet networks:** Make sure the connectors are properly crimped. (The RJ-45 connectors should make solid contact with the wires in the unshielded twisted-pair cable.) A concentrator or hub is required as the connection backbone for the network. Note that 10Base-T equipment has a *link light*, which indicates whether you have a connection to your concentrator. Finally, make sure you have not exceeded the recommended cable length (usually 100 meters from the repeater to your computer, including all path cables and cross-connects).

- **10Base-F networks (or FDDI or any other fiber-optic networks):** You must pay special attention to the cabling. Fiber-optic cable is extremely fragile and can easily be broken. Make sure the cable has not been bent or broken.

  When diagnosing faults in fiber-optic cables, never look directly into the end of a live cable. Retinas can be damaged easily, even by low-level emissions.

- **Asynchronous Transfer Mode (ATM) networks:** ATM networks have very strict requirements for cabling. Be sure to follow all the manufacturer's recommendations for your cabling plant.

- **Token-ring networks:** Make sure your cabling connections are reliable. As with 10Base-T, a centralized network connection point known as a Media Access Unit (MAU) is required. Diagnostic tools can diagnose and resolve problems with the token-ring environment.

B.   Configuration-Related Problems

During Windows NT installation, you are asked several questions that can lead to problems if not answered correctly. Common mistakes made during installation include the following:

- Computer name
- Role of server
- Inability to communicate with the Primary Domain Controller (PDC)

1.   Computer Name Issues

The computer name for each participating computer must be unique within the network. The NetBIOS name is limited to 15 characters, none of which can be the following:

```
/ \ []":;|<>+=,?*
```

If a duplicate name is detected, the computer's network services will not start.

2.   Computer Role Issues

During Windows NT Server installation, the installer is asked what role the computer will play in the network. The choices are Primary Domain Controller, Backup Domain Controller, and Member Server. This selection is critical because an incorrect selection generally requires reinstallation of the NT Server product into a new directory. Installing a Primary Domain Controller requires that a unique domain name be entered. This name must be a unique NetBIOS name on the network (including computer names and other domain names). When installing a Backup Domain Controller, make sure the domain name is entered correctly.

3. Communication with the Primary Domain Controller

If you install a Backup Domain Controller (BDC) or a member server that participates in the domain, the Windows NT Server computer requires communication with the Primary Domain Controller (PDC). The BDC needs to communicate with the PDC at two stages of the installation:

- During the creation of the computer account for the BDC
- During the initial synchronization of the Accounts database

A member server that participates in the domain requires communication with the PDC during the creation of the computer account in the PDC's Accounts database. If the PDC is not available during installation, a member server can be initially installed as a member of a workgroup. The member server then can join a domain when the PDC is available on the network.

C. Automating the Installation Process

When performing large numbers of Windows NT installations, the main areas of concern are speed and consistency. Windows NT enables you to script, or automate, installation. This provides a consistent method of performing the installations and reduces the amount of user interaction required during the installation process. Automated installation makes use of two files: an unattended script and a uniqueness database file.

The *unattended script* can be configured using the SETUPMGR.EXE utility. This application is located on the Windows NT Server CD in the \support\deptools\%platform% directory. SETUPMGR.EXE generates a text file containing all the basic information required for installation of Windows NT. The script can be configured for either Windows NT Workstation or Windows NT Server.

The *uniqueness database file* defines unique parameter settings for individual computers when multiple installations are performed using the same unattended script. The uniqueness database file defines what definitions are included in the file and what included sections are referenced by the definitions.

1. Performing an Unattended Installation

To perform an automated installation, run the WINNT program with the following parameters:

```
WINNT /t:<drive letter> /s:<source directory> /u:<unattended file> /udf:<id,udf file>
```

The /t parameter defines to which drive letter Windows NT will be installed. The rule is: Where the temp files go, so goes the Windows NT installation. The /s option enables you to select the source file directory. This is especially useful when installing from a local or network directory location. The /u option enables the installation to make use of a preconfigured unattended-installation script file. Use the full path when defining the filename. The /udf option enables the installation to use unique entries for each machine. The ID is used to identify which computer is being installed with the script. The ID also identifies the sections of the UDF file that will be used for the installation process.

2. Including Applications in the Unattended Installation

The Windows NT Server CD includes another deployment application that assists with the installation of application software during unattended installations. The application is called SYSDIFF.EXE and is located in the \support\deptools\%platform% directory of the Windows NT Server CD-ROM.

The SYSDIFF utility is run in three phases. The first phase takes a snapshot of a computer before any applications are installed. The second phase takes a snapshot of all changed files, *.ini configuration files, and Registry entries after the applications have been installed. The final phase applies these changes to other systems that do not yet have the applications installed. The parameters of the SYSDIFF utility are as follows:

- **SYSDIFF /SNAP** *snapfile*: Creates the original snapfile that contains the current files, the *.ini configuration files, and the Registry settings before applications are installed.

- **SYSDIFF /DIFF** *snapfile diff-file*: After all applications are installed, this command creates the difference file based on the original snapfile. The file outlines what files, *.ini settings, and Registry entries have been added during the installation of the application software.

- **SYSDIFF /APPLY** *diff-file*: This command is used to apply the difference file to a workstation on which applications have not yet been installed.

- **SYSDIFF /INF** *diff-file oemroot*: This command applies the contents of a difference file to an installation directory. It generates an .inf file to perform .ini file and Registry changes contained in a Sysdiff package. It also generates an OEM\ directory tree for file changes contained in a SYSDIFF package. This information can be incorporated into an automated installation.

6.1.1   Exercise: Creating Windows NT Startup Disks

This exercise shows you how to create the three Windows NT startup disks.

1. Format three 1.44 MB floppy disks by right-clicking the A drive icon in My Computer. Repeat for each disk.

2. Insert the Windows NT CD into your CD-ROM drive.

3. From the Start menu, select Run and type the following command:

    ```
    WINNT32 /ox
    ```

4. When prompted, insert Windows NT disk #3 into your floppy drive.

5. When prompted, insert Windows NT disk #2 into your floppy drive.

6. When prompted, insert the Windows NT Startup disk into your floppy drive.

6.1.2   Exercise: Viewing Your Current Hardware Resource Allocations

This exercise shows how the Windows NT diagnostics program can be used to determine what resources your computer system has.

1. From the Start menu, select Programs, Administrative Tools, Windows NT Diagnostics.

2. Select the Resources tab.

3. The Resources tab shows the currently allocated hardware interrupts (IRQs). You should note common interrupt assignments, such as the floppy drive being assigned IRQ 6. If you were to install a new network adapter, you could scrutinize the IRQ listing to determine which IRQs are free, and therefore, where to install the network adapter.

4. By clicking the I/O Port button near the bottom of the dialog box, you likewise can determine which I/O ports are in use on your system.

5. The DMA button enables you to determine which DMA channels are in use.

6

6.1   Practice Problems

1. The most likely cause of a dependency service failure during Windows NT installation is which of the following?

    A. Improper configuration of the Service applet.

    B. Incorrect service account information.

    C. The network adapter is improperly configured.

    D. You must be a member of the Administrators group to install Windows NT.

2. What must be configured correctly for a newly created BDC to communicate with a PDC on a remote TCP/IP subnetwork? Select all that apply.

    A. WINS server IP address

    B. DNS server IP address

    C. LMHOSTS file

    D. HOSTS file

3. In a Master Domain Model, where are Windows NT computer accounts most commonly created? Select all that apply.

    A. Master domain

    B. Resource domain

    C. Trusted domain

    D. Trusting domain

4. You are upgrading a Windows 95 system to Windows NT Workstation. You notice that none of your applications are running now. This is due to which of the following?

    A. You must run SETUP.EXE and select the Search for All Applications option.

    B. They are now located under Programs in the Start Menu.

    C. Only 32-bit applications are migrated to Windows NT Workstation.

    D. You cannot upgrade Windows 95 to Windows NT Workstation.

5. You are upgrading a Windows NT 3.51 Workstation to Windows NT Server. Which role can the newly created NT Server take on during the upgrade?

    A. Primary Domain Controller

    B. Backup Domain Controller

    C. Windows NT Member Server

    D. All the above

6. You are upgrading a Windows NT 3.51 Member Server to Windows NT Server. Which role can the newly created NT Server take on during the upgrade?

    A. Primary Domain Controller

    B. Backup Domain Controller

    C. Windows NT Member Server

    D. All the above

7. You are installing Windows NT Server on a RISC-based system. The system partition can be formatted as which file system?

    A. FAT

    B. NTFS

    C. CDFS

    D. HPFS

8. During Windows NT Server installation, you accidentally chose to install the computer as a Member Server. How do you change the role of the computer to a Backup Domain Controller?

    A. Reinstall Windows NT Server.

    B. In Server Manager, promote the Member Server to a Backup Domain Controller.

C. Edit the Registry.

D. In the Networks applet, change the role of the computer on the Identification tab.

9. Which situation causes the installation of a Backup Domain Controller named MARKETING in the HEAD_OFFICE domain to fail? Select all that apply.

A. The PDC for the HEAD_OFFICE domain is not available.

B. The MARKETING BDC does not share a common protocol with the PDC.

C. There are no other BDCs in the domain.

D. Another computer named MAR-KETING already exists on the network.

E. All the above.

10. If the incorrect video driver is selected during Windows NT Workstation installation, what should be the next course of action?

A. Reinstall Windows NT Server.

B. Select the LastKnownGood boot option.

C. Select the [VGA Mode] option from the Boot menu.

D. Hold Shift during the boot process to enable the VGA driver.

11. Which Windows NT utility do you use to troubleshoot the failure of a dependency service to start?

A. Server Manager

B. Windows NT Event Viewer

C. Windows NT Diagnostics

D. The Services applet in the Control Panel

12. If your CD-ROM drive is not on the Windows NT Hardware Compatibility List, what alternative method can be used to install Windows NT? Select all that apply.

A. Run the installation over the network using WINNT /B.

B. Generate the three startup disks using WINNT32 /ox.

C. Copy the installation files to a local directory and run WINNT /B from the directory.

D. Order the 3.5-inch floppy installa-tion disk set from Microsoft.

13. How many PDCs can be installed in a single domain?

A. 4

B. Any number

C. 1

D. 100

14. Which of the following systems meet the minimum hardware specifications to run Windows NT Server? Select all that apply.

A. Pentium 100 MHz, 16 MB RAM, 100 MB free disk space

B. 486 33 MHz, 16 MB RAM, 200 MB free disk space

C. Dec Alpha, 12 MB RAM, 300 MB free disk space

D. Pentium II 233 MHz, 32 MB RAM, 500 MB free disk space

15. Which of the following computers can be upgraded to a Windows NT 4.0 Primary Domain Controller? Select all that apply.

A. Windows NT 3.51 PDC

B. Windows NT 3.51 BDC

C. Windows NT 3.51 Member Server

D. Windows NT 3.51 Workstation

6

16. Which computer types require computer accounts when participating in a domain environment? Select all that apply.

    A. Backup Domain Controllers

    B. Windows NT Workstations

    C. Windows 95 Computers

    D. Windows for Workgroups Computers

17. Which methods can be used to add a computer account during the installation process? Select all that apply.

    A. Have an administrator precreate a computer account using User Manager.

    B. Have an administrator precreate a computer account using Server Manager.

    C. Indicate the domain that the computer will be a member of.

    D. Indicate the domain that the computer will be a member of and provide an account/password combination that is a member of the domain's Administrators local group.

18. Which program is used to speed up the installation of client software during the deployment of computers?

    A. APPDIFF.EXE

    B. USERDIFF.EXE

    C. SYSDIFF.EXE

    D. SOFTDIFF.EXE

The following scenario applies to questions 19 and 20. A different solution to the scenario is proposed for each question.

Scenario: The Orion Organization has hired a consultant to assist with the deployment of 1,000 new computer systems, all of which will all be running Windows NT 4 Workstation.

Required Result: The IS Manager wants the installations to be completely automated and be consistent between computers. *Optional Result 1:* The workstations should be installed to different resource domains based on their geographic locations and should have the correct time zone settings. *Optional Result 2:* All applications used in the Orion Organization should be included in the deployment process.

19. *Proposed Solution:* Create an unattended script file for the installation process. Install all necessary software onto the first system using the unattended script file. Run the SYSDIFF utility to take a snapshot of all the software installed. Perform all remaining installations using the unattended script file and the SYSDIFF snapshot.

    This solution:

    A. Meets the required result and both optional results

    B. Meets the required result and only one optional result

    C. Meets only the required result

    D. Does not satisfy any required or optional results

20. *Proposed Solution:* Create an unattended script file for the installation process. Create a uniqueness database file to contain the computer names, domains, and time zone settings for each computer. Install the first system using the unattended script file. Run the SYSDIFF utility using the /SNAP option to capture the current configuration of the system. Install all necessary software onto the system. Run the SYSDIFF utility using the /DIFF option to take a snapshot of all the software installed. Run the SYSDIFF utility a third time using the /INF option to create a OEM directory structure. Modify the unattended script file to include this software in the installation. Perform all remaining installations using the unattended script file and the uniqueness database file.

This solution:

A. Meets the required result and both optional results

B. Meets the required results and only one optional result

C. Meets only the required results

D. Does not satisfy any required or optional results

21. Which of the following is not required for using Windows NT Workstation?

A. Hard disk

B. Mouse

C. 12 MB memory

D. VGA monitor

22. During the installation of Windows NT Workstation, the installation program does not recognize a SCSI adapter. How can the third-party driver be installed?

A. Install with the default SCSI driver and apply the third-party driver after the installation is complete.

B. Press **S** to specify the third-party driver when the SCSI device-selection screen is presented.

C. If the SCSI adapter cannot be selected, it is not on the NT Hardware Compatibility List and cannot be used.

D. Replace the SCSI adapter with an adapter on the HCL list.

23. When installing Windows NT onto a SCSI drive, what issue can arise that does not come into play when installing to EIDE drives?

A. Unique SCSI IDs.

B. Master/Slave settings.

C. Whether the SCSI controller is BIOS-enabled.

D. There are no issues when using SCSI drives.

24. If you want to install the TCP/IP protocol to test Internet Information Server, but you do not have a physical network card, what can you install that will provide an adapter for TCP/IP to bind to?

A. Any supported Network Adapter Driver.

B. Microsoft Loopback Adapter.

C. Virtual Network Adapter.

D. This cannot be done.

25. Windows NT Workstation can be dual-booted with which of the following? Select all that apply.

A. Windows NT Server

B. Windows 95 (upgrade version)

C. Windows 95 (OSR2) using FAT

D. Windows for Workgroups

E. Windows 95 (OSR2) using FAT32

6.1.1 Answers and Explanations: Exercise

Exercise 6.1.1 reviewed how to create the three startup disks for Windows NT. These disks can be used for either of the following:

- Performing an installation of Windows NT

- Performing an emergency repair process on a Windows NT system

You should be aware that the startup disks are operating system dependent. If you have both a Windows NT Workstation and Windows NT Server, you need a separate set of boot disks for each operating system.

6.1.2 Answers and Explanations: Exercise

Exercise 6.1.2 reviewed how to determine your existing hardware configuration. The process described in this exercise often is used when installing a new adapter on a

6

system. Inspecting the current resources in use can greatly reduce installation time because open resources are already known.

This process also should be used to document what resource allocations have been performed on a computer. This can greatly reduce reinstallation scenarios if the actual resource allocations are known before the installation occurs.

6.1 Answers and Explanations: Practice Problems

1. **C** All Windows NT networking services depend on the initialization of the network adapter drivers to start.

2. **A, C** Both WINS and LMHOSTS provide NetBIOS name resolution. For a BDC to be installed successfully, it must be able to communicate with the PDC, even if it is on a remote subnet. The NetBIOS name of the PDC must be resolved to an IP address for this to occur.

3. **B, D** Computer accounts generally reside in the Resource (or trusting) domain. This reduces the size of the SAM database in the Master (or account) domain.

4. **C** You cannot upgrade Windows 95 to Windows NT Workstation. Upgrades are supported only for Windows 3.x and Windows NT 3.x.

5. **C** A Windows NT Workstation can only be upgraded to a Windows NT Member Server. Its Registry does not contain the necessary entries to become a Primary or Backup Domain Controller.

6. **C** A Windows NT Member Server can only remain a Windows NT Member Server. Its Registry does not contain the necessary entries to become a Primary or Backup Domain Controller.

7. **A** A RISC-based system requires that the SYSTEM partition be formatted using the FAT file system.

8. **A** To change the role of an NT Server computer from Member Server to Backup Domain Controller, you must reinstall the software.

9. **A, B, D** The installation of a BDC will fail if the BDC cannot communicate with the PDC. Lack of a common protocol or the unavailability of the PDC can cause this. Likewise, if another computer named MARKETING exists on the network, the networking services on the BDC will fail. This also prevents communication with the PDC.

10. **C** You can choose to boot Windows NT using the /BASEVIDEO option, which loads Windows NT using a VGA 16-color, 600×480 display driver.

11. **B** The Windows NT Event Viewer's system log reports the cause of a dependency service failure.

12. **A, C** Without the generation of boot disks, the installation of Windows NT can be performed from a local folder or from a network share if the CD-ROM is not on the HCL.

13. **C** There can be only a single PDC in a domain.

14. **B, D** The only systems that meet the minimum requirements for installing Windows NT Server are the 486-33 and Pentium II systems. The Pentium 100 does not meet the minimum disk space requirement, and all RISC-based installations require 16 MB of RAM.

15. **A, B** Only domain controllers can be upgraded to domain controllers. The Backup Domain Controller would technically be upgraded to a Backup Domain Controller. It then can be promoted to a Primary Domain Controller.

16. **A, B** Only Windows NT–class computers require computer accounts when participating in a domain environment.

17. **B, D** Either an Administrator can create the account before the installation is performed, or the installer can create the account by providing the logon credentials of a member of the Administrators local group.

18. **C** The SYSDIFF utility captures the files, *.ini settings, and Registry entries associated with a software installation.

19. **D** Although this solution appears to answer the required result, a uniqueness database file is required to do 1,000 installs. The UDF provides the unique settings required by each computer. Without the UDF, the computers would have to be renamed manually after the install is completed. In addition, the SYSDIFF procedure is performed incorrectly. The initial snapshot must be performed before the software is installed to the master template system.

20. **A** This solution meets all the business requirements. The unattended script and the UDF file methodology meet the required results. The first optional result also is met with the UDF file. The second optional result is met with the proper use of the SYSDIFF utility.

21. **B** A mouse is not required to use Windows NT (although it is desired).

22. **B** You can specify third-party SCSI drivers during the SCSI-detection routine of the Windows NT installation.

23. **A** When installing SCSI drives, each SCSI drive must have a unique SCSI ID to be accessible. EIDE drives are configured using a master/slave relationship.

24. **B** The MS Loopback Adapter can be used to assign an IP configuration if no network card is present in the local system.

25. **A, B, C, D** Windows NT Workstation can be dual-booted with all the operating systems listed. Windows 95 OSR2 cannot be dual-booted with Windows NT when the FAT32 file system is used, however, because Windows NT does not recognize this file system.

6.1 Key Words

10Base2

10Base-T

Concentrator

Enhanced integrated drive electronics (EIDE)

Hardware Compatibility List (HCL)

Hardware Quantifier Tool

Media Access Unit (MAU)

NetBIOS name

Small computer system interface (SCSI)

SYSDIFF

6

6.2   Solving Boot Failures

When configuration changes take place on a Windows NT system, they sometimes result in the inability to restart Windows NT. This section reviews common problems that occur during the boot process and their resolutions. This section discusses the boot process, the emergency repair process, and using the Last Known Good (LKG) configuration.

A.   The Boot Process

The boot process is a series of operations that load, initialize, and start the various subsystems, services, and device drivers required to operate Windows NT. Knowing the sequence of the boot process and the files involved can help troubleshoot Windows NT boot failures. The process differs slightly on Intel- and RISC-based platforms.

1.   Files Involved in Booting

The Windows NT boot process involves several files working together to start the Windows NT operating system. On the Intel and RISC platforms, the initialization files initially are platform specific, then are common during the later stages of the boot process. The platform-specific files required for the startup of an Intel-platform Windows NT system are as follows:

- **NTLDR:** The NTLDR file loads the Windows NT operating system. It is located in the root directory of the C: drive.

- **BOOT.INI:** This text file contains the entries for the Operating System Selection menu that appears during the startup of the computer. It is located in the root directory of the C: drive.

- **BOOTSECT.DOS:** This file contains the boot sector of the hard disk that existed before Windows NT was installed. It is machine specific and should not be copied between systems. It is loaded by NTLDR if an operating system other than Windows NT is selected during the boot process. It is located in the root directory of the C: drive.

- **NTDETECT.COM:** This file examines the available hardware on the system and builds the hardware list that will be contained in the HKEY_LOCAL_MACHINE\Hardware key of the Registry. It is located in the root directory of the C: drive.

- **NTBOOTDD.SYS:** This driver is used by Windows NT systems that have a non-BIOS–enabled SCSI adapter. This driver is used to access devices attached to the adapter. It is located in the root directory of the C: drive. It is not required for BIOS-enabled SCSI adapters.

The platform-specific files required for the startup of an RISC-platform Windows NT system are as follows:

- **OSLOADER.EXE:** This is the operating system loader file (similar in function to NTLDR on Intel systems).

- ***.pal:** On Alpha systems, these files contain software subroutines that enable the Windows NT operating system to directly control the microprocessor.

The common files involved in the boot sequence include the following:

- **NTOSKRNL.EXE:** The Windows NT kernel file. It is located in the `%SystemRoot%\System32` directory.

- **SYSTEM hive:** This file contains the SYSTEM hive of the Registry. It contains the configuration settings for the device drivers and servers loaded during the initialization process of the operating system. The SYSTEM hive is stored in the `%SystemRoot%\System32\Config` directory.

- **Device drivers:** All hardware on the computer requires device drivers that can interface with Windows NT. They are commonly stored in the `%SystemRoot%\System32\drivers` directory.

- **HAL.DLL:** The hardware abstraction layer (HAL) protects the NT Kernel and the Windows NT Executive from recognizing platform-specific hardware differences. All procedures make their calls to the HAL layer, and the HAL controls the underlying hardware.

2.   The Boot Sequence

The boot sequence in Windows NT is composed of five distinct phases:

- Boot-up
- Kernel load
- Kernel initialization
- Services load
- Win32 Subsystem start

These phases are the same for both Intel- and RISC-based computers; however, there are some differences in implementation.

a.   The Boot-Up Phase

On an Intel system, the boot-up phase proceeds as follows:

1. The power on self-test (POST) determines what hardware components are present on the system, including memory and disks.

2. The master boot record (MBR) is loaded into memory from the system's boot device. The program stored in the MBR is executed.

3. The MBR program locates the active partition for the system by scanning the partition boot record. The boot sector on the active partition is loaded into memory.

4. NTLDR is loaded and initialized on a Windows NT system.

5. NTLDR switches the CPU to a 32-bit flat memory model.

6. The minifile system drivers are started by NTLDR to enable NT to read the hard disk. There are minifile system drivers for FAT and NTFS.

7. The BOOT.INI file is read, and the Boot Loader Operating System Selection menu is presented to the user.

8. If an operating system other than Windows NT is selected, NTLDR runs BOOTSECT.DOS. NTLDR then passes control to the selected operating system, and the NT boot process is completed. If Windows NT is selected, the boot process continues.

9. NTDETECT runs and detects installed hardware components. The list of detected hardware is passed back to NTLDR for inclusion in the HKEY_LOCAL_MACHINE\Hardware key of the Registry.

10. NTLDR loads NTOSKRNL.EXE, HAL.DLL, and the SYSTEM hive.

11. NTLDR scans the SYSTEM hive and loads the device drivers that are configured to start at boot time.

12. NTLDR starts NTOSKRNL.EXE and the boot-up phase is complete.

The RISC boot-up phase is more streamlined than the Intel boot-up phase. This is a result of the RISC architecture. The RISC boot-up phase process is as follows:

1. The ROM firmware—system software—selects a boot device by reading the boot precedence table in non-volatile RAM(NVRAM).

2. The firmware reads the Master Boot Record (MBR) and determines whether the Windows NT system partition is present.

3. The firmware reads the first sector of the system partition into memory. It examines the BIOS parameter block to make sure the volume's file system is supported by the firmware.

4. The firmware loads OSLOADER.EXE from the root directory of the system partition. It then passes control to the OSLOADER.EXE, along with the list of available hardware on the system (from the RISC POST routines).

5. OSLOADER.EXE loads NTOSKRNL.EXE, HAL.DLL, the *.pal files, and the SYSTEM hive.

6. OSLOADER.EXE scans the SYSTEM hive and loads any device drivers that are configured to start at boot time.

7. OSLOADER.EXE passes control to NTOSKRNL.EXE, and the boot-up phase is complete.

b. The Kernel Load Phase

From this phase forward, the boot process is identical on the Intel and RISC platforms. The kernel load phase is the actual loading of NTOSKRNL.EXE. The HAL is loaded after the kernel to mask differences in the underlying hardware. Finally, the SYSTEM hive is loaded and scanned again. This time, it is scanned for device drivers and services that are configured to a System Startup type. The drivers and services are loaded into memory but are not initialized. They are loaded in the order set by the ServiceGroupOrder subkey found in the Registry under:

```
HKEY_LOCAL_MACHINE\System\CurrentControlSet\Contrl\ServicesGroupOrder
```

c. The Kernel Initialization Phase

The screen is now blue. The drivers and services loaded during the kernel load phase are now started. The SYSTEM hive again is scanned. This time any drivers configured to start automatically are loaded. They are initialized after the kernel is fully initialized. The CurrentControlSet is saved, and the Clone set is created and initialized for the creation of the Last Known Good configuration.

Finally, the Hardware key of the Registry is created based on information passed from NTDETECT.COM (for Intel systems) or OSLOADER.EXE (for RISC systems).

d. The Service Load Phase

This phase starts the Session Manager, which then starts the higher-order subsystems for Windows NT. These include the following:

- The BootExecute item runs programs (such as the NT version of Checkdisk) and performs conversions of FAT volumes to NTFS.

- The Memory Management key sets up the defined Paging files.

- The DOS Devices key is used by the Session Manager to create symbolic links. These links direct certain classes of commands to the correct components in the file system.

- The Subsystems key loads the required subsystems on the computer. By default, this only includes the Win32 subsystem.

e. Win32 Subsystem Start Phase

When the Win32 subsystem starts, the WINLOGON.EXE process is started. The WINLOGON.EXE process calls the local security authority that displays the Press Control+Alt+Delete logon dialog box.

The service controller makes a final pass through the SYSTEM hive, looking for services that are configured to start automatically. They are loaded based on their configured dependencies. The Last Known Good configuration is not saved until the user successfully logs on to the system.

B. Troubleshooting the BOOT.INI File

The BOOT.INI file presents a menu of selectable operating systems during the boot-up phase on an Intel system. An error in BOOT.INI can lead to a boot failure of Windows NT. BOOT.INI also can contain additional parameters to help troubleshoot a system failing to start or suffering from Blue Screen STOP errors.

1. Use of ARC Names in the BOOT.INI File

The BOOT.INI file makes use of Advanced RISC Computing (ARC) names to represent the locations of installed operating systems on a computer. A typical ARC name is as follows:

```
multi(0)disk(0)rdisk(1)partition(1)
```

The ARC name components can be described as:

- **MULTI/SCSI:** This component identifies the hardware adapter/disk controller that is controlling the disk on which the operating system is installed. SCSI is used as the first parameter only if the adapter is a SCSI adapter with BIOS disabled. All other controllers (including SCSI controllers with BIOS enabled) use the designation MULTI.

> The multi() syntax indicates to Windows NT that it should rely on the system BIOS to load system files. This means that NTLDR, the boot loader for x86-based computers, will be using interrupt (INT) 13 BIOS calls to find and load NTOSKRNL.EXE and any other files it needs to get the system running. The scsi() syntax indicates that Windows NT needs to load a SCSI device driver and use that driver to access the boot partition.

- **DISK:** The SCSI bus number (or ID) of the disk. If the first parameter is MULTI, the value is set to 0.

- **RDISK:** The ordinal number of the disk. If the disk is a SCSI disk (controlled by a BIOS-enabled SCSI controller), it is the SCSI ID of the disk.

- **PARTITION:** The ordinal number of the partition on which the operating system is installed.

Errors that can occur due to a misconfigured BOOT.INI file include the following:

- **The BOOT.INI file is missing:** If the BOOT.INI file is missing, the Windows NT operating system will not start unless it is located on the first partition of the first disk of the first controller in a directory named WINNT. All other locations will fail because the NTLDR file only looks in the default installation directory.

- **An entry for NT (default) appears in the Boot menu:** This entry appears only if the ARC name for the default entry does not match the ARC name for an entry on the [operating system] section of BOOT.INI.

- **An invalid path name exists in BOOT.INI:** If BOOT.INI points to the incorrect partition or path for the Windows NT installation, the following error appears:

```
Windows NT could not start because the following file was missing or corrupt:
<winnt root>\system32\ntoskrnl.exe

Please reinstall a copy of the above file.
```

- **An invalid device is referenced by BOOT.INI:** If the BOOT.INI file points to a nonexistent disk or partition, the following error message displays:

```
OS Loader v4.0

Windows NT could not start because of a computer disk hardware configuration
problem.
Could not read from the selected boot disk. Check boot path and disk hardware.

Please check the Windows NT (TM) documentation about hardware disk
configuration and your hardware reference manuals for additional
information.
```

2. Additional Parameters Within BOOT.INI

Within BOOT.INI, a series of options can be added to entries for troubleshooting and debugging purposes. The following switch options can be appended to the multiline in the BOOT.INI file:

- **/SOS:** Displays kernel and driver names during system startup. If you suspect a driver is missing or corrupted, append the /SOS switch to the BOOT.INI line that loads Windows NT.

- **/MAXMEM:##:** Enables you to specify the quantity of memory Windows NT will use. If you suspect a problem with a faulty memory chip, for example, this option enables you to boot your system using less than the total quantity of available RAM. A value of less than 12 MB should never be specified because Windows NT Workstation requires at lest 12 MB for normal operation (NT Server requires 16 MB). If you want to limit the amount of memory to 16 MB, enter the parameter as **/MAXMEM:16**.

- **/BASEVIDEO:** Forces Windows NT to use the standard VGA display driver. If your display no longer appears correctly, or if a driver upgrade has made your display unreadable, this option can be added to BOOT.INI.

- **/DEBUG:** Tells NT to load the kernel debugger during boot and to keep it in memory.

- **/CRASHDEBUG:** Similar to the /DEBUG option, except the debugging code is available only if the system crashes. In most cases, this is a better option because the debugger code will not be in memory and, therefore, won't interfere with the problem.

- **/DEBUGPORT:** Indicates the communications port you use.

- **/BAUDRATE:** Selects the baud rate for the connection you use for debugging.

- **/NOSERIALMICE:** This parameter disables NTDETECT from looking for serial mice on the designated serial port. This often is used when a UPS is connected to a COM port. The technique that NTDETECT.COM uses can cause many UPSs to think a power failure has occurred. The setting /NOSERIALMICE:COM1 indicates not to detect serial mice on COM1. If no COM port is indicated, no COM ports are searched for serial mice.

C. Creating a Windows NT Boot Disk

A boot disk can be created for a Windows NT system. This disk enables you to reboot your system if the startup files located in the system partition are damaged or missing. The procedure to create a boot disk is quite straightforward, as follows:

- Format the disk from within Windows NT. This is required because the boot sector must look for the NTLDR file, not the IO.SYS file as under DOS or Windows 95.

- For Intel systems: Using My Computer, Windows NT Explorer, or a command prompt, copy the following files to the disk: NTLDR, BOOT.INI, NTDETECT.COM, and possibly NTBOOTDD.SYS (if using a non-BIOS–enabled SCSI controller).

- For RISC systems: Copy the following files to the newly formatted disk: OSLOADER.EXE, HAL.DLL, and *.pal (for Alpha systems only). Note that for RISC systems, a few more steps are required. In order to boot from a disk, you have to add an alternate boot selection in your system firmware. Refer to your system's documentation for information about how to add a boot selection.

D. Using the Last Known Good Configuration

The Last Known Good option can be selected during the boot process to select the prior successful boot configuration. Basically, the Last Known Good option enables you to boot your system using the Registry settings in effect the last time you successfully booted your system and logged on. If your system configuration has changed, and you are no longer able to boot your computer, this option reverts your configuration to the settings in effect the last time you successfully booted your computer.

It should be noted that the Last Known Good configuration is available to the users only when they have successfully logged on to the system. To use the Last Known Good option, press the space bar when prompted during the Windows NT boot sequence. You will be presented with a screen informing you that the Last Known Good option can be used. Press the L key to use the Last Known Good configuration.

6

E. The Emergency Repair Process

An emergency repair disk can be used to rebuild corrupted Registry files. The repair process requires an emergency repair disk and the three Windows NT startup disks.

1. Creating the Three Windows NT Startup Disks

For Intel-based systems, place the Windows NT CD-ROM into a system running Windows NT or any other operating system, and then locate either WINNT.EXE or WINNT32.EXE. (WINNT is for 16-bit operating systems and Windows 95; WINNT32 is for 32-bit operating systems.) Execute the appropriate file using the /OX command-line parameter. You are prompted to insert startup disks 3, 2, then 1. These disks can be used to install the operating system or to perform an emergency repair process. RISC-based systems, unlike Intel systems, do not require startup disks. Instead, the firmware is used to provide a series of boot options.

2. Creating an Emergency Repair Disk

The emergency repair disk is created during the actual installation of the Windows NT operating system. It should be updated whenever changes are made to the computer. The application file for creating and updating the emergency repair disk is RDISK.EXE. This executable file starts the repair disk utility.

Update Repair Info updates the data files stored in the `%SystemRoot%\System32\Config` directory. If no emergency repair disk is provided during an emergency repair process, the information in this directory is used.

> By default, the Security and SAM hives are not updated when updating the repair information. If you want this information to be updated, you must run RDISK /S.

The Create Repair Disk is used for the initial creation of a recovery disk, and it requires a blank floppy disk. Note that the disk need not be formatted (or even blank) because RDISK formats the disk.

A recovery disk has copies of a Windows NT system's configuration files. Thus, a recovery disk created for one specific computer cannot be used on a different computer. In addition, recovery disks should be updated whenever your system configuration changes. The recovery disk contains the following files:

- **SETUP.LOG:** A log of files installed and the cyclic redundancy check (CRC) checksums for each file. This file is Read Only, Hidden, and System.
- **SYSTEM._:** The contents of the HKEY_LOCAL_MACHINE\SYSTEM Registry key in compressed format.
- **SOFTWARE._:** The contents of the HKEY_LOCAL_MACHINE\SOFTWARE Registry key in compressed format.
- **SECURITY._:** The contents of the HKEY_LOCAL_MACHINE\SECURITY Registry key in compressed format.
- **SAM._:** The contents of the HKEY_LOCAL_MACHINE\SAM Registry key in compressed format.

- **DEFAULT._:** The contents of the HKEY_LOCAL_MACHINE\DEFAULT Registry key in compressed format.

- **NTUSER.DA_:** The contents of `%systemroot%\Profiles\Default User\Ntuser.day` in compressed format.

- **AUTOEXEC.NT:** A copy of `%systemroot%\System32\Autoexec.nt` (a configuration file for the MS-DOS environment under Windows NT).

- **CONFIG.NT:** A copy of `%systemroot%\System32\Config.nt` (a configuration file for the MS-DOS environment under Windows NT).

3. Performing the Emergency Repair Process

The following options apply to the standard emergency repair on an Intel-based machine. These options, however, are similar for other systems. Insert the Windows NT Server Disk 1 and boot the computer. When prompted, insert Disk 2 and proceed. At the next prompt, select R in order to begin the recovery process. The following four options are presented:

- Inspect Registry files

- Inspect startup environment

- Verify Windows NT system files

- Inspect boot sector

All four tasks are selected by default, but tasks can be deselected as required. Note that to select or deselect items, you must use the cursor keys because no mouse driver is loaded at this point. These four tasks perform the following operations:

- **Inspect Registry files:** This option can be used to repair Registry keys. When this option is selected, you are provided with a list of Registry files it can restore. A warning also is shown, indicating that information can be lost. Proceed until you are prompted with a list of information that can be restored. Select the Registry keys you want to restore, and then select Continue.

- **Inspect startup environment:** This option verifies that the Windows NT files in the system partition are not missing or corrupted. If required, Repair will replace these with files from the Windows NT Server CD. On Intel-based systems, Repair ensures that Windows NT is listed in BOOT.INI. If this is not the case (or if BOOT.INI is missing), Repair changes or creates it as required. On RISC-based systems, startup information in NVRAM is inspected and repaired if required.

- **Verify Windows NT system files:** This option verifies that the Windows NT system files are not corrupt or missing. The file SETUP.LOG on the recovery disk contains a list of every file installed. It also has a cyclic redundancy check (CRC) checksum for every file. The checksums are computed for each file present on the system and are compared with SETUP.LOG. If the checksums do not match, the repair process asks whether it should replace the files from the Windows NT Server CD. If you have applied service packs to your system, these might need to be reinstalled after the repair process is completed.

- **Inspect boot sector:** On Intel systems, this option verifies that the boot sector on the system partition is configured to load NTLDR on startup. If this is not the case, the boot sector will be repaired. This part of the recovery process is not required for RISC systems. After the entire process has been completed, your system is configured as a bootable system, and all errors encountered are repaired.

6.2.1   Exercise: Creating a Windows NT Boot Disk

This exercise reviews the steps necessary to create a Windows NT boot disk. This disk can be used if any files are damaged in the system partition of a Windows NT computer.

1. Insert a new 1.44 MB disk into your floppy drive.

2. Open the My Computer icon on the desktop.

3. Right-click the A: drive icon and choose Format.

4. Ensure that the format is set to 1.44 MB and the FAT file system, and then select OK. (You can perform a quick format if you want.)

5. From the Start menu, select Programs, and then select Windows NT Explorer.

6. From the View menu, select Options.

7. Make sure the Show all Files option is selected, and then click OK.

8. Copy the following files to the A: drive:

   - NTLDR

   - BOOT.INI

   - NTDETECT.COM

   - NTBOOTDD.SYS (if it exists)

9. Shut down Windows NT.

10. Leaving the newly created boot disk in the A: drive, restart the system. If created correctly, the computer should boot as normal.

6.2.2   Exercise: Updating the Emergency Repair Disk

This exercise reviews how to update the emergency repair information for a system.

1. From the Start menu, select Run.

2. Type **RDISK** and click OK.

3. In the Repair Disk Utility dialog box, click the Update Repair Info button. This updates the information stored in the `%SystemRoot%\System32\Config` directory.

4. Place a 1.44 MB floppy disk into the A: drive.

5. Click the Create Repair Disk button. This copies the files in the `%SystemRoot%\System32\Config` directory to the floppy disk.

6. Label the disk as the emergency repair disk for the system and store it in a secure location.

6.2   Practice Problems

1. Which files are located in the Windows NT boot partition on an Intel system? Select all that apply.

   A. HAL.DLL

   B. NTLDR

   C. BOOT.INI

   D. NTOSKRNL.EXE

2. The file NTBOOTDD.SYS is used to what end?

   A. To identify whether Windows NT is installed on a system

   B. To activate a BIOS-enabled SCSI adapter

   C. To activate a non-BIOS–enabled SCSI adapter

   D. By Windows 95

3. Which NT startup files are common to both the Intel and RISC platforms? Select all that apply.

   A. OSLOADER.EXE

   B. BOOT.INI

   C. NTOSKRNL.EXE

   D. HAL.DLL

4. Which files are located in the Windows NT system partition on an Intel system?

   A. HAL.DLL

   B. NTLDR

   C. BOOT.INI

   D. NTOSKRNL.EXE

5. What information is included in the SYSTEM hive of the Registry?

   A. The operating system version

   B. The name of the file system in use

   C. The configuration settings for the device drivers and services

   D. A listing of all installed operating systems on the computer

6. What is contained in the boot partition?

   A. The files necessary to start Windows NT

   B. The previous operating system before Windows NT was installed

   C. The BOOT.INI file

   D. The \WINNT directory structure

7. What is used to collect a list of all the hardware present on an Intel computer system?

   A. NTDETECT.COM

   B. NTLDR

   C. OSLOADER.EXE

   D. CMOS information

8. How can you force a user to select an operating system from the Boot menu when starting Windows NT?

   A. Do not enable a default choice.

   B. Set the timeout value to 0 in BOOT.INI.

   C. Set the timeout value to –1 in BOOT.INI.

   D. In the System applet of the Control Panel, set the Show List option on the Startup/Shutdown tab to 999 seconds.

9. Which Registry subkey is used to determine the order in which device drivers and services are started?

   A. HKEY_CURRENT_USER\ So ftware\Microsoft\Windows NT

   B. HKEY_LOCAL_MACHINE\ Software \Microsoft\ Windows NT

6

    C.   HKEY_LOCAL_MACHINE\
System\CurrentControlSet\Control\
ServiceGroupOrder

    D.   HKEY_LOCAL_MACHINE\
System\CurrentControlSet\Services\
ServiceGroupOrder

10.   When is the Last Known Good Configuration saved?

    A.   When control is passed to the
NTOSKRNL

    B.   When the kernel has completed
initialization

    C.   When the user successfully logs on
to the computer

    D.   When the Control+Alt+Delete to
Logon dialog box appears

11.   Where is the Last Known Good configuration stored in the Registry?

    A.   HKEY_LOCAL_MACHINE\
System\ControlSet001

    B.   HKEY_LOCAL_MACHINE\
System\Select

    C.   HKEY_LOCAL_MACHINE\
Software\Select

    D.   HKEY_LOCAL_MACHINE\
System\Startup

12.   If Windows NT was installed on the
second partition of the slave disk in a
directory named WINNT4, the ARC
name in the BOOT.INI for this installation would be which of the following?

    A.   SCSI(0)disk(1)rdisk(0)partition
(1)\WINNT4

    B.   MULTI(0)disk(1)rdisk(0)partition
(1)\WINNT4

    C.   SCSI(0)disk(0)rdisk(2)partition
(2)\WINNT4

    D.   MULTI(0)disk(0)rdisk(1)
partition(2)\WINNT4

13.   Your system has been encountering
frequent STOP errors resulting in a blue
screen on the computer. What settings
can be added to BOOT.INI to assist in
debugging the problem? Select all that
apply.

    A.   /SOS

    B.   /DEBUG

    C.   /ENABLEDEBUG

    D.   /BAUDRATE

14.   Under what circumstances might Windows NT boot when the BOOT.INI file
has been deleted?

    A.   When Windows NT is the only
operating system on the computer.

    B.   When Windows NT is installed in
the directory C:\WINNT.

    C.   When the boot sequence in the
BIOS has been set to C: then A:.

    D.   It is not possible to boot Windows
NT without a BOOT.INI file.

15.   You have received an error message stating
`<WINNT ROOT>\SYSTEM32\NTOSKRNL.EXE`
`IS MISSING OR CORRUPT` during the
startup of Windows NT. The cause of the
problem could be which of the following?
Select all that apply.

    A.   The file NTOSKRNL.EXE is
missing or corrupt.

    B.   The file NTLDR is corrupt and
cannot find NTOSKRNL.EXE.

    C.   The Registry contains the incorrect
location for NTOSKRNL.EXE.

    D.   The BOOT.INI file has an incor-
rect ARC name path for the
Windows NT installation.

16.   You want to test a software package on
your computer. The actual computer that
will run the software has only 32 MB of
RAM while your computer has 128 MB

of RAM. What setting do you add to
BOOT.INI to restrict memory usage to
32 MB of RAM?

A. /RESTRICTMEM:32000

B. /RESTRICTMEM:32

C. /MAXMEM:32000

D. /MAXMEM:32

17. What settings are added to the ARC
name path for the [VGA mode] entry in
the BOOT.INI? Select all that apply.

A. /DEBUG

B. /VGA

C. /SOS

D. /BASEVIDEO

18. When creating a boot disk for a RISC-
based system, what files must be included
on the boot disk? Select all that apply.

A. NTLDR

B. OSLOADER.EXE

C. HAL.DLL

D. BOOT.INI

19. Which file is not located on the emergency repair disk?

A. SETUP.DAT

B. SETUP.LOG

C. SAM._

D. AUTOEXEC.NT

20. After adding a new network adapter to
your Windows NT Workstation computer, the computer suffers a blue screen
STOP error when restarting. To repair
this problem, you have to do which of the
following?

A. Use a Windows NT boot disk and
remove the adapter using the
Network applet in the Control
Panel.

B. Perform an emergency repair
process.

C. Use the Last Known Good configuration.

D. Reinstall Windows NT
Workstation.

21. To create the three startup disks for
Windows NT, which command do you use?

A. WINNT /B

B. WINNT /O

C. WINNT /OX

D. RDISK /S

22. To back up the entire Registry to the
emergency repair disk, which command
do you use?

A. REGBACK.EXE

B. RDISK

C. RDISK /E

D. RDISK /S

23. Which files are normally not adjusted
when the repair disk utility is run to
update configuration info? Select all that
apply.

A. SAM._

B. SOFTWARE._

C. SYSTEM._

D. SECURITY._

24. After performing an emergency repair
process, all the user accounts in the
domain have been lost. This is most likely
due to which of the following?

A. Somebody has deleted all the
accounts.

B. The SAM database was restored.

C. The Registry is still corrupt.

D. The emergency repair process
always removes all user accounts
from the domain.

6

6.2.1 Answers and Explanations: Exercise

In Exercise 6.2.1, a Windows NT boot disk was created. This is useful for troubleshooting corrupt files in the Windows NT system partition. It can be used in the following circumstances:

- When NTLDR, NTDETECT.COM, or BOOT.INI has been deleted or corrupted.

- When somebody has run the DOS SYS command and changed the boot sector of the computer to look for IO.SYS instead of NTLDR.

- If the system partition has been mirrored and a disk failure has occurred, the BOOT.INI file on the boot disk can be modified to boot to the other disk of the mirror set.

The only issue that might arise is when the computer CMOS settings have been adjusted to use the boot sequence C,A rather than A,C. This must be set to A,C for the Windows NT boot disk to work.

6.2.2 Answers and Explanations: Exercise

In Exercise 6.2.2, an emergency repair disk was created. This process should be repeated whenever a configuration change is made to the Windows NT system. This includes:

- The addition of a new hard disk

- The changing of a partition's file format from FAT to NTFS

- New software installed to the computer

It should be noted that repair information can only be updated by members of the Administrators or Power Users local groups.

6.2 Answers and Explanations: Practice Problems

1. **A, D** Remember that the Windows NT boot partition is where the operating system is located.

2. **C** If you do not have a non-BIOS–enabled SCSI adapter, the file NTBOOTDD.SYS will not be installed.

3. **C, D** Both the Intel and RISC versions of Windows NT use the NTOSKRNL.EXE and HAL.DLL files during the boot sequence.

4. **B, C** Remember that the system partition is where platform-specific startup files are located in Windows NT.

5. **C** The System hive contains configuration information for all device drivers and services. This includes parameter settings, dependency services, and how to handle errors during startup.

6. **D** The operating system itself is stored in the boot partition for Windows NT.

7. **A** NTDETECT.COM collects a list of all detected hardware on an Intel-based Windows NT computer.

8. **C** Setting the timeout value to –1 eliminates the countdown timer for selecting the default operating system.

9. **C** The List value is found in HKEY_LOCAL_MACHINE\ System\CurrentControlSet\Control\ ServiceGroupOrder. It sets the order for starting services.

10. **C** The Last Known Good configuration is saved after a user successfully logs on to the system.

11. **B** The Last Known Good configuration's location in the Registry is stored in the value LASTKNOWNGOOD in the HKEY_LOCAL_MACHINE\System\Select key.

12. **D** Because Windows NT was installed to a slave disk, the disk is not a SCSI disk. Therefore, the first parameter in the ARC name must be MULTI. Remember that partitions start numbering at 2; therefore, answer D is correct in referring to the second partition as partition(2).

13. **B, D** To enable debugging on a Windows NT system, you need to add /DEBUG, /BAUDRATE, and /DEBUGPORT to an ARC name in the BOOT.INI.

14. **B** When the BOOT.INI file is missing, Windows NT boots only if it is installed to the first partition of the first disk in the directory \WINNT.

15. **A, D** This error appears when NTOSKRNL.EXE is missing or corrupt and when an ARC name in the BOOT.INI points to the wrong partition.

16. **D** The correct setting to restrict memory usage on a Windows NT system to 32 MB is /MAXMEM:32. This also is useful if you suspect you have a defective memory SIMM module.

17. **C, D** The [VGA Mode] entry in the BOOT.INI file has both the /SOS and /BASEVIDEO parameters. You only need /BASEVIDEO to start up in VGA 16-color mode.

18. **B, C** The boot disk for a RISC system requires the OSLOADER.EXE, HAL.DLL, and *.pal files. The *.pal files are required only on an Alpha system.

19. **A** The file SETUP.DAT is not located on an emergency repair disk.

20. **C** When the computer prompts you to press the spacebar for the Last Known Good configuration, do so. Also remember to press L to select the Last Known Good configuration.

21. **C** The command WINNT /OX generates the three startup disks for Windows NT. They are used to install Windows NT and to perform emergency repairs.

22. **D** The parameter /S, when included with the RDISK command, also backs up the SECURITY and SAM hives that are not normally backed up.

23. **A, D** The SAM and SECURITY hives normally are backed up only during the initial installation of the Windows NT system into the directory `%SystemRoot%\System32\Config`. Running RDISK /S updates these two files along with the rest of the recovery files.

24. **B** If all Registry files are recovered, the SAM will be restored to its initial state from installation. The SAM now must either be re-created or restored from backup. If RDISK /S has been run, the accounts created up until that point of time are restored.

6.2 Key Words

BOOT.INI

Cyclic redundancy check (CRC)

Last Known Good option

SETUP.LOG

RDISK

6

6.3   Solving Configuration and Registry Failures

The Registry is used to store most of the configuration information for Windows NT. It is organized as a series of keys, subkeys, and values. A file system is similar in organization: a file is stored with a filename consisting of a drive letter, a directory, and a filename (C:\USERS\ MYFILE.TXT), and the file can contain data. In much the same way, the Registry stores information as a key, subkey, and value (HKEY_LOCAL_MACHINE\MySubkey\MyValue).

A.   NT Registry Subtrees

The primary keys located in the Registry (known as the subtrees of the Registry) are:

- **HKEY_LOCAL_MACHINE:** Contains information about the hardware installed on the computer as well as operating system data, device drivers configuration, service configuration information, and startup control data.

- **HKEY_USERS:** Contains all actively loaded user profiles (including HKEY_CURRENT_USER) and the default profile. The currently active user profile is listed as a subkey under the user Security ID.

- **HKEY_CURRENT_USER:** Contains the user profile for the currently logged on user. The profile includes desktop settings, network connections, the installed printer, and user-based configuration information.

- **HKEY_CURRENT_CONFIG:** Contains configuration data for the current hardware profile.

- **HKEY_CLASSES_ROOT:** Contains information about how all installed applications open and print their data files. Application extensions are associated to the applications. This key also contains information about object linking and embedding for the applications.

You might also see the term *hive* when reading about the Registry. A hive is a section of the Registry that is backed up to a combination of a data file and a .log file. Hives are located either in the `%SystemRoot%\System32\Config` or the `%SystemRoot%\Profiles\%Username%` directories.

The Registry can be viewed using REGEDT32, a tool provided with Windows NT. This tool provides a graphical interface to examine and modify Registry information on either local or remote computers. All information in the Registry can be edited using this tool. Much of the key information, however, also can be changed using standard administrative tools such as the Control Panel. It is preferable to use standard tools to modify the Registry; this reduces the likelihood of accidental changes or deletions. The most common standard tools used are the applets in the Control Panel.

Wherever possible, use administrative tools such as the Control Panel and System Policy Editor to make configuration changes, rather than editing the Registry. It is safer to use administrative tools because they are designed to store values properly in the Registry. If you make errors while changing values with a Registry editor, you are not warned. Registry-editing applications do not recognize and cannot correct errors in syntax or other semantics.

> Note that REGEDIT also can be used to edit the Registry files. REGEDIT has better search capabilities but cannot edit all value types. Also, you cannot set security permissions on the Registry using the REGEDIT command.

B.   Datatypes in the Registry

Each value in the Registry stores data as a specific value type. Some value types, however, can be used only for certain types of data. The value types used in Windows NT are as follows:

- **REG_BINARY:** Binary information, entered either as a sequence of binary digits or as hexadecimal digits.

- **REG_SZ:** A string value (human-readable text).

- **REG_EXPAND_SZ:** A string value that also contains a variable, such as %SystemRoot%.

- **REG_DWORD:** A four-byte hexadecimal value.

- **REG_MULTI_SZ:** A large string value (multiple lines of text, such as a list of configured IP addresses).

Values can be added anywhere in the Registry by selecting the desired key, and then selecting Edit, Add Value from the REGEDT32 menu. You then are asked for the name of the new value, its data type, and the data itself.

Existing Registry values can be modified by double-clicking the desired value in its Registry key. Depending on the value type of the selected value, you are presented with an appropriate editor. After the desired modifications have been completed, click OK to save the new value.

C.   Setting Permissions in the Registry

Windows NT defines a series of Registry permissions that can be set for users and groups. The following list describes the permissions:

- **Read:** Users or groups are allowed to read the Registry key, but they cannot change its information.

- **Full control:** Users or groups have permission to read, modify, delete, or take ownership of a key.

- **Special access:** Allows fine-tuning of access permissions and is broken down as follows:

  - **Query value:** Permission to read a value.

  - **Set value:** Permission to modify a value.

  - **Create subkey:** Permission to create a subkey under an existing key.

  - **Enumerate subkey:** Permission to list the subkeys of a Registry key.

  - **Notify:** Permission to open a key with notify access.

  - **Create link:** Permission to create a symbolic link (a "shortcut") for a Registry key.

  - **Delete:** Permission to delete a Registry key.

  - **Write DAC:** Permission to modify permissions (discretionary access control) for a key.

  - **Write owner:** Permission to take ownership of a Registry key.

  - **Read control:** Permission to read the security information for a key.

6

These permissions can be changed by selecting Security, Permissions from the REGEDT32 menu.

D. Backing up the Registry

The REGEDT32 tool can be used to back up the Registry of other computers in the domain as well. In REGEDT32, select Save from the Registry menu. You are prompted to enter a filename. This procedure creates a binary file containing the selected Registry information.

Select Restore from the Registry menu to restore this information at a later time. You are prompted to select a file to be restored. Note that because the Registry is open when Windows NT is running, you cannot restore the entire Registry from within REGEDT32. This is because some of the keys currently are opened by the operating system. After a file has been selected, a warning message displays before the Registry values are restored.

Another way to back up the Registry is to use the RDISK utility. The RDISK utility saves the current configuration to the %SystemRoot\Repair directory and can be used by the emergency repair process. The RDISK utility saves all information except the SAM and SECURITY hives. If you want to save the complete Registry using RDISK, you must run RDISK /S. This also creates a backup, compressed version of the Registry that includes updated versions of the SAM and SECURITY hives.

The Windows NT Resource Kit includes the REGBACK and REGREST utilities, which also can be used to back up the Registry. These utilities enable you to back up the entire Registry to a specified directory. A separate file is created for each hive of the Registry.

A final method to back up the Registry is to use the Windows NT Backup program. If you select the Backup Local Registry option and at least one file on the Windows NT boot partition, Windows NT Backup also can back up the local Registry. If you are running NTBACKUP from a batch file, you must include the /b option to back up the local Registry. Remember, you must include at least a single file from the boot partition of Windows NT to back up the Registry.

> **The Backup Local Registry option cannot be used to back up remote Registries. NT Backup only supports backing up the local Registry.**

6.3.1   Exercise: Using the Policy Editor to Modify the Registry

The System Policy Editor can be used to edit the local Registry. It provides an easy-to-use interface that prevents syntax errors when modifying values in the Registry. The System Policy Editor is installed on any domain controller in the environment. It also can be installed on a Windows NT Workstation or a Windows NT Member Server. This is accomplished by installing Server Tools for Windows NT from the Windows NT Server CD-ROM.

1. From the Start menu, select Programs, Administrative Tools, System Policy Editor.

2. In the System Policy Editor, select Open Registry from the File menu. A window appears containing two icons. The Local Computer icon affects settings in the HKEY_LOCAL_MACHINE subtree of the Registry. The Local User icon affects the HKEY_CURRENT_USER subtree.

3. Double-click the Local User icon.

4. In the Local User Properties window, select the '+' next to the Shell option in the list of items.

5. Beneath the Shell option, open the Restrictions option.

6. Enable the Hide Network Neighborhood option.

7. Click OK to finish the settings.

8. From the File menu, select Save.

9. Close the System Policy Editor. Note that the Network Neighborhood icon still exists on the desktop.

10. Log off, and then log on to the system again. Note that the Network Neighborhood icon now has disappeared.

6.3.2 Exercise: Comparing the Search Utilities of REGEDT32 and REGEDIT

This exercise compares the search capabilities of the REGEDT32 and REGEDIT utilities. Although both utilities can be used to view the Windows NT Registry, each has its own strengths. Knowing these strengths can help you decide which editor to use under specific circumstances.

1. From the Start menu, select Run and type **REGEDT32.EXE** to start the native format of the Registry Editor.

2. From the Start menu, select Run and type **REGEDIT.EXE** to start the Windows 95 version of the Registry Editor.

3. Right-click an open space on the Taskbar and select Tile Windows Horizontally from the pop-up menu. This arranges both versions of the Registry Editor on your screen.

4. Note that the Windows 95 Registry Editor uses a single window, whereas the Windows NT version uses a separate window for each subtree of the Registry.

5. In each window, select the HKEY_LOCAL_MACHINE subtree.

6. In the Windows NT Registry Editor, select Find Key from the View menu. Note that you only can search for keys in this version of the Registry Editor. Search for the string ServiceGroupOrder. Note that the value in the right window is named LIST and is a REG_MULTI_SZ data type.

7. In the Windows 95 Registry Editor, select Find from the Edit menu. Note that you can search for Keys, Values, or Data in this version. Enter the string ServiceGroupOrder in the Find dialog box and click OK. The LIST value also appears in this version of the Registry Editor.

8. Double-click the List value. Note that this version of the Registry Editor determines List is a binary value. The Windows 95 editor does not recognize the REG_MULTI_SZ data type.

9. Close both Registry Editors.

6

6.3 Practice Problems

1. What information is stored in the Registry? Select all that apply.

   A. Programs

   B. Configuration information

   C. Hardware detected during the startup process

   D. Only application information

2. Which utilities can be used to view portions of the HKEY_LOCAL_ MACHINE subtree of the Registry? Select all that apply.

   A. Windows NT Diagnostics

   B. The System applet of the Control Panel

   C. The SCSI applet of the Control Panel

   D. Solitaire

3. You have updated your video drive, and when you reboot, Windows NT fails to start. What can you do to fix this problem? Select the best answer.

   A. Boot using the [VGA Mode] setting.

   B. Use the Last Known Good configuration.

   C. Perform an emergency repair procedure.

   D. Boot into DOS and rename the REG.BAK file REG.DAT.

4. You have updated your tape backup device's driver, and when you reboot, Windows NT fails to start. What can you do to fix this problem? Select the best answer.

   A. Boot using the [VGA Mode] setting.

   B. Use the Last Known Good configuration.

   C. Perform an emergency repair procedure.

   D. Boot into DOS and rename the REG.BAK file REG.DAT.

5. What is the organization of the Registry?

   A. Keys, values

   B. Keys, text, values

   C. Values

   D. Keys, subkeys, values

6. How do you create a mandatory user profile?

   A. In the System applet of the Control Panel, change the user's profile type to Mandatory on the User Profile tab.

   B. Rename the NTUSER.DAT file to NTUSER.MAN in the `%Systemroot%\profiles\ %username%` directory.

   C. In the System Policy Editor, configure the user profile to be Mandatory.

   D. In User Manager, configure the Profile path to a central network location.

7. Which Windows NT Resource Kit file can be used to research an unknown Registry entry?

   A. Windows NT Server Resource Guide

   B. Windows NT Workstation Resource Guide

   C. RESGUIDE.HLP

   D. REGENTRY.HLP

8. What is a hive?

   A. The file that contains the entire Registry

   B. Another name for the HKEY_LOCAL_MACHINE subtree

C. A portion of the Registry contained in a single file/.log file combination

D. A multiple-value data type in the Registry

The following scenario applies to questions 9 and 10. A different solution to the scenario is proposed for each question.

Scenario: The Grabling Group has installed two Windows NT Server computers in its Vancouver office. It has set up the RESOURCE server as the primary file location. It also is functioning as the print server for the office.

The BACKEND server is running Microsoft Exchange and SQL Server. It also is functioning as the PDC for the GRABLING domain. A consultant has been hired to configure these computers to optimize network performance.

Required Result: The Grabling group wants to make sure its PDC is running efficiently, so the 100 users do not suffer any delays when authenticating with the network. *Optional Result 1:* The users need fast access to their data stores. *Optional Result 2:* The Grabling group is planning to install a BDC next year and wants to make sure its user account database is protected.

9. *Proposed Solution:* Configure the Server service of the BACKEND server to Maximize Throughput for Network Applications. Configure the RESOURCE server's Server service to be Balanced. Install a tape backup unit on the RESOURCE server. Configure NT Backup to back up the Registries of both the BACKEND and RESOURCE servers as well as all the data files on the BACKEND and RESOURCE servers.

This solution:

A. Meets the required result and both optional results

B. Meets the required result and only one optional result

C. Meets only the required results

D. Does not satisfy any required or optional results

10. *Proposed Solution:* Configure the Server service of the RESOURCE server to Maximize Throughput for File Sharing. Configure the BACKEND server's Server service to Maximize Throughput for Network Applications. Install a tape backup unit on the BACKEND server. Configure NT Backup to back up the local Registry as well as all the data files on the BACKEND and RESOURCE servers.

This solution:

A. Meets the required result and both optional results

B. Meets the required result and only one optional result

C. Meets only the required result

D. Does not satisfy any required or optional results

11. Using REGEDT32.EXE, where do you look to determine which subkey contains the Last Known Good configuration?

A. The LastKnownGood subkey in the HKEY_LOCAL_MACHINE subtree.

B. The LastKnownGood value located in HKEY_LOCAL_MACHINE\ Select.

C. The LastKnownGood value located in HKEY_LOCAL_MACHINE\ System\CurrentControlSet.

D. The LastKnownGood value located in HKEY_LOCAL_MACHINE\ System\Select.

12. Which editing tools can be used to edit the Registry? Select all that apply.

A. Notepad

B. REGEDIT

    C.   REGEDT32

    D.   SysEdit

13. How can you optimize the pagefile to provide better virtual memory performance? Select all that apply.

    A.   Spread the paging file across multiple logical disks.

    B.   Spread the paging file across multiple physical disks.

    C.   Include the paging file on the volume that contains the Windows NT boot partition.

    D.   Exclude the paging file from the volume that contains the Windows NT boot partition.

14. Which of the following is the text version of the Windows NT Diagnostics program that can be used to read Registry information from a command prompt?

    A.   WINMSDT.EXE

    B.   WINMSD.EXE

    C.   WINMSDP.EXE

    D.   WINDIAG.EXE

15. Which of the following data types can be used in the Registry? Select all that apply.

    A.   REG_HEX

    B.   REG_BYTE

    C.   REG_BINARY

    D.   REG_SZ

16. The text string values in the Registry are stored as which type?

    A.   REG_SZ

    B.   REG_TEXT

    C.   REG_WORD

    D.   REG_EXPAND

17. What is the purpose of the ServiceGroupOrder subkey?

    A.   It contains the order in which services were installed on a system.

    B.   It organizes the services into logical groups.

    C.   It determines the order in which device drivers and services are loaded.

    D.   It determines where memory services and device drivers are loaded.

18. Where would you find the TCP/IP settings for a DHCP client in the Registry of a computer that had an IEEPRO network card?

    A.   HKEY_LOCAL_MACHINE\ System\CurrentControlSet\Services\ TCPIP\Parameters

    B.   HKEY_LOCAL_MACHINE\ System\CurrentControlSet\Services\ IEEPRO\Parameters\TCPIP

    C.   HKEY_LOCAL_MACHINE\ System\CurrentControlSet\ Control\TCPIP\Parameters

    D.   HKEY_LOCAL_MACHINE \System\CurrentControlSet\Services\ IEEPRO1\Parameters\TCPIP

19. Where are the physical data files that store the Registry on the computer? Select all that apply.

    A.   %SystemRoot%\Repair

    B.   %SystemRoot%\System32\Config

    C.   %SystemRoot%\Profiles\ %Username%

    D.   %SystemRoot%\Config

20. When editing the Registry file, what is true of each data type?

    A.   Only the text data can be edited.

    B.   Each has its own editor.

C. All are edited with the same editor.

D. All are edited in hex.

21. On the Intel platform, the information collected by NTDETECT.COM during the startup process is stored in which key of the HKEY_LOCAL_MACHINE subtree?

    A. SAM

    B. SOFTWARE

    C. HARDWARE

    D. SECURITY

22. What does RDISK /S do?

    A. Copies only selected Registry keys.

    B. Copies boot files, not Registry files.

    C. It is not a valid program.

    D. Makes a complete copy of the Registry, including the SAM and SECURITY.

23. If the start value for a driver is set to Automatic, when is the driver loaded during the Windows NT startup process?

    A. By NTLDR

    B. During the NTOSKRNL.EXE initialization

    C. During the system startup phase

    D. By a dependency service

24. From within REGEDT32, which of the following is true?

    A. You cannot save the resource profiles.

    B. You cannot save or restore the entire Registry.

    C. You can save only selected keys.

    D. You cannot save the information.

25. What is the difference between REGEDIT and REGEDT32?

    A. They are the same program.

    B. REGEDIT allows saving the Registry, REGEDT32 doesn't.

    C. REGEDT32 allows restoring the Registry, REGEDIT doesn't.

    D. REGEDIT provides better search options.

6.3.1 Answers and Explanations: Exercise

Exercise 6.3.1 reviewed using the System Policy Editor to edit the Registry. Another use of the System Policy Editor is to create system policies that can be merged with the Registry.

When using the System Policy Editor to work with policy files, the information is stored in a separate file named NTCONFIG.POL for Windows NT systems. The contents of NTCONFIG.POL merge with the user's and the computer's Registry settings when they authenticate with their domain. NTCONFIG.POL is read from the NETLOGON share of the authenticating domain controller.

You also can connect to a remote Registry using File, Connect and can edit the Registry using the System Policy Editor. It is common practice to create your own system policy templates to modify the Registry more safely.

6.3.2 Answers and Explanations: Exercise

Exercise 6.3.2 outlined the differences between REGEDT32.EXE and REGEDIT.EXE. REGEDT32.EXE is best used for editing information under Windows NT because it has native data editors for all data types stored in the Windows NT Registry. REGEDIT.EXE is best used for finding information in the Registry because it allows searches to be performed on keys, values, and data. REGEDT32.EXE can search only for keys.

6

6.3   Answers and Explanations: Practice Problems

1. **B, C**   The Registry contains information about hardware detected during startup and configuration information for installed devices, services, and applications.

2. **A, B, C**   Windows NT Diagnostics, the System applet, and the SCSI applet all can be used to view configuration information stored in the Windows NT Registry.

3. **A**   Windows NT has BOOT.INI settings that enable Windows NT to boot in a VGA 16-color mode. The setting that performs this is /BASEVIDEO. It is listed as [VGA Mode] in the Windows NT boot menu.

4. **B**   If your computer fails to start due to a newly installed driver, you can use the Last Known Good configuration to revert to the previous setup. Remember, you must not log on to Windows NT if you plan to use the Last Known Good configuration.

5. **D**   The Registry is organized into keys, subkeys, and values contained in the subkeys.

6. **B**   You create a mandatory profile by renaming the user's NTUSER.DAT file as NTUSER.MAN. NTUSER.DAT is stored in the `%SystemRoot%\Profiles\ %Username%` directory. Remember that if the user has been configured with a roaming profile, you must rename the NTUSER.DAT file in the configured roaming profile directory.

7. **D**   The Windows NT Resource Kit contains a help file named REGENTRY.HLP that holds all Registry entries, data types, and default values.

8. **C**   A hive is a portion of the Registry that is stored in a single distinct file/.log file combination. The combination is stored in the `%SystemRoot%\System32\ Config` directory.

9. **C**   The RESOURCE server should have been set to Maximize Throughput for File and Print Sharing. In addition, Windows NT Backup can perform only a local Registry backup. Because the tape backup unit is located on the resource server, the NT account database will not be backed up in this scenario.

10. **A**   This solution meets all the requirements. The BACKEND server is configured to Maximize Throughput for Network Applications, which increases login response for authentication. The RESOURCE server is optimized for file and print sharing. By locating the tape backup unit on the RESOURCE server, the NT account database will be backed up.

11. **D**   The LastKnownGood value stored in the HKEY_LOCAL_MACHINE\ System\Select subkey contains a REG_DWORD data type that contains a number. If the number is 2, it means that HKEY_LOCAL_MACHINE\System\Current ControlSet002 contains the Last Known Good configuration information.

12. **B, C**   You can use the REGEDT32 and REGEDIT programs to edit the Registry.

13. **B, D**   To obtain the best virtual memory performance, spread the paging file across multiple physical drives to increase system performance. Excluding it from the boot partition drive also increases performance because this drive is frequently accessed by the operating system, which can cause delays in access for virtual memory. Remember that if you do not include the page file on the boot partition, Windows NT cannot store crashdump information because it requires a paging file the size of physical RAM on the boot partition.

14. **C**   The WINMSDP.EXE utility can access the same information from the Registry as Windows NT Diagnostics. It can be run through a remote command session on a remote computer.

15. **C, D**   REG_BINARY and REG_SZ are recognized data types in the Windows NT Registry.

16. **A**   String values in the Registry are stored in the REG_SZ data type.

17. **C**   The ServiceGroupOrder subkey contains a list of service groups. It determines the order in which these groups are loaded during the Windows startup process.

18. **D**   DHCP configuration information is stored under the HKEY_LOCAL_MACHINE\System\CurrentControlSet\Services\ Netcard1\Parameters\TCPIP subkey. A common mistake is to look only in the NETCARD subkey. The configuration is in the specific instance of the network card.

19. **B, C**   The hives located in HKEY_LOCAL_MACHINE are stored in `%SystemRoot%\System32\Config`. The current user information is stored in the `%SystemRoot%\Profiles\ %UserName%\ NTUSER.DAT` file.

20. **B**   Each data type has its own editor in the Windows NT Registry Editor.

21. **C**   The information collected by NTDETECT is stored in the Hardware subkey. This information is volatile and is rebuilt every time Windows NT is restarted.

22. **D**   Running RDISK with the /s parameter backs up the entire Registry to the `%SystemRoot%\Repair` directory. It also includes updated copies of the SAM and SECURITY hives.

23. **C**   A driver configured to start automatically starts during the system startup phase.

24. **B**   You cannot restore or save the entire Registry using the REGEDT32 utility because a portion of the Registry is always open when operating Windows NT.

25. **D**   The REGEDIT utility allows searches for keys, values, and data; REGEDT32 only allows searches for keys.

6.3   Key Words

Hive

NT Backup

RDISK

REGEDIT

REGEDT32

System Policy Editor

6

6.4   Solving Printer Problems

Before examining the print model, it is necessary to discuss the vocabulary used by Microsoft to explain the model. Microsoft does not use the same terminology as other network operating systems, and this can lead to some confusion when first working with the Windows NT print model.

Print devices are the actual hardware devices that produce hard copy output. *Printers* are the software interfaces between the operating system and the print device. A printer can be configured to send output to multiple physical printer devices. Multiple printers also can be configured to send output to the same printing device at different priority levels or at different hours of the day. A *print spooler* is the software responsible for receiving, distributing, and processing print jobs. A spooler consists of many components that perform the functions.

A *print job* is data destined for a print device. It can be sent in various formats in the Windows NT print model. A *queue* is a series of print jobs waiting to be printed. *Print processors* work with the print drivers to de-spool the spooled print jobs during print spool file playback. The print processor makes the final alterations to print jobs, based on the data type of the print job. Data types include Text, Enhanced Metafile (EMF), RAW FF(Appended), and RAW FF(Auto).

A.   Files Involved in the Windows NT Print Process

Most files involved in printing are in the %systemroot%\SYSTEM32 directory. One notable exception is the spooler's workspace, which can be placed on any given drive or directory. By default, it is located in %systemroot%\SYSTEM32\SPOOL\Printers. You can change this location in the Advanced Property page of the Server Properties dialog box. You can access this dialog box from the Printers applet by selecting Server Properties from the File menu. The following list shows the major print-related files used under Windows NT:

- The print spooler uses WINSPOOL.DRV, SPOOLSS.EXE, and SPOOLSS.DLL.

- Local print providers (used for printers connected to a local port, such as LPT1 or COM1) use LOCALSPL.DLL.

- Remote print providers (used for printers not connected to a local port, such as a printer equipped with a network interface card) use WIN32SP.DLL for NT print servers. For NetWare print servers, NWPROVAU.DLL is used instead. For AppleTalk print servers, SFMPSPRT.DLL is used.

- Print monitors (used to send jobs from the spooler to the print device) can use one of a series of files, depending on how the printer is connected. For local printers, LOCALMON.DLL is used. For network-connected printers, a DLL specific to the network connection is used (HPMON.DLL or LPRMON.DLL).

B.   The Printing Process

When a job is printed from a remote client to a printer located on a Windows NT printer server, the following process occurs:

1. The application (such as MS Word) makes a series of GDI calls. The GDI uses the printer driver to perform a partial rendering of the print job.

> **Windows 16-bit programs and DOS applications perform full rendering of the print job.**

2. The print job is sent to the print spooler on the workstation that generated the print job.

3. The print job is sent using a remote print provider, which connects the workstation to the remote print spooler.

4. The print spooler on the NT system receives the print job and performs whatever final processing is required (if any).

5. Finally, the print job is sent to the actual print device. If all is OK, a paper copy is generated.

C. Support for Other Operating Systems

Windows NT supports printing from other operating systems. Special services are required to provide support for UNIX, NetWare, and Macintosh clients.

1. Print Support for UNIX Hosts

Windows NT includes an LPD service (the Microsoft TCP/IP Print Server service), which can accept print jobs from UNIX clients using Line Printer Remote (LPR) clients. Windows NT clients also can use the LPR command when they have installed the TCP/IP Print Server service. The syntax of the LPR command is as follows:

```
lpr -S{server} - P{printer} -J{job} -C{class} -o {option} -x -d {filename}
```

> **The options -S and -P are case sensitive. They must be uppercase.**

Another command included with the TCP/IP Print Server service is the LPQ command, which can display the queue information for an LPD Print Server. The syntax of the LPQ command is:

```
lpq -S{server} - P{printer}
```

2. Print Support for NetWare Clients

Two services provide print support when the NetWare operating system is involved. Gateway services for NetWare enables Windows NT clients to print to NetWare print servers. File and print services for NetWare enables Windows NT Server printers to receive print jobs from NetWare clients.

3. Print Support for Macintosh Clients

The Services for Macintosh print processor (SFMPSPRT.DLL) enables Macintosh clients to send print jobs to Windows NT printers. This print processor has a specific data type named PSCRIPT1. This data type enables Macintosh clients to send Level 1 PostScript jobs to non-PostScript printers. The spooler sends the PostScript code through a Microsoft TrueImage raster image processor (RIP), supplied with Services for Macintosh. The raster image processor creates a series of one-page, monochrome bitmaps at a maximum of 300 DPI. The Windows NT print spooler sends the rasterized images, or bitmaps, to the print driver for the target printer. The print driver returns a job that prints the bitmaps on the page. If the printer is a PostScript printer, the Services for Macintosh print processor sends the job using the RAW data type.

D.　Typical Print Problems

Typical problems encountered during the printing process include:

- The print device is turned off.
- The print device is offline.
- The print device is out of paper.
- The print permissions do not allow a user access to the printer.
- The print driver on the client is corrupt.
- The print spooler on either the client or the print server is corrupt.
- The print spool directory is out of disk space.

The following basic troubleshooting steps can be used to diagnose a printing problem:

1. Make sure the print device is properly connected, is online, and has paper.

2. On the print server, click the Print Test Page button. This determines whether the print driver on the print server is corrupt. If the test page does not print correctly, make sure all required files are present on the print server. This can be done by reloading the print driver.

3. On the printer's Sharing property page, make sure all necessary operating systems' print drivers are loaded for the printer. This enables the auto-downloading of drivers for each installed operating system's print drivers.

4. If the test print works correctly, try printing using a basic application such as Notepad or WordPad. If printing works for these applications, you might need to reinstall the application that does not print correctly.

5. If only specific users cannot print, verify that the permissions for the printer have been set correctly by inspecting the Permissions option on the Security page of the Printer dialog box. The permissions that can be set include:

   - **Full Control:** Allows the configured groups or users to change printer settings. This is assigned by default to members of the Administrators, Server Operators, Print Operators, and Power Users groups.

   - **Manage Documents:** Allows the configured groups or users to pause documents in the queue, to delete jobs, and to reorder jobs. The Creator/Owner special group has this permission assignment by default.

   - **Print:** Allows the configured groups or users to print a job. This permission is assigned to the Everyone special group by default.

   - **No Access:** Prevents the configured users and groups from printing. This is not assigned to any groups or users by default.

E. Downloading Print Drivers

Automatic downloading of print drivers can be configured for the following platforms:

- Windows NT Alpha platforms (Windows NT versions 3.1, 3.5x, and 4.0)

- Windows NT MIPS platforms (Windows NT versions 3.1, 3.5x, and 4.0)

- Windows NT PPC platforms (Windows NT 3.51 and 4.0)

- Windows NT Intel platforms (Windows NT versions 3.1, 3.5x, and 4.0)

- Windows 95 (true 32-bit print drivers only)

When a Windows NT client connects to a printer on a remote print server, its version of the print driver is compared to the version on the print server. If the version on the print server is newer, the newer version is downloaded and then used on the client. If the driver does not exist on the client, it also is downloaded and then used on the client.

On Windows 95 clients, the driver is downloaded only during the initial installation of the printer. If the Windows 95 print driver on the print server has been updated at all, the printer should be deleted from all Windows 95 clients and then reloaded.

6.4.1   Exercise: Installing Multiple Print Drivers for a Printer

This exercise reviews the steps necessary to install multiple print drivers for a Windows NT printer. Installing all necessary platforms' drivers to a print server assists in the distribution of updated print drivers on the network.

1. From the Start menu, select Settings and then select Printers.

2. Double-click the Add Printers icon to start the Add Printer Wizard.

3. Select My Computer and click the Next button.

4. Select the Enable Printer Pooling option to enable the creation of a printing pool. Select LPT1:, LPT2:, COM1:, and COM2: from the list of ports.

   The order in which you select the ports is extremely important because it is the order in which the ports are accessed when sending a print job to the pool.

5. From the Manufacturer listing, select LexMark. From the Printers listing, select the LexMark 4039 Plus PS printer. Click the Next button to continue.

   When configuring a printer pool, all component printing devices must be able to use the same print driver.

6. Accept the default for printer name. Do not set this printer to be your default printer. Click the Next button to continue.

7. Share the printer with the name LEXMARK. The share name can be up to 256 characters in length. Click the Next button to continue.

6

> **Although print shares can be up to 256 characters in length, this is not supported by all operating systems. Windows NT 4 clients can connect to printer shares up to 256 characters in length. Windows 95 and Windows NT 3.x clients can connect to printer shares up to 12 characters in length. Win16 and DOS clients can only connect to print shares up to 8.3 characters in length.**

8. Answer No when asked whether you want to print a test page. Click the Finish button to complete the printer installation.

9. When prompted, insert the Windows NT Server CD-ROM and indicate the <Drive Letter>:\i386 directory to install the necessary support files.

6.4.2   Exercise: Installing the TCP/IP Print Server Service

This exercise reviews the steps to install the TCP/IP Print Server service. It then reviews usage of the LPR and LPQ commands. This exercise assumes that the printer created in Exercise 6.4.1 exists and that the current user is a member of the Administrators local group.

1. From the Start menu, select Settings and then select Control Panel.

2. Double-click the Printers applet.

3. Right-click the LexMark 4039 Plus PS printer and select the Pause Printing option.

4. Switch back to the Control Panel and double-click the Network applet.

5. Select the Services tab of the Network Properties dialog box.

6. Click the Add button, and then select the Microsoft TCP/IP Printing option to install the TCP/IP Print Server service.

7. When prompted, indicate the path for the Windows NT Server CD-ROM and the %platform% directory (such as d:\i386).

8. When prompted to restart the computer, select Yes.

> **If you have installed any service packs on your Windows NT Server computer, you should always select No when asked any question about restarting the computer until you have reinstalled the service pack. If you do not reapply the service pack at this point, you could end up with a STOP error that will not allow Windows NT to start.**

9. When the computer restarts, log on as Administrator.

10. Start the Control Panel again.

11. In the Control Panel, double-click the Service applet.

12. Change the Startup setting for the TCP/IP Print Server service to Automatic, and then start this service.

13. Start a command prompt.

14. Make C:\ the current directory.

15. Type the following command to print the BOOT.INIfile to your LEXMARK print share:

    ```
    LPR -S<Your Computer Name> -PLEXMARK c:\boot.ini
    ```

    You should replace <Your Computer Name> with the NetBIOS name of your computer.

16. To view the queue of the paused printer, type the following command:

    ```
    LPQ -S<Your Computer Name> -PLEXMARK
    ```

17. Switch back to the Printers Window. Double-click the LexMark 4039 Plus PS printer to view the contents of the queue. The contents should be the same as you saw in step 16.

6

6.4   Practice Problems

1. When a new printer is installed on a print server, which of the following statements is true about the default permissions assigned to the printer? Select all that apply.

   A. Everyone can delete any job in the printer.

   B. Only Administrators can change the properties of the printer.

   C. Administrators, Server Operators, and Printer Operators can change the properties of the printer.

   D. The owner of a job can delete the job.

2. What does the print spooler do?

   A. Receives, processes, and prints jobs

   B. Receives jobs and reroutes to remote printers

   C. Reprints jobs

   D. Translates hex to ASCII

3. Which operating systems support the automatic downloading of printer drivers by Windows NT? Select all that apply.

   A. Windows NT Server

   B. Windows NT Workstation

   C. Windows 95

   D. Windows for Workgroups

4. Which service must be installed to enable a UNIX system to print to a Windows NT printer?

   A. TCP/IP

   B. Simple TCP/IP services

   C. SNMP Service

   D. TCP/IP Printing service

5. Where are permissions for a print share set?

   A. Windows NT Explorer

   B. Property pages of a printer

   C. Print Manager

   D. Server Manager

6. Your department is using an HP LaserJet 3 SI printer that is unable to switch dynamically between PCL and PostScript modes. Which separator page do you use before all PostScript jobs to make sure the printer is in PostScript mode?

   A. PCL.SEP

   B. PSCRIPT.SEP

   C. SYSPRINT.SEP

   D. SWITCH.SEP

7. You are supporting a mainframe emulation program that requires form feeds appended to each job. You want to change the default data type for the WINPRINT print processor to which of the following?

   A. RAW

   B. RAW (FF After)

   C. FF After

   D. Text (FF After)

8. Users in your office are unable to print large documents. You suspect that the drive where your spool files are stored has run out of disk space. How do you change the default location for the spool directory?

   A. Change the location on the Spool tab of the Printer's Properties dialog box.

   B. Change the Spool Settings in the System Applet of the Control Panel.

   C. On the Advanced tab of the Server Properties dialog box, which can be reached from the Server Properties option in the File menu of the Printer dialog box.

D. This setting cannot be changed. You must delete files to free up disk space.

9. If you find there is a job in the printer that will not print and cannot be deleted, how can you remove this job from the printer?

   A. Delete all files in the %System Root%\System32\spool\PRINTERS directory.

   B. Log on as Administrator and delete the job. The Administrator account has the right to delete stuck jobs.

   C. Ignore the job. After the configured time-out period has passed, the job removes itself from the queue.

   D. Stop and start the Spooler Service.

10. What factors must be considered when creating a printer pool? Select all that apply.

   A. All printers should be in the same area of the office.

   B. The print server must have a digiboard installed.

   C. The HP JetAdmin utility must be installed on the print server.

   D. The printers that make up the printer pool must be able to use the same print driver.

   E. The order in which the ports are selected determines the order in which the printing devices are accessed.

11. What is the name of the administrative share that is set up to download print drivers?

   A. PRINTER$

   B. SPOOL$

   C. PRINT$

   D. SPOOLER$

12. What is the syntax of the command a UNIX client would use to print the file OUTPUT.DOC to a share named HPLJ on the server SPARKY?

   A. `lpd -SSPARKY -PHPLJ output.doc`

   B. `lpr -SSPARKY -PHPLJ output.doc`

   C. `lpd -SHPLJ -PSPARKY output.doc`

   D. `lpq -SHPLJ -PSPARKY output.doc`

13. You have installed all your HP Laserjet printers with HP Jet Direct cards, yet you cannot manage any of them with Windows NT. What is the missing component that enables Windows NT to manage these printers?

   A. HP Jet Direct Service

   B. HP Print Service

   C. DLC Protocol

   D. Need to install the NT Patch to the HP Laserjet firmware on each printer

14. Can a Windows NT Server support the automatic downloading of print drivers for Intel, PPC, Alpha, and MIPS clients on the same print server?

   A. Yes

   B. No

15. What permissions are required to pause, delete, and reorder jobs in the print queue?

   A. No Access

   B. Print

   C. Manage Documents

   D. Full Control

16. What is the main difference in the printing process when a Windows 3.x client prints to a Windows NT print share compared to when a Windows NT client prints to a Windows NT print share?

6

A. There is no difference.

B. Windows 3.x clients cannot print to a Windows NT print share.

C. Windows 3.x clients can only submit text jobs.

D. Windows 3.x clients fully process their jobs before submitting them to a Windows NT print share.

17. You have installed the TCP/IP Print Server service on your print server and have restarted the print server, yet UNIX clients cannot print to any of the print shares. Which of the following could be the reason for this?

A. Windows NT does not support printing for UNIX clients.

B. The SNMP Service also must be installed.

C. The TCP/IP Print Server service is set to be manually started. It should be switched to start automatically.

D. The UNIX clients must first capture the print port.

18. What must be installed to enable Macintosh clients to print to a Windows NT printer?

A. TCP/IP Print Server service

B. Services for Macintosh

C. Mac Print Services

D. AppleTalk Protocol

The following scenario applies to questions 19–22. A different solution to the scenario is proposed for each question.

Scenario: The Xavier group has offices in Boston, Montreal, and Seattle. Each office has its own domain, with the Boston domain functioning as the master domain in a Master Domain Model. Global groups have been created to represent the Boston users, the Montreal

users, and the Seattle users. The resource domains each have their own printer resources that are shared throughout the entire enterprise.

Required Result: The Systems group comprised of Bob, Mary, and Jane should be the only users with Full Control on all printers in the enterprise. *Optional Result 1:* The Xavier group wants all print servers to be capable of hosting jobs sent by UNIX computers. *Optional Result 2:* The Xavier group wants to provide printing support to all Macintosh clients in the enterprise.

19. *Proposed Solution*: When a printer is installed, change the permissions on each print share to assign Bob, Mary, and Jane to manage all documents for the printer. Be sure to install the TCP/IP and AppleTalk Protocols on each print server. This enables print support for UNIX and Macintosh clients.

This solution:

A. Meets the required result and both optional results

B. Meets the required result and only one optional result

C. Meets only the required result

D. Does not satisfy any required or optional results

20. *Proposed Solution:* In each domain, add the user accounts for Bob, Mary, and Jane to the Print Operators local group. At each print server, install the TCP/IP protocol and the SNMP Service. Also add the Services for Macintosh service.

This solution:

A. Meets the required result and both optional result

B. Meets the required result and only one optional result

C. Meets only the required result

D. Does not satisfy any required or optional results

21. *Proposed Solution*: In the Boston domain, add the user accounts for Bob, Mary, and Jane to the Print Operators local group. At each print server, install the TCP/IP protocol and the Microsoft TCP/IP Print Server service. Also add the Services for Macintosh service.

    This solution:

    A. Meets the required result and both optional results

    B. Meets the required result and only one optional result

    C. Meets only the required result

    D. Does not satisfy any required or optional results

22. *Proposed Solution*: In each domain, add the user accounts for Bob, Mary, and Jane to the Print Operators local group. At each print server, install the TCP/IP protocol and the Microsoft TCP/IP Printing service. Also add the Services for Macintosh service.

    This solution:

    A. Meets the required result and both optional results

    B. Meets the required result and only one optional result

    C. Meets only the required result

    D. Does not satisfy any required or optional results

23. You have updated the HP LaserJet 4 print driver on your print server for Windows 95 to enable duplex printing. Your Windows 95 clients are not able to take advantage of this new option. What is the problem?

    A. Windows 95 clients do not support duplex printing.

    B. You must load Windows 95 print drivers at the client systems.

    C. You must restart the Windows 95 system for the changes to take effect.

    D. You have to delete the existing printer and reconnect to the printer to download the newer version of the driver.

24. How can you prevent print job information events from being written to the System Log of the Event Viewer?

    A. In the Registry, configure which events are logged to the Event Viewer for the Spooler service.

    B. In the Printers dialog box, select Server Properties from the File menu. On the Advanced tab, deselect the Log Spooler Information Events option.

    C. On a printer's Advanced Property page, configure the printer so it does not record information events to the Event Viewer.

    D. This cannot be done.

25. What is the syntax a login script uses to connect the printer shared as SHOPPRINT that is located on the print server named SHOP_FLOOR to LPT2:?

    A. `Capture l=2 s=SHOP_FLOOR q=SHOPPRINT`

    B. `NET PRINT LPT2: Error! Reference source not found. \SHOPPRINT`

    C. `CAPTURE LPT2:=\\SHOP_FLOOR\SHOPPRINT`

    D. `NET USE LPT2: \\SHOP_FLOOR\SHOPPRINT`

26. If a physical printing device has broken down, and the printer that was sending jobs to the printing device still has jobs in its queue, how do you redirect the jobs to a similar printing device?

    A. You cannot redirect jobs.

    B. Have the users recall their jobs and readdress them to a different printer.

    C. Add a new local port to the printer using the UNC name of a printer that prints to a similar printing device.

    D. Use the Redirect option in the printer's property pages.

6

27. What data type is used when a Macintosh client sends a print job to a LaserJet III printer that does not have PostScript support?

   A. RAW

   B. PSCRIPT1

   C. EMF

   D. You cannot print PostScript to a PCL printer.

28. What data type is used when a Macintosh client sends a print job to a PostScript Laser printer?

   A. RAW

   B. PSCRIPT1

   C. EMF

   D. TEXT

6.4.1 Answers and Explanations: Exercise

Exercise 6.4.1 reviewed the steps necessary to create a printer pool. The following are the key concerns when creating a printer pool:

- Make sure the print devices are near each other in the office because it is not known which print device is used to output a job.

- All printers must be able to use the same print driver.

- When selecting the ports for a printing pool, be sure to select the fastest ports first.

- If the print devices are different models, select the faster print devices before the slower print devices.

6.4.2 Answers and Explanations: Exercise

Exercise 6.4.2 reviewed the steps to install the TCP/IP Print Server service. This service also added a new print monitor, known as the LPR Print Monitor (LPRMON.DLL). This print monitor can be used to redirect print jobs to an LPD print server.

When configuring an LPR print port, you must configure the network address of the LPD print server and the name that the LPD service associates with its print device.

6.4 Answers and Explanations: Practice Problems

1. **C, D** The default permissions grant Administrators, Print Operators, and Server Operators the Full Control permissions. The special group Creator Owner is granted the Manage Documents permissions, which enable users to delete their own print jobs.

2. **A** The spooler receives jobs from clients, performs further processing on jobs received from 32-bit clients, and prints the jobs.

3. **A, B, C** Windows NT Server, Windows NT Workstation, and Windows 95 all support the automatic downloading of print drivers. Windows 95 has this support only when working with true 32-bit drivers.

4. **D** The TCP/IP Printing service enables a UNIX system to print to a Windows NT printer. After installation, it is referred to in the list of installed services as the TCP/IP Print Server service.

5. **B** Print permissions are set from the Security tab of a printer's properties. The Print Manager application was used in Windows NT 3.x.

6. **B**   The PSCRIPT.SEP separator page switches the printer into PostScript mode before a job is printed.

7. **B**   The data type RAW (FF After) is used to automatically eject the page after printing has been completed.

8. **C**   On the Server Properties pages, you can set the default spool directory when configuring the advanced properties.

9. **D**   Stopping and starting the Spooler service flushes all jobs from the printer.

10. **A, D, E**   When setting up a printer pool, the printers should be in the same general location and must use the same print driver. When selecting the ports used for the printer pool, be sure to select faster ports before slower ports.

11. **C**   The print drivers are downloaded from the administrative share named PRINT$ on the print server.

12. **B**   The syntax of the LPR command is `LPR –S<Server name or IP address> –P<printer or share name>`. Remember, the –S and –P are case sensitive and must be uppercase.

13. **C**   The HP print monitor is loaded when the DLC protocol is added to a Windows NT computer.

14. **A**   Yes. You must install print drivers for each platform that will connect to the print server for printing.

15. **C**   The Manage Documents permission allows a user to pause, delete, and reorder print jobs.

16. **D**   Windows for Workgroups uses its own 16-bit drivers to fully process a job before sending the job to a Windows NT print share. Windows NT clients partially process their print jobs, and then send them to the print share. The print share's spooler completes the processing of the job.

17. **C**   The TCP/IP Print Server service is not configured to automatically start after installation. You must change its startup setting to automatically start the service.

18. **B**   Services for Macintosh installs the Services for Macintosh print processor (SFMPSPRT), which enables Macintosh clients to print to Windows NT print shares.

19. **D**   According to the requirements, Bob, Mary, and Jane require Full Control permissions, not Manage Documents permissions. This could have been achieved without granting excess permissions by making them members of the Print Operators local group in each of the three domains.

20. **B**   This solution grants the three users sufficient permissions to meet the primary requirement. Only Macintosh clients, however, can access the print shares. You need the TCP/IP Print Server service to grant print access to UNIX hosts.

21. **D**   This does not meet the primary requirement. Bob, Mary, and Jane are only able to fully manage the printers in the Boston domain. They must be added to the Print Operators local group in each of the three domains.

22. **A**   This solution fully meets all requirements. Remember that if any member servers or Windows NT workstation computers are functioning as print servers, the three users must be added to the Print Operators local group in the account database on each of the member servers or NT Workstation computers.

23. **D**   Windows 95 clients only download the server's version of the print driver when they initially connect to the printer. You must delete the printer and then reinstall it to download the new version of the driver. Windows NT clients *do* check the version of their driver and the version stored on the print server. If the version on the print server is newer, they download the newer version.

24. **B**   You can choose whether to log information, warnings, and STOP errors

6

for the print spooler in the Advanced properties page of the Server Properties dialog box.

25. **D**   The syntax for connecting a print share to a DOS print port is NET USE <PORT>Error! Reference source not found.**Error! Reference source not found.** SHARE>.

26. **C**   A local port can be added that points to the UNC name of a printer. The printer must use the same print driver as the original printer because the job will be fully processed when downloaded to the new printer.

27. **B**   The Services for Macintosh print processor (SFMPSPRT) downloads the job using the PSCRIPT1 data type. This data type indicates that the job is Level 1 PostScript code from a Macintosh client, but the target printer is not a PostScript printer.

28. **A**   When a Macintosh client prints to a PostScript printer, the data is downloaded in its native RAW format.

6.4   Key Words

LPD Service

LPQ

LPR

Print device

Print drivers

Print job

Print spooler

Printer

Queue

6.5   Troubleshooting Remote Access Service

One of the many challenges faced by network administrators today is the user's need to dial in to the network. The popularity and convenience of laptops and telecommuting makes this process necessary. Windows NT comes with a dial-in service known as Remote Access Service (RAS). This section presents an overview of RAS and investigates troubleshooting the RAS client and server.

A.   An Overview of RAS

Essentially, RAS enables users to function as if they are physically connected to a remote network. RAS has two main components—the server (Remote Access Service) and the client (Dial-Up Networking). The RAS server can be Windows NT Server, Windows NT Workstation, or Windows 95 (either through Service Pack 1 or OEM Service Release 2). The RAS server enables users to connect to the network from a remote location. The Microsoft RAS server always uses the Point-to-Point Protocol (PPP) when users are dialing in to the network.

When clients connect to a server using a modem, there are two popular line protocols. *Serial Line Internet Protocol* (SLIP) frequently is used in UNIX implementations. SLIP is the older of the two line protocols and is geared directly for TCP/IP communications. Windows NT can dial in as a client to a SLIP server. However, it does not provide a SLIP server. Because SLIP requires a static IP address and does not provide secured logon (passwords are sent as clear text), Microsoft's RAS server uses Point-to-Point Protocol (PPP).

PPP, developed as a replacement for SLIP, provides several advantages over the earlier protocol. PPP can automatically provide the client computer with an IP address and other configuration. It provides a secure logon and has the capability to transport protocols other than TCP/IP (such as AppleTalk, IPX, and NetBEUI).

Two important extensions to PPP are implemented in Windows NT RAS Server. These extensions are the Multilink Protocol (MP) and the Point-to-Point Tunneling Protocol (PPTP). Windows NT supports both of these protocols.

Multilink Protocol enables a client station to connect to a remote server using more than one physical connection. This capability provides better throughput over standard modems. You will, however, need multiple phone lines and modems to enable this protocol. This can be an easy interim solution if you need to temporarily connect to offices, but do not have the time or budget to set up a leased line or other similar connection.

Point-to-Point Tunneling Protocol facilitates secure connections across the Internet. Using PPTP, users can connect to any Internet Service Provider (ISP) as well as the office network. During the session initialization, the client and server negotiate a 40-bit session key. This key then is used to encrypt all packets to be sent back and forth over the Internet. The packets are encapsulated into PPP packets as data. The PPTP-encapsulated protocol can be NetBEUI, NWLink IPX/SPX, or TCP/IP.

You can connect to the Windows NT server in other ways. In addition to connections over Public Switched Telephone Networks (PSTN), RAS can connect networks in two other ways—using Integrated Services Digital Networks (ISDN) and using X.25 (a wide area networking standard).

1. ISDN

ISDN is becoming a common method of communicating. It is a good choice for connecting to remote sites or for individuals and small organizations connecting to the Internet. Whereas today's standard phone lines can handle transmission speeds of up to 56 Kbps, ISDN transmits at 64 or 128 Kbps—depending on whether it is one or two channels.

ISDN is a point-to-point communications technology, and special equipment must be installed at both the server and the remote site. You need to install an ISDN card (which acts as a network card) in place of a modem in both computers. As you probably have guessed by now, ISDN connections are more expensive than modems. If you truly require the higher speed, however, the cost most likely is justified. Be aware that in some parts of the world, this is a metered service; the more you use, the more you pay.

2. X.25

The X.25 protocol is not a communication device; rather, it is a standard protocol for connections. It is a packet-switching communication protocol designed for WAN connectivity.

RAS supports X.25 connections using Packet Assemblers/Disassemblers (PADs) and X.25 smart cards. These are installed as a network card, just like ISDN.

B. Client Issues When Using RAS

Several issues must be investigated when configuring and troubleshooting the Dial-Up Networking client. These issues include installing and configuring the modem, configuring dialing locations, creating phonebook entries, setting dial-in permissions, and setting callback security levels on a user-by-user basis.

1. Installing and Configuring Modems

Installing a modem is simple in Windows NT. After the hardware is connected, go to the Control Panel and double-click the Modems icon. If no modem is installed, the modem installer starts automatically. This wizard steps you through the installation of the modem.

If you have already used the installer once and it was unable to detect the modem, you probably have one of two problems. Either the modem cannot be detected and you will have to install it manually, or the system can't see the modem, in which case you should check the port. If you need to install the modem manually, check the option Don't detect my modem, I will select it from a list. This selection brings up a screen that enables you to select the modem.

> **Windows NT can use Windows 95 configuration files to install a modem. If you are unable to find a Windows NT 4.0 driver, you can use a Windows 95 driver in its place.**

When you have installed the modem, you can check modem properties using the Modems icon in the Control Panel. After you have selected the modem to configure, you can change the configuration of the modem using its property pages. On the General tab of the modem's properties, you can set the following items:

- **Port:** Displays the port that the modem was installed on. You should check this if the hardware has been changed. Also check the port settings if the modem is not working.

- **Speaker Volume:** Determines the volume of the speaker during the connection phase. This should be turned up so you can verify the dial tone and that the other end is, in fact, a modem.

- **Maximum Speed:** Sets the fastest rate attempted by the system when communicating with the modem. If this is set too high, some modems are not able to respond to the system. In this case, try lowering the rate.

- **Only connect at this speed:** Instructs the modem to connect to the remote site at the same speed you set for communications with the modem. If the other site is unable to support this speed, you are not able to communicate.

In the Connection tab of the modem's properties dialog box, you also can set the manner in which the modem connects. Settings that might need to be adjusted include

- **Call Preferences:** Configures how the modem reacts to events that occur during a dial-up session. Options include:

  - Wait for Tone Before Dialing

  - Cancel the Call if Not Connected Within…

  - Disconnect a Call if Idle for More Than…

- **Advanced Modem Settings:** The advanced modem settings are configured by clicking the Advanced button on the Connection page. This enables the configuration of the following properties of a modem:

  - **Use Error control:** Turns on or off some common settings that affect the way the system deals with the modem.

  - **User flow control:** Overrides the flow control setting for the port. Both types of flow control (Xon/Xoff and hardware) are available. In most cases, you should choose to use hardware flow control. Using flow control enables you to set the speed of the transmission between the computer and the modem.

  - **Modulation Type:** Enables users to set the modem's frequency modulation to match that of the phone system being used. The modulation is either standard or Bell, and deals with the sound frequency that is used for the send and receive channels of the communicating hosts.

  - **Extra settings:** Enables you to enter extra modem initialization strings to be sent to the modem whenever a call is placed.

  - **Record a log file:** Enables you to record a file that permits you to see the communications that take place between the modem and the computer during the connection phase of the communications. This is probably the most important setting from the troubleshooting perspective.

6

2. Configuring Dialing Locations

Some dial-in users call from varying locations. Depending on their location, they might need to dial long distance to reach the office network or use different prefixes to access an outside line. You can create various Dialing Locations from the Telephony applet in the Control Panel. This information is used with a phonebook setting to determine how to dial an access number to dial-in to the office network. If a user cannot reach the point in which the two modems are attempting to connect, dialing location is generally one of the first areas to check. The settings that can be configured for a dialing location include:

- **I am dialing from:** This is the configured name of the location. To create a new entry, click the New button and enter a name in the box. The user needs to know which entry to use when dialing. Be sure to use a descriptive name that has meaning for the user.

- **The area code is:** The computer uses this information to determine whether it needs to dial the number as a long distance number or as a local number.

- **I am in:** Sets the country code for dialing purposes, so the system is able to connect to international numbers.

- **To access an outside line, first dial:** Sets the prefix to be used to access an outside line. This setting enables configuration of separate prefixes for local and long distance calls.

- **Dial using Calling Card:** Enables you to have the computer enter calling card information to make the connection with the remote host. Click the Change button to review or change the calling card information. You can select from common calling cards available or create your own template for your calling card.

- **This location has call waiting:** The call waiting tone often causes a connection to be dropped. You can enter information here to temporarily disable call waiting for the location you are dialing from.

- **The phone system at this location uses:** Enables you to select whether the system you are calling from uses tone or pulse dialing.

3. Configuring the Phonebook Entry

After your modem has been configured and dialing locations have been created, you need to configure a phonebook entry for the network you want to dial-in to. Dial-Up Networking is the component used to connect to the RAS server. In Dial-Up Networking, you create a phonebook entry for each remote network you call. The steps required to create an entry are as follows:

1. Double-click the My Computer icon, and then double-click the Dial-Up Networking folder.

2. Click the New button to create an entry. You also can select an existing entry from the list, click More, and choose Edit the Entry.

    If you choose New, the New Entry Wizard appears. You have the option to enter information manually. Because this chapter discusses troubleshooting, this section covers manual entries (they provide more options).

3. The New (or Edit) Phonebook Entry dialog box appears. Enter or verify the information. The options are as follows:

    - **Entry Name:** The name of the entry.

    - **Comment:** Any comment you want to make about the entry.

- **Phone Number:** This is the phone number for the entry; you should verify this. You can enter multiple numbers by clicking the Alternates button. These numbers are tried in the sequence entered. You also have the option to move a successful number to the top of the list.

- **Use Telephony-Dialing Properties:** This tells the system to use the properties set for your location when dialing the number.

- **Dial Using:** Informs the system which modem you want to use when dialing. Verify that the modem exists. If Multilink is selected, choose Configure and verify the phone numbers entered for each modem listed.

- **Use Another Port if Busy:** This tells the system to use another modem if the modem specified is busy.

4. Select the Server tab, and enter or verify the information. The options are as follows:

- **Dial-up server type:** Tells the system what type of server you are trying to connect to. You can use three different types of servers—PPP (such as Windows NT), SLIP, and Windows NT 3.1 RAS.

- **Network protocols:** Select the protocols you want to be able to use. If the client computer uses the Internet, TCP/IP needs to be selected. If the client uses the services of a remote NetWare server, IPX/SPX must be selected.

- **Enable software compression:** If you are working with a Windows NT server, you can select this to turn on software compression. For troubleshooting purposes, you should turn this off.

- **Enable PPP LCP extensions:** Tells the system that the PPP server can set up the client station and can verify the user name and password. This also should be turned off when you are troubleshooting.

5. If you are using TCP/IP for this connection, you also should set or verify the TCP/IP settings. The TCP/IP setting screen appears; the screen is different depending on the type of server you selected. The options are as follows:

- **Server Assigned IP Address:** Tells the computer that the server will assign the IP address for this station. The server must have some means of assigning IP address to use this option.

- **Specify an IP Address:** Enables you to give the station an IP address. The address needs to be unique and must be correct for the server's network. The server also must enable the client to request an IP address.

- **Server Assigned Name Server Addresses:** Tells the system that the server will assign IP addresses for DNS and WINS servers.

- **Specify Name Server Addresses:** Enables you to set the addresses for DNS and WINS servers. This enables you to see if the server is giving you correct addresses.

- **Use IP Header Compression:** Using IP header compression reduces the overhead transmitted over the modem. For troubleshooting, you should disable this.

- **Use Default Gateway on the Remote Network:** If you are connected to a network and dialed-in to a service provider, this tells Windows NT to send information bound for a remote network to the gateway on the dial-in server.

6. Set the script options on the Script tab, as follows:

- **After dialing (logon):** You can choose three different settings here; make sure the correct one is used. For NT-to-NT communications, you can select None. For other connections, you might have to enter information. For troubleshooting, you should try the terminal window. This enables you to enter the information manually rather than using the script. If this works, you should verify the script.

- **Before dialing:** If you click this button, you are presented with basically the same options. This can be used to bring up a window or to run a script before you dial the remote host.

7. Enter or check the security information on the Security tab. This security should be set to the same level as the security on the server or the connection will probably fail. The options are as follows:

- **Authentication and encryption policy:** Set the level of security you want to use. For troubleshooting, you can try Accept any authentication including clear text. This setting should be set to match the setting on the server.

- **Require data encryption:** If you are using Microsoft-encrypted authentication, you have the option to encrypt all data being sent over the connection. This option should be set the same as the server.

- **Use current name and password:** Enables Windows to use the current username and password as your logon information. If you are not using the same name and password on the client as you do on the network, do not check this box. You will be prompted for the username and password to log on, just as when you attempted to connect.

- **Unsave password:** If you told the system to save the logon password for a connection, you can clear it by clicking this button. You should do this in the case of a logon problem.

8. Finally, you can check or enter the information for X.25 connections.

You can configure many different options; therefore, a great potential exists for errors. Client errors tend to be either validation problems or errors in the network protocols. Remember that you also might need to check the configuration of the server to verify that the client configuration is correct.

4. Dial-In Permissions

Remote Access Server uses integrated Windows NT security. To access the network using Dial-Up Networking, a client has to provide the same account/password combination that is used when connecting directly to the network. In addition, the account needs to have dial-in permissions set.

You can grant users dial-in permissions through the User Manager (or User Manager for Domains) or through the Remote Access Admin program. If you receive an error message that you do not have permission to dial in to the network, this is one of the first things you should check. In User Manager for Domains, the dial-in permissions are set in the property pages for an individual user. Each user has a Dial-in button. From the Dial in property page, the user can be configured as a dial-in user.

You also can set dial-in permissions from the Remote Access Admin utility. In the Remote Access Admin program, select Permissions from the Users menu. You can select each user and set whether the user has dial-in permissions or not. You also can use the Grant All button to grant dial-in permissions to all accounts in the domain.

> You can only grant dial-in permissions on a user-by-user basis. You cannot grant dial-in permissions to a global group or a local group.

5. Configuring Call-Back Security

You also can set call-back options in the Dial-in property pages of User Manager for Domains or Remote Access Admin. Call-back adds another level of security to your network. It also is used to assign long distance charges primarily to the RAS server rather than to the dial-in clients. The call-back levels that can be set include the following:

- **No Call Back:** This is the default; it means the call-back feature is disabled.

- **Set By Caller:** With this option, the user is able to specify the number to be be used when the server calls back. This is useful if you have a large number of users that travel and you want to centralize long distance.

- **Preset To:** This enhances the security of the network by forcing the user to be at a predetermined phone number. If this option is set, the user only can call from that one location.

> In some cases, call-back security cannot be implemented. If the user dials in from a hotel and does not have a direct line to the room, call-back security cannot be implemented.

6

6. Troubleshooting Other Issues with the Client

As mentioned earlier, Windows NT acts as a PPP server. This means the client station and the server undergo a negotiation during the initial phase of the call.

During the negotiation, the client and the server decide on the protocol to be used and the parameters for the protocol. If there are problems when attempting to connect, you might want to set up PPP logging to actually watch the negotiation between the server and the client. This is set up on the server by changing the Logging option, as follows:

```
HKEY_LOCAL_MACHINE\SYSTEM\CurrentControlSet\Services\RASMAN\PPP\Parameters
```

The log file is in the system32\RAS directory and, like the modem log, can be viewed using any text editor. Some other problems you might encounter when dialing in to the network include:

- You must make sure the protocol you are requesting is available on the RAS server. There must be at least one common protocol or the connection fails.

- If you are using NetBEUI, make sure the name used on the RAS client is not in use on the network you are attempting to connect to.

- If you are attempting to connect using TCP/IP, the RAS server must be configured to provide you with an address.

C. Server Issues When Using Remote Access Server

The server side of the dial-in process also can have some configuration and installation issues that affect whether a successful dial-in session is established.

After Remote Access Server is installed, several configuration issues can affect the dial-in clients. You can configure Remote Access Service by opening the Network applet in the Control Panel. On the Services tab, select the Remote Access Service and click the Properties button. The Remote Access Setup dialog box contains the following configuration options:

- **Add:** Enables you to add another port to the RAS server. This could be a modem, an X.25 PAD, or a PPTP Virtual Private Network. Note that to add a Virtual Private Network port, you also must have installed the PPTP Protocol.

- **Remove:** Removes the port from RAS.

- **Configure:** Brings up a dialog box that enables you to configure how this port is used. You can configure the port to be used only for dialing out, only for receiving calls, or it can support both. Check this option if users are not able to dial in.

- **Clone:** This setting enables you to copy a port. Windows NT Server has been tested with up to 256 ports.

> **Due to product restrictions, Windows NT Workstation and Windows 95 (with service pack 1 or the OSR2 release) can only enable one client to dial in.**

After the ports are configured, you need to configure the network settings. These affect what users are able to see, how they are authenticated, and what protocols they are able to use when they dial in to the network. The network settings include:

- **Configuring Dial Out Protocols:** Sets which protocols you can use to dial in to another server.

- **Configuring Dial in Protocols:** Sets the protocols used to connect to you. The following sections detail protocol-specific configuration options.

- **Configuring Server-Side Encryption Settings:** As with the client side of Remote Access Service, encryption levels can be set. The level of security you choose also must be set on the client computer. If the client cannot use at least the same level of security, it cannot be validated by the server.

- **Enabling Multilink Connections:** By enabling the multilink option, the RAS server can accept multilink connections from clients.

a. Configuring NetBEUI on the RAS Server

Very little configuration is required for the NetBEUI protocol. Only one option can be configured—whether to give dial-in users access to the entire network or just to the RAS server.

Built within the NetBEUI protocol is a NetBIOS gateway. The NetBIOS gateway can take requests bound for a server that does not speak NetBEUI and forward them on your behalf. In other words, you can dial in to a server using NetBEUI and connect to file shares on a remote server that only runs NWLink or TCP/IP.

b. Configuring IPX on the RAS Server

If your environment is a mix of both Windows NT and NetWare, you probably want to enable the IPX protocol on the RAS server. This enables clients to communicate with the NetWare servers over the RAS connection (if they also are using a NetWare client).

Again, you have the option to let clients see either the entire network or only this computer. The other options deal with the IPX node numbers that identify a station using IPX. Normally, you do not need to change the defaults; if you are having problems, however, try resetting the dialog box to the default.

The only case in which you might have a problem is when a secure package reads the node number. In this case, do not assign the same node number to all clients. If the numbers need to be entered in the software, either assign a group of node numbers you are able to enter or enable the client to request a specific number.

c. Configuring TCP/IP on the RAS Server

If you run a mixed network that could include UNIX hosts, you should enable the TCP/IP protocol on the RAS server. This also enables your clients to use an Internet connection on your network.

The TCP/IP configuration dialog box enables the administrator to restrict network access to the RAS server or to allow access to the entire network. The other options all deal with assigning TCP/IP addresses to clients dialing in. By default, the RAS server uses a Dynamic Host Configuration Protocol (DHCP) server to assign the addresses. If your DHCP server has a long lease period, you might want to assign the numbers from a pool of addresses given on the server. If you enable the client to request an address, you need to configure the client stations for all the other parameters.

If your clients are having problems connecting, assign a range of addresses to the RAS server. This eliminates any problems related to the DHCP server and still enables you to prevent clients from requesting specific IP addresses.

D. Monitoring the Dial-In Connections

When you are unable to determine whether the client or server portion is causing the problem in a failed dial-up session, you might need to monitor the actual connection. Tools that can be used include the Remote Access Admin monitoring option and the Dial-Up Network Monitor.

1. Monitoring from the RAS Server

From the server, you can use the Remote Access Admin tool to monitor the ports. Select the server you want to look at and double-click it. A list of communication ports appears. For each port available on the server, you will see the user currently connected and the time connected.

From this dialog box, you can disconnect users or you can send a message to all users (or a single user) connected to the server. You also can check the port status, which shows you all the connection statistics for the selected port.

2. Dial-Up Networking Monitor

On the client side, the Dial-Up Networking Monitor is an application you can use to check the status of communications. There are three tabs in the monitor:

- **The Status tab:** Provides the dial-in user with basic information about the connection. From here, you have the option to hang up the connection or to view details about the connection. The details include names the client has registered on the network and the IP address assigned to the client (if using TCP/IP).

- **The Summary tab:** Summarizes all the connections the client currently has open.

- **The Preferences tab:** Enables the dial-in user to control the settings for Dial-Up Networking. Options that can be set include controlling when a sound is played and how the Dial-Up Networking monitor is presented to the user.

D. Other Issues that Affect RAS Connections

Other issues can affect a RAS connection, including authentication problems and the use of multilink when call-back security is enabled. Authentication can be a problem in two areas. First, a client might attempt to connect using the incorrect username and password. This easily can happen if the user is dialing from a home system. The RAS client can be set to attempt the connection using the current username and password, or it might have to unsave the previous password if it has changed on the network.

The other authentication problem occurs if the security settings on the server and the client do not match. You can get around this using the Allow Any Authentication setting or possibly by using the After Dial terminal window. If connection can be achieved using clear text, you must increase the encryption level on both the client and the server to use the highest level of encryption shared by both.

In the case of using call-back security with the multilink protocol, it is not supported over a Public Switched Telephone Network. The initial connection to the server uses multilink. When the server hangs up, however, it only has one number configured for the call-back configuration. The client only uses one line from this point on.

> The only case in which call-back can be enabled for a multilink session is over an ISDN connection using two channels. The two channels must share the same phone number for this to work.

6.5.1 Exercise: Creating a New Dialing Location

This exercise reviews the steps to create a new dialing location. The scenario is this—you are on the road and need to create a new dialing location to access an outside line from your hotel room to access your office network.

1. Open the Windows NT Control Panel by selecting Settings, Control Panel from the Start menu.

2. Open the Telephony applet to create a new dialing location.

3. Click the New button and name the new location Hotel.

4. Set the Area Code to 604 and the country to Canada.

5. Configure the options so you dial 8 to access an outside line for a local call and dial 9 to access an outside line for a long distance call.

6. Enable the checkbox to use a calling card and click the Change button to select the calling card type.

7. Select the Calling Card via 0 option. Enter the card number 80755512121234.

8. Click OK to save the new dialing location.

6.5.2   Exercise: Configuring a Phonebook Entry

This exercise creates a new phonebook entry and uses the dialing location setup in Exercise 6.5.1.

1. Double-click the My Computer icon on the desktop.

2. Double-click the Dial-Up Networking folder in the My Computer window.

3. Click the New button to create a new phonebook entry.

4. Name the new entry New Riders.

5. Set the phonebook entry to use Telephony properties.

6. Set the Area Code to 317.

7. Set the phone number to 555-1234.

8. Click the Alternates button to enter alternative phone numbers.

9. Add the phone number 555-2345. Try reordering the phone numbers. You also can select the option to move successful numbers to the top of the list.

10. Select the modem you want to use for the dial-up entry.

11. On the Server tab, select the NetBEUI protocol.

12. On the Security tab, select to use Microsoft Encrypted Authentication with data encryption. Note that on this tab, you can configure to use the current user and password combination. You also can erase a saved password.

13. Click OK to save the configuration.

14. In the Dial-Up Networking dialog box, set Hotel as the location. Note that the phone number appears as `9 0 317 555-1234 [Calling Card via 0]`.

15. Click the Location button.

16. Change the area code for the Hotel to 317 and click OK.

17. Note that the phone number now has changed to `8 555-1234`.

6.5   Practice Problems

1. Windows NT RAS Server can accept connections using which line protocols? Select all that apply.

   A. SLIP

   B. PPTP

   C. PPP

   D. TCP/IP

2. What does the Multilink Protocol provide?

   A. The capability to connect to a RAS server with multiple protocols.

   B. The capability to dial in to a RAS server from two or more clients at the same time.

   C. The capability to connect to a RAS server using multiple phone lines from the same client.

   D. The capability to connect with ADSL.

3. You have purchased a new modem for use with Dial-Up Networking in Windows NT Workstation., There is only a Windows 95 driver on the modem driver disk, and the Windows NT Workstation CD-ROM does not contain a driver for your new modem. How do you configure your modem for use?

   A. Edit the SWITCH.INFfile.

   B. Edit the MODEM.INFfile.

   C. Use a driver for an older version of the modem.

   D. Use the Windows 95 driver.

4. What advantages does PPP offer over SLIP when connecting to the Internet? Select all that apply.

   A. Auto configuration of TCP/IP

   B. Advanced scripting options for PPP versus SLIP

   C. Support for dial-in protocols other than TCP/IP

   D. Encrypted user authentication

5. How can RAS Server be configured to auto assign IP addresses to dial-in clients? Select all that apply.

   A. Use a DHCP server.

   B. Use the current IP address of the client.

   C. Have its own pool of IP addresses to assign to clients.

   D. This cannot be done. Clients must request their own IP addresses.

6. You want to install Internet tunnels to allow access to the corporate network over the Internet. What must be installed before you configure RAS to provide this capability?

   A. VPN Service

   B. PPTP protocol

   C. L2TP protocol

   D. This functionality is built into RAS and just needs to be configured.

7. You want to install an ISDN adapter on your Windows NT Server. Where do you add the adapter?

   A. On the Adapters page of the Networks applet in the Control Panel.

   B. In the Modems applet of the Control Panel.

   C. In the SCSI Adapter applet of the Control Panel.

   D. In the WAN Adapter applet of the Control Panel.

8. What is the maximum number of inbound connections supported by Windows NT Server?

   A. 1

   B. 64

C. 256

D. Unlimited

9. What network protocols can be used over a PPP connection? Select all that apply.

A. NetBEUI

B. NWLink

C. TCP/IP

D. AppleTalk

10. Under what conditions can a dial-in Windows NT Workstation client access NetWare resources by dialing into a Windows NT Server? Select all that apply.

A. The client dials in via a SLIP connection to a RAS Server running Gateway Services for NetWare.

B. The client dials in via a PPP connection to a RAS Server running Gateway Services for NetWare.

C. The client dials in via a NWLink PPP connection and has Client Services for NetWare installed.

D. The client dials in via a NetBEUI PPP connection and has Client Services for NetWare installed.

11. What security features are included with RAS Server? Select all that apply.

A. Call-back Security

B. Integrated Domain Security

C. Kerberos Server Certificates

D. Support for Intermediary Security Hosts

12. Ruby is dialing in to the RAS server on your network. She complains that the line disconnects right after her user name has been authenticated. This happens every time she attempts to connect to the network, and no further communication

exists. This is most likely due to which of the following?

A. The client is using the wrong network protocol.

B. Ruby has entered the wrong password for her account.

C. Ruby does not have dial-in permissions.

D. Call-back security has been set to a specific phone number for the client and is configured incorrectly.

13. What utilities can be used to assign dial-in permissions to user accounts? Select all that apply.

A. Remote Access Admin

B. Server Manager

C. User Manager for Domains

D. Registry Editor

14. What operating systems can be used to connect to a RAS Server over a PPTP tunnel? Select all that apply.

A. Windows for Workgroups 3.11

B. Windows 95

C. Windows NT Workstation 3.51

D. Windows NT Workstation 4.0

The following scenario applies to questions 15-17. A different solution to the scenario is proposed for each question.

Scenario: Your office wants to enable users to access the office network from home. The office is connected to the Internet through a fractional T1 line.

Required Result: The office has decided to provide only managers with dial-in access to the network. *Optional Result 1:* Because the network is being accessed from the homes of personnel, the office wants to encrypt all information transferred to and from the network. *Optional Result 2:* Due to the nature of the files the managers

6

have access to on the network, it has been determined that call-back security will be implemented. The managers will be called back at a predetermined phone number.

15. *Proposed Solution*: Install a RAS Server that contains a digiboard on the local network. Set up four modems to enable the users to access the network. In User Manager for Domains, create a global group containing all the managers' accounts. In Remote Access Admin, assign the newly created global group the Dial-In permission. Set call-back security on the global group so the users can set the number to be called back at.

This solution:

A. Meets the required result and both optional results.

B. Meets the required result and only one optional result.

C. Meets only the required result.

D. Does not meet the required result.

16. *Proposed Solution*: Install a RAS Server that contains a digiboard on the local network. Set up four modems to enable the users to access the network. Configure so that all clients require Microsoft Encrypted Authentication using data encryption. In User Manager for Domains, select each of the managers' user accounts and grant them Dial-In permissions. Set call-back security on each user account so the users can set the number at which to be called back.

This solution:

A. Meets the required result and both optional results.

B. Meets the required result and only one optional result.

C. Meets only the required result.

D. Does not meet the required result.

17. *Proposed Solution*: Install a RAS Server that contains a digiboard on the local

network. Set up four modems to enable the users to access the network. Configure so that all clients require Microsoft Encrypted Authentication using data encryption. In Remote Access Admin, select each of the managers' user accounts and grant them dial-in permissions. Set call-back security on each user account so each user is called back at a preconfigured phone number.

A. Meets the required result and both optional results.

B. Meets the required result and only one optional result.

C. Meets only the required result.

D. Does not meet the required result.

18. What methods can clients use to connect to RAS servers? Select all that apply.

A. ISDN

B. X.25

C. RadioLan

D. PSTN

19. What methods can be used to reduce dial-in phone charges? Select all that apply.

A. Have all users use the same Internet account.

B. Set call-back security by user.

C. Establish a modem on an 800 line for remote users.

D. Set logon preferences so each dial-in client disconnects if idle for at least 120 seconds.

20. A user notes that when logging on to the network using Dial-Up Networking, it seems to take an exceptionally long time for the logon process to complete. This is most likely due to which of the following?

A. A roaming profile is being downloaded.

B. A login script is being executed.

C. A virus scan is being run.

D. Authentication is always slow over a dial-in connection.

21. A user dials in to your RAS Server using multilink. The server uses call-back security to a user-specified number. The server successfully calls the user back, but the connection is not using multilink anymore. This is due to which of the following?

A. The user must provide both phone numbers for multilink to work.

B. The call-back security feature only works with multilink if it is configured to call back a preconfigured phone number.

C. The user's modems are not on the multilink HCL.

D. Multilink is not supported for call-back security.

22. Autodial can be enabled by which of the following?

A. NetBIOS name

B. Location

C. IP address

D. Time of day

23. Which service needs to be running to enable Autodial functionality?

A. Server Service

B. Remote Access Service

C. Remote Access Autodial Manager

D. Dial-Up Networking Service

24. Where is the file PPP.LOG stored on a NT Server?

A. %SystemRoot%

B. %SystemRoot%\System32

C. %SystemRoot%\System32\PPP

D. %SystemRoot%\System32\RasMan

25. Where can a network administrator view which users have connected to the network using the RAS service, how much data they transferred to and from the network, and how long the users were connected to the RAS server?

A. PPP.LOG

B. Remote Access Admin

C. Event Viewer's System Log

D. Dial-Up Network Monitor

26. Where can a network administrator view actual compression ratios as the user is connected to a Remote Access Server?

A. PPP.LOG

B. Network Monitor

C. Event Viewer

D. Dial-Up Network Monitor

27. What is the one case in which callback security over a multilink connection works?

A. All modems on the server and the client are the same brand and model.

B. The client is using Windows NT Server as the operating system.

C. The connection is established using PPTP.

D. The link between the server and the client uses ISDN with two channels that have the same phone number as the client.

28. A remote client has connected to the office's RAS Server using a NetBEUI PPP connection. The RAS Server is running the NWLink, TCP/IP, and NetBEUI protocols. The DATA server is only running the TCP/IP protocol, and the OFFICE server is only running the NWLink protocol. The MAIL server is only running the NetBEUI protocol. Which servers can the remote client connect to (and use file shares) if the

NetBEUI protocol has been configured to allow access to the entire network? Select all that apply.

A. The RAS server

B. The DATA server

C. The OFFICE server

D. The MAIL server

6.5.1 Answers and Explanations: Exercise

This exercise configured a new dialing location for use with Dial-Up Networking. By configuring a dialing location, you can automate how a phonebook entry is dialed. Dialing locations enable you to configure information such as the area code you are in, prefixes for accessing outside lines, whether the phone line is tone or pulse, and whether you want to use a calling card.

6.5.2 Answers and Explanations: Exercise

This exercise guided you through creating a new phonebook entry. It then investigated how the phone number changes as the location is modified.

You also could investigate changing your location rather than editing the existing location. This indicates how Dial-Up Networking can be configured to change the phone number dialed simply by changing the dialing location.

6.5 Answers and Explanations: Practice Problems

1. **B, C** PPP and PPTP are the only line protocols that a Windows NT RAS Server can accept connections over. SLIP is supported as a client protocol only in Windows NT RAS.

2. **C** Multilink enables multiple phone lines to be used to provide more bandwidth to the client.

3. **D** Windows 95 and Windows NT Workstation can use the same modem configuration files.

4. **A, C, D** PPP provides for auto-configuration, dial-in support for NetBEUI and NWLink, and the encryption of a user's name and password when authenticating.

5. **A, C** When using TCP/IP as a dial-in protocol, a RAS server can assign IP addresses using the network's DHCP server or from its own private pool.

6. **B** By installing the PPTP protocol, you can add Virtual Private Networks (VPNs) to RAS Server.

7. **A** Wide Area Network (WAN) adapters are added in the Adapters property page of the Network applet in the Control Panel.

8. **C** Windows NT has been tested to support 256 inbound RAS connections.

9. **A, B, C** NetBEUI, NWLink, and TCP/IP are all supported network protocols for a PPP session.

10. **B, C** A dial-in client can access a NetWare server if the dial-in server is running Gateway Services for NetWare or if the client is running Client Services for NetWare and using the NWLink protocol when dialing in to the network.

11. **A, B, D** Windows NT RAS Server includes support for call-back security, fully integrated domain authentication, and third-party security hosts such as radius servers.

12. **D** This situation can occur if call-back security has been implemented for a specific user and is set to call the user back at a predetermined number. In this case, the predetermined number is either incorrect or entered incorrectly.

13. **A, C** Dial-in permissions can be set in Remote Access Admin and User Manager for Domains.

14. **B, D** The PPTP protocol can be used in Windows 95 (using Dial-Up Networking version 1.2) and Windows NT Workstation 4.0.

15. **D** Dial-in permissions are granted to individual users, not groups.

16. **B** This solution fulfills the required result of granting secure access to the network. It also assigns the managers access using the User Manager for Domains. It does not meet the second optional result because if a user breaks into the network with a manager's account, he can configure the network to call him back at his own phone number.

17. **A** This solution fulfills all requirements. Remember that dial-in permissions also can be granted in Remote Access Admin. Implementing predetermined phone numbers ensures that the managers are calling in from an approved phone number.

18. **A, B, D** Remote Access Server supports connections via Public Switched Telephone Networks, ISDN, and X.25 networks.

19. **B, C, D** Setting call-back security can reduce costs if the office network is able to take advantage of reduced long distance charges. Likewise, use of an 800 number reduces long distance charges. Setting auto-disconnect times prevents charges from accumulating if the line is not active.

20. **A** If a roaming profile has been configured for a user, configure the client to use a locally cached version of the profile if a slow connection is detected. This is set in the User Profiles tab of the System applet in the Control Panel.

21. **D** Multilink is not supported for call-back security when using modems over Public Switched Telephone Networks.

22. **B** You configure auto-dial functionality by dialing location. This is enabled on a location-by-location basis by viewing the User Preferences in the Dial-Up Network Phonebook.

23. **C** The Remote Access Autodial Manager must be running for Autodial to be available.

24. **D** The PPP.LOG file is stored in the %Systemroot%\System32\RasMan directory.

25. **C** The Windows NT Event Viewer shows an information event after a RAS session has ended. The event contains information about who was connected, how long they were connected, and how much data was transferred over the connection.

26. **D** The Dial-Up Network Monitor shows actual compression information for incoming and outgoing data during a dial-up session.

27. **D** Multilink functionality is available only if the link between the client and the server is an ISDN line using two channels configured to use the same phone number. This is because call-back accepts only a single phone number as a parameter.

28. **A, B, C, D** All servers can be accessed because NetBEUI functions as a NetBIOS gateway, enabling access to servers not running the NetBEUI protocol

6.5 Key Words

Call-back Security

Multilink Protocol (MP)

PPP

PPTP

RAS

SLIP

6.6　Solving Connectivity Problems

Network connectivity problems center around the inability of a client to find the destination server on the network. This can be due to:

- Protocol issues

    - The protocol does not allow routing in a Wide Area Network.

    - The client and the server do not share a common protocol.

    - The protocol is configured improperly.

- Name resolution not being performed correctly

- A physical problem with the network

A.　Protocol Issues that Affect Connectivity

Each protocol has issues that can affect network connectivity. Common to all protocols is the use of NetBIOS computer names in the Windows NT Networking model. When a client connects to a server, the client uses the Computer Name in the Universal Naming Convention (UNC) address. A UNC name is represented in the format *SERVER**SHARE*.

If a Microsoft networking-participant computer starts and finds that another computer has already registered its NetBIOS name, the networking services will not start. The remedy is to give the computer a unique name on the network. This problem can be diagnosed in the Windows NT Event Viewer in the System Log.

Each protocol has specific issues that can affect connectivity. The following sections detail potential problems with the NetBEUI, NWLink, and TCP/IP protocols.

1.　NetBEUI Configuration Issues

NetBEUI is the simplest protocol to use on the network because it automatically configures itself to perform at its best possible level. The major issue with NetBEUI is that it is non-routable. If your network is broken into separate segments, clients using NetBEUI cannot communicate with servers on remote segments of the network. The only physical device that enables this connectivity is a bridge. A bridge logically connects two physical network segments into one large segment.

2.　NWLink Configuration Issues

NWLink is Microsoft's 32-bit implementation of the IPX/SPX protocol standard. NWLink is a routable network commonly associated with Novell NetWare networks.

By default, NWLink alone enables you to interact with client/server class applications running on NetWare servers. It also enables a NetWare client to connect to a SQL server running on a Windows NT box. (The client must be running NetBIOS, which is optional in NetWare.)

If you want to be able to work with the file and print services of a Novell NetWare system, you need to add either Client Services for NetWare (on Windows NT Workstation) or Gateway (and Client) Services for NetWare (on Windows NT Server). These services enable your Windows NT system to become a Novell client.

If you want NetWare clients to use file and print resources on a Windows NT Server, you must load File and Print Services for NetWare. This enables a Windows NT server to emulate a NetWare 3.12 server, which a NetWare client can connect to using its native protocols.

> **Client Services for NetWare enables a user to authenticate to a Novell NetWare 4.x server by indicating the Preferred Tree and the default context. Unfortunately, you cannot manage the Directory Services using NetAdmin or NWAdmin because you have not fully authenticated into the Directory Services. You can do this only if you use NetWare's Windows NT client.**

The only configuration that needs to be checked when NWLink is installed is the frame type. NetWare servers use different frame types depending on the network topology and the version of NetWare in use. If you are having problems communicating with a Novell server, make sure the frame types are the same.

When the frame type is set to Automatic, only a single frame type is loaded. If both Ethernet 802.2 (the default for NetWare 3.12 and later versions) and Ethernet 802.3 (the default for NetWare 3.11 and later versions) are loaded, Windows NT defaults to the Ethernet 802.2 frame type. This prevents communication with any NetWare servers using only the 802.3 frame type.

3. TCP/IP Configuration Issues

The TCP/IP protocol is designed to enable wide area networking and is a routable protocol.

Most problems you encounter using the TCP/IP protocol deal with the actual configuration of the protocol. TCP/IP uses a 32-bit binary address to uniquely identify each host connected to a network. These 32 bits are separated into a network component and a host component.

The number of bits used to identify the network and host components is determined by the subnet mask configuration setting. The network portion is set to all 1s, and the host portion is set to all 0s. This is used to extract the network ID from the IP address, so the computer is able to determine whether a given address is local or remote. (If the network IDs match, it is local; otherwise, it is remote.)

Normally, the IP address is not viewed as a string of 32 1s and 0s; rather, look at it as four decimal numbers between 0 and 255, separated by dots (hence the name *dotted decimal notation*).

You can configure TCP/IP in two ways. You can enter all the information manually, or you can use a DHCP server that provides all the configuration information automatically for the participating hosts.

a. Manual IP Configuration

Be sure you enter each and every IP address used in communication correctly. A common problem with assigning IP addresses manually is that duplicate addresses can be assigned. It is imperative to use an organized method to distribute IP addresses when working with manual IP addresses.

After you have manually configured TCP/IP, you can use the Packet Internet Groper (ping) utility to verify your connectivity to the network.

After you have verified that you are able to communicate using these steps, you should attempt to ping other computers using their Fully Qualified Domain Names (FQDNs).

b. Automatic TCP/IP Configuration

For dynamically allocating IP address, the DHCP Server service is used to create a pool of IP addresses to be assigned to DHCP clients.

When a DHCP server is installed, the first configuration issue is setting up a pool of IP addresses to assign to DHCP clients. Another common issue is that the pool should not contain any IP addresses that have already been assigned on the network. In addition, if there are multiple DHCP servers on the network, the pool of addresses on each DHCP server should not overlap.

The DHCP server also must be assigned a lease duration. When setting the lease duration, keep these factors in mind:

- If the number of clients is very close to the number of IP addresses available to lease, the lease duration should be kept short.

- If the number of clients is low compared to the number of IP addresses available, longer lease durations can be set.

- Lease duration is applied on a scope-by-scope basis.

- DHCP clients renew their DHCP lease every time the computer is restarted, at 50 percent of the lease duration and at 87.5 percent of the lease duration.

In order to verify the IP configuration that a DHCP server has assigned to a DHCP client, you can use the IPCONFIG command. The IPCONFIG command—when entered without parameters—returns your IP address, your subnet mask, and your default gateway settings.

Microsoft DHCP clients not only can get their IP addresses and subnet mask settings from the DHCP server, several other options can be assigned as well, including:

- **[003] Router:** The Router setting contains the IP address for the default gateway for the subnet the DHCP client is on.

- **[006] DNS Server:** The DNS Server setting contains the IP addresses of the DNS server that the DHCP client can query when it needs to resolve a hostname or Fully Qualified Domain Name to an IP address.

- **[015] Domain Name:** The Domain Name setting contains the domain name the host is using in an intranet. The host www.company.com, for example, has its domain name set to company.com and its hostname to www.

- **[044] WINS/NBNS Servers:** The WINS/NBNS (NetBIOS Name Server) setting contains the IP addresses of servers that will provide a NetBIOS name to IP address-resolution services.

- **[046] WINS/NBT Node Type:** The WINS/NBT (NetBIOS over TCP/IP) Node Type determines what methods will be implemented (and in what order) to resolve a NetBIOS name to an IP address.

- **[047] NetBIOS Scope ID:** The NetBIOS Scope ID setting can segment NetBIOS clients into working groups that cannot communicate with each other (even if they are on the same network segment).

B. Name Resolution Issues

Microsoft networking clients use two methods of name resolution in their day-to-day transactions. When performing native Windows NT networking, they commonly use *NetBIOS name resolution*. When using intranet or Internet technologies, they use *hostname resolution*.

All protocols included with Windows NT support NetBIOS name resolution methods. The TCP/IP protocol requires that an additional service be installed for efficient resolution of NetBIOS names to IP addresses. This service is known as the WINS Server service.

Only the TCP/IP protocol provides the capability to resolve hostnames or Fully Qualified Domain Names to IP addresses. The TCP/IP protocol requires that a Domain Name Service (DNS) server assist in the resolution of hostnames to IP addresses.

1. The WINS Server Service

The WINS Server service provides a centralized database of NetBIOS names to IP address mappings. WINS clients automatically register their NetBIOS names and IP address to the WINS server every time they start.

WINS clients can be configured to use the WINS server as their primary method of NetBIOS name resolution. There are four methods of NetBIOS name resolution that the WINS clients can use: B-node, P-Node, M-Node, or H-Node.

2. The DNS Server Service

The DNS Server service provides hostname-to-IP address resolution. Hostnames are used for most common Internet applications, such as FTP, Web browsing, Telnet, and IRC. The resolution of hostnames to IP addresses is performed by three components:

- **Domain Name Space:** Every host on the Internet requires a unique Fully Qualified Domain Name. The registration of each unique name is managed by Internic to ensure that duplication does not occur.
- **Name Resolver:** Any client that needs to resolve a hostname to an IP address is functioning as a name resolver.
- **Name Server:** The name server contains lists of hostnames and their IP addresses. The name server can contain records that represent services (for example, a Mail Exchanger record to represent that a host is the mail server for a domain) or aliases for hosts.

If you are unable to resolve hostnames on the Internet using a Web browser or FTP client, you must check whether you have configured the correct IP address for your DNS server. The NSLOOKUP command can be used to determine whether the hostname is being resolved correctly on your DNS Server. The NSLOOKUP commands syntax is as follows:

```
NSLOOKUP <hostname>
```

This returns the resolved IP address for the entered hostname. It also can be run in a batch mode by simply typing **NSLOOKUP**.

C.   Physical Network Problems

If the network has suffered breakdowns in its physical components, this also can lead to the inability of clients to connect to servers. If information cannot flow between two sites due to a downed router, connectivity cannot take place. A Simple Network Management Protocol (SNMP) management utility can assist in diagnosing a breakdown in the physical network in a timely fashion. Windows NT includes SNMP services that enable an NT client to be managed by an SNMP manager. It does not provide any management software itself. These are generally third-party products such as HP OpenView.

D.   Tools for Troubleshooting Connectivity Problems

Windows NT contains several tools that can be used to troubleshoot connectivity problems. These include

- The Network Monitor

- The Server Manager

- The TRACERT command

- The NETSTAT command

The Network Monitor application can be used to examine network traffic and to monitor network performance. The Network Monitor is a network sniffer and can be used to check for the following:

- **Bad packet cyclic redundancy checks (CRCs):** A packet with a bad CRC value indicates that the packet is corrupted.

- **Network saturation:** This is caused by a network card constantly sending broadcast packets.

- **Packet Recognition:** Understanding what common traffic flows should look like can help in diagnosing a communication error. Detecting where communication is breaking down can assist in determining where the problem lies and can lead to a quicker resolution. You might notice, for example, that the DHCP client is placing Discover packets onto the network, but the DHCP server is not sending offers. You can rule out that the problem is on the client.

The Server Manager program can be used to manage services running on a Windows NT computer. If the workstation or server service is not functioning on a Windows NT computer, this can lead to connectivity failure if the computer is part of an equation.

The TRACERT command can be used to determine what route is taken when a computer attempts to communicate with a host on a remote network. It also reports how many routers have been crossed when the remote host is communicated with.

The NETSTAT command can be used to determine what ports are in use when a communication session is taking place. TCP/IP Winsock applications use preconfigured ports to connect. Many networks now have firewalls in place that prevent certain ports from being used. The NETSTAT command can be used to determine which ports might need to be opened on a firewall.

6.6.1 Exercise: Investigating NetBIOS Names

This exercise guides you through using the NBTSTAT command to investigate what NetBIOS names your computer has registered on the network. This exercise assumes that the TCP/IP protocol is installed on your system.

1. Start a command prompt.

2. At the command prompt, type the following command:

   `C:\>nbtstat -n`

   You will see output similar to the following:

```
Node IpAddress: [131.107.2.200] Scope Id: []

        NetBIOS Local Name Table

   Name           Type      Status
   ─────────────────────────────────────
   SIDESHOWBRI    <00> UNIQUE    Registered
   CLASSROOMB     <00> GROUP     Registered
   CLASSROOMB     <1C> GROUP     Registered
   SIDESHOWBRI    <20> UNIQUE    Registered
   CLASSROOMB     <1B> UNIQUE    Registered
   SIDESHOWBRI    <03> UNIQUE    Registered
   CLASSROOMB     <1E> GROUP     Registered
   INet~Services <1C> GROUP      Registered
   IS~SIDESHOWBRI.<00> UNIQUE    Registered
   CLASSROOMB     <1D> UNIQUE    Registered
   .._MSBROWSE__.<01> GROUP      Registered
   ADMINISTRATOR <03> UNIQUE     Registered
```

3. Based on the information you see, is this computer a Primary Domain Controller? If so, what entry tells you this? What is the name of the domain?

4. What is the name of the user logged in to this system? Which entry tells you this?

5. Is the computer a master browser on the subnet where it is located? Which entry tells you this?

6.6.2 Exercise: Troubleshooting NWLink Configuration Errors

This exercise shows you how to troubleshoot if a client is unable to connect to any resources when using the NWLink protocol. This exercise assumes the NWLink protocol is installed on your computer.

1. Start a command prompt.

2. Type the following command:

   `C:\>ipxroute config`

You should see output similar to the following:

```
NWLink IPX Routing and Source Routing Control Program v2.00
net 1: network number 00000000, frame type 802.2, device CE31
(0080c72254bf)
```

3. What is the network number assigned to your network card?

4. When would you see multiple network numbers?

5. What is the MAC address of your network adapter?

6. What issues are involved with the frame type configuration?

6.6   Practice Problems

1. What connectivity feature of Windows NT enables secure access to a Windows NT network over public networks?

   A. PPP

   B. SLIP

   C. PPTP

   D. NetBIOS Scope ID

2. The two offices of MNO Office Supplies are linked by a dedicated T1 line. The network is configured to use NetBEUI as its network protocol. Users can connect to any servers on their network segment, but cannot view resources on the remote network segment. This is due to which of the following?

   A. They require a WINS server.

   B. They need to configure LMHOSTS files at each computer.

   C. A static route needs to be added on the router to direct traffic between the two segments.

   D. NetBEUI does not support routing.

3. You want to connect to a client/server application located on a NetWare server. What must be configured on your Windows NT Workstation to enable connectivity?

   A. NWLink protocol

   B. RIP for IPX

   C. Client Services for NetWare

   D. SAP Agent

4. You want to connect to a printer hosted by a NetWare server. What must be configured on your Windows NT Workstation to enable connectivity? Select all that apply.

   A. NWLink protocol

   B. RIP for IPX

   C. Client Services for NetWare

   D. SAP Agent

The following scenario applies to questions 5–7. A different solution to the scenario is proposed for each question.

Scenario: Your network is running a mix of NetWare and Windows NT servers. All your client systems are using the Windows NT Workstation operating system.

5. *Required Result:* Connectivity must be established to file and print services in both the NetWare and Windows NT environments. *Optional Result 1:* You want to be able to manage the users in the Windows NT domain from your own Windows NT Workstation computer. *Optional Result 2:* You want to be able to manage the users on the NetWare 4.x servers in your environment.

   Proposed Solution: Add Client Services for NetWare and the NWLink protocol to all your Windows NT client systems. Configure Client Services for NetWare to authenticate to the correct Directory Tree and to set the correct default context. Perform user management on the Windows NT domain with the User Manager utility, and use the NWADMIN.EXE utility to manage the NetWare servers.

   This solution:

   A. Meets the required result and both of the optional results.

   B. Meets the required result and only one of the optional results.

   C. Meets only the required result.

   D. Does not meet the required result.

6. *Required Result:* Connectivity must be established to file and print services in both the NetWare and Windows NT environments. *Optional Result 1:* You want to be able to manage the users in the Windows NT domain from your own Windows NT Workstation computer. *Optional Result 2:* You want to be able to manage the users on the NetWare 3.x servers in your environment.

Proposed Solution: Add Client Services for NetWare and the NWLink protocol to all your Windows NT client systems. Configure Client Services for NetWare with the correct Preferred Server setting. Perform user management on the Windows NT domain with the User Manager utility, and use the SYSCON.EXE utility to manage the NetWare servers.

This solution:

A. Meets the required result and both optional results.

B. Meets the required result and only one optional result.

C. Meets only the required result.

D. Does not meet the required result.

7. *Required Result:* Connectivity must be established to file and print services in both the NetWare and Windows NT environments. *Optional Result 1:* You want to be able to manage the users in the Windows NT domain from your own Windows NT Workstation computer. *Optional Result 2:* You want to be able to manage the users on the NetWare 3.x servers in your environment.

Proposed Solution: Add Client Services for NetWare and the NWLink protocol to all your Windows NT client systems. Configure Client Services for NetWare with the correct Preferred Server setting, and install Server Tools for Windows NT. Perform user management on the Windows NT domain using the User Manager for Domains utility, use the SYSCON.EXE utility to manage the NetWare servers.

This solution:

A. Meets the required result and both optional results.

B. Meets the required result and only one optional result.

C. Meets only the required result.

D. Does not meet the required result.

8. Your network has a mix of NetWare 3.x and NetWare 4.x servers. A Windows NT workstation cannot connect to all the NetWare servers even though Client Services for NetWare and NWLink appear to be properly configured. What potentially is the problem?

A. There are frame type issues.

B. Preferred Server is configured incorrectly.

C. The default context is set incorrectly.

D. You need to switch the default network provider to NetWare from Microsoft.

9. What service is used in TCP/IP networks to resolve NetBIOS names to IP addresses?

A. DNS

B. WINS

C. DHCP

D. SNMP

10. What service is used in TCP/IP networks to resolve Fully Qualified Domain Names to IP addresses?

A. DNS

B. WINS

C. DHCP

D. SNMP

11. Which protocol in the TCP/IP protocol suite is used to resolve an IP address to a physical MAC address?

A. WINS

B. Services for Macintosh

C. SNMP

D. ARP

The following scenario applies to questions 12–14. A different solution to the scenario is proposed for each question.

Scenario: The Cosmos Corporation wants to use TCP/IP as the primary protocol on the wide area network between two sites. The corporation has had issues assigning IP addresses to all the hosts on its network and has brought in your consulting firm to assist with the IP address rollout.

Required Result: The Cosmos Corporation wants to reduce the number of hosts that require manual IP address configuration. *Optional Result 1:* The Cosmos Corporation wants to provide fault tolerance in case the primary IP address-assignment server fails. *Optional Result 2:* The Cosmos Corporation wants to reduce the broadcast traffic on the network.

12. *Proposed Solution:* Set up two DHCP servers on separate segments with the Scope of IP addresses set as shown in Table 6.6.1:

    Also configure a DHCP relay agent on each network segment to forward any DHCP packets to the DHCP server on the remote segment.

    This solution:

    A. Meets the required result and both optional results.

    B. Meets the required result and only one optional result.

    C. Meets only the required result.

    D. Does not meet the required result.

13. *Proposed Solution:* Set up two DHCP servers on separate segments with the Scope of IP addresses set as shown in Table 6.6.2:

    Also configure a DHCP relay agent on each network segment to forward any DHCP packets to the DHCP server on the remote segment.

    This solution:

    A. Meets the required result and both optional results.

    B. Meets the required result and only one optional result.

    C. Meets only the required result.

    D. Does not meet the required result.

14. *Proposed Solution:* Set up two DHCP servers on separate segments with the Scope of IP addresses set as shown in Table 6.6.3:

    Also configure a DHCP relay agent on each network segment to forward any DHCP packets to the DHCP server on the remote segment.

    This solution:

    A. Meets the required result and both optional results.

    B. Meets the required result and only one optional result.

    C. Meets only the required result.

    D. Does not meet the required result.

Table 6.6.1

	Server1	Server2
Scope	192.168.2.10–192.168.3.254 with subnet mask 255.255.0.0	192.168.2.10–192.168.3.254 with subnet mask 255.255.0.0
Scope Options	Def Gateway—192.168.2.1 DNS Server—192.168.3.9	Def Gateway—192.168.3.1 DNS Server—192.168.3.9

Table 6.6.2

	Server1	Server2
Scope1	192.168.2.10–192.168.2.200 with subnet mask 255.255.255.0	192.168.3.10–192.168.3.200 with subnet mask 255.255.255.0
Scope2	192.168.3.201–192.168.3.254 with subnet mask 255.255.255.0	192.168.2.201–192.168.2.254 with subnet mask 255.255.255.0
Scope1 Options	Def Gateway—192.168.2.1 WINS Server—192.168.2.8 WINS Node Type—Mixed	Def Gateway—192.168.3.1 WINS Server—192.168.2.8 WINS Node Type—Mixed
Scope 2 Options	Def Gateway—192.168.3.1 WINS Server—192.168.2.8 WINS Node Type—Mixed	Def Gateway—192.168.2.1 WINS Server—192.168.2.8 WINS Node Type—Mixed

Table 6.6.3

	Server1	Server2
Scope1	192.168.2.10–192.168.2.200 with subnet mask 255.255.255.0	192.168.3.10–192.168.3.200 with subnet mask 255.255.255.0
Scope2	192.168.3.201–192.168.3.254 with subnet mask 255.255.255.0	192.168.2.201–192.168.2.254 with subnet mask 255.255.255.0
Scope1 Options	Def Gateway—192.168.2.1 WINS Server—192.168.2.8 WINS Node Type—Hybrid	Def Gateway—192.168.3.1 WINS Server—192.168.2.8 WINS Node Type—Hybrid
Scope 2 Options	Def Gateway—192.168. 3.1 WINS Server—192.168.2.8 WINS Node Type—Hybrid	Def Gateway—192.168.2.1 WINS Server—192.168.2.8 WINS Node Type—Hybrid

15. What file can be used instead of WINS to provide NetBIOS name resolution?

    A. HOSTS
    B. LMHOSTS
    C. LMHOSTS.SAM
    D. HOSTS.SAM

16. How do you optimize network protocol usage when multiple protocols are installed on a system?

    A. Adjust the network bindings.
    B. Set a default protocol.
    C. Install the protocols in the order you prefer to use them.
    D. This cannot be done.

17. Which methods are used to reduce browser traffic on a network? Select all that apply.

    A. Disable file and print sharing on any clients that do not require these services.
    B. Disable the Browser service on all clients.
    C. Adjust the binding order on all clients.
    D. Reduce the number of protocols on the network.

The following scenario applies to questions 18–20. A different solution to the scenario is proposed for each question.

Scenario: The Pelican Insurance Company wants to enable file and print connectivity to its Windows NT server for its NetWare clients. Pelican created the following requirements for this system.

Required Result: Pelican wants to create common file-storage locations for both the NetWare and Windows NT clients. *Optional Result 1*: Pelican wants to establish common drive-letter mappings for both NetWare and Windows NT users. *Optional Result 2*: Pelican wants to limit the number of protocols in use on the network.

18. *Proposed Solution*: Install Gateway Services for NetWare on the Windows NT server to enable connectivity to Windows NT resources. Set a login script in the %systemroot%\System32\ repl\import\scripts directory that establishes common drive letters for NetWare and Windows NT clients. Install the TCP/IP protocol on all servers and clients.

    This solution:

    A. Meets the required result and both optional results.

    B. Meets the required result and only one optional result.

    C. Meets only the required result.

    D. Does not meet the required result.

19. *Proposed Solution*: Install File and Print Services for NetWare on the Windows NT server to enable connectivity to Windows NT resources by NetWare clients. Set a login script in the %systemroot%\System32\repl\import\scripts directory that establishes common drive letters for Windows NT clients. Install the NWLink protocol on all servers and clients.

    This solution:

    A. Meets the required result and both optional results.

    B. Meets the required result and only one optional result.

    C. Meets only the required result.

    D. Does not meet the required result.

20. *Proposed Solution*: Install File and Print Services for NetWare on the Windows NT server to enable connectivity to Windows NT resources by NetWare clients. Set a login script in the %systemroot%\System32\repl\import\scripts directory that establishes common drive letters for Windows NT clients. Configure a login script in the NetWare compatibility settings so that each NetWare client uses the same drive mappings. Install the NWLink protocol on all servers and clients.

    This solution:

    A. Meets the required result and both optional results.

    B. Meets the required result and only one optional result.

    C. Meets only the required result.

    D. Does not meet the required result.

21. Which protocol offers routing capabilities with the least amount of configuration?

    A. NetBEUI

    B. NWLink

    C. TCP/IP

    D. DLC

22. Your Windows NT server is configured with both the TCP/IP and NWLink protocols. The TCP/IP protocol is used only for enabling connections from Microsoft clients; the NWLink protocol is used to connect to a client/server application hosted on a NetWare server. What binding adjustments can be performed to optimize the network protocols? Select all that apply.

    A. Disable the TCP/IP protocol for the Workstation Service.

    B. Disable the NWLink protocol for the Workstation Service.

    C. Disable the TCP/IP protocol for the Server Service.

    D. Disable the NWLink protocol for the Server Service.

23. Which protocols can be used to connect to IBM mainframes? Select all that apply.

    A.　NetBEUI

    B.　NWLink

    C.　TCP/IP

    D.　DLC

24. You use the network monitor to diagnose why clients on a remote subnet are taking a long time to authenticate on the network. It is discovered that the clients are all authenticating with a BDC on a remote subnet rather than the local BDC. What setting should you use to configure the NetBIOS node type on this subnet to speed up authentication, yet enable authentication from remote BDCs if the local BDC is down?

    A.　Pointed

    B.　Broadcast

    C.　Mixed

    D.　Hybrid

25. Which command can be used to determine how many routers are crossed when communicating with a remote TCP/IP network?

    A.　ROUTE.EXE

    B.　TRACERT.EXE

    C.　NETSTAT.EXE

    D.　NET CONFIG

26. What command can be used to determine which ports are in use during a network session?

    A.　ROUTE.EXE

    B.　NBTSTAT.EXE

    C.　NETSTAT.EXE

    D.　NET CONFIG

27. Which commands can be used to view your network adapter's MAC address? Select all that apply.

    A.　IPCONFIG /ALL

    B.　ARP -A

    C.　NBTSTAT -n

    D.　NET CONFIG WORKSTATION

28. You can connect to any computers on your local network segment using TCP/IP, but not to any computers on remote network segments. Which of the following is a likely cause of the problem?

    A.　Incorrect subnet mask

    B.　Incorrect default gateway

    C.　Incorrect DNS setting

    D.　Incorrect WINS setting

29. What line can be entered in the LMHOSTS file to preload the address 172.16.3.16 for the Primary Domain Controller XERXES in the XANADU domain?

    A.　`172.16.3.16  XERXES  #CACHE #DOM:XANADU`

    B.　`XERXES  172.16.3.16 #CACHE #DOM:XANADU`

    C.　`172.16.3.16  XERXES  #PRE #DOM:XANADU`

    D.　`XERXES  172.16.3.16 #PRE #DOM:XANADU`

6.6.1　Answers and Explanations: Exercise

This exercise helped you recognize the NetBIOS names a computer registers on the network. Knowing the NetBIOS name registrations can help you recognize when a service has failed. You also can use the NBTSTAT command to view your NetBIOS name cache. The NetBIOS name cache contains the NetBIOS names that have been resolved by your computer. The answers to the specific questions posed in the exercise are:

3. This computer is a Primary Domain Controller. The entry CLASSROOMB <1B> is registered only by the PDC for a domain. This computer is a PDC for the CLASSROOMB domain.

4. The Administrator is currently logged on to the system. This is based on the Administrator <03> entry. The <03> entry is registered by the messenger service.

5. Yes. This computer is a master browser on the subnet. This is based on the ..__MSBROWSE__.<01> entry. The master browser for a workgroup or domain on a subnet registers this NetBIOS name.

6.6.2 Answers and Explanations: Exercise

This exercise investigated the use of the IPXROUTE command. The IPXROUTE command also can be used to determine which servers are using the Server Advertising Protocol (SAP) and to display routing statistics if RIP for IPX/SPX is installed. The answers to the specific questions asked in this exercise are:

```
NWLink IPX Routing and
Source Routing Control
Program v2.00
net 1: network number
00000000, frame type
802.2, device CE31
(0080c72254bf)
```

3. The network number assigned to this network card is 00000000. This is the default value used when automatic frame configuration is chosen.

4. You would see multiple network numbers in one of two cases. First, if the network card has been configured to use multiple frame types, each frame type would be assigned a unique network number. The other case is when multiple network cards

are installed on the system. Each card would have a unique network number.

5. The MAC address of the network card in question is 0080C72254BF.

6. If the Windows NT computer is using a different frame type than the rest of the computers on the network, then communication will not take place on the network segment using NWLink.

6.6 Answers and Explanations: Practice Problems

1. **C** PPTP enables secure tunnels to be established over public networks such as the Internet.

2. **D** NetBEUI is fast performing and requires no configuration, but it does not support routing. This protocol cannot be used to link two remote offices.

3. **A** Connecting to a client/server application on a NetWare server only requires the NWLink protocol.

4. **A, C** To use file and print services on a NetWare server, a Windows NT Workstation computer requires both the NWLink protocol and Client Services for NetWare.

5. **A** This solution meets only the required result. You must use User Manager for Domains (not User Manager) to manage users in a Windows NT domain. The NWAdmin utility cannot be used with Client Services for NetWare because the user has not logged in to the directory services of NetWare. To run NWAdmin, you must load the NetWare client for Windows NT.

6. **B** You can manage a NetWare 3.x server running both Client Services for NetWare and SYSCON.EXE, but you must run User Manager for Domains to manage users in a Windows NT domain.

7. **A** If you install the Server Tools for Windows NT Workstation, you can manage the Windows NT domain with User Manager for Domains.

8. **A** If Windows NT is set to auto-detect frame types, it defaults to an Ethernet 802.2 frame if it detects both Ethernet 802.2 and Ethernet 802.3 frame types on the network. NetWare 3.11 (and earlier versions) used 802.3 as the default frame type. NetWare 3.12 and 4.x use Ethernet 802.2 as the default frame type.

9. **B** WINS provides NetBIOS-to-IP address resolution in a Windows NT network.

10. **A** DNS provides FQDN-to-IP address resolution in a Windows NT network.

11. **D** The Address Resolution Protocol (ARP) is used to resolve an IP address to a MAC address.

12. **A** This solution does not work. You do not want to create overlapping scopes on the two servers. Even though the DHCP relay agent would pass requests to the other server, the clients would receive incorrect default gateway information if they received an IP address from the other subnet's server.

13. **B** The first two requirements are met. Using DHCP assists in reducing manual configuration by properly configuring the scopes on each server to not overlap. By using a mixed node type, however, NetBIOS name resolution is performed first using a broadcast and then a WINS lookup.

14. **A** This solution meets all the requirements.

15. **B** The LMHOSTS file can be used to provide NetBIOS name resolution in Microsoft networking. It must be located in the %Systemroot%\System32\Drivers\Etc directory.

16. **A** To optimize network protocols, you should order the bindings for each network service to use the desired protocols first.

17. **A, D** By disabling file and print sharing on unnecessary clients, you reduce the number of computers making browser announcements on the network. By reducing the number of protocols on the network, you reduce the total number of browser election packets as a separate election for browse masters that occur for each protocol.

18. **D** Gateway Services for NetWare enable Microsoft clients to intermittently use file and print services on a NetWare server. This scenario requires NetWare clients to connect to resources on a Windows NT server.

19. **B** Only Windows NT clients can process login batch files in the NETLOGON share. This does not meet the first optional result.

20. **A** This solution meets all requirements.

21. **B** NWLink requires the least configuration for a routable protocol.

22. **A, D** The TCP/IP protocol is not used when acting as a client, and the NWLink protocol is not used to enable other systems to connect to file shares. You can disable these bindings to optimize the network bindings on the system.

23. **C, D** TCP/IP and DLC can be used to connect to IBM mainframes.

24. **C** By using Mixed for the NetBIOS node type, the client first broadcasts and then uses a WINS lookup.

25. **B** The TRACERT command indicates how many routers are crossed when communicating with a remote host.

26. **C** The NETSTAT command shows which ports are in use during a network session.

27. **A, D** The IPCONFIG /ALL and NET CONFIG WORKSTATION commands can be used to view your network adapter's MAC address.

6

28. **B** If the default gateway is configured incorrectly, you can connect only to local hosts.

29. **C** The correct syntax for an LMHOSTS entry is `<IP Address> <NetBIOS Name>  #PRE   #DOM:<Domain name>`.

6.6   Key Words

Client Services for NetWare (CSNW)

File and Print Services for NetWare

Frame types

Gateway Services for NetWare

IPCONFIG

NBTSTAT

NetBEUI

NetBIOS

NETSTAT

NWLink

Ping

TCP/IP

TRACERT

6.7   Solving Resource Access and Permissions Problems

When resources cannot be accessed, and there is not a network connectivity problem, it generally can be attributed to incorrect share or NTFS permissions. This section discusses how to trouble-shoot resource access problems that result from incorrect permissions, and how share and NTFS permissions interact with each other.

Another issue is group usage in a multidomain environment. Planning your domain environment for growth and using groups in your security assignments can assist you in creating a security environment that will expand into a multidomain environment.

A.   Share Permissions

In Windows NT networking, shares provide an access point into a server's file stores. Setting share permissions determines which users have access to a file share and what level of access they have.

Share permissions do not change from the entry-point directory. In other words, if a user only has Read access to a shared directory, that user also only has Read access to all subdirectories. The shared permissions that can be assigned to a directory include:

- **No Access:** No Access permissions override all other permissions assigned to a shared directory. If a user (or a group the user is a member of) is assigned No Access permissions, he cannot gain access to the file share.
- **Read:** Read permissions enable the assigned user to view documents, to copy information from the shared directory, and to run programs.
- **Change:** Change permissions include all the privileges of the Read permission, plus the capability to modify and to delete any files contained in the shared directory.
- **Full Control:** Full Control permissions include all the privileges of the Change permission, plus the capability to change the share permissions on the shared directory.

By default, a newly created file share is assigned to the EVERYONE special group with Full Control permissions. This default generally should be changed because it grants access rights to the file share.

> It is recommended that you never use the EVERYONE special group when assigning permissions. The EVERYONE special group includes all users that connect to the file share, including users you do not know about. It is better to use the local group USERS.

Some final issues that must be considered when you use share permissions are:

- Share permissions can be applied only to directory objects. You cannot apply share permissions to the file's level of access.
- On FAT volumes, share permissions are the only level of security that can be applied.
- Share permissions can be applied only to users connecting through the network. Share permissions do not apply to local security.

B.   NTFS Permissions

When you use NTFS volumes, you can apply NTFS permissions. NTFS permissions can be applied to both directories and files. This enables the administrator to assign varying levels of access to files within the same directory structure. It is therefore possible to have many different files in a directory that have their own individual permissions. There are six specific NTFS permissions that can be assigned to directories and files. They are:

- **Read (R):** Allows viewing the names of files and subdirectories.
- **Write (W):** Allows adding files and subdirectories.
- **Execute (X):** Allows changing to subdirectories in the directory.
- **Delete (D):** Allows deleting the directory.
- **Change Permissions (P):** Allows changing the directory's permissions.
- **Take Ownership (O):** Allows taking ownership of the directory.

Due to POSIX compliance, Windows NT has an exception rule that appears to break the NTFS permissions. If an NTFS folder is assigned the NTFS Full Control permissions, users can delete a file even if they have been assigned No Access permissions on the file. This is because, under POSIX, if users have full control of a directory, they can perform any task to the underlying files.

If you do not want this to be the case, assign the special permissions Read, Write, Execute, Delete, Permissions, and Ownership. Even though this is equivalent to Full Control permissions, the Windows NT operating system recognizes that they have been assigned separately. The Windows NT operating system then does not allow the deletion of a file if file-level permissions prevent it.

C.   Combining Permissions

One thing that complicates matters is that you can assign both NTFS permissions and share permissions to a folder. In addition, the files in a share also can have NTFS file permissions. The effective permissions will be the most restrictive of the share and NTFS permissions. Evaluate each set of permissions separately, then compare them to determine which is most restrictive.

A good rule of thumb is to set the share permissions to the maximum level of NTFS permissions required within the directory structure. If you use this rule, you only have to troubleshoot the NTFS permissions. This is because the NTFS permissions are always the most restrictive.

D.   Implementing Permissions in a Multidomain Environment

When assigning permissions, make sure you use the Account-Global Groups-Local Groups-Permissions (AGLP) methodology, as follows:

- An account is created for each user.
- The accounts are grouped together into global groups. Global groups can only contain accounts from the same domain. If multiple domains exist, you need to create a global group in each of the domains.

- The global groups are made members of local groups in the domain in which the resource exists. If the resource exists on a domain controller, the local group is created in the domain account database. If the resource exists on a Windows NT Member Server or NT Workstation, you create the local group in the account database of that system.

> You do not have to go to the specific system to add a local group to a Member Server or NT Workstation account database. In User Manager for Domains, you can modify a computer's account database by typing **computername** in the dialog box presented when you choose Select Domain from the User menu.

- The local group(s) are assigned the appropriate permissions.

This methodology should be applied to both NTFS and share permissions. If you use this methodology, it expands well into a multidomain environment.

Remember that in a multidomain environment, appropriate trust relationships must be established. A trust relationship should be established so the Resource domains trust the Account domains. In this case, local groups in the Resource domains can have global groups from the Account domains assigned as members.

E. Other Issues with NTFS Permissions

When a file is copied or moved on an NTFS partition, the permissions might change. This can lead to unexpected resource access problems when the NTFS permissions are not what was expected. Remember the following rules for moving and copying files:

- When a file is copied into an NTFS directory, the file assumes the NTFS permissions of the target directory.

- If a file is moved to an NTFS directory on the same NTFS partition, the file retains its original NTFS permissions.

- If a file is moved to an NTFS directory on a different NTFS partition, the file assumes the NTFS permissions of the target directory.

- If a file is moved or copied to a non-NTFS partition, all NTFS permissions are lost.

6.7.1 Exercise: Testing NTFS Permissions

This exercise requires a single NTFS partition to test NTFS permission assignments.

1. Open the Windows NT Explorer.

2. Select the NTFS drive in the left pane and select File, New, Folder from the menus. Name the folder NTFSTEST.

3. Right-click the NTFSTEST folder and select Properties from the pop-up menu.

4. Select the Security tab and click the Permissions button.

5. Note that security is set to EVERYONE with Full Control permissions by default. Click the Remove button to remove the EVERYONE permission assignment.

6. Click the Add button and select the Users local group. Set the type of access to Change.

7. Click the OK button to set the new permissions and click the following OK button to close the properties of the folder.

8. Select the NTFSTEST folder in the left pane.

9. Select File, New, Text File from the menu to create a new document in the folder. Name it RIGHTS.

10. Right-click the RIGHTS file in the right pane and select Properties.

11. From the menu, select the Security tab and select Permissions.

12. Note that the permissions for the newly created file also are Change permissions. This is because new files inherit the permissions of the parent directory.

13. Change the type of access to No Access. You are warned that No Access permissions prevent any users from accessing the object after you click the OK button to change the permissions. Click the Yes button to acknowledge the warning.

14. Attempt to open the file. What is the error message you receive?

15. Start a command prompt and change the current directory to NTFSTEST.

16. Attempt to delete the file. Can you delete the file? Why or why not?

17. Change the permissions on the directory to Full Control for the Users group. Be sure not to apply the changes to the files in the directory.

18. Attempt to delete the file again. Can you delete the file? Why or why not?

6.7.2   Exercise: Testing the Effects of Copying and Moving

This exercise tests how copying and moving affects NTFS permissions. This exercise assumes the NTFSTEST directory still exists and the USERS group has Full Control permissions.

1. Start the Windows NT Explorer.

2. In the root directory of your NTFS partition, create a new text file. Name it Change.

3. Assign the new text file Administrators permissions and Change permissions.

4. Create another text file in the root directory. Name it READ.

5. Assign this file Administrators permissions and Read permissions.

6. Copy the Change file to the NTFSTEST directory.

7. Move the Read file to the NTFSTEST directory.

8. What are the permissions on each file?

6.7 Practice Problems

1. What are the default permissions assigned to a new file share?

   A. Users, Change permissions

   B. Everyone, Change permissions

   C. Users, Full Control

   D. Everyone, Full Control

2. The ACME Corporation has offices in St. Louis, Vancouver, and New Orleans. Each office has been installed with its own Windows NT domain. The ACME Corporation wants all user accounts in the domain to be managed at the head office in St. Louis. Select the trust relationships that must be established. Select all that apply.

   A. St. Louis must trust Vancouver.

   B. Vancouver must trust St. Louis.

   C. New Orleans must trust St. Louis.

   D. St. Louis must trust New Orleans.

3. The ACME Corporation wants all administrators in the St. Louis domain to be able to manage the two remote domains. What group memberships must be implemented to accomplish this?

   A. Assign the Administrators group from the St. Louis domain to be a member of the Domain Admins group in the New Orleans and Vancouver domains.

   B. Assign the Administrators group from the St. Louis domain to be a member of the Administrators group in both the New Orleans and Vancouver domains.

   C. Assign the Domain Admins group from the St. Louis domain to be a member of the Administrators group in the New Orleans and Vancouver domains.

   D. Assign the Domain Admins group from the Vancouver and New Orleans domains to be members of the Administrators group in the St. Louis domain.

4. Which Windows NT utilities can be used to set share permissions on the local computer? Select all that apply.

   A. User Manager for Domains

   B. Server Manager

   C. Windows NT Explorer

   D. File Manager

5. When Jim attempts to log on to a Windows NT workstation, he receives the message that he cannot log on locally. What configuration change must be made to grant Jim permission to log on locally?

   A. Make Jim a member of the Administrators local group.

   B. Configure Jim's account so he only can log on to the workstation that he has problems logging on to.

   C. Configure Jim's account to ignore warnings.

   D. Grant Jim's account the user right Log on Locally.

6. The Red domain trusts the Blue domain. The Blue domain trusts the White domain. If you are attempting to log on to the network at a Windows NT workstation that is a member of the Red domain, what account databases can you authenticate with? Select all that apply.

   A. The Red domain

   B. The White domain

   C. The Blue domain

   D. The Windows NT Workstation account database

7. Which Windows NT utilities can be used to set NTFS permissions on the local computer? Select all that apply.

   A. User Manager for Domains

   B. Server Manager

   C. Windows NT Explorer

   D. File Manager

Questions 8–10 are based on a two-domain network in which DOMAIN1 trusts DOMAIN2. The computers involved in each question are located in the domains as shown in Figure 6.7.1

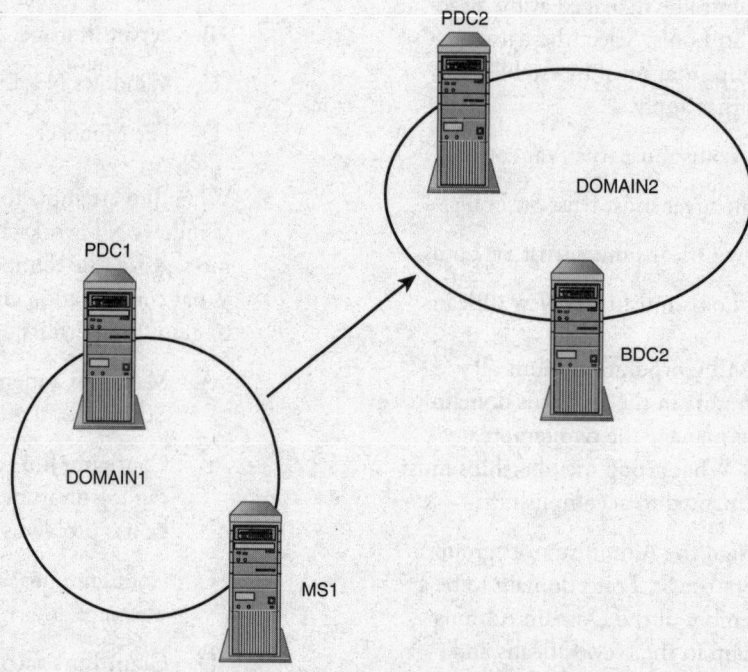

Figure 6.7.1   The Omaha National Network.

8. Greg's account on the Omaha National Network is located in DOMAIN1. If you were to grant Greg access to a printer located on BDC2, what permission assignments need to be performed?

   A. Create a new global group in DOMAIN1 and make Greg's account a member of the group. Create a local group in DOMAIN2 and assign it Print permissions. Remove the Everyone group from the permissions for the printer. Finally, assign the global group from DOMAIN1 to the local group in DOMAIN2.

   B. Create a new local group in DOMAIN1 and make Greg's account a member of the group. Create a local group in DOMAIN2 and assign it Print permissions. Remove the Everyone group from the permissions for the printer. Finally, assign the local group from DOMAIN1 to the local group in DOMAIN2.

   C. Create a new local group in DOMAIN1 and make Greg's account a member of the group. Create a global group in DOMAIN2 and assign it Print permissions. Remove the Everyone group from the permissions for the printer. Finally, assign the local group from DOMAIN1 to the global group in DOMAIN2.

   D. This cannot be done because the trust relationship has been established in the wrong direction.

9. Charlene and Ron have user accounts in DOMAIN2. Anthony and Bernice have accounts in DOMAIN1. You need to grant all these users access to the accounting system on the member server MS1 in DOMAIN1. What group assignments must be performed?

   A. Create a global group in DOMAIN1 and make all four users members of the group. Create a local group on PDC1 and assign permissions to it on the MS1 computer. Make the global group a member of the local group.

   B. Create a global group in DOMAIN1 and make all four users members of the group. Create a local group on MS1 and assign permissions to it on the MS1 computer. Make the global group a member of the local group.

   C. Create a global group in DOMAIN1 and make Anthony and Bernice members. Create another global group in DOMAIN2 and make Charlene and Ron members. Create a local group on PDC1 and assign permissions to it on the MS1 computer. Make the two global groups members of the local group.

   D. Create a global group in DOMAIN1 and make Anthony and Bernice members. Create another global group in DOMAIN2 and make Charlene and Ron members. Create a local group on MS1 and assign permissions to it on the MS1 computer. Make the two global groups members of the local group.

10. Adam has an account in DOMAIN2 and needs to manage file and print shares on the PDC1 computer in DOMAIN1. What group assignments enable Adam to perform this task without assigning excess rights?

   A. Assign Adam to the Server Operators group in DOMAIN2 and make the group a member of the Server Operators group in DOMAIN1.

B. Assign Adam to the Domain Admins group in DOMAIN2 and make the group a member of the Administrators group in DOMAIN1.

C. Assign Adam to a newly created global group in DOMAIN2 called FILENPRINT. Make the FILENPRINT global group a member of the Server Operators group in DOMAIN1.

D. Assign Adam to a newly created global group in DOMAIN2 called FILENPRINT. Make the FILENPRINT global group a member of the Account Operators group in DOMAIN1.

11. Which of the following groups are not found in Windows NT Workstation?

A. Backup Operators

B. Server Operators

C. Power Users

D. Administrators

12. Which of the following are the default groups for new users?

A. Administrators, users

B. Users, domain users

C. Domain users

D. Logon users

13. When you log on to Windows NT Workstation as an Administrator, you notice that the sharing symbol no longer appears below any of your shared folders. Which of the following is the probable cause of this?

A. The View options in Windows NT Explorer have been configured to not show the shared folder symbol.

B. The Server service has stopped.

C. The Workstation service has stopped.

D. On Windows NT Workstation, shares are only viewed in the Server Manager.

14. A file within Users local group that is assigned NTFS Change permissions is located in the c:\USERS directory. The directory d:\DATA has been assigned the NTFS Administrators permissions with Full Control permissions. If the file is moved to the d:\DATA directory, what are the permissions after the file is moved?

A. Everyone, Full Control

B. Users, Change

C. Administrators, Full Control

D. Users, Change Administrators, Full Control

15. A file in the Users local group that is assigned NTFS Change permissions is located in the c:\USERS directory. The directory C:\DATA has been assigned the NTFS Administrators permissions with Full Control permissions. If the file is moved to the C:\DATA directory, what are the permissions after the file is moved?

A. Everyone, Full Control

B. Users, Change

C. Administrators, Full Control

D. Users, Change Administrators, Full Control

16. All users' home directories have been generated using the setting \\SERVER\USERS\%USERNAME% in the home directory field of each user's properties. What permissions are assigned to the home directories by default?

    A. Users, Full Control

    B. Everyone, Full Control

    C. %USERNAME%, Change

    D. %USERNAME%, Full Control

17. The file DATA.TXT has been assigned the NTFS permissions Users, Read. The directory the file is in has the NTFS permissions Users, Change. The share permissions for the folder are set to Administrators, Full Control and Users, Full Control. What are the effective permissions on the file DATA.TXT?

    A. Users, Read

    B. Users, Change

    C. Users, Full Control

    D. Users, Full Control
       Administrators, Full Control

Questions 18 and 19 are based on the directory structure shown in Figure 6.7.2. The SALARIES.XLS file is located in the Payroll folder, which is located in the Accounting folder, which is located in the Data folder. Varying share and NTFS permissions are set on these directories and files in each question.

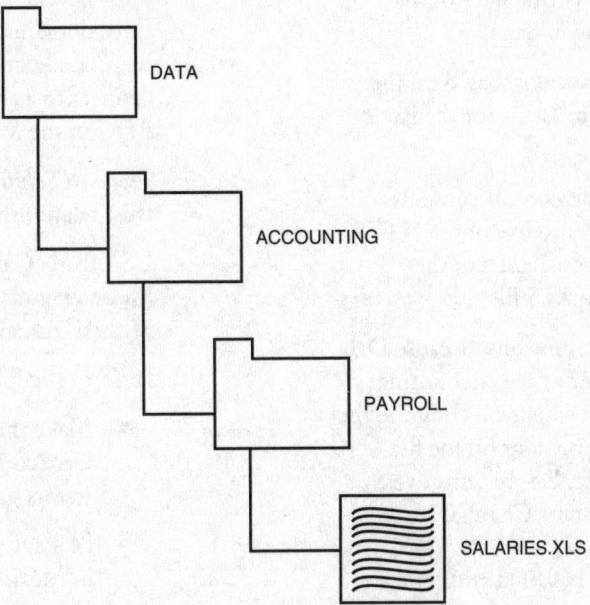

Figure 6.7.2 A sample directory structure.

18. Using the directory structure in Figure 6.7.2, the following security has been set. The Data directory has been shared with the Administrators group, which is assigned Full Control permissions. The Accounting folder has been shared with the Accountants local group, which is assigned Full Control permissions. The Payroll folder has NTFS Read permissions assigned to the Accounting group, and the SALARIES.XLS file has been assigned NTFS Change permissions. Dale, an accountant, has been assigned NTFS Read permissions. What are Dale's effective permissions on the file SALARIES.XLS if he connects using the Accounting share? Choose the best answer.

A. Full Control permissions, based on the shared permission for the Accounting folder.

B. Read permissions, based on the NTFS permissions for the Payroll folder.

C. Read permissions, because Read is the more restrictive of the NTFS permissions assigned to the SALARIES.XLS file.

D. Change permissions, because Dale is a member of the Accounting group and, when you combine the NTFS permissions on the file SALARIES.XLS, his effective permissions are Change.

19. The Data folder is shared with Full Control permissions for the Users group. The Accounting folder has been shared with the Change permission assigned to the Users group. Finally, the Payroll folder has been assigned the Read share permission to the Users group. What are the effective permissions on the SALARIES.XLS file if Anna connects using the Data share and the default NTFS permissions are in effect?

A. Full Control

B. Change

C. Read

D. No Access

The following scenario applies to questions 20–22. A different solution to the scenario is proposed for each question.

Scenario: The Really Big Corp. has three domains in its organization: Canada, USA, and Mexico. It wants to set up a Windows NT domain structure that meets the following requirements.

Required Result: Administrators in the Canada domain must be able to administer all three domains. *Optional Result 1:* Backup Operators in the Mexico domain must be able to perform backups in all three domains. *Optional Result 2:* Users in the Canada domain must be able to connect to a shared program located on a BDC in the Mexico domain.

20. *Proposed Solution:* Set up the following trust relationships:

USA trusts Canada
Mexico trusts Canada
Mexico trusts USA

Perform the following group assignments:

- Make the Domain Admins group in Canada a member of the Administrators groups in USA and Mexico.

- Make the Backup Operators group in Mexico a member of the Backup Operators groups in USA and Canada.

- Make the Users group in Canada a member of a newly created local group in Mexico that has been assigned appropriate permissions for the shared program.

This solution:

A. Meets the required result and both optional results.

B. Meets the required result and only one optional result.

C. Meets only the required result.

D. Does not meet the required result.

21. *Proposed Solution:* Set up the following trust relationships:

USA trusts Canada
Mexico trusts Canada
USA trusts Mexico
Canada trusts Mexico

Perform the following group assignments:

- Make the Domain Admins group in Canada a member of the Administrators groups in USA and Mexico.

- Make the Backup Operators group in Mexico a member of the Backup Operators groups in USA and Canada.

- Make the Domain Users group in Canada a member of a newly created local group in Mexico that has been assigned appropriate permissions for the shared program.

This solution:

A. Meets the required result and both optional results.

B. Meets the required result and only one optional result.

C. Meets only the required result.

D. Does not meet the required result.

22. *Proposed Solution:* Set up a complete trust model between the three domains.

Perform the following group assignments:

- Make the Domain Admins group in Canada a member of the Administrators groups in USA and Mexico.

- Create a new global group in Mexico that includes all members of Mexico that perform backups. Make this new global group a member of the Backup Operators groups in Mexico, USA, and Canada.

- Make the Domain Users group in Canada a member of a newly created local group in Mexico that has been assigned appropriate permissions for the shared program.

This solution:

A. Meets the required result and both optional results.

B. Meets the required result and only one optional result.

C. Meets only the required result.

D. Does not meet the required result.

Questions 23, 24, and 25 are based on the permissions outlined in Table 6.7.1, which are assigned to the DATASTORE folder on the RESOURCES server.

6

Table 6.7.1

Share Permissions	NTFS Permissions
Users, Change	Users, Read
Accountants, Full Control	Accountants, Change
Actuaries, Read	Actuaries, Full Control
Irwin, No Access	Irwin, Read

23. If Alexander, a member of the Accountants group, attempted to access the \\RESOURCES\DATASTORE share, what would his effective permissions be?

    A. Full Control

    B. Change

    C. Read

    D. No Access

24. If Amy, a member of the Accountants and Actuaries groups, attempted to access the \\RESOURCES\DATASTORE share, what would her effective permissions be?

    A. Full Control

    B. Change

    C. Read

    D. No Access

25. If Amy were to walk over to the actual RESOURCES server and use Windows NT Explorer to view the DATASTORE folder, what would her effective permissions be?

    A. Full Control

    B. Change

    C. Read

    D. No Access

26. An organization has three domains named Alberta, Saskatchewan, and Manitoba. The trust relationships have been established so that Alberta trusts Saskatchewan and Saskatchewan trusts Manitoba.

Andrea's account is in the Alberta domain, Sandy's account is in the Saskatchewan domain, and Max's account is in the Manitoba domain. Select all statements that are correct.

    A. Max can use resources in the Saskatchewan domain.

    B. Max can use resources in the Alberta domain.

    C. Sandy can use resources in the Alberta domain.

    D. Sandy can use resources in the Manitoba domain.

    E. Andrea can use resources in the Saskatchewan domain.

27. In a multimaster domain mode, how many trust relationships must be implemented if there are three master domains and four resource domains?

    A. 7

    B. 10

    C. 14

    D. 18

28. Which of the following groups can Account Operators modify the membership of?

    A. Replicators

    B. Backup Operators

    C. Domain Users

    D. Administrators

29. Harry, a user who handed in his resignation three weeks ago, had his account deleted. He now has returned to his former job. When you re-create his account, he can no longer access the files that he accessed before his resignation. Why is this?

    A. The account should have been undeleted in the User Manager for Domains.

    B. The account now has a new SID.

    C. The password has changed.

    D. The account must be regenerated.

6.7.1   Answers and Explanations: Exercise

This exercise tested the POSIX-compliant feature of Windows NT. This feature enables users with NTFS Full Control permissions to delete a file to which they have been assigned No Access permissions.

It should be noted that if you are working in the Graphical environment of Windows NT Explorer, you are prevented from actually deleting the file when the permissions are set to No Access. This is because you are working entirely in the Windows NT environment. For a command prompt, you could be working in a POSIX environment, so the POSIX rules are enforced.

6.7.2   Answers and Explanations: Exercise

This exercise investigated the effects of moving and copying a file in an NTFS environment. When you copied the Change file from the root directory to the NTFSTEST directory, the permissions changed to Users, Full Control from the original settings of Administrators, Full Control.

This exercise helps you recognize that permissions can be affected when files are moved or copied between directories. This realization can help you troubleshoot permission problems.

6.7   Answers and Explanations: Practice Problems

1. **D**   The default permissions assigned to a shared directory are Everyone, Full Control.

2. **B, C**   If St. Louis is going to act as the Master Domain, both Vancouver and New Orleans must trust St. Louis.

3. **C**   If you assign the Domain Admins group from the St. Louis domain to the Administrators group in the Vancouver and New Orleans domains, administrators in the St. Louis domain are able to manage the remote domains.

4. **B, C, D**   Server Manager, Windows NT Explorer, and File Manager all can be used to set share permissions on the local computer.

5. **D**   If you grant the users' accounts (or groups that they have membership in) the user right Log on Locally, users can log on to the NT Workstation computer.

6. **A, C, D**   You are able to authenticate with all account databases except the White domain. This is because trust relationships are non-transitive. Even though the Blue domain trusts the White domain, there is not an explicit trust relationship between the Red and White domains.

7. **C, D**   Only Windows NT Explorer and File Manager can be used to set NTFS permissions on the local computer.

8. **D**   The trust relationship is pointing in the wrong direction. If you want Greg to access any resources in DOMAIN2, DOMAIN2 must trust DOMAIN1.

6

9. **D** Because the resource is located on a Member Server in DOMAIN2, the local group must be created in the account database of the Member Server.

10. **C** The Server Operators group in DOMAIN1 grants Adam sufficient rights to manage file and print shares. He also could do this with the answer in B, but this grants excess rights.

11. **B** The Server Operators group is only found on a Windows NT domain controller.

12. **C** Users are members of the Domain Users global group by default. They have membership in the Users local group only because the global group Domain Users is a member of the Users local group.

13. **B** If the Server service stops operating, share symbols do not appear below shares because they are not being shared at that time. When you restart the Server service, the share symbols reappear.

14. **C** Because the file is moved between NTFS partitions, the file assumes the NTFS permissions of the target directory.

15. **B** Because the file is moved to a directory on the same NTFS partition, it retains its original permissions.

16. **D** When a home directory is generated on an NTFS partition, only the user's account is granted the Full Control permission.

17. **A** File permissions always take precedence over directory permissions in NTFS permissions assignments. Because the share permissions will effectively be Full Control, the Read permissions on the file DATA.TXT are the most restrictive and are the effective permissions.

18. **D** Dale's effective rights would be Change. Even though he has been assigned NTFS Read permissions, he also is a member of the Accounting group, which has Change permissions. When

you combine Read and Change permissions, they are effectively Change permissions.

19. **A** The default NTFS permissions are Everyone with Full Control permissions. This means they are definitely not the most restrictive. The user is entering the directory structure at the Data directory, which has shared permissions of Full Control. This is the permission for the entire directory structure. Only Windows 95 looks at the share permissions assigned to subdirectories.

20. **C** This solution only meets the required result. You cannot assign local groups to other local groups. The Users group and the Backup Operators group are both local groups. Also, the trust relationships do not allow the optional requirements to work.

21. **B** This answer does not meet the requirement to have Backup Operators in the Mexico domain perform backups in all three domains. You cannot make a local group a member of another local group.

22. **A** This solution meets all objectives, but it uses excess trust relationships. There is no need for Canada to trust USA. There also is no need for Mexico to trust USA. Because there was no objective to minimize trust relationships, however, this meets all the objectives.

23. **B** Alexander would have share permissions of Full Control and NTFS permissions of Change. The most restrictive permissions are the NTFS permissions. This gives him effective permissions of Change.

24. **D** Amy has been assigned the explicit No Access permission on the share. This always overrides any other permission assignments.

25. **A** Because Amy is not connecting to the DATASTORE folder over the network, share permissions are not in effect. Her

effective NTFS permissions on the folder would be Full Control, due to her membership in the Actuaries local group.

26. **A, C** An account can only use resources in its own domain or in a domain that explicitly trusts its domain. Trust relationships are not transitive.

27. **D** The formula for calculating the number of trust relationships in a multimaster domain model is

$$M*(M-1) + M*R$$

where M is the number of Master domains, and R is the number of Resource domains.

28. **A, C** Account Operators are not allowed to affect the membership of the Administrators group, the Domain Admins group, or any of the Operators groups.

29. **B** When you delete an account and re-create it with the same User ID, the account has a different SID and does not retain any of its previous group memberships.

6.7 Key Words

Accounts-Global Groups-Local Groups-Permissions (AGLP) global group

Local group

NTFS permissions

Share permissions

SID

6.8   Solving Fault-Tolerance Failures

There are two levels of fault tolerance that are built into Windows NT Server: disk mirroring/duplexing (RAID 1) and disk striping with parity (RAID 5). Each fault-tolerant method has advantages and issues when being implemented. No matter which fault-tolerant method you implement, a good backup strategy is essential to prevent data loss in an organization. This section details issues with disk mirroring, stripe sets with parity, and backup strategies.

A.   RAID 1: Disk Mirroring

Disk mirroring writes the contents of a single disk on two physical disks. Mirroring duplicates each write action to both disks in the mirror set. This protects against a disk failure because the system can continue to function using the other disk in the mirror set. If the disks are on separate controllers, this also protects against a controller failure. If they are on separate controllers, this is commonly known as disk duplexing. The cost associated with disk mirroring is 50%, which means that 50% of the total disk space in the mirror set is used to maintain fault-tolerant information.

Disk mirroring is the only fault-tolerant partitioning scheme provided with Windows NT that can contain the System and boot partitions. There are some issues to consider when you do mirror the System or boot partitions. It is possible that the disk that the computer uses to start the system may not be functioning at that time. For that, you need a fault-tolerant boot disk.

> **Remember that any time you update the disk configuration, you must update the Emergency Repair Disk. Doing so copies the disk configuration changes so that you can recover the fault-tolerant set in case of Registry problems.**

1.   Recovering from a Mirror Set Failure

If a mirror set fails, you may need to use a fault-tolerant boot disk. You only need to do use this if the Boot or system partitions of Windows NT are located on the failed drive in the mirror set. If the Boot or system partitions were located on the failed disk, the following steps must be followed:

1. Diagnose which disk is the failed hard disk in the mirror set. This disk probably needs to be replaced.

2. Start the system using the fault-tolerant boot disk. Select the startup entry for the functioning disk in the system.

3. Start the Disk Administrator program.

4. Select the mirror set. (You may not be able to determine which disk has failed until you have started the Disk Administrator program.)

5. From the Fault Tolerant menu, select Break Mirror.

6. Assign to the remaining member of the mirror set the original drive letter assigned to the mirror set.

7. After the defective drive has been replaced, you should reestablish the mirror. This is done by selecting the remaining member of the mirror set, and then Ctrl-clicking an area of free disk space on the newly installed disk that is the same size or larger than the original member of the mirror set.

8. When prompted, restart the computer.

B. RAID 5: Stripe Sets with Parity

Disk striping with parity also protects against the failure of a single disk on a Windows NT system. A stripe set with parity writes data across all the disks in a 64 KB stripe. On a different disk in each stripe, parity information is written that assists in recovering from a disk failure. The movement of the parity information between the drives in the stripe set with parity helps to improve performance when a disk fails. If a disk fails, the information that was on the missing disk can be rebuilt using the information on the remaining disk and the information stored in the parity information for that stripe. For some of the stripes, the parity information will have been stored on the disk that failed. No calculations are required to read information for stripes where this scenario occurs.

Windows NT–created stripe sets with parity cannot be used to store the Windows NT System and boot partitions. For data partitions, they offer better write and read performance due to the additional disk controllers involved in a stripe set with parity. A stripe set with parity requires a minimum of three disks and can be created using up to 32 disks. These disks can be any mix of disk formats, including SCSI, IDE, EIDE, and ESDI.

6

> **Windows NT can store its System and boot partitions on hardware RAID 5 stripe sets with parity because Windows NT sees the stripe set with parity as a single physical disk.**

The cost of utilizing a stripe set with parity is $1/n$, where n is the number of disks involved in a stripe set with parity. If you have six disks making up your stripe set with parity, 1/6th of the total disk space is used to store parity information.

> **If you are asked a question about fault-tolerant disk schemes, remember that although stripe sets and volume sets are supported under Windows NT, they provide absolutely NO fault tolerance.**

1. Recovering from a Disk Failure with RAID 5

When a disk fails in a stripe set with parity, the Windows NT system can continue to use the disk array. When reading information from a stripe, the computer rebuilds any of the missing information from the failed disk using the parity information and the remaining disks for that stripe.

An example might be the best way to explain how parity information is calculated and used when a single disk fails in a stripe set with parity. Stripe sets with parity use the Exclusive OR function to create the parity information for each stripe. The Exclusive OR function is based on the following series of calculations:

- 0 Exclusive OR 0 = 0
- 0 Exclusive OR 1 = 1
- 1 Exclusive OR 0 = 1
- 1 Exclusive OR 1 = 0

Table 6.8.1 shows how the parity information would have been calculated for a single stripe as the data was written to the stripe.

Table 6.8.1

Calculating the Parity Information for a Stripe Set with Parity

Drive	Drive Status	Bit Pattern
Data drive 1	Running	11100011
Data drive 2	Running	11101101 XOR
Check Byte drive	Running	00001110

If Data drive 1 were to fail, the calculation shown in Table 6.8.2 would be used to re-create the data missing from Data drive 1.

Table 6.8.2

Calculating the Parity Information for a Stripe Set with Parity

Drive	Drive Status	Bit Pattern
Data drive 1	Running	11100011
Check Byte drive	Running	00001110 XOR
Data drive 2	Failed	11101101

The system regenerates the information from Data drive 2 in memory on-the-fly. Due to the amount of calculations that are required, system performance suffers. Therefore, you need to quickly replace the failed disk and regenerate the stripe set with parity.

> If two or more disks fail in a stripe set with parity, the only way to recover is to restore from a backup tape.

2. Recovering from a Failed Stripe Set with Parity

If a stripe set with parity fails, you should replace the defective disk as quickly as possible. The following process is used:

1. Start the Disk Administrator program to determine which disk has failed.

2. Replace the failed disk. Windows NT does not support hot swapping functionality, so the system must be shut down to replace the drive with a new drive that is at least the same size as the original drive.

3. Start the Disk Administrator again.

4. Click the stripe set with parity that you need to repair, and then Ctrl+click the free space of the drive you want to add to the stripe set with parity.

5. From the Fault Tolerant menu, select Regenerate. Note that this process can take some time, although it takes less time than restoring from tape.

6. If there were any other partitions on the failed drive, they may need to be restored from a tape backup.

> You cannot increase the size of a stripe set with parity unless you back up its information. To back up a stripe set with parity, delete the previous stripe set with parity and create a new one made up of additional disks. After the new stripe set with parity is running, you have to restore the original data from the backup.

C. Backup Strategies for Disaster Recovery

Windows NT comes with its own proprietary backup software named NT Backup. Windows NT Backup can be run in either a graphical mode or a command-line mode. Both modes require a Windows NT HCL-compliant tape backup unit. Windows NT supports five different backup types, as follows:

- **Normal:** Backs up all selected files during the backup process and resets the archive bit to an off position on each file to indicate that the file has been backed up.

- **Differential:** Backs up only the files that have the archive bit set on from the selected files. A differential backup does not reset the archive bit.

- **Incremental:** Backs up the files that have the archive bit set to an on position from the selected files. After the files have been backed up, the archive bit for the backed up files is reset to an off position.

- **Copy:** Backs up all files that are selected for backup, but does not change the status of the archive bit.

- **Daily Copy:** Backs up only the files that have their archive bits set to an on position and were modified on that day. This backup type does not reset the archive bit for the files it backs up.

Other options that can be set during a backup include the following:

- Verify After Backup

- Backup Local Registry

> Selecting the Backup Local Registry option works only if at least one file located on the Windows NT boot partition is selected.

- Restrict Access to Owner or Administrator

- Hardware Compression

- Log Options

1. Scheduling Backups

The Windows NT Backup program does not support the scheduling of backups. If you want to schedule backups, you must use the text version of the NTBACKUP command and the Automatic Transaction (AT.EXE) command that comes with Windows NT. The NTBACKUP command uses the following syntax:

```
NTBACKUP BACKUP paths [/A] [/V] [/R] [/D "TEXT"] [/B] [/HC:ON¦OFF] [/T type]
[/L "LOGFILE"]
```

Where:

- /A indicates that the new backup operation should be appended to the tape.

- /V indicates that the backup set should be verified after the backup process is completed.

- /R indicates that restoration should be restricted to Administrators or Owners of the file.

- /D "Text" enables an electronic description to be associated with the backup.

- /B indicates that the local Registry should be included in the backup operation.

- /HC:ON|OFF turns the hardware compression feature on or off.

- /T sets the backup type. Options include Normal, Incremental, Differential, Copy, or Daily.

- /l "logfile" indicates that logging should occur and should be written to the indicated log file.

A batch file can be written that can be called by the Windows NT AT.EXE command. The AT command enables you to schedule a batch file to be run at regular intervals.

```
AT time [ /EVERY:date[,...] ¦ /NEXT:date[,...]] "command"
```

For example, if you created a batch file named fullback.bat that you want to run every Friday at 11:30 p.m., you use the command.

```
AT 23:30 /EVERY:Friday "FULLBACK.BAT"
```

> **The AT command requires that the Schedule service be running on the computer on which you want to run the scheduled backup.**

2. Backup Strategies

There are some very common backup strategies that are implemented to ensure that data is not lost on a system. These include the following:

- Daily full backups

- Weekly full backups with differentials

- Weekly full backups with incrementals

A backup methodology of full backups can be implemented when the total amount of data that needs to be backed up can be handled by your tape backup device and can be performed in a timely fashion. As the size of your backup set increases, this backup methodology generally evolves into a weekly full backup set with differentials or incremental occurring on the other days of the week. With the increase in data storage over the last few years, this often requires that a tape changer be in place to enable the automatic changing of tapes. If data is lost and needs to be restored from tape, it takes a single restore function to restore the entire system to the state it was in after the last completed backup.

When using a backup with differential method, full backups are usually run once a week. During the other days of the week, a differential backup is run. The differential backs up all the files that have changed since the previous week's full backup. If the system needs to be restored fully from backup, it requires two restore operations—one from the previous week's full backup and one from the previous day's differential backup. A common practice is to store the full backups off-site to prevent a loss of data from a natural disaster or fire.

When using a backup with incremental method, full backups are usually run once a week. During the other days of the week, an incremental backup is run. The incremental backups save all the files that have changed since the last backup. It does not matter whether it was a full or incremental backup the day before. If the system needs to be restored fully from backup, it requires many restore operations. You first restore the previous week's full backup. You then restore, in order, the incremental backups. A common practice is to store the full backups off-site to prevent a loss of data from a natural disaster or fire.

6.8.1　Exercise: Choosing a Disk Partitioning Scheme

Your computer has Windows NT Server installed. Your computer currently contains a single 2 GB drive. You want to install another 4 GB disk and two 2 GB disks to your computer. Based on this scenario, answer the following questions:

1. What fault-tolerant disk-partitioning schemes would you use to protect your Windows NT Server System and boot partitions and to provide the best access speeds for data stores?

2. What disks would you use to create these fault-tolerant disk-partitioning schemes?

3. If the 4 GB disk were to fail, could you still access all data on the computer?

4. If the 4 GB disk were to fail, what steps would you have to perform to restore the computer back to its fault-tolerant status?

6.8.2　Exercise: Creating a Batch File for Backup

In this exercise, you write a batch file that meets the following backup scenario. The computer that you are backing up is named MARKETING and has Windows NT Server installed into the default directory location.

- You need to back up all the data files in the \\CORPORATE\DATA network share.

- You need to back up all data on the local D: drive.

- You want to verify that the backup proceeded correctly.

- You want to create a logfile named BIGBACK.LOG and store it in the d:\LOGS directory.

- You want to back up the local Registry.

- You want to take advantage of the hardware compressions of your tape backup unit.

6.8 Practice Problems

1. How many total disks can be combined into a stripe set with parity?

   A. 3

   B. 10

   C. 32

   D. As many as can be installed in the system

2. What is required to boot a system that has a mirrored system partition and a default startup disk that is not operating?

   A. Emergency Repair Disk

   B. Fault-tolerant boot disk

   C. DOS boot disk

   D. Windows NT startup disks

   The following scenario applies to questions 2–5. A different solution to the scenario is proposed for each question.

   Scenario: Your computer system has four 8 GB hard disks. You want to configure the system to be fault tolerant based on the following specifications:

   Required Result: Protect the operating system from a boot failure. *Optional result 1:* The user data must be available at all times. *Optional result 2:* You want to get the best performance with the lowest cost for the user data.

3. *Proposed Solution:* Create a mirror set between the first two disks and install the Windows NT boot and System partitions to the mirrored disks. Create a second mirror between the remaining two disks and install the user data to the remaining disk in the system.

   This solution:

   A. Meets the required solution and both optional solutions.

   B. Meets the required solution and only one optional solution.

   C. Meets only the required solution.

   D. Does not meet the required solution.

4. *Proposed Solution:* Create a software-based stripe set with parity using all four disks and install the Windows NT boot partition, Windows NT System partition, and the user data to the newly created stripe set with parity. This solution:

   A. Meets the required solution and both optional solutions.

   B. Meets the required solution and only one optional solution.

   C. Meets only the required solution.

   D. Does not meet the required solution.

5. *Proposed Solution:* Create a hardware-based stripe set with parity using all four disks and install the Windows NT boot partition, Windows NT System partition, and the user data to the newly created stripe set with parity.

   This solution:

   A. Meets the required solution and both optional solutions.

   B. Meets the required solution and only one optional solution.

   C. Meets only the required solution.

   D. Does not meet the required solution.

6. Which option in backup can prevent unauthorized users from restoring the data on the backup tapes? Select all that apply.

   A. Select the Only Approved Users check box.

   B. Select the Restrict Access to Owner or Administrator check box.

   C. Run the backup command from a command prompt using the /r parameter.

   D. Run the ntbackup command from a command prompt using the /r parameter.

6

7. What software-fault-tolerant solutions can be used to protect the System and boot partitions of Windows NT? Select all that apply.

    A. Disk mirroring

    B. Stripe set

    C. Disk duplexing

    D. Stripe set with parity

8. How do you recover from a MIRROR failure?

    A. Use the Disk Regenerate command in Disk Administrator.

    B. Use the Rebuild Mirror command in Disk Administrator.

    C. Break the mirror, replace the defective disk, and re-establish the mirror.

    D. Replace the defective disk. The Disk Administrator automatically re-creates the mirror set.

9. Does a Windows NT system keep running if a single disk fails in a mirrored solution?

    A. Yes

    B. No

10. Is data still accessible if two disks fail in a stripe set with parity solution?

    A. Yes

    B. No

11. What disk driver does Windows NT use when implementing a mirror set?

    A. NTFS.SYS

    B. FTDISK.SYS

    C. MIRROR.SYS

    D. DISK.SYS

12. In your computer, you have four disks with free disk space. Disk 0 has 300 MB of free disk space. Disks 1, 2, and 3 have 500 MB of free disk space each. What is the largest usable disk space that can be provided using a stripe set with parity

made up of any combination of disks in the computer?

    A. 900 MB

    B. 1500 MB

    C. 1200 MB

    D. 1000 MB

13. What types of disks can be combined to form a stripe set with parity in Windows NT 4.0 Server?

    A. SCSI

    B. EIDE

    C. JAZZ

    D. ESDI

14. Under what conditions can the Windows NT boot partition be installed to a RAID 5 stripe set with parity?

    A. It cannot be done.

    B. The RAID 5 stripe set with parity is formatted using NTFS.

    C. If the system partition is installed to the same partition.

    D. If the RAID 5 stripe set with parity is implemented as a hardware RAID solution.

15. What program is used to create a stripe set with parity?

    A. FTDISK

    B. Disk Administrator

    C. FDISK

    D. RAIDUTIL

16. Your stripe set with parity is running out of disk space. You add a new 4 GB drive to your system and want to expand the stripe set with parity to include the new disk. What must be done?

    A. In Disk Administrator, select the previous stripe set with parity, Ctrl-click the free space in the new disk, and select Disk Regenerate from the Fault Tolerant menu.

B. In Disk Administrator, select previous stripe set with parity, Ctrl-click the free space in the new disk, and select Disk Expand in the Fault Tolerant menu.

C. Back up all the data on the existing stripe set with parity, delete the partition, and create a new stripe set with parity using all the disks of the previous stripe set with parity, including the new disk. After the system has been restarted, restore all data and re-create any shares that were on the partition.

D. In Disk Administrator, select previous stripe set with parity, Ctrl-click the free space in the new disk, and select Expand Stripe Set with Parity from the Disk Menu.

17. What can be done to protect against both a disk and a disk controller failure?

A. Stripe set

B. Stripe set with parity

C. Disk mirroring

D. Disk duplexing

18. If Windows NT is installed to a Windows NT RAID 5 disk set, what would the ARCNAME appear as?

A. SCSI(0)DISK(0)RDISK(3) PARTITION(0)\WINNT

B. MULTI(0)DISK(0)RDISK(3) PARTITION(0)\WINNT

C. SCSI(0)DISK(0)RDISK(3) PARTITION(1)\WINNT

D. Windows NT cannot be installed to a software RAID 5 disk set.

19. Which disk-partitioning scheme provides the best disk access performance?

A. Striping

B. Mirror set

C. Striping with parity

D. Volume set

20. Two disks have failed in a stripe set with parity. How do you recover?

A. Replace the two disks, restart the system, and allow the automatic recovery to take place.

B. Replace the two disks, re-create the stripe set with parity, and restore from a tape backup.

C. Replace the two disks and select the Disk Regenerate command from the Fault Tolerant menu in Disk Administrator.

D. Replace the two disks. Start the Disk Administrator, right-click the remaining disks in the stripe set with parity, and select Rebuild.

21. Which fault-tolerant methodology is the most efficient in its usage of disk space?

A. Disk duplexing

B. Disk mirroring

C. Disk striping

D. Disk striping with parity

22. Which fault-tolerant disk strategy results in only 50% disk utilization?

A. Disk duplexing

B. Disk mirroring

C. Disk striping

D. Disk striping with parity

23. What steps are required to recover from a failed disk in a mirror set? Select all that apply.

A. Boot with a fault-tolerant boot disk.

B. Replace the defective disk.

C. Select Regenerate from the Fault Tolerant menu.

D. Re-create the mirror.

E. Assign the desired drive letter to the remaining member of the mirror set.

24. What RAID levels are supported in Windows NT Server?

    A. 0

    B. 1

    C. 3

    D. 5

25. What RAID levels are supported in Windows NT Workstation?

    A. 0

    B. 1

    C. 3

    D. 5

The following disk space scenario applies to questions 26 and 27.

Scenario: Disk 0 has 1000 MB of free disk space, Disk 1 has 1200 MB of free disk space, Disk 2 has 200 MB of free disk space, Disk 3 has 400 MB of free disk space, and Disk 4 has 500 MB of free disk space.

26. What is the largest usable disk space RAID 5 stripe set with parity that can be created using any available disks?

    A. 1500 MB

    B. 1600 MB

    C. 1200 MB

    D. 1000 MB

27. What is the largest stripe set that can be created using any of the available disks?

    A. 2200 MB

    B. 2000 MB

    C. 1600 MB

    D. 1500 MB

The following scenario applies to questions 28–30. A different solution to the scenario is proposed for each question.

Scenario: The Omega Organization needs to establish a backup strategy. It has two Windows NT Server computers named

PDC and BDC that require backups to be performed. Both computers have the System and boot partitions on the C drive, and all organizational data is stored to the D drive. The tape backup device is on the Windows NT HCL and is located on the PDC. The following requirements have been defined:

Required functionality: The backup of the PDC must include the Registry.

Optional result 1: The backup process should be automated.

Optional result 2: The backup process should restrict access to the data files to the owner or to an administrator.

28. *Proposed solution:* Map a network drive on the PDC connecting to the D$ share on the BDC computer. Run the Windows NT Backup program, and then select to back up all files on the local D: drive and the drive letter mapped to the \\BDC\D$ share. Select the options to restrict access to the owner or administrator, backup the Registry, and run the backup process each night at midnight.

    This solution:

    A. Meets the required solution and both optional solutions.

    B. Meets the required solution and only one optional solution.

    C. Meets only the required solution.

    D. Does not meet the required solution.

29. *Proposed solution:* Create the following batch file to perform the backup:

    ```
    Ntbackup backup
    c:\boot.ini d:\*.*
    \\BDC\D$\*.* /t:normal
    /r /b /23:00
    ```

    This solution:

    A. Meets the required solution and both optional solutions.

    B. Meets the required solution and only one optional solution.

C. Meets only the required solution.

D. Does not meet the required solution.

30. Proposed solution: Create the following batch file to perform the backup:

```
Ntbackup backup
c:\boot.ini d:\*.*
\\BDC\D$\*.* /t:normal
/r /b
```

Run the following command to automate the backup procedure:

```
AT 23:00 /
EVERY:MONDAY,TUESDAY,WEDNESDAY,
THURSDAY,FRIDAY
"batchfile.bat"
```

This solution:

A. Meets the required solution and both optional solutions.

B. Meets the required solution and only one optional solution.

C. Meets only the required solution.

D. Does not meet the required solution.

6.8.1 Answers and Explanations: Exercise

Your computer has Windows NT Server installed. Your computer currently contains a single 2 GB drive. You want to install another 4 GB disk and two 2 GB disks to your computer.

1. A mirror set would provide fault tolerance for the boot and System partitions on the original 2 GB disk. You could then create a stripe set with parity to provide the best disk access times for data.

2. You would probably choose to create a mirror set between the original disk in the computer using 2 GB of the 4 GB disk. You could then create a stripe set with parity using the 2 GB of disk space from the 4 GB drive and the two 2 GB drives.

3. Yes. Because the 4 GB disk has failed, you would still be able to boot into Windows NT using the original boot disk without requiring a fault-tolerant boot disk. If the original 2 GB disk had failed, you would require a fault-tolerant boot disk with the BOOT.INI configured to point to the 4 GB disk's first partition instead. You would also be able to access data on the stripe set with parity, as it can rebuild the missing information from the 4 GB disk using the parity information that it has stored.

4. You would have to turn off the computer and replace the 4 GB drive with another 4 GB or larger disk drive. When the system restarted, you would need to start the Disk Administrator program. You would re-create the mirror set to provide fault tolerance to the boot and System partitions. You would then select the stripe set with parity and the remaining 2 GB of disk space on the newly added disk. You would restore the stripe set with parity using the Disk Regenerate command on the Fault Tolerance menu.

6.8.2 Answers and Explanations: Exercise

The following batch file would meet the backup scenario in this question:

```
Net use X:
\\Corporate\DATA
NTBACKUP BACKUP
C:\boot.ini d:\*.* x:\*.*
/V /l
"D:\LOGS\BIGBACK.LOG" /B
/HC:ON
NET USE X: /D
```

Another correct answer is:

```
NTBACKUP BACKUP
C:\boot.ini d:\*.*
\\corpoarte\data\*.* /V /
l "D:\LOGS\BIGBACK.LOG" /
B /HC:ON
```

You need to back up the file BOOT.INI because the /b option to back up the local Registry only works if you back up a file on the partition where the Windows NT Registry is stored. Because Windows NT was installed to the default location, you must assume that this is c:\WINNT.

6.8   Answers and Explanations: Practice Problems

1.   **C**   A stripe set with parity requires a minimum of three disks and can use up to 32 disks.

2.   **B**   A fault-tolerant boot disk contains the necessary files for the operating system to start. On an Intel system, these include NTLDR, BOOT.INI, NTDETECT.COM, and possibly NTBOOTDD.SYS. You edit the BOOT.INI to use the other component disk of the mirrored set.

3.   **B**   This solution does protect all user data and protects the operating system from boot failure. A mirrored partition does not give a performance boost for disk access for the user data volume.

4.   **D**   This solution does not meet the required solution because Windows NT cannot have its System or boot partition located on a software-created stripe set with parity.

5.   **A**   Windows NT can have its System and boot partitions installed on a hardware-created stripe set with parity. This protects the operating system and user data from a single disk failure. It also gives the best performance. The cost of this setup is 1/4 of the disk space; 8 GB will be used to store parity information.

6.   **B, D**   By selecting the Restrict Access to Owner or Administrator option in the GUI version of Windows NT Backup or by using the /r parameter in the NTBACKUP command-line version of the backup, you can restrict who can restore from the backup.

7.   **A, C**   Windows NT can only protect the System and boot partitions using disk mirroring or disk duplexing when using a software raid solution.

8.   **C**   You must replace the defective disk and then re-establish the mirror using the remaining disk of the mirror set and the free space of the new disk.

9.   **A**   Yes, the computer continues to operate; however, if the system is rebooted, it may not restart. It depends on whether the failed disk is the disk referenced in the BOOT.INI file.

10.   **B**   Stripe sets with parity only protect against a single disk failure. You can only be protected from two disks failing if you are using a hardware RAID 10 solution in which two disk stripes with parity are mirrored.

11.   **B**   Windows NT uses the fault-tolerant disk driver (FTDISK.SYS) when implementing a mirrored set.

12.   **D**   The largest usable disk space that you can create from this set of disks is 1000 MB. This is done by creating a stripe set with parity using the three 500 MB disks. 500 MB is allocated to parity information.

13.   **A, B, D**   Jazz drives cannot be component drives in a stripe set with parity.

14.   **D**   Windows NT can only have its boot partition installed on a stripe set with parity if the stripe set with parity is hardware-based. Windows NT recognizes only the disk array as a single disk.

15.   **B**   The Disk Administrator program is used to create all disk partitioning schemes in Windows NT.

16.   **C**   Windows NT does not support increasing the number of disks in the stripe set with parity without re-creating the stripe set with parity and reloading the contents from a tape backup.

6

17. **D**   A disk duplexing scheme protects against both disk and controller failure as each disk in the mirror set is controlled by an independent disk controller.

18. **D**   Windows NT cannot be installed to a software RAID 5 disk array.

19. **A**   Disk striping offers the fastest disk access performance, but offers no fault tolerance.

20. **B**   Disk striping with parity only protects against a single disk failure. You must re-create the stripe set with parity with new disks and restore the data from backup.

21. **D**   Disk striping with parity only uses 1/n of the total disk space for parity information (where n is the total number of disks in the array).

22. **A, B**   Both disk mirroring and disk duplexing use 50% of their total disk space to maintain a fault-tolerant copy of the data.

23. **A, B, D**   To recover from a failed mirror set, you may have to boot with a fault-tolerant disk if the failed disk is the disk and partition referenced in the BOOT.INI. You must also replace the defective disk and re-create the mirror set in Disk Administrator.

24. **A, B, D**   Windows NT supports RAID 0 (stripe sets), RAID 1 (mirror sets), and RAID 5 (stripe sets with parity).

25. **A**   Windows NT does not provide any fault-tolerant disk schemes.

26. **C**   The largest stripe set with parity that can be created using any of these five disks is 1200 MB. It would be created using 400 MB from disks 0, 1, 3, and 4.

27. **C**   The largest stripe set that can be created using any of the available disks is 1600 MB, using 400 MB from disks 0, 1, 3, and 4.

28. **D**   To back up the Registry using Windows NT Backup, you must include at least a single file from the partition where the Registry is stored.

29. **B**   The required objective is met because /b for backing up the Registry is included in the NTBACKUP statement and a file is being backed up from the C drive of the PDC. The /r parameter does restrict access to the data to owners or administrator. There is no such parameter as /time.

30. **A**   This solution meets all the requirements. The use of the AT command enables the backup to be scheduled for 11:00 p.m. Monday through Friday.

6.8   Key Words

Disk duplexing

Disk mirroring

Disk striping

Disk striping with parity

Exclusive OR function

NTBackup

6.9   Advanced Problem Resolution

Advanced problem resolution requires the use of the Event Log, the System Log, and the Application Log to determine what is causing the problem. Often, what the user sees is the result of a more significant failure. The three event logs that are maintained by Windows NT are as follows:

- **The system event log:** Used to record events generated by Windows NT system components, such as drivers and services.

- **The security event log:** Records events related to system security. In the case of the security log, the system audit policy determines which events are logged. System audit policies are created and maintained with User Manager for Domains.

- **The application event log:** Used to record messages generated by applications.

The first place you should look for information is the Event Viewer. There are five basic events that you see in the logs. The first is informational items that are letting you know when things are happening on the system. These are represented by blue circles with the letter "i" in them. Warning messages indicate there are more severe problems, but do not stop the system. These are yellow circles with an exclamation point (!) in them. Warnings often lead to a STOP error. Most STOP errors indicate that some part of Windows NT is not functioning and are shown as red stop signs. Event fields are described in the following list:

- **Date:** The date the event message was logged.

- **Time:** The time the event message was logged.

- **User:** The user who caused the event.

- **Computer:** The name of the computer where the event occurred.

- **Event ID:** A numeric value for a specific message as defined by the source of the message.

- **Source:** The application or system component that logged the event.

- **Type:** A Windows NT classification of the event, such as an Error, Warning, or Information message.

- **Category:** A classification of the event, as defined by the source of the message.

- **Description:** A textual explanation of the event.

- **Data:** Binary data specific to an event, shown either as a series of Byte or Word values.

A.   Filtering

Thousands of events that can be listed in the event logs. To make the job of finding the problem easier, you can filter the log. Filters can be set on any of the event fields in the preceding list. To filter the log, choose View, Filter from the menu.

B.   Searching for Events

Searching for an Event is similar to Filtering, but in many cases it is more useful for troubleshooting, because it enables you to see the events around the one for which you are looking. You can find an event by going to View, Find.

The Find dialog box appears, which enables you to enter the search criteria. The options are almost the same as the Filter Events dialog box; however, you will notice that dates are missing. You can now look for any piece of text in the details of the event and choose to search up or down.

C. Other Errors

There are two other errors that are normally found in the security log. Violations of security are shown as locks, and access events are shown as keys. Blue screen errors are cases in which the operating system fails to start or abruptly stops working.

There are two ways to deal with a blue screen. You may reboot the system, and if the problem continues, you may have to diagnose which driver or component of Windows NT is causing the STOP error. Interpreting the information reported when a STOP error has occurred can help in diagnosing which driver may be at fault. You can also use some of the tools that are provided by Windows NT to diagnose the problem and fix it.

Debug port status indicators, bugcheck information, driver information, kernel build number and stack dump, and debug port information are the informational items used to determine the root of a system crash.

You can also configure the computer to create a dump file and debug it, or use a kernel debugger to isolate the problem. Boot options associated with a debug are /DEBUG, /CRASHDEBUG, /DEBUGPORT, and /BAUDRATE. You can keep the system debug-ready by setting the /DEBUG switch in the BOOT.INI. This enables the host computer running a kernel debugger to interrupt processing on the target computer whenever it is desired. If you use the /CRASHDEBUG switch, kernel debugging is enabled only after a STOP error has occurred.

D. Information on the Blue Screen

When a STOP error occurs and the system gives the character mode stop screen, there are five main sections on the screen. The five are listed here:

- **Debug Port Status Indicators:** Describes the status of the serial port. If it is in use, that information is used for debugging.

- **BugCheck Information:** Displays the actual error code and any parameters that the developer included in the error trapping routines. If only the top line is displayed, the error has also affected the areas that are used to display such information. This is the most useful portion of information for diagnosing the cause of the STOP screen.

- **Driver Information:** In this area, the drivers that were loaded when the STOP error occurred are listed. There are three items of information given for each driver:

  1. The memory location into which the driver was loaded.

  2. The time the driver was created (this is the offset in seconds from Jan 1, 1970; use CVTIME.EXE to convert these to readable dates).

  3. The name of the driver is listed. The BugCheck Information sometimes includes a pointer to the instruction that caused the ABEND (abnormal end), and you can use this information to discover which driver was involved.

- **Kernel Build Number and Stack Dump:** Provides the information on the current build number and a dump of the last instructions that were executed.

- **Debug Port Information:** Indicates the baud rate and other COM settings for the debug port in use.

E. Interactive Debugging

In some cases you need to go further than just looking at the screen. You can do this in two ways. You can set up the problematic computer to create a dump file and use utilities to verify it, or you can interactively debug the problematic computer using another computer, either with a RAS null modem cable or remotely using a modem.

In the \support\debug directory on the distribution CD, there is a kernel debugger for each platform that can be used for installation. The kernel debuggers use basic serial communications and each needs some configuration. The steps involved in preparing for a debugging session are listed here:

1. Set up the serial connection.

2. Configure the problematic computer (target).

3. Place the symbol tree on the diagnostic computer (host).

4. Start the computer in debugging mode.

5. Start the debugger on the diagnostic computer.

1. Setting up the Serial Connection

You may not be able to use an off-the-rack null modem cable to perform kernel debugging. Table 6.9.1 shows the cabling requirements for a 9-pin cable. Table 6.9.2 shows the cabling specifications for a 25-pin cable. Kernel debugging does not function correctly if the null modem cable you used does not meet these specifications.

Table 6.9.1

9-Pin Null Modem Cabling		
Remote host	Calling system	Signal
3	2	Transmit Data
2	3	Receive Data
7	8	Request to Send
8	7	Clear to Send
6,1	4	Data Set Ready and Carrier Detect
5	5	Signal Ground
4	6,1	Data Terminal Ready

Table 6.9.2

25-Pin Null Modem Cabling

Remote host	Calling system	Signal
3	2	Transmit Data
2	3	Receive Data
4	5	Request to Send
4	4	Clear to Send
6,8	20	Data Set Ready and Carrier Detect
7	7	Signal Ground
20	6,8	Data Terminal Ready

After you have created the null modem cable, connect the host and target computers. Be sure to plug the Remote Host end of the null modem cable into the target computer and the Calling System end of the cable into the host computer.

2. Configuring the Target Computer

For the system that you debug to properly route the information (to the serial port rather than the screen), you need to modify the BOOT.INI file. The following list provides the switches that you should add to the version of Windows NT you will boot:

- **/Debug:** Tells NT to load the kernel debugger during boot and kept it in memory.

- **/Crashdebug:** Similar to the /Debug option; however, the debugging code is available only if the system crashes. In most cases, this is a better option because the debugger code is not in memory and therefore doesn't interfere with the problem.

- **/Debugport:** Indicates the communications port that you use.

- **/Baudrate:** Selects the baud rate for the connection that you use for debugging.

You must also configure the target computer to not reboot in the case of a STOP error so that kernel debugging can be performed at that time. This is done by deselecting the Automatically Reboot option on the Startup/Shutdown tab of the System applet in Control Panel.

3. Configuring the Host Computer

The host computer requires that the necessary tools for debugging are located on a local disk drive. The symbol tree is used in debugging to provide the information about what the code does at various locations. This information is different for every version of Windows NT. The symbol library for a standard single processor version of Windows NT is in the `\support\debug\` `%platform%\symbols` directory on the CD-ROM.

If you have installed a service pack or you are working with a HAL other than the basic single processor HAL, you need to create a symbol set for the system. The following list outlines how to do this:

1. Copy the correct directory structure from the Support directory on the CD to your hard drive.

2. For the updates you have applied, copy the symbols from the distribution media for them in the same order that you applied them. Depending on your service pack version, these may need to be expanded first.

3. For multiprocessor systems, you have to rename some of the symbol files. The standard kernel debugger files are named NTOSKRNL.DBG for kernel and HAL.DBG for the HAL. On a multiprocessor computer, you need to rename NTKRNLMP.DBG to NTOSKRNL.DBG. These files are in the \Exe subdirectory.

Next, you need to set up the host with a series of environment variables so that the debugger has the basic information that it needs. You can do this using the SET command (for help on this, type **SET /?** at a prompt).

- **_NT_DEBUG_PORT:** COM port being used.

- **_NT_DEBUG_BAUD_RATE:** Baud rate for port.

- **_NT_SYMBOL_PATH:** Directory in which the symbols directory is located.

- **_NT_LOG_FILE_OPEN:** The name of a log file; this is optional.

> **To automate the process of performing kernel debugging, you may want to create a batch file that sets the previous environment variables and starts the kernel debugger.**

4. Starting the Target Computer in Debugging Mode

After the necessary parameters have been added to the BOOT.INI file and the computer has been configured so as not to automatically reboot in the case of a STOP error, you must restart the target computer so that the debug parameters are enabled.

5. Starting the Debugger on the Host Computer

After you have restarted the host system, you can perform kernel debugging on the remote system. To do this, you run the kernel debugger for the platform of the target machine. You need to be aware of some command-line switches, as follows:

- **-b:** Sends a debug breakpoint to the remote system, which causes execution on the target computer to stop as soon as possible.

- **-c:** Requests a communications resync when the systems connect.

- **-m:** Watches the modem control lines. This places the debugger in terminal mode if there is no CD (carrier detect).

- **-n:** Loads the symbols immediately. They usually are loaded in a deferred mode.

- **-v:** Activates verbose mode.

- **-x:** Forces the debugger to immediately break in when an exception occurs. The application is usually left to deal with it.

If you want to invoke the debugger, you must use the Ctrl+C combination. After you have started the debugger, you need to use some of the commands in Table 6.9.3 to diagnose the problems.

Table 6.9.3

Kernel Debugging Commands

Command	Usage
!reload	Reloads the symbol files if an updated symbol file has been copied to the host system.
!trap	Dumps the computer state when the trap frame occurs. It shows the state of the computer when an access fault has occurred.
!errlog	Displays the contents of an error log that the system builds as kernel errors occur. If there are contents in the log, this can assist in determining which component or process has caused the STOP error.
!process	Lists information about the current process running on the active processor.
!process 0 0	Lists all running processes and their headers.
!thread	Lists all the currently running threads.
!drivers	Displays a list of all drivers currently loaded. The most useful information can be the link date, which can be used to determine whether non-service pack versions of drivers are used correctly.
!vm	Lists the system's virtual memory usage.
g	Releases the target computer if kernel debugging was invoked by the person performing kernel debugging.
.reboot	Restarts the target computer.

F. Analyzing Memory Dump Files

Sometimes you are unable to resolve the problem using the kernel debugger. When this happens, you might want to have Windows NT create a dump file and either try to analyze it yourself or send it to Microsoft for analysis.

To create a dump file, you must have the page file existing on the boot partition of Windows NT. The page file on this partition must be larger in size than the total memory installed on the computer because the contents of memory are copied into the page file when a STOP error occurs.

After the system is restarted, the contents of the page file are copied to the configured memory dump file. The default is %SystemRoot%\memory.dmp. This can be configured in the System applet of Control Panel on the Startup/Shutdown tab. You must ensure that there is enough free disk space on the partition where the MEMORY.DMP file is to be created. It will be the size of the installed RAM on the system.

1. Configuring NT to Create a Dump File

Configuring Windows NT to create a dump file is very easy. You must configure the DumpCrash settings. The steps for setting this up are as follows:

1. Right-click the My Computer Icon.

2. Choose the Startup/Shutdown tab.

3. Under Recovery, click the "Write debugging information to" check box.

    You can select to overwrite an existing dump file by checking "Overwrite any existing file."

    You can enter another location for the dump file by entering the location (and name) into the text box.

4. Click OK.

2. Dump File Utilities

Three utilities come with Windows NT that enable you to work with the memory dump files. These utilities are listed here with a brief description:

- **DUMPCHK:** Checks that the dump file is in order by verifying all the addresses and listing the errors and system information.

- **DUMPEXAM:** Creates a text file that can provide the same information that was on the blue screen at the time the STOP error occurred. You need the symbol files and the kernel debugger extensions, as well as IMAGEHLP.DLL to run dump exam. The DUMPEXAM utility can only be used for STOP 0×0000000A and 0×0000001E errors.

- **DUMPFLOP:** Backs up and compresses the dump file to a series of floppies so that they can be sent to Microsoft.

G. Finding More Information

If you have worked with the event logs in Windows NT, you know that the information displayed in the event details can sometimes be cryptic. This means that you need to be able to find more information using the event ID or other clues that are in the information. There are three very good sources for information about Windows NT errors:

- Microsoft TechNet is a solid and very current source of information that is available as a monthly subscription. TechNet is probably the best source for troubleshooting information for Windows NT and all the Microsoft products. Shipped to subscribers on a monthly basis, it comes on at least two CDs.

- The Microsoft Support site, at `http://www.microsoft.com/support`, has a full suite of information about problems that other users have already experienced. One of the more helpful items on the support site is a group of the troubleshooting wizards. These wizards step you through the process of troubleshooting and provide you with solutions that come from the Microsoft technical staff.

- The Microsoft Knowledge Base contains articles on errors with the Windows NT operating system and their solutions. The Knowledge Base is accessible on the Internet at `http://www.microsoft.com/kb`.

6.9.1 Exercise: Configuring the Target Server for Kernel Debugging

This exercise guides you through the necessary steps to enable kernel debugging on a Windows NT computer that will be functioning as the target computer.

1. Start the Windows NT Explorer.

2. From the View menu, select Options. Ensure that the option to Show all files is enabled and the Hide file extensions for known file types is deselected. Click the OK button to confirm your changes.

3. In the c:\ directory, right-click the BOOT.INI file and select properties.

4. Clear the Read-only attribute and click the OK button.

5. Double-click the BOOT.INI file to edit the file.

6. In the section titled [Operating Systems], add the following parameters to the end of the line:

```
/debug /debugport=com1 /baudrate=9600
```

7. Save and close the file.

8. Restart Windows NT. Note that the Boot menu now displays the words [Debugger Enabled] for the selection to which you have added the parameters.

6.9.2 Exercise: Configuring the Host Server for Kernel Debugging

This exercise guides you through the necessary steps to enable kernel debugging on a Windows NT computer that will be functioning as the host computer. This exercise assumes that your CD-ROM is assigned the drive letter Z.

1. Insert the Windows NT Server CD in the CD-ROM drive.

2. Start a command prompt.

3. On the C drive, create a new directory named \debug.

4. On the Z drive (the CD-ROM), make the current directory \support\debug.

5. Run the following command to install the symbol files on the host computer:

```
expandsym z: c:\debug
```

where z: is the drive letter of your CD-ROM and the c:\debug directory is the target directory where you want to install the symbol files.

6. Now copy the contents of the directory z:\support\debug\i386 to the c:\debug folder.

7. Close the command prompt.

8. In the c:\debug folder, create a DBG.BAT file. It should contain the following information:

```
REM loca debug batch file
Set _NT_DEBUG_PORT=com2
Set _NT_DEBUG_BAUD_RATE=9600
Set _NT_SYMBOL_PATH=c:\debug\symbols
Set _NT_LOG_FILE_OPEN=c:\debug\debug.log
-i386kd -M -v
```

9. Close the DBG.BAT file and save changes.

6.9   Practice Problems

1. When running a kernel debugger, what key combination interrupts processing on the target computer and enables the technician to perform kernel debugging?

   A. Ctrl+D

   B. Ctrl+C

   C. End

   D. Ctrl+Break

2. How does Windows NT provide the capability to perform kernel debugging?

   A. By providing checked versions of all programs.

   B. By providing debug files of all programs.

   C. By providing symbol files for all programs.

   D. By providing kernel files for all programs.

3. Although checked versions of files provide the capability to perform kernel debugging, which of the following is a performance issue?

   A. They cannot be run in a production environment.

   B. They cannot be run in debug mode.

   C. They result in larger, possibly slower executables.

   D. They can only be used on the Intel platform.

4. In Windows NT debugging, the host computer is which of the following?

   A. The computer that is suffering the STOP errors.

   B. The computer running the kernel debugger.

   C. The computer running the Remote Access Service.

   D. The file where the Windows NT Symbol files are stored on the network.

5. In Windows NT debugging, the target computer is which of the following?

   A. The computer that is suffering the STOP errors.

   B. The computer running the kernel debugger.

   C. The computer running the Remote Access Service.

   D. The file where the Windows NT Symbol files are stored on the network.

6. What program writes the contents of memory to a disk file when a STOP error occurs?

   A. CRASHDUMP

   B. DUMPCHK.EXE

   C. DUMPFLOP.EXE

   D. DUMPEXAM.EXE

7. What settings must be set in the BOOT.INI of the system that is encountering STOP errors? Choose all that apply.

   A. /DEBUG

   B. /CRASH

   C. /BAUDRATE

   D. /DEBUGPORT

8. Which setting in the BOOT.INI file enables debugging ionlyn the event of a STOP error?

   A. /DEBUG

   B. /CRASH

   C. /CRASHDEBUG

   D. /WAIT

9. Where are CRASHDUMP parameters set?

   A. Registry

   B. Server Manager

   C. RDISK

   D. Startup/Shutdown tab of the System Applet in Control Panel

6

10. In which file are the contents of a CRASHDUMP stored by default?

   A. Paging file

   B. %SystemRoot%\crashdmp.log

   C. %SystemRoot%\memdump.log

   D. %SystemRoot%\memory.dmp

11. Which Windows NT dump analysis tool validates the contents of a dump file after a STOP error has occurred?

   A. CRASHDUMP

   B. DUMPCHK.EXE

   C. DUMPFLOP.EXE

   D. DUMPEXAM.EXE

12. What size will the crash dump file be when it is created?

   A. 16 MB

   B. 32 MB

   C. 64 MB

   D. Size of physical RAM on computer

13. For a memory dump to be successful, what conditions must be met? Choose all that apply.

   A. The paging file must be at least 64 MB.

   B. The paging file must be at least as large as physical RAM.

   C. The paging file must be located on the Windows NT boot partition.

   D. The paging file must be located on the Windows NT system partition.

14. What utility can be used to reduce the size of a memory dump file by extracting the crucial information that Microsoft Technical services requires to diagnose a problem?

   A. CRASHDUMP

   B. DUMPCHK.EXE

   C. DUMPFLOP.EXE

   D. DUMPEXAM.EXE

15. What utility can be used to copy the contents of a memory dump to floppy disks to be sent to Microsoft technical support?

   A. DUMPDISK.EXE

   B. DUMPCHK.EXE

   C. DUMPFLOP.EXE

   D. DUMPEXAM.EXE

16. When troubleshooting errors occur during the startup of Windows NT, which event log should be viewed in the Windows NT event viewer?

   A. Startup

   B. System

   C. Application

   D. Security

17. How can you narrow down the number of items being viewed in the Windows NT Event Viewer?

   A. Use the Extract command in the NT Event Viewer.

   B. Export the contents of the Windows NT Event Viewer to a comma-separated value file and import into a database product.

   C. Use Crystal Reports.

   D. Apply a filter.

18. What is the default behavior for the Windows NT Event viewer when an Event log becomes full?

   A. Overwrite Events as Needed.

   B. Overwrite Events older than seven days.

   C. Do not overwrite events (Clear log Manually).

   D. Shut down the Windows NT Server.

19. When running a kernel debugger, what command is entered to display all device drivers in use and their link dates?

   A. devices

   B. !devices

C. drivers

D. !drivers

20. When performing kernel debugging on a multiprocessor computer, what additional steps must be performed before starting the debugging process?

    A. Add the /MULTI parameter to the BOOT.INI file of the target computer.

    B. Set the environment variable _DEBUG_PROCESSOR to MULTI on the host computer.

    C. Rename the file NTKRNLMP.DBG to NTOSKRNL.EXE on the host computer.

    D. Rename the file NTKRNLMP.DBG to NTOSKRNL.EXE on the target computer.

21. What must be configured on both the host and target computers for successful kernel debugging to take place?

    A. Debug ports

    B. Identical version of the kernel debugger

    C. Port speed settings

    D. The NT Symbol path

22. If you encounter a STOP error that you do not recognize, where can you research information that may help troubleshoot the problem?

    A. The knowledge base on the Microsoft web site

    B. TechNet Compact Disks

    C. The Windows NT README.DOC file

    D. The Windows NT Help files

23. Which STOP errors are supported by the DUMPEXAM utility? Select all that apply.

    A. STOP: 0x0000007F UNEXPECTED_KERNEL_MODE_TRAP

    B. STOP: 0x0000000A IRQL_NOT_LESS_OR_EQUAL

    C. STOP: 0x0000001E KMODE_EXCEPTION_NOT_HANDLED

    D. STOP: 0x0000007B INACCESSIBLE_BOOT_DEVICE

24. What utility on the Windows NT Server CD-ROM enables a dial-in client to perform kernel debugging on a computer?

    A. REMOTE.EXE

    B. REMDEBUG.EXE

    C. KRNDEBUG.EXE

    D. RCMD.EXE

25. If you have installed a Windows NT Service Pack, what additional steps must be completed to perform kernel debugging?

    A. No additional steps are required.

    B. Ensure that the same level of service packs is applied to the computer performing the kernel debugging.

    C. Delete the previous symbol files and install the new symbol files for the service pack.

    D. Download the symbol files for the service pack and replace all updated symbol files.

The following scenario applies to questions 26–29. A different solution to the scenario is proposed for each question.

Scenario: You have a computer that is crashing several times a day. You want to have Microsoft Technical Support assist you with diagnosing the cause of the problem.

Required Result: You want to be able to perform kernel debugging at any time, even when a STOP error has not

6

occurred. *Optional Result 1:* You want to have the Administrator of the network notified when a STOP error has occurred. *Optional Result 2:* When a STOP error occurs, you want to have the system restart automatically, because the computer is housing crucial information that must be available at all times.

26. *Proposed Solution:* On the computer that is crashing, add the parameter /CRASHDEBUG to the BOOT.INI file. Also configure the messenger service to forward all alerts to the Administrator's computer. Finally, set the computer to reboot in the event of a STOP error.

    This solution:

    A. Meets the required solution and both optional solutions.

    B. Meets the required solution and only one optional solution.

    C. Meets only the required solution.

    D. Does not meet the required solution.

27. *Proposed Solution:* On the computer that is crashing, add the parameters /DEBUG and /REBOOT to the BOOT.INI file. Configure the computer to send an administrative alert to the Administrator of the network.

    This solution:

    A. Meets the required solution and both optional solutions.

    B. Meets the required solution and only one optional solution.

    C. Meets only the required solution.

    D. Does not meet the required solution.

28. *Proposed Solution:* On the computer that is crashing, add the parameter /DEBUG to the BOOT.INI file. Configure a computer that will be connected directly to the machine that is suffering the STOP errors. Run the following command on the host computer:

```
    remote /s "i386kd
-v" debug
```

Configure a separate RAS server to allow Microsoft Technical support to dial in to the network. Configure the RAS server to allow access only to that computer. Provide Microsoft with an account to access the network, grant that account the dial-in permission, and tell them to run the command:

```
    Remote /c
\\hostcomputername debug
```

Whenever a crash occurs, run the DUMPFLOP utility to transfer the dump the memory dump file to floppy disks.

This solution:

A. Meets the required solution and both optional solutions.

B. Meets the required solution and only one optional solution.

C. Meets only the required solution.

D. Does not meet the required solution.

29. *Proposed Solution:* On the computer that is crashing, add the parameter /DEBUG to the BOOT.INI file. Configure a computer that will be connected directly to the machine that is suffering the STOP errors. Run the following command on the host computer:

```
    remote /s "i386kd
-v" debug
```

Configure the RAS service on the host computer to enable Microsoft Technical support to dial in to the network. Configure the RAS server to allow access only to that computer. Provide Microsoft with an account to access the network, grant that account the dial-in permission, and tell them to run the command:

```
    Remote /c
\\hostcomputername debug
```

Any time that a crash occurs, run the DUMPFLOP utility to transfer the dump the memory dump file to floppy disks.

This solution:

   A. Meets the required solution and both optional solutions.

   B. Meets the required solution and only one optional solution.

   C. Meets only the required solution.

   D. Does not meet the required solution.

30. If you have not configured your computer to store the results of a STOP error into a memory dump file, where might you look to see what the actual STOP error was?

   A. Server Manager

   B. DRWATSON.LOG

   C. MEMORY.DMP

   D. Windows NT Event Viewer

6.9.1 and 6.9.2 Answers and Explanations: Exercises

These two exercises investigated how to configure the host and target computers to perform kernel debugging.

Additional steps must be included to complete the debugging process. The target computer could have been configured with the /crashdebug switch instead of the /debug switch. This would have only enabled kernel debugging when a STOP error occurred. The /debug switch enables the kernel debugger to STOP processing at any time and investigate the target system.

6.9 Answers and Explanations: Practice Problems

1. **B** Ctrl+C interrupts processing on the target computer and enables a technician to perform kernel debugging without a crash taking place.

2. **C** Windows NT provides symbol files for all Windows NT operating system files. These symbol files are used with the actual executable files when kernel debugging is performed.

3. **C** Checked versions of files do provide debugging capabilities, but are larger in size and can result in slower execution.

4. **C** The host computer is the computer running the kernel debugging software.

5. **A** The target computer is the computer in which the STOP errors are occurring. This computer is the target of the kernel debugging.

6. **A** Although not a true executable, the CRASHDUMP routine writes the contents of memory to the page file with an indicator that a memory dump has been written to the page file. When the system is restarted, the contents of the page file are written to the file %SystemRoot%\Memory.dmp by default.

7. **A, C, D** The parameters /DEBUG, /BAUDRATE, and /DEBUGPORT must be included in the BOOT.INI of the target computer in kernel debugging.

8. **C** The /CRASHDEBUG parameter in the BOOT.INI of the target computer enables kernel debugging only in the event of a STOP error. It does not enable kernel debugging when the host computer presses Ctrl+C to interrupt processing.

9. **D** The CRASHDUMP parameters are set on the Startup/Shutdown tab of the System applet in Control Panel.

10. **D** The contents of a memory dump are stored in the file %SystemRoot%\memory.dmp by default. The actual memory dump is originally written to the page file on the boot partition in Windows NT with an indicator that a memory dump has taken place. When the

system is restarted, the page file contents are then copied to the MEMORY.DMP file. You might receive a warning that you are running out of virtual memory space when the system initially restarts.

11. **B**   The DUMPCHK utility verifies that the contents of a MEMORY.DMP file are not corrupt.

12. **D**   The MEMORY.DMP file will be the size of physical RAM on the computer. If the computer has 512 MB of RAM, the MEMORY.DMP file will be 512 MB in size. Be sure to have enough available disk space for the file.

13. **B, C**   The Paging file must be located on the Windows NT boot partition and be at least as big as the physical RAM pool for a memory dump to occur successfully.

14. **D**   The DUMPEXAM utility reduces the size of a memory dump file for transport to Microsoft Technical support. It includes only the relevant information and, by default, stores the information in a file named MEMORY.TXT.

15. **C**   Not only does the DUMPFLOP copy the entire MEMORY.DMP file to floppy disk, it also compresses the information.

16. **B**   The System log in Windows NT Event Viewer will contain errors related to the Windows NT startup process.

17. **D**   You can apply a filter to reduce the displayed events in the Windows NT Event Viewer. Filters can include error codes, reporting services, and event types.

18. **B**   The default Event Log behavior is to overwrite events that are older than seven days.

19. **D**   The command !drivers is executed within the kernel debugger. The command drivers is a Windows NT resource kit tool that displays the same results for the computer on which the program is run.

20. **C**   You must rename the NTKNRLMP.DBG file on the host com-puter to NTOSKRNL.EXE. A multiprocessor computer will be using the multiprocessor and the symbol file must match the executable.

21. **A, C**   Both the target and host computer must configure which port and what speed will be used for the debugging to take place.

22. **A, B**   You can research STOP error messages by searching the knowledge base at www.microsoft.com/support/ or searching the TechNet CD with the actual STOP message error.

23. **B, C**   The DUMPEXAM utility only works with 0x0000000A or 0x0000001E errors.

24. **A**   The REMOTE.EXE command enables a dial-in client to take over a remote session on the host computer that is connected by a direct cable to the target computer.

25. **D**   You must update each symbol file to match the current version of the Win-dows NT system file. Some of the files may not have been updated in the service pack, so replacing all symbol files with the new symbol files for the service pack may omit some necessary files.

26. **D**   The /CRASHDEBUG setting in the BOOT.INI only enables kernel debug-ging when a STOP error occurs. This does not meet the required result.

27. **B**   There is no such setting as /REBOOT in the BOOT.INI. To set the reboot parameters, you edit the Start/Shutdown tab of the System applet in Control Panel.

28. **B**   With the RAS Server only enabling a connection to resources on the local computer, Microsoft Technical Support will not be able to connect to the host computer to perform the kernel debug-ging.

29. **A** When the RAS Server is running on the host computer, the remote user can connect to the host computer using the REMOTE.EXE program. It does not matter that the target computer is running on a separate computer.

30. **D** The Windows NT Event Viewer's System log can contain an entry with the actual STOP error message if the Startup/Shutdown tab in the System applet has been configured to write an event to the system log.

6.9   Key Words

Application event log

DUMPCHK

DUMPEXAM

DUMPFLOP

Host computer

Kernel debugger

Memory dump file

Security event log

Stop event

System event log

Target computer

6

Practice Exam: Troubleshooting

Use this practice exam to test your mastery of "Troubleshooting." The passing Microsoft score is 76.4 percent.

1. What is the syntax of the SYSDIFF command that applies the changes created by a new application to another system?

   A. SYSDIFF /APPLY SNAPFILE

   B. SYSDIFF /DIFF SNAPFILE

   C. SYSDIFF /APPLY DIFFFILE

   D. SYSDIFF /DIFF DIFFFILE

2. Why must a Backup Domain Controller communicate with a Primary Domain Controller during the installation process? Choose all that apply.

   A. To verify that the account being used to install the BDC has sufficient permissions.

   B. To synchronize the BDC's copy of the accounts database.

   C. To create the computer account for the BDC in the accounts database.

   D. To verify the network protocols that must be installed on the BDC.

3. During the installation of an NT Workstation, you encounter an error message that states the hard disk cannot be accessed. The error message is 0x4,0,0,0. The cause of this error is which of the following?

   A. Another installation of NT Workstation using the same serial number has been found on the network.

   B. There is insufficient disk space on the NT Workstation.

   C. The CD-ROM is damaged.

   D. A boot sector virus is on the computer.

4. Which program is used to add a Tape Backup Device to an existing installation of Windows NT Server?

   A. The Add/Remove Hardware applet in the Control Panel.

   B. The Tape Devices applet in the Control Panel.

   C. The Windows NT Setup program.

   D. The SCSI Devices applet in the Control Panel.

5. What partitions can Windows NT Server be installed to? Select all that apply.

   A. Mirrored sets

   B. Volume sets

   C. Stripe sets

   D. Stripe sets with parity

6. When starting your computer, Windows NT's boot menu is not presented and the computer starts Windows 95 immediately. Some of the likely causes of this are which of the following?

   A. Windows NT has been removed from the computer.

   B. Windows 95 has been set as the default operating system.

   C. Somebody has run the SYS command on drive C.

   D. The timeout setting in BOOT.INI has been set to 0.

7. You have been asked to update the Emergency Repair Disk, but it appears to be failing. What is the probable cause?

   A. The Emergency Repair Disk that you have tried to update is corrupt.

   B. The Emergency Repair Disk must be blank and formatted under Windows NT.

   C. You must be a member of the local group Administrators or Power Users to run RDISK.

D.   The Registry must have been in use when you tried to update the Emergency Repair Disk.

8.   During the start of Windows NT, you encounter an error message that states that the file NTFS.SYS is corrupt. You decide to perform an emergency repair on the system. Which option do you select to fix this problem?

A.   Inspect Registry Files

B.   Inspect Startup Environment

C.   Verify Windows NT System Files

D.   Inspect Boot Sector

9.   After creating a stripe set with parity on your computer, Windows NT refuses to restart. You receive an error message that states <WINNT ROOT>\SYSTEM32\ NTOSKRNL.EXE IS MISSING OR CORRUPT. You decide to perform an emergency repair on the computer. Which option do you select?

A.   Inspect Registry Files

B.   Inspect Startup Environment

C.   Verify Windows NT System Files

D.   Inspect Boot Sector

10. If the Windows NT boot sector has been replaced with the Windows 95 Boot sector, how do you reinstall the Windows NT boot sector?

A.   Reinstall Windows NT.

B.   Run an Emergency Repair Process and select the Inspect Startup Environment option.

C.   Run an Emergency Repair Process and select the Inspect Boot Sector option.

D.   Boot with a Windows NT Boot disk and select the SYS option in Disk Administrator.

11. If you wanted to determine the name of each file installed by Windows NT, what file could be viewed on the Emergency Repair Disk that contains this information?

A.   LOADED.LOG

B.   SETUP.LOG

C.   FILES.LOG

D.   EVENTS.LOG

12. NTBackup enables what options on Registry files?

A.   All Registry files on the network can be backed up and restored.

B.   Backup on the Registry file is not enabled.

C.   Only the local Registry file can be backed up and restored.

D.   Only the changes from the prior Registry file can be saved.

13. If the Registry becomes corrupted, how can the entire Registry be restored?

A.   It can't be; you must reinstall it.

B.   By using the Emergency Repair Disk.

C.   By copying an older version to registry.sys.

D.   By renaming the backup Registry to registry.nt.

14. Which of the following is the name of the registry file?

A.   REG.DAT

B.   It has multiple names.

C.   SYSTEM.INI

D.   SYSTEM.REG

15. If the start value is set to System for a driver, when is the driver loaded during the Windows NT startup process?

A.   By NTLDR

B.   During the NTOSKRNL.EXE initialization

C. During the system startup phase

D. By a dependency service

16. When are changes to the Registry file implemented? Choose all that apply.

    A. At boot up for the local machine

    B. When changed

    C. When acknowledged by the administrator

    D. When the user logs in again

17. Your printer is unable to send any jobs to the physical print devices and you have verified that the correct port has been selected. What other configuration property can you change?

    A. Start printing after last page is spooled

    B. Start printing immediately

    C. Stop the Spooler Service

    D. Print directly to printer

18. Which option can be set for a Printer to prevent PostScript jobs from being printed to a connected PCL Print Device?

    A. Print directly to printer

    B. Hold mismatched jobs

    C. Print spooled documents first

    D. Check print format

19. What can be configured in the Telephony applet of Control Panel? Choose all that apply.

    A. Modem configuration

    B. Dialing locations

    C. Calling card information

    D. Whether the phone line uses pulse or tone

20. Mary, a user, receives a message that her user account could not be authenticated. Which debugging feature can be used to troubleshoot this problem?

A. Use the Event Viewer

B. Enable the logging option in Remote Access Admin

C. Enable PPP logging in the Registry

D. Server Manager

21. You want to use a centralized LMHOSTS file for all your servers and want to reference this LMHOSTS file located in the PUBLIC share of the computer name LOCALSRV. What entries are required in the LMHOSTS file if the LOCALSRV computer is located on a remote subnet?

    A. #BEGIN_ALTERNATE

       #INCLUDE
       \\localsrv\public\lmhosts

       #END_ALTERNATE

       172.16.2.1 LOCALSRV

    B. 172.16.2.1 LOCALSRV

       #BEGIN_ALTERNATE

       #INCLUDE
       \\localsrv\public\lmhosts

       #END_ALTERNATE

    C. #INCLUDE
       \\localsrv\public\lmhosts

    D. 172.16.2.1 LOCALSRV

       #INCLUDE
       \\localsrv\public\lmhosts

22. You want to have Jody use her account and password to make Windows NT computers members of the SCHOOL-HOUSE domain. What methods can be used to enable Jody to add computers to the domain?

    A. Make Jody a member of the Administrators group in the SCHOOLHOUSE domain.

    B. Make Jody a member of the Account Operators group in the SCHOOLHOUSE domain.

C. Make Jody a member of the Server Operators group in the SCHOOL-HOUSE domain.

D. Grant Jody the User Right to "Add Workstations to Domain."

Answers and Explanations: Practice Exam

1. **C**   The syntax for applying a difference file is SYSDIFF /APPLY DIFFFILE.

2. **B, C**   During the installation of a BDC, the SAM database is synchronized to the BDC, and a computer account is created in the SAM database for the BDC.

3. **D**   This message occurs when a boot sector virus is found during the installation of Windows NT.

4. **B**   Tape Devices are added via the Tape Device applet in Control Panel.

5. **A**   Windows NT can be installed only to mirror sets in the list of options. Volume sets and stripe sets have no fault tolerance and cannot house the Boot or system partitions. The Boot and system partitions also cannot be stored on a Windows NT created RAID 5 partition. This is supported only under hardware RAID 5.

6. **B, C, D**   If Windows 95 is set to be the default operating system and the timeout value in the BOOT.INI is set to 0, the computer will automatically start Windows 95 without presenting a boot menu. Likewise, if the SYS command was run in Windows 95 on the C drive, this would replace the boot sector and now look for IO.SYS instead of NTLDR.

7. **C**   To update the Emergency Repair Disk, you must be a member of either the Administrators or Power Users local group and using the computer on which you are running RDISK.

8. **C**   To replace a corrupted driver file, you select the Verify Windows NT System Files option. If you had applied any service packs, they must be re-applied after this, because the file is restored to the pre-service-pack version.

9. **B**   The Inspect Startup Environment option searches for the partition and disk on which Windows NT is installed and rebuilds the BOOT.INI. If the SYSTEM partition was installed on a FAT partition, editing the BOOT.INI also could have been performed to fix this problem (as long as you knew the new partition number for the installation).

10. **C**   By inspecting the boot sector, the Emergency Repair Process resets the boot sector to load the file NTLDR.

11. **B**   The file SETUP.LOG contains the name of every file installed under Windows NT. It also contains a CRC value to determine whether a file has been corrupted.

12. **C**   The NTBackup utility only enables the local Registry to be backed up to tape.

13. **B**   By performing an Emergency Repair process, you can read in a previously saved version of the Registry, assuming that you have updated the repair information using RDISK.

14. **B**   The Windows NT 4 Registry is made up of several hives that are stored in the %SystemRoot%\System32\Config directory.

15. **B**   System drivers are started at the same time that the Windows NT kernel is initialized.

16. **A, B, D**   It depends on what you have adjusted. Some of the changes are immediate, some require the system to be restarted, and some take effect the next time the user logs in to the network.

17. **D**   When you print directly to the printer, you bypass the Print Spooler entirely. You can do this to test for a corrupt print spooler.

18. **B**   When you choose the option to Hold mismatched jobs, the print spooler detects that the job was intended for a PostScript printer when the printer only supports PCL jobs. It prevents the job from printing, but enables other jobs to continue printing.

6

19. **B, C, D**   The Telephony applet enables dialing locations to be configured. The dialing location information includes calling card information and indicates whether the phone line used pulses or tones.

20. **C**   By enabling PPP logging in the Registry, authentication problems can be determined using the PPP.LOG file.

21. **B, D**   When you reference a centrally stored LMHOSTS file, you must first have an entry for the SERVER where the LMHOSTS file is located. If the entry does not exist, there is no way for the client to resolve the NetBIOS name to an IP address when the LMHOSTS file resides on a remote subnet. The LMHOSTS file is parsed sequentially line by line.

22. **A, B, D**   The Administrators and Account Operators groups can add Workstations to the domain by default. You can also grant users this right by granting them the user right Add Workstations to Domain.

Practice Exam 1

Implementing and Supporting Microsoft Windows NT Server 4.0

The Windows NT Server Enterprise exam is an adaptive test—meaning that the number of questions you must answer is indeterminate. The following describes how an adaptive test works:

- The test covers six categories: Planning, Installation and Configuration, Managing Resources, Connectivity, Monitoring and Optimization, and Troubleshooting. Test questions are associated with these categories.

- The testing system asks an extremely difficult question for one of the five test categories. If you answer correctly, the testing system asks you a few easier questions to pass the category.

  If you answer incorrectly, the testing system presents you with at least one less difficult question for the category. If you continue to incorrectly answer questions for the category, the questions become increasingly less difficult until the testing system determines that you do not have sufficient knowledge to pass the category.

  If you finally answer a question correctly, the testing system asks increasingly difficult questions for the category until you correctly answer a certain number of questions (the number is unknown to you or me).

You are not asked the questions in order. The testing system presents questions for all six categories in a seemingly random order. The following are the two types of questions in the test:

- Multiple-choice questions—Select the correct answer.
- Scenario-based questions—Select the response or best scenario from the scenario description.

It is suggested that you set a timer to track your progress while taking the practice exam, because the time restrictions on the tests are often the biggest obstacles to overcome. Begin the following practice exam after you set your time.

Practice Exam Begins

Questions 1 and 2 are based on the following scenario:

Your company has chosen to replace its current network platform with Windows NT. The current network has 1600 users—21 file servers located at four wide-area sites.

Day-to-day business requires a substantial amount of file sharing and remote printing among sites.

To date, each site has its own information systems department that manages and supports all users and resources at the respective site. Your company has decided to maintain this network management structure.

1. What directory services architecture is the best choice for the new Windows NT network?

   A. Double domain

   B. Single master domain

   C. Single domain

   D. Complete trust domains

2. In addition to the 1600 users, it is estimated that the new Windows NT network requires 200 global groups, 55 local groups on domain controllers, and 1150 computer accounts. The average global group has 35 members and the average local group has five members. If all this information were installed in a single SAM database, approximately how large would the database be?

   A. 1 megabyte

   B. 2.45 megabytes

   C. 4.4 megabytes

   D. 700 kilobytes

3. A large number of your company's employees work at more than one of the wide-area sites that comprise the network. Generally, what directory services architecture is best suited for "traveling" users?

   A. Full-trust domains so that the traveling users can have a logon ID for each site and still access resources at other sites.

   B. Single domain so that each user has one logon ID, and all resources on the network are accessible.

   C. Full-trust domains so that the user has one logon ID and can use any local domain controller for the logon process.

   D. None of the above.

4. The Widget company network consists of three domains, DM_Sales, DM_Mfg, and DM_Admin. At present, the three domains do not share resources. Users in the DM_Sales domain need to access some resources that belong to the DM_Mfg domain. How would you enable access to the resources in DM_Mfg for users in DM_Sales?

   A. Establish a two-way trust relationship between DM_Mfg and DM_Sales.

   B. Configure DM_Mfg to trust DM_Sales.

   C. Configure DM_Mfg to trust DM_Sales and DM_Sales to allow DM_Mfg to trust DM_Sales.

   D. Set up user accounts in the DM_Mfg domain with the same username and password as the corresponding accounts in DM_Sales.

5. When a trust relationship is broken by a failed network connection, you can easily reestablish the trust relationship (after the network connection is restored) by which method?

   A. Rebooting the domain controllers.

   B. Reestablishing the network connection restores the trust relationship.

   C. Reestablishing the network connection and rebooting the Primary Domain Controller for each domain.

   D. Reestablishing the network connection, deleting the trust relationship in both domains, and creating a new trust relationship.

6. What are the limitations of local user accounts?

   A. They cannot be used to access resources across domains.

   B. Their passwords cannot be synchronized.

   C. They do not support the interactive logon process.

   D. All of the above.

7. Which of the following statements is true about the local Administrator account on a Windows NT domain controller?

   A. It cannot be deleted.

   B. It is by default a member of the local Server Operators group.

   C. It cannot be renamed.

   D. None of the above.

8. After a trust relationship has been established between two domains, users may access resources across domains because:

   A. Establishing the trust relationship merges the user account databases from the two domains.

   B. The logon services from the trusted domain pass the resource access request to the trusting domain's logon services, where the resource access permissions are authenticated.

   C. Duplicate logon IDs are created in the trusting domain's account database when you assign permissions.

   D. The trust relationship allows logon services from the trusting domain to access the trusted domain's account database.

9. Which RAID fault-tolerance levels are built in to Windows NT Server?

   A. Levels 1, 2, and 3

   B. Levels 1, 2, and 5

   C. Levels 0, 1, and 5

   D. All levels of RAID fault-tolerance

10. What is the maximum number of physical disks that Windows NT Server RAID fault-tolerance supports?

   A. There is no limit.

   B. 16

   C. 32

   D. 128

11. Which is the best Windows NT disk fault-tolerance configuration for read performance?

    A. RAID Level 1

    B. Disk mirroring

    C. Disk striping

    D. Disk striping with parity

12. What is the method by which Windows NT Server protects against writing data to a bad sector on its fault-tolerant volume of a hard disk?

    A. RAID Level 5

    B. Hot swapping

    C. Sector sparing

    D. Hot fixing

13. What is one reason why TCP/IP is the protocol of choice for most networks?

    A. It allows connectivity between dissimilar networks and devices.

    B. TCP/IP is more easily installed and configured than other protocols.

    C. It is a *self-encrypting* protocol that provides secure communications.

    D. All the above.

14. If you shut down a Windows NT Server that is a master browser, you must:

    A. Do nothing; the network will elect a new master browser when the time limit on the downed browser expires.

    B. Promote a domain controller to master browser.

    C. Manually trigger a WINS replication for the entire network.

    D. None of the above.

15. What switch is used with the Windows NT Server installation program to suppress the creation of floppy startup disks?

    A. /B

    B. /N

    C. /NOBOOT

    D. /SI

16. To promote a member Windows NT Server to domain controller, you must:

    A. Select the Domain Controller option from Add/Remove software in the Control Panel.

    B. Run the Windows NT installation program using the /DC switch.

    C. Reinstall the server and configure it as a domain controller during installation.

    D. Promote the server to domain controller using Server Manager.

17. You are the network administrator for a small network that consists of 12 workstations and a single Windows NT Server. Your boss asks you to set up an intranet web site. What is required to install Internet Information Server?

    A. Purchase Internet Information Server and install it on the current server.

    B. Install Internet Information Server from the Windows NT Server CD-ROM if you did not install it during the initial installation of the Windows NT Server software.

C. Install Internet Information Server from the Windows NT Server CD-ROM only if the Windows NT Server is a domain controller.

D. Activate Internet Information Server, which is automatically included in the Windows NT Server installation process.

18. The NETLOGON service is used to:

A. Facilitate SAM database synchronization.

B. Process logon requests.

C. Facilitate pass-through authentication.

D. All the above.

19. To promote a Backup Domain Controller to a Primary Domain Controller, you must:

A. Reinstall Windows NT Server and specify the server as a PDC during installation.

B. Choose the Primary Domain Controller option from the Networks applet in the Control Panel.

C. Choose Promote to Primary Domain Controller in the File menu for Server Manager.

D. Backup Domain Controllers cannot be manually promoted. This is handled automatically by Windows NT.

20. A Windows NT Server that has more than one network adapter installed is called:

A. A routable server.

B. A multihomed server.

C. A proxy server.

D. None of the above. A Windows NT Server is limited to a single network interface card.

21. DHCP can be used on a Windows NT Network to:

A. Set the default gateway for DHCP clients.

B. Assign IP addresses to DHCP clients.

C. Set the WINS server addresses for DHCP clients.

D. All the above.

22. The TCP/IP subnet mask 255.255.255.0 is:

A. Class A

B. Class B

C. Class C

D. Class A or Class B, depending on the value of the first octet.

23. What happens when duplicate IP addresses are assigned to two Windows NT Workstations on the same network?

A. All network communications stop.

B. When the second workstation is started, a warning message is issued, and it does not connect to the network.

C. DHCP automatically assigns a new, unique address to the second workstation that starts.

D. WINS automatically translates communications to and from the second workstation started.

24. Your Microsoft network is a single domain network to the Internet via an ISDN router. You use Windows NT DNS service to provide access to your web server. How do you configure the DNS service to *know* your web server name and IP address?

    A. The web server automatically registers its name and IP address with any DNS services running in its domain.

    B. The web server registers its name and IP address with WINS and WINS automatically updates the DNS server.

    C. The web server name and IP address must be added to the DNS service's database manually.

    D. The web server automatically registers its name and IP address with WINS. When the DNS service cannot find the name request, it interrogates WINS and finds the web server IP address.

25. The purpose of a DHCP relay agent is:

    A. To facilitate communication between WINS servers across routers.

    B. To forward DHCP broadcasts to DHCP servers across routers.

    C. To redirect NetBIOS broadcasts to the domain master browser.

    D. To provide communication between WINS-enabled hosts and WINS servers across routers.

26. A multihomed Windows NT Server can be used in which capacities?

    A. As a NetBEUI router

    B. As an IPX router

    C. As an IP router

    D. As either an IPX router, an IP router, or both

27. When configuring a Windows NT Server to connect to a NetWare 3.11 Server using Ethernet, it is very likely that the correct frame type will be:

    A. 802.5

    B. Ethernet_SNAP

    C. 802.2

    D. 802.3

28. For development purposes, a Windows NT Server is installed on your network to use both as a workstation and a test server for no more than three programmers. What server service optimization option should be selected for this server?

    A. Minimize Memory Used

    B. Balance

    C. Maximize Throughput for File Sharing

    D. Maximize Throughput for Network Applications

29. You can edit the Windows NT Server Registry using:

    A. Any text editor

    B. NOTEPAD.EXE

    C. REGEDT32.EXE

    D. REDIT.EXE

30. To better manage traffic on your network, you manually configure one of the Windows NT Servers to be the master browser. What should you know about manually configured master browsers?

A. The Windows NT Server configured to be the master browser will remain the master browser until it is manually reconfigured.

B. The Windows NT Server cannot be manually configured to act as a master browser.

C. The Windows NT Server may loose its status as a master browser if it is downed or disconnected from the network.

D. The Windows NT Server must be a domain controller to be a master browser.

31. The users on your company's network require different configurations. As a result, many users require a special logon script. You have just installed the second Windows NT Server on your network and configured it as a Backup Domain Controller. Because users will now be logging on to one of two domain controllers, how are the special logon scripts best managed?

A. Place all logon scripts in the default logon script location, configure user profiles to use the default location for logon scripts, and configure the Windows NT directory replication service to replicate the logon script directory between the domain controllers.

B. Leave all logon scripts on one domain controller, and then modify the profile for each user to access the logon script from only the domain controller that contains the scripts.

C. Create a logon script for each user and place it in their respective home directories; change all user profiles to access logon scripts in home directories.

D. Place all logon scripts in the default logon script directory on the Primary Domain Controller. Logon scripts are automatically replicated to all domain controllers in the domain.

32. Configure the Directory Replication service using what utility?

A. Server Manager.

B. The Services applet in Control Panel.

C. Directory Replication service must be configured when Windows NT Server is installed.

D. Directory Replication Manager.

33. Which of the following volume formatting types support volume extension?

A. FAT

B. VFAT

C. NTFS

D. CDFS

34. What utility can you use to convert a FAT file system to NTFS format?

A. NTDETECT.COM

B. SCANDISK.EXE

C. CONVERT.EXE

D. NTFS.EXE

35. Which of the following are required to configure a mirrored drive set on a Windows NT Server? Choose all that apply.

    A. A minimum of four gigabytes storage space.

    B. At least two physical disk drives.

    C. Disk volumes must use NTFS file formatting.

    D. None of the above.

36. What Windows NT Server utility is used for disk fault-tolerance configuration?

    A. Server Manager

    B. Disk Manager

    C. Server Administrator

    D. Disk Administrator

37. One way to configure a printer on a Windows NT Server is:

    A. Using the Printers applet in Control Panel.

    B. Using Printer Manager.

    C. Using Printer Administrator.

    D. None of the above.

38. One possible disadvantage to printer pooling is:

    A. If one printer is taken offline, the pooled print queue is disabled.

    B. All printers must use the same print driver.

    C. The print queue assigned to the pooled printers can only be written to by one user at a time.

    D. A print driver must be installed for each printer in the pool.

39. What Windows NT Server utility is used to share client-based Windows NT administration tools?

    A. Network Client Administrator

    B. Disk Administrator

    C. Server Manager

    D. User Manager for Domains

40. Which of the following workstation platforms can join a Windows NT domain?

    A. Windows NT Servers and Windows NT Workstations

    B. Windows NT Servers only

    C. Windows NT Workstations and Windows 95 Workstations

    D. Windows NT Servers, Windows NT Workstations, Windows 95 Workstations

41. Which of the following Windows NT Server programs can you use to create user accounts? Select all correct answers.

    A. Network Client Administrator

    B. NET.EXE

    C. Server Manager

    D. User Manager for Domains

42. Which of the following groups can lock out global user accounts in a Windows NT domain?

    A. Domain Admins

    B. Administrators

    C. Account Operators

    D. System

43. A Windows NT logon script can be of which types? Select all that apply.

    A. *.BAT

    B. *.CMD

    C. *.EXE

    D. *.SYS

    E. All the above.

44. Windows NT passwords must include which of the following character types? Choose all that apply.

    A. At least one non-alphanumeric character.

    B. At least one numeric character.

    C. At least one uppercase alpha character.

    D. None of the above.

45. Which of the following statements about global groups is true? Choose all the correct answers.

    A. Global groups can have local groups as members.

    B. Global groups can be accessed across domains.

    C. Global groups can be members of local groups.

    D. Members of local groups inherit file rights assigned to global groups.

46. What Windows NT tool is used to create global groups?

    A. Domain Administrator

    B. User Manager

    C. Server Manager

    D. User Manager for Domains

47. What are the global groups created when you create a Windows NT domain?

    A. Domain Admins, Domain Controllers, Domain Guests

    B. Domain Admins, Domain Guests, Domain Users

    C. Domain Administrators, Domain Users, Everyone

    D. Domain Admins, Domain Guests, Everyone

48. Which built-in local group is found only on domain controllers? Choose all that apply.

    A. Everyone

    B. Administrators

    C. Domain Admins

    D. Account Operators

49. A user needs sufficient file access to a Windows NT member server to administer file backups. As a member of the Power Users group on that server, how would you grant the appropriate rights to the user?

    A. Make the user a member of the local group Backup Operators on the member server.

    B. Make the user a member of the local group Administrators on the member server.

    C. Explicitly assign the appropriate rights for the user to all files and directories on the server.

    D. None of the above.

50. After adding a Windows NT Workstation or Server to a domain, what must you do to allow Domain Admins to manage this workstation?

    A. Add the global group Domain Admins to the workstation's local Administrators group.

B. No additional configuration is required. The global group Domain Admins is automatically added to the local group Administrators when a Windows NT workstation successfully joins a domain.

C. Add the local group Administrators to the global group Domain Admins.

D. Set the local user Administrator's password to be the same as the local group Administrator's password on the Primary Domain Controller.

51. A user must have what right in order to create a page file on Windows NT Server?

A. The Create Permanent Shared Objects right

B. The Log On as a Service right

C. The Create Token Object right

D. The Create a Pagefile right

52. Where is the user profile for Windows NT Workstations stored?

A. On the workstation's local hard drive.

B. In the same directory as the Windows NT Registry.

C. In the user's home directory as defined in the user account properties.

D. In the directory specified by the Profile Path in the user account properties (the local hard drive if the Profile Path field is blank).

53. What Windows NT utility do you use to set system policies for users?

A. Domain Administrator

B. User Manager for Domains

C. System Policy Editor

D. Policy Editor for Domains

54. Which of the following restrictions can you assign to users on a Windows NT network? Choose all that apply.

A. Disallow creation of drive mappings.

B. Disable booting from the A drive.

C. Lock out access to the C: prompt (DOS command line).

D. All the above.

55. When a Windows NT Workstation reads a machine policy file, how does the workstation store the information?

A. The information is merged into the HKEY_CURRENT_MACHINE subtree of the Workstation Registry.

B. It is stored in the home directory of the current user.

C. It is merged into the HKEY_LOCAL_MACHINE subtree of the Windows NT Workstation Registry.

D. It replaces the HKEY_CURRENT_MACHINE subtree of the Windows NT Workstation registration.

56. A user requires which permissions on a file share in order to change directories within that share? Choose all that apply.

A. Change

B. Read & Add

C. Full Control

D. Modify

E. None of the above.

57. What implicit file share permission do you assign to all users that do not have explicit permission to a give file share?

   A. Read Only.

   B. Read and Execute.

   C. Access Denied.

   D. Users not assigned explicit rights to a file share have no rights assigned.

58. A user belongs to a local group on a domain controller that is assigned No Access rights to a file share on that server. This user also belongs to another local group that is assigned Change permissions to the same file share. What is this user's effective permission to the file share?

   A. No Access

   B. Change

   C. Change and No Access

   D. Access Denied

59. Why might the FAT file format be used on a Windows NT volume?

   A. The FAT file structure offers a greater degree of flexibility in assigning permissions to directories than NTFS.

   B. FAT may be needed to provide filename compatibility with Windows for Workgroups workstations connected to the network.

   C. Due to hardware resource limitations, your only option for disk fault-tolerance is disk mirroring, and you want to mirror the boot sector.

   D. None of the above.

60. What NTFS directory permission is minimally required to change the current NTFS permissions?

   A. Change Permission

   B. Change

   C. Full Control

   D. List

61. What NTFS file permission is minimally required to view the contents of a file?

   A. Read

   B. Read and Execute

   C. Execute

   D. Full Control

62. You have just added a new disk drive to your Windows NT Server, formatted it (NTFS), and configured the new drive as a volume. Several local groups will store data on the new volume in separate directories. How should you configure the directory permissions?

   A. You should assign Full Control to the root directory for the group Everyone, create the required directories, and assign appropriate permissions to the subdirectories.

   B. You should assign the No Access permission to the group Everyone in the root directory, create the required directories, and add the appropriate permissions to the directories.

   C. You should assign permissions to the root directory for all groups that will access the volume.

   D. The group Everyone is automatically assigned Full Control to the root directory. You remove the group Everyone from the root directory permissions list, create the required directories, and assign appropriate rights to groups for the directories.

63. Some data files are stored on a Windows NT Server in the (NTFS) directory C:\INVENTORY\DATA. You assign Read permission for the Accounting local group and Change permission for the Management local group. They are copied to (NTFS) directory C:\INVENTORY\SECRET, which is located on the same server volume. The target directory for these files has Read permission for both Accounting and Management. What access permissions will Management have to these files after they are copied to the target directory?

    A. Read

    B. Change

    C. Access Denied

    D. List

64. Some data files are stored on a Windows NT Server in the (NTFS) directory C:\INVENTORY\DATA. You assign Read permission for the Accounting local group and Change permission for the Management local group. They are moved to the (NTFS) directory C:\INVENTORY\SECRET on the same server. The target directory for these files has Read permission for both Accounting and Management. What access permissions will Management have to these files after they are moved to the target directory?

    A. Read

    B. Change

    C. Access Denied

    D. List

65. Directory C:\TEST\DATA is shared with Read permissions for the group Users. The NTFS permissions for C:\TEST\DATA is set to Change for the group Domain Users. What permission does Domain Users have for directory C:\TEST\DATA?

    A. Change

    B. Read

    C. Change and Read

    D. None of the above.

66. DomainA and DomainB have a one-way trust relationship: DomainA trusts DomainB. What can you do in terms of adding users from one domain to groups in the other?

    A. You can add users in DomainA to global groups in DomainB.

    B. You can add users in DomainB to global groups in DomainA.

    C. You can add users from DomainA to local groups in DomainB.

    D. You can add users from DomainB to local groups in DomainA.

    E. None of the above. Domains must have a full-trust relationship to add users from one domain to a group in the other.

67. The marketing department has some files stored in a directory on an NTFS volume. All users on the network need read access to some of these files and write access to others. The Mktg group requires read and write access to all the files. How would you configure the file share and NTFS permissions to satisfy the requirements?

    A. You should assign Read permission for Everyone to the file share and Change permission to the NTFS directory for the Mktg group.

B. You should assign Full Control permission for Everyone to the file share, Change permission to the Mktg group, and the appropriate Change or Read permissions to each file in the directory for Everyone.

C. You should assign Change permission for Everyone in the file share, assign the NTFS Read permission to Everyone for all files in the directory, and assign the NTFS Change permission to all files for the Mktg group.

D. You should assign Change permission for Everyone in the file share, for each file in the directory assign the appropriate NTFS Change or Read permission for Everyone, and assign the NTFS Change permission for the Mktg group to all files in the directory.

68. John requires access to a Windows NT resource. He is assigned to a local group that has permission to access the resource. John attempts to access the resource, but is greeted with an Access Denied message. What is the most likely reason that John cannot access the resource?

A. John has not logged in since he was added to the local group.

B. Another group that John belongs to has the default Access Denied permission assigned for that resource.

C. John is not a member of the domain to which the local group belongs.

D. Users can be added only to global groups.

69. You suspect that an unauthorized person attempted to log on to your network. What audit policy could you activate to check for attempted unauthorized logons?

A. Process Tracking: Look for excessive failed logon processes.

B. Use of User Rights: Look for excessive failed logon attempts.

C. Lockout Tracking: Track the user lockout count.

D. Logon and Logoff: Look for excessive failed logon attempts.

70. To use file-level auditing on a given Windows NT Server, you must first do what?

A. Enable File and Object Access Auditing on the target file server.

B. Assign Full Control NTFS permission for the built-in group, System, to all volumes that you will audit.

C. Rebuild the file tables on the target volume by using NTFSCVT.EXE.

D. Add Change permission for the built-in group, Administrators, to the target volume using CACLS.EXE.

71. You are required to audit an NTFS directory, C:\DATA\ACCTG, on your Windows NT Server for changes to all files in that directory. You are asked to move C:\DATA\ACCTG to a new location under directory C:\COMMON on the same Windows NT Server. What must you do to continue to audit the ACCTG directory?

A. You should do nothing. The audit information in the ACCTG directory will not change.

B. You should reestablish the auditing configuration using Windows NT Explorer.

C. You should not move the directory because all auditing information to date will be lost.

D. You should maintain the auditing configuration on the ACCTG directory by first copying the directory to the new location and then deleting the original directory.

72. Which of the following IP addresses is a valid Class C address?

A. 222.18.22.4

B. 191.255.255.1

C. 127.34.56.199

D. 225.275.8.44

73. Your IP network is assigned the Class B address range of 129.48.0.0–129.48.255.255. You are using a subnet mask of 255.255.192.0. How many subnets can you have on your network using this subnet mask?

A. 8

B. 5

C. 4

D. 64

74. Using the IP address information from the previous question, which of the following IP addresses does not belong to the subnet 129.48.128.0? Choose all that apply.

A. 129.48.128.8

B. 129.48.191.123

C. 129.48.127.17

D. 129.48.132.255

75. What service is used to facilitate bi-directional print services between Windows NT Server and UNIX (IP) hosts?

A. LPR

B. TCP/IP Printing Support

C. LPD

D. UNIX Gateway for Windows NT

76. What service does Windows NT Server use to connect to NetWare servers?

A. IPX

B. Gateway Service for NetWare

C. SPX

D. NWLink

77. What utility do you use to manage and configure DHCP on a Windows NT network?

A. DHCP Administrator

B. Server Manager

C. DHCP Manager

D. Protocol Manager

78. What utility do you use to migrate Novell directories and files to a Windows NT domain controller?

A. NTFSCVT.EXE

B. NWCONV.EXE

C. NET.EXT

D. NW2NT.EXE

79. Which of the following protocols are network protocols supported by Windows NT Remote Access Service? Choose all that apply.

A. SLIP

B. NetBIOS

C. IPX

D. TCP/IP

80. Although you can substantially improve system performance on a Windows NT Server by moving the paging file from the default location on the system partition to another partition, what is one disadvantage?

    A. The paging file uses more disk space.

    B. The CRASHDUMP utility is disabled.

    C. Physical stress increases on the partition to where you moved the paging file.

    D. There are no disadvantages.

81. In terms of network protocols on a Windows NT network, what is the simplest way to optimize network performance?

    A. Always use TCP/IP.

    B. Use NetBEUI on segmented networks.

    C. Match the network size and load requirements to the protocol.

    D. Use compressed network packets.

82. What tool would you typically use to view processes running on a Windows NT Server or Workstation?

    A. Server Manager

    B. Windows Diagnostics

    C. MSD.EXE

    D. Task Manager

83. What Windows NT utility is used to monitor network activity?

    A. Performance Monitor

    B. Network Monitor

    C. Network Manager

    D. Windows Diagnostics

84. Which of the following are counter types used by Performance Monitor? Choose all that apply.

    A. Averaging

    B. Instantaneous

    C. Delayed

    D. Difference

85. What might a high rate of hard page faults on a Windows NT Server indicate?

    A. Not enough disk space in the system partition.

    B. Not enough physical memory.

    C. The paging file is not large enough.

    D. Memory errors.

86. The hardware address of a device on an Ethernet network is called the:

    A. IP address

    B. Socket number

    C. Port number

    D. MAC address

87. How might a Windows NT Workstation client locate a domain controller to log on? Choose all the correct answers.

    A. The address of the domain controller is in the client's Registry.

    B. The client sends out a broadcast looking for a NETLOGON mail slot.

    C. The client sends a request for a NETLOGON address to a WINS Server.

    D. The client uses a browse list to locate the domain controller.

88. How do you change the update interval time on master and backup Windows NT browsers?

   A. Run WINS Manager, select the browser, choose Configuration from the File menu.

   B. Modify the browser's Registry.

   C. Run Server Manager, select the browser, choose the Browser option from the File menu.

   D. None of the above. The interval time for browsers cannot be changed from their default 12 minutes.

89. What is the purpose of the `%systemroot%\System32\Autoexec.nt` file?

   A. It runs as a batch command file when the Windows NT Server is initialized.

   B. It is used as the AUTOEXEC.BAT file for DOS sessions.

   C. The boot process uses this file to locate the system partition.

   D. None of the above.

90. You perform an emergency repair to a Windows NT computer using what utility?

   A. SETUP.EXE

   B. RDISK.EXE

   C. WINNT.EXE or WINNT32.EXE

   D. WINREP.EXE

   E. None of the above.

91. You are installing Windows NT Server on a computer that has multiple SCSI adapters. For Windows NT to install correctly on this computer, what must you do?

   A. You must enable the BIOS on all SCSI adapters.

   B. You must enable the BIOS on only the first physical SCSI adapter.

   C. You must disable the BIOS for all the SCSI adapters.

   D. Windows NT automatically configures for multiple SCSI adapters regardless of their BIOS configuration.

92. Which program provides hardware detection when an Intel-based Windows NT Server boots?

   A. NVRAM

   B. NTLDR

   C. NTDETECT

   D. NTMENU

93. What Windows NT utility do you use to view log files created by the Remote Access Service?

   A. Any text editor

   B. Event Viewer

   C. Server Manager

   D. Windows NT Diagnostics

94. What utility do you use to monitor RAS connections from the Windows NT Server console?

   A. RAS Admin

   B. Windows Diagnostics

   C. Network Monitor

   D. RAS Monitor

95. Assuming that all workstations on the network are Windows NT or Windows 95, how do you know that there is a duplicate workstation (NetBIOS) name on a Windows NT network?

A. A warning message displays on all domain controllers on the network.

B. A warning message displays on the offending workstation during initialization, and the workstation will not connect to the network.

C. A warning message sends to any Domain Admins that are logged on to the network.

D. The offending workstation issues a warning, and then automatically renames itself at startup time.

96. Which of the following is a utility that you can use to discover the IP address and subnet mask assigned to a Windows NT computer?

A. PING

B. CONFIG

C. INETD

D. IPCONFIG

97. Which of the following is a utility that you can use to test the connectivity between two IP hosts?

A. PING

B. IPFIND

C. SEARCHIP

D. GROPE

98. The protocol you use to translate Ethernet MAC addresses to IP addresses on a TCP/IP network is:

A. RARP

B. ARP

C. WINS

D. DNS

99. The Windows NT utility you use to view the current NetBIOS names registered by the client, as well as to view the cache of NetBIOS names to IP addresses that have been resolved by a Windows NT client, is:

A. NETSTAT.EXE

B. NBTSTAT.EXE

C. ROUTE.EXE

D. NET.EXE

100. How does a differential backup data set differ from an incremental backup data set?

A. An incremental backup data set contains files that have been modified since the last incremental backup was performed; a differential backup data set contains files that have been modified since the last full backup was performed.

B. An incremental backup data set contains files that have been modified since the last full backup was performed; a differential backup data set contains files that have been modified since the last differential backup was performed.

C. An incremental backup data set contains files that have been modified since the last incremental or full backup was performed; a differential backup data set contains files that have been modified since the last full or differential backup was performed.

D. An incremental backup data set contains files that have been modified since the last differential backup was performed; a differential backup data set contains files that have been modified since the last full backup was performed.

Answers and Explanations

1. **D**   Complete trust domains is the best choice because management wants to retain distributed administration of users. (Planning.)

2. **B**   The SAM database size is calculated as follows:

   - Add 1024 (1 KB) bytes per user in the account.
   - Add 512 (0.5 KB) bytes per local group on domain controllers plus 36 bytes per member for each group.
   - Add 512 (0.5 KB) bytes per global group plus 12 bytes per member for each group.
   - Add 512 (0.5 KB) bytes per computer account.

   Using this information, you can calculate as follows:

   1600 users * 1024 bytes = 1638400 bytes + 200 global groups * 512 bytes = 102400 bytes + 200 global groups * 35 members * 12 bytes = 84000 bytes + 55 local groups * 512 bytes = 28160 bytes + 55 local groups * 5 members * 36 bytes = 9900 bytes + 1150 computer accounts * 512 bytes = 588800 bytes + = 2451660 bytes = 2.45 MB. (Planning.)

3. **B**   Single domain directory services are best suited for *traveling* users so that each user has one logon ID, all resources on the network are accessible, and logon authentication is performed at the nearest domain controller. The single domain directory services architecture may not work best for networks that have few traveling users, but it is the best

choice of the options offered when only traveling users are considered. (Installation and Configuration.)

4. **C**   To enable access to the resources in DM_Mfg for users in DM_Sales, use the User Manager for Domains utility to configure DM_Mfg to trust DM_Sales and to configure DM_Sales to allow DM_Mfg to trust DM_Sales. (Managing Resources.)

5. **A**   When a trust relationship breaks, it is easily reestablished by rebooting the domain controllers. (Managing Resources.)

6. **D**   All the listed issues are limitations of local user accounts. (Managing Resources.)

7. **A**   You cannot delete the local Administrator account on a Windows NT domain controller. (Managing Resources.)

8. **B**   After a trust relationship is established between two domains, users may access resources across domains because the trust relationship allows logon services from the trusted domain to pass through access requests to the trusting domain. (Managing Resources.)

9. **C**   RAID fault-tolerance levels 0, 1, and 5 are built in to Windows NT Server. (Installation and Configuration.)

10. **C**   Windows NT Server RAID fault-tolerance supports at maximum 32 disks. (Installation and Configuration.)

11. **D**   The best Windows NT disk fault-tolerance configuration for read performance is disk striping with parity. (Installation and Configuration.)

12. **C**   Sector sparing is the method by which Windows NT Server protects against writing data to a bad sector on its hard disk drive(s). (Installation and Configuration.)

13. **A**   TCP/IP is the protocol of choice for most networks because it is the network industry standard and allows connectivity between dissimilar networks and devices. (Connectivity.)

14. **A**   If you shut down a Windows NT Server that is a master browser, you do nothing; the network elects a new master browser when the time limit on the downed browser expires. (Managing Resources.)

15. **A**   Use the /B switch with the Windows NT Server installation program to suppress the creation of floppy startup disks. (Installation and Configuration.)

16. **C**   You must configure a Windows NT Server as a domain controller at installation time. To promote a member server to domain controller, you must reinstall Windows NT Server. (Installation and Configuration.)

17. **B**   Internet Information Server ships with Windows NT Server. You may install IIS on any Windows NT Server (domain controller or not), and you have the option of installing IIS when you install Windows NT Server. (Installation and Configuration.)

18. **D**   The NETLOGON service facilitates SAM database synchronization, processes logon requests, and processes authentications for trusted domains (pass-through authentication). (Troubleshooting)

19. **C**   You can promote a Backup Domain Controller to a Primary Domain Controller by starting Server Manager, selecting the target Backup Domain Controller, and choosing the Promote to Primary Domain Controller option in Server Manager's File menu. (Managing Resources.)

20. **B**   A multihomed server is a Windows NT Server that has more than one network adapter installed. (Connectivity.)

21. **D**   DHCP can set a number of configuration parameters on a DHCP client, including setting the default gateway, assigning an IP address to the client, and setting the IP address for the (usually nearest) WINS server. (Connectivity.)

22. **C**   By definition, a TCP/IP address that uses the first three octets for the network address is a Class B IP address. Note that any valid subnet mask may be used for any Class IP network address: the subnet mask in this question is the standard Class C subnet mask. (Installation and Configuration.)

23. **B**   When a Windows NT Workstation starts up, it looks for a duplicate of its IP address on the network before connecting to the network. If the Windows NT Workstation finds a duplicate IP address, it issues a warning message, and it does not connect to the network. (Connectivity.)

24. **C**   The DNS database is static. You must add addresses manually. (Connectivity.)

25. **B**   DHCP relay agents are configured with the IP address(es) of one or more DHCP servers that are connected to another network segment.

The agents capture client DHCP broadcasts and send them to the DHCP server. (Connectivity.)

26. **D** NetBEUI is not routable. You can configure Windows NT Server to be both an IPX router and an IP router. Windows NT Server can also route both protocols simultaneously. Note that answers B and C are correct answers, but D is the most correct answer. (Installation and Configuration.)

27. **D** 802.3 is the default frame type for NetWare 3.11. (Installation and Configuration.)

28. **A** Minimize Memory Used is the server optimization option that you should select for this server. Minimize Memory Used is the setting when fewer than 10 connections are guaranteed as the maximum. (Installation and Configuration.)

29. **C** You can also use REGEDIT.EXE. (Troubleshooting.)

30. **C** The Registry setting can change if the computer is rebooted, or if it is disconnected from the network long enough for the other browsers on the network to hold a master browser election. (Connectivity.)

31. **A** Answers A, B, and C all work; however, A provides the best way to manage a messy situation. If logon scripts are replicated among domain controllers, any additional logon scripts or edits to existing logon scripts are replicated to other domain controllers. The logon scripts run regardless of which domain controller processes the logon. (Managing Resources.)

32. **A** Configure the Directory Replication service using Server Manager. (Installation and Configuration.)

33. **C** VFAT is a non-existent file format, CDFS is a CD-ROM file format. Of FAT and NTFS, only NTFS supports volume extension. (Installation and Configuration.)

34. **C** CONVERT.EXE is used to convert a FAT file system to NTFS format. (Installation and Configuration.)

35. **D** You can mirror any size disk; you can use a single physical drive to mirror a volume. The boot partition cannot be mirrored, but you can mirror FAT file format disks. (Installation and Configuration.)

36. **D** Use Disk Administrator to configure disk fault-tolerance. (Installation and Configuration.)

37. **A** One way to configure a printer on a Windows NT Server is to use the Printers applet in Control Panel. (Managing Resources.)

38. **B** Because printer pooling sends jobs to a single print queue, all printers that belong to a given printer pool must use the same print driver. (Managing Resources.)

39. **A** Use Network Client Administrator to share client-based Windows NT administration tools. (Managing Resources.)

40. **A** Windows 95 computers cannot join the domain. (Managing Resources.)

41. **B, D** User Manager for Domains is normally the tool you use to create new user accounts. NET.EXE is a command-line utility that is useful for batch processing of new user accounts. The Windows NT Server Resource kit also comes with a tool, ADDUSER.EXE, for batch processing of user accounts. (Managing Resources.)

42. **D** Only System can lock out accounts. Note that users with the appropriate permissions can disable user accounts. (Installation and Configuration.)

43. **A, B, C** A Windows NT logon script can be either a batch file (*.BAT, *.CMD) or an executable (*.EXE). (Managing Resources.)

44. **D** Although you can configure Windows NT password security to require any or all the character types listed, none are required by default. The Windows NT Server Resource Kit includes a toolset that can enable the character types feature, as well as other password security enhancement features. (Installation and Configuration.)

45. **B,C** Global groups may be accessed across domains, and they can be members of local groups. (Managing Resources.)

46. **D** User Manager for Domains is one tool you use to create global groups. (Managing Resources.)

47. **B** When you create a Windows NT domain, the global groups Domain Admins, Domain Guests, and Domain Users are automatically created. Domain Controllers is not a standard group, and Everyone is a special group. (Installation and Configuration.)

48. **D** The built-in group Account Operators is created automatically on Windows NT Servers only when you configure the server as a domain controller. (Installation and Configuration.)

49. **D** As a member of the Power User group, you do not have the necessary rights to perform A, B, or C. Only members of the local group

Administrators may add or delete members from the local group Backup Operators. (Installation and Configuration.)

50. **B** The global group Domain Admins is automatically added to the local Administrators group when a Windows NT computer joins a domain. (Managing Resources.)

51. **D** Users must have the Create a Pagefile right to create a page file on a Windows NT Server. The right is assigned by default to the local groups Administrators and Power Users. (Managing Resources.)

52. **D** The user profile for a Windows NT Workstation is stored in the directory specified by the Profile Path in the user account properties. If you do not specify the profile path in the user account, the user profile is stored on the local hard drive of the Windows NT Workstation. Although a user profile is stored somewhere other than the Windows NT Workstation hard drive, a copy of the profile is also stored on the Windows NT Workstation hard drive as a backup in case the system cannot locate the server-stored copy of the profile at boot time. (Installation and Configuration.)

53. **B** You use the User Manager for Domains to set system policies for users. (Managing Resources)

54. **D** You can assign all the listed restrictions to users. The best source of information on this subject is the Windows NT Server Resource Kit. (Managing Resources.)

55. **C** When a Windows NT Workstation reads a machine policy file, the information merges into the HKEY_LOCAL_MACHINE subtree of the workstation's registry. Machine policy files are one method of updating network and workstation security. (Managing Resources.)

56. **A, C**   The Change and the Full Control permissions are the only two valid file share permissions listed. The three file share permissions that enable any access to a shared directory are Read, Change, and Full Control. These three permissions enable the user to change directories. (Managing Resources.)

57. **C**   Users and groups for which you do not assign explicit rights to a file share have an implied Access Denied right. (Managing Resources.)

58. **A**   In this case, the user's effective permission to the file share is No Access because when an access request to a file share is authenticated, the system uses the most restrictive right assigned to the user. (Managing Resources.)

59. **D**   The FAT file structure is less flexible than NTFS in terms of file and directory permissions. The FAT file structure on a Windows NT Server employs the same long names and associated shorthand 8.3 format short names as NTFS. On mirrored drives, the boot partition is mirrored for both FAT file systems and NTFS. (Planning.)

60. **A**   Change Permissions is the minimally required right for changing file permissions. You can explicitly set or clear this right for a user or group by using the Special file permissions option when you assign file and directory permissions. (Managing Resources.)

61. **A**   The NTFS file permission of Read is minimally required to view the contents of a file. (Managing Resources.)

62. **D**   By default, the group Everyone is granted Full Control rights to the root directory of a newly created volume. You should delete this group from the permissions list for the root directory, so that the directories you subsequently create do not inherit the permissions. Removing Everyone also blocks any users from creating new directories and changing permissions on existing directories. After removing Everyone from the root directory permission list, you should create the required directories and assign appropriate permissions. (Managing Resources.)

63. **A**   When files are copied from one NTFS directory to another, the files inherit the permissions of the target directory. (Managing Resources.)

64. **B**   Management will have Change permissions after the files move to the target directory. Files that are moved within the same NTFS volume retain their original permissions. (Managing Resources.)

65. **B**   After you share an NTFS directory, the most restrictive permissions. (Managing Resources.)

66. **B**   You can add users from a trusted domain to global groups in the trusting domain. You cannot add users to local groups across domain lines. (Managing Resources.)

67. **D**   When Windows NT determines file access permissions for a shared NTFS directory, the system compares NTFS permissions and the file share permissions, and the most restrictive permissions of the two are the effective permissions. Conversely, when a user is a member of two groups that are both assigned permissions to an NTFS file or directory, the least restrictive permissions are the effective permissions. (Managing Resources.)

68. **A**   After permissions change, users must re-log on to a Windows NT network to rebuild their access tokens. (Troubleshooting.)

69. **D** Logon and Logoff is the correct audit category where you set the audit flag for failed logon attempts. (Managing Resources.)

70. **A** To use file-level auditing on a Windows NT Server, you must first enable File and Object Access Auditing on the target file server. (Managing Resources.)

71. **A** Audit policies associated with files operate under the same copy/move rules as NTFS permissions. (Managing Resources.)

72. **A** 222.18.22.4 is a valid Class C address because the first octet of the address is within the range of Class C IP addresses (192–224). (Planning.)

73. **C** The four subnets are defined by the third octet in the subnet mask, 192 (binary 11000000). This is referred to as a two-bit subnet mask. The possible values for these two bits are: 00, 01, 10, and 11. The four subnet address ranges are:

    (a) 129.48.0.0 to 129.48.63.255,

    (b) 129.48.64.0 to 129.48.127.255,

    (c) 129.48.128.0 to 129.48.191.255, and

    (d) 129.48.192.0 to 129.48.255.255. (Planning.)

74. **C** Refer to the listing of IP address ranges in the answer to question 73. (Planning.)

75. **B** TCP/IP Printing Support is the service you use to facilitate bidirectional printing between Windows NT networks and UNIX hosts. Note that LPD and LPR are components of TCP/IP Printing Support. (Installation and Configuration.)

76. **B** Use Gateway Service for NetWare with the NWLink protocol to connect Windows NT networks to Novell servers. (Connectivity.)

77. **C** You use DHCP Manager to configure DHCP. (Installation and Configuration.)

78. **B** Use NWCONV.EXE to migrate Novell directories and files to a Windows NT domain controller. (Installation and Configuration.)

79. **C, D** RAS does not support NetBIOS, and SLIP is a line protocol. (Connectivity.)

80. **B** When the paging file is located on any partition other than the system partition, the CRASHDUMP utility is disabled. (Monitoring and Optimization.)

81. **C** The overall network requirements and size are important factors to consider when you select the appropriate protocol for a new Microsoft network. Although TCP/IP is the de facto standard for network protocols, NWLink or NetBEUI is a better choice in some cases. (Planning.)

82. **D** You use Task Manager on Windows NT Workstations to view running processes on that workstation. (Troubleshooting.)

83. **B** You can use Network Monitor to view network activity on a Windows NT network. (Monitoring and Optimization.)

84. **A, B, D** The three types of counters used by Performance Monitor are: Averaging, Instantaneous, and Difference. (Monitoring and Optimization.)

85. **B** Insufficient physical memory on a Windows NT Server or Workstation usually causes excessive hard-page faults. (Troubleshooting.)

86. **D** MAC (Media Access Control) address is the hardware address of a device on an Ethernet network. (Monitoring and Optimization.)

87. **B, C**   After a Windows NT Workstation attempts to find a domain controller by sending a request to a WINS Server (if the Windows NT Workstation has been assigned at least a primary WINS Server), and the WINS Server fails to respond, the Windows NT Workstation sends out a broadcast request for a NETLOGON service mailbox. (Troubleshooting.)

88. **B**   The only way to change the update interval time for browsers is to manually modify the Registry. (Monitoring and Optimization.)

89. **B**   The `%systemroot%\system32\Autoexec.nt` runs at the start of a Windows NT DOS session. (Monitoring and Optimization.)

90. **E**   To perform an emergency repair, you boot the Windows NT Server using the original installation diskettes. The system prompts you to repair the file server. (Troubleshooting.)

91. **B**   You must enable the BIOS on only the first physical SCSI adapter (generally the SCSI adapter located in the lowest slot number). (Connectivity.)

92. **C**   NTDETECT provides hardware detection when an Intel-based Windows NT Server boots. (Troubleshooting.)

93. **A**   Remote Access Service log files are ordinary ASCII text files. You can use any text editor to view them. (Troubleshooting.)

94. **A**   RAS Admin is the tool you use to monitor RAS connections from the Windows NT Server console.

(Troubleshooting.)

95. **B**   As with duplicate TCP/IP addresses, when a Windows 95 or Windows NT workstation boots, it checks the network for a duplicate NetBIOS name. If the system finds a duplicate NetBIOS name, the workstation issues a warning message and does not connect to the network. (Troubleshooting.)

96. **D**   The command-line utility IPCONFIG displays, as well as other information, such as the IP address and subnet mask assigned to the workstation. (Troubleshooting.)

97. **A**   PING is a utility that you can use to test the connectivity between two IP hosts. (Troubleshooting.)

98. **A**   The protocol used to translate Ethernet MAC addresses to IP addresses on a TCP/IP network is RARP (Reverse Address Resolution Protocol). (Troubleshooting.)

99. **B**   Use NBTSTAT.EXE to view the current NetBIOS names registered by the client and view the cache of NetBIOS names to IP addresses that a Windows NT client resolved. (Troubleshooting)

100. **C**   Remember that both incremental and differential backup processes are based on file archive flags. Full backups clear the archive flag when a file successfully saves. Incremental backups save only files with the archive flag set and then clear the archive flag. Differential backups save only files with the archive flag set and leave the archive flag set. (Installation and Configuration.)

Practice Exam 2

Implementing and Supporting Windows NT Server 4.0 in the Enterprise

The Windows NT Server Enterprise exam is an adaptive test—meaning that the number of questions you must answer is indeterminate. The following describes how an adaptive test works:

- The test covers six categories: Planning, Installation and Configuration, Managing Resources, Connectivity, Monitoring and Optimization, and Troubleshooting. Test questions are associated with these categories.

- The testing system asks an extremely difficult question for one of the five test categories. If you answer correctly, the testing system asks you a few easier questions to pass the category.

  If you answer incorrectly, the testing system presents you with at least one less difficult question for the category. If you continue to incorrectly answer questions for the category, the questions become increasingly less difficult until the testing system determines that you do not have sufficient knowledge to pass the category.

If you finally answer a question correctly, the testing system asks increasingly difficult questions for that category until you correctly answer a certain number of questions (the number is unknown to you or me).

You are not asked the questions in order. The testing system presents questions for all six categories in a seemingly random order. The following are the two types of questions in the test:

- Multiple-choice questions—Select the correct answer.
- Scenario-based questions—Select the response or best scenario from the scenario description.

It is suggested that you set a timer to track your progress while taking the practice exam, because the time restrictions on the tests are often the biggest obstacles to overcome. Begin the following practice exam after you set your time.

Practice Exam Begins

1. A user on your Windows NT network requires full access to all services, files, and directories on a Windows NT applications server. Which of the following actions is the best solution?

   A. Assign the user to the Domain Admins group.

   B. Create a global group, add the user to the global group, and add the global group to the local Administrators group for the target file server.

   C. Grant the user full access to all files and directories on the target server.

   D. A and C.

   E. B and C.

2. A large number of your company's employees work at more than one of the wide-area sites that comprise the network. Generally, what directory services architecture is best suited for *traveling* users?

   A. Full trust domains so that the traveling users can have a logon ID for each site and still access resources at other sites.

   B. Single domain so that each user has one logon ID, and all resources on the network are accessible.

   C. Full trust domains so that the user has one logon ID and can use any local domain controller for the logon process.

   D. None of the above.

3. DomainA trusts DomainB. DomainB trusts DomainC. Which of the following statements is true? Choose all correct answers.

   A. DomainA trusts DomainC.

   B. DomainC trusts DomainA.

   C. Domains A, B, and C have a full-trust relationship.

   D. None of the above.

4. When establishing a trust relationship between two domains, which of the following is true?

   A. The Administrator password is used to establish the communications link between the domains.

   B. After the trust relationship is established, the domain controllers generate a password to secure their communications link.

   C. After the trust relationship is established, it can break only if both domain controllers agree to break the trust relationship.

   D. None of the above.

5. To assign administrative control to the global group Domain Admins when adding domain controllers to an existing domain, what should you do?

   A. You should do nothing. Domain Admins is automatically added to the local group Administrators.

   B. You should add Domain Admins to the local group Administrators, and then delete the local (built-in) user Administrator.

C. You should assign full permissions to Domain Admins and to all volumes on the server, and then add Domain Admins to the local (built-in) group Administrators.

D. You should add Domain Admins to the local (built-in) group Users, and then assign the Administrate This Computer permissions to Users.

6. To assign permissions across a trust relationship, you should:

A. Directly assign permissions to a local user account belonging to the trusted domain.

B. Create a local group in the trusting domain, assign permissions to a local group in the trusting domain, add a global group from the trusted domain to the local group, and add users to the global group from the trusted domain.

C. Assign permissions to a global group from the trusting domain.

D. Assign permissions to a local group from the trusting domain.

7. A complete-trust directory services model is effective on large networks because:

A. You manage all users in one domain.

B. Any user can use resources on any of the trusted domains.

C. It is the best way to configure a *one user, one account* network.

D. None of the above.

8. Of the disk fault-tolerance methods supported by Windows NT Server, which method offers the best protection for data recovery?

A. Disk striping

B. Disk striping with parity

C. Disk compression

D. Sector swapping

E. None of the above

9. What is the name of disk mirroring in combination with independent disk controller cards for each physical disk drive?

A. Disk balancing

B. Disk duplexing

C. RAID Level 0

D. Parallel disks

10. Disk striping with parity offers better data recovery characteristics than disk striping without parity because:

A. The assumption is false. Disk striping without parity offers better data recovery characteristics than disk striping with parity.

B. Exact copies of all data are stored on different disk volumes. If one volume fails, you can replace the volume and restore the data from the other parity volume. Disk striping without parity stores blocks of data across at least two physical drives. If one of the drives fails, you have no way to recover the data.

C. Data is stored in blocks across at least three physical disk drives along with parity information. Because parity information is stored, you can regenerate data on any one drive if the drive fails. Without parity information, you cannot recover any data from the striped set.

D. Disk striping with parity employs *hot swapping* technology, which enables you to replace a failed physical disk drive without downing the server and without data loss. Disk striping without parity does not support the *hot swapping* feature.

11. The NetBEUI protocol is best suited for large, segmented networks because:

A. It is efficient and easily routed.

B. NetBEUI is the Internet standard protocol.

C. It offers scalability.

D. None of the above. NetBEUI is not well-suited for large, segmented networks.

12. How do you exclude a Windows NT Server from functioning as a master browser?

A. Disable the Master Browser setting on the Browsing tab in Network Neighborhood properties.

B. Set the Registry entry MaintainServerList to False.

C. Set the IsBrowser setting in WIN.INI to 0.

D. Do not use the NetBEUI protocol.

13. What program do you use to install Windows NT Server? Choose all correct responses.

A. WINNT.EXE

B. WINNT32.EXE

C. SETUP.EXE

D. SETUP32.EXE

14. What is the default installation directory for Windows NT Server?

A. \WINDOWS

B. \WINNT on the system partition

C. \WINNT on the first available NTFS volume

D. \SYSTEM32

15. After installing and configuring a Primary Domain Controller, it is a good idea to: Choose all that apply.

A. Delete the local Administrator account.

B. Delete the local group Administrators.

C. Add the global group Domain Admins to the local group Administrators.

D. None of the above.

16. Windows NT network logon requests are processed by:

A. Primary Domain Controllers

B. Backup Domain Controllers

C. Both Primary and Backup Domain Controllers

D. Any Windows NT Server that has an account on the domain

17. What is the software interface that communicates between system hardware and Windows NT?

    A. Hardware Interface Layer

    B. Hardware Abstraction Layer

    C. Windows Hardware Interface

    D. MPR

18. How many browsers are on a Windows NT network?

    A. There is a master browser and a backup browser.

    B. At least one master browser for each network segment and a domain master browser.

    C. One browser for each Windows NT Server on the network.

    D. One browser for each network segment.

19. A TCP/IP subnet mask is used to:

    A. Define the host and network portions of an IP address.

    B. Hide the IP address from non-domain resources.

    C. Determine which DHCP clients must be renewed.

    D. None of the above.

20. One difference between WINS and DNS is:

    A. WINS is completely dynamic; DNS is a static service.

    B. WINS services Internet Names; DNS handles NetBIOS names.

    C. DNS services Internet Names; WINS handles NetBIOS names.

    D. DNS is a dynamic service; WINS is a static service.

21. The DNS domain name must be the same as the Windows NT domain name on a Windows NT network because:

    A. WINS and DNS exchange information to translate NetBIOS names to Internet Names.

    B. The Windows NT domain name and the DNS name are not required to be the same on a Windows NT network.

    C. Microsoft Network clients use their assigned WINS servers to locate the nearest DNS server.

    D. Microsoft Network clients use their assigned DNS servers to locate the nearest WINS server.

22. You just installed a Windows NT member server on your multisegment TCP/IP network. You configure this new server as the first DHCP server on your network and configure workstations on several different segments as DHCP clients. Workstations not connected on the same segment as the DHCP server are unable to obtain an IP address from the DHCP server. Which of the following describes the possible reason that the workstations cannot connect to the DHCP server and the solution? Choose all that apply.

    A. The DHCP clients must be members of the same domain as the DHCP server. Add the workstations to the appropriate domain.

    B. The routers that connect the network segments are configured with BOOTP broadcasts disabled. Enable BOOTP broadcasts on the routers that connect the DHCP server's segment.

C. The workstations do not know the IP address of the DHCP server. You must add the IP address of the DHCP server to the LMHOSTS file on each workstation.

D. The workstations do not know the IP address of the DHCP server. You must configure the workstation to query its assigned WINS server for the IP address of the DHCP server.

23. You are the network administrator for a small (20-user) single-segment Windows NT network using NWLink protocol. Your boss asks you to create an additional segment on the network for a special development project. Four new Windows NT Workstations will connect to the additional segment. All network cabling is in place for the new segment. You have been instructed to create this new segment as inexpensively as possible. Which of the following offers the best solution?

A. Add a network adapter to one of the new workstations and configure the workstation as a router.

B. Add a network adapter to the Windows NT Server and configure the server as a router.

C. Change the network protocol to TCP/IP, add a network adapter to the Windows NT Server, and configure the server as a router.

D. Purchase an inexpensive network bridge and connect the bridge between the two physical segments.

24. What is the primary purpose of NWLink?

A. To guarantee connectivity between domain controllers.

B. NWLink is used only for communication between Windows NT and Windows 95 workstations.

C. To facilitate communications with Novell NetWare hosts.

D. None of the above.

25. The binding order of network services on a Windows NT Server can be important to network and server performance because the binding order determines which of the following?

A. The order in which Windows NT services network requests.

B. The order in which Windows NT services network clients.

C. The amount of memory used by protocol drivers.

D. The number of broadcasts that the server must issue.

26. The best server service optimization setting for a Windows NT Server running Microsoft Exchange is:

A. Minimize Memory Used

B. Balance

C. Maximize Throughput for File Sharing

D. Maximize Throughput for Network Applications

27. Select all statements that are true:

A. Unless specifically excluded, all Windows NT Servers act as browsers.

B. Browsers maintain a list of workstations and their IP addresses.

C. All the domain controllers on the network elect master browsers.

D. Browsers maintain information only about the domain to which they belong.

28. The criteria used to elect a browser are:

A. Operating system type

B. Operating system version

C. Whether the computer is currently a browser, master browser, or able to become a browser

D. All the above

29. Directory replication requires which of the following user accounts?

A. A service account.

B. A user account assigned to the global group Domain Admins.

C. A user account that belongs to the local group Administrators on each server that is a replication partner.

D. None of the above.

30. You configure import and export servers to use with Directory Replication service using what utility?

A. Server Manager

B. The Services applet in Control Panel

C. You must configure Directory Replication service when Windows NT Server is installed

D. Directory Replication Manager

31. Your Windows NT Server has 64 MB of RAM and a single 4 GB hard drive. The hard drive is configured as a single FAT partition that serves as the system partition. You are installing another 4 GB hard drive. After installing and partitioning the new disk drive, what must you do to add the additional disk space to the existing partition?

A. You must extend the existing volume.

B. You must format the new disk drive as FAT, and then extend the existing volume.

C. You must convert the existing disk partition to NTFS file format, configure the new partition to NTFS file format, and then add the new partition to the existing volume as an extended volume.

D. You must reinstall Windows NT, defining both physical disk drives as a single volume.

32. What utility do you use to extend a volume set?

A. Server Manager

B. Disk Manager

C. Server Administrator

D. Disk Administrator

33. The most secure disk fault-tolerance supported by Windows NT Server is:

A. Disk duplexing

B. Disk striping with parity

C. Disk striping

D. Sector swapping

34. Assigning multiple printers to a single print queue is called:

    A. Printer sharing

    B. Printer pooling

    C. Printer polling

    D. Printer integration

35. What Windows NT Server utility do you use to create client startup disks?

    A. Network Client Administrator

    B. Disk Administrator

    C. Server Manager

    D. User Manager for Domains

36. What utility do you use to create a domain account for a Windows NT client system?

    A. Server Administrator

    B. User Manager for Domains

    C. Server Manager

    D. Server Manager for Domains

37. How do you install Network Services for Macintosh on a Windows NT Server?

    A. Use the Services tab in the Network applet in Control Panel

    B. Use Server Manager

    C. Use the Windows NT Server installation program

    D. None of the above

38. Which of the following Windows NT programs are used to create local user accounts, but not global accounts? Choose all correct answers.

    A. User Manager

    B. Disk Administrator

    C. Server Manager

    D. User Manager for Domains

39. Which of the following statements is true about the Primary Group property of a user account?

    A. It is used by Services for Macintosh.

    B. It is used to assign default user account permissions.

    C. You assign a primary group only to users that use Macintosh services.

    D. All the above.

40. Your new company's home office has a new computer training facility. You are asked to create user accounts for each of the eight training workstations that can log on to the domain at the home office. What can you do to limit the use of these user accounts to their intended role as training tools?

    A. Remove the training account from the Domain Users group.

    B. Limit account access to the training workstations.

    C. Set logon times to office hours at the home office.

    D. Both B and C.

41. A user at your office succumbs to marital bliss and takes her husband's last name. You must change her logon ID and the full name field in her user account. Using User Manager for Domains, what is the best way to make these changes?

    A. You must create a new account from scratch that reflects the user's new name and adds this account to the appropriate groups.

    B. You can create a new account by copying the old account and assigning the new logon ID, Full Name. This preserves the

original user account group
membership and user profile.

C. You can change the logon ID
name and edit the Full Name
field in the existing account.

D. You can create a new account
from scratch, and then use the
CACLS command-line utility to
copy security information from
the original user account to the
newly created user account.

42. What Windows NT utility do you use
to set user account policies for domain
user accounts?

A. User Manager

B. Server Manager

C. User Manager for Domains

D. Domain Administrator

43. To increase logon security on a
Windows NT Server, which of the
following can you do? Choose all that
apply.

A. Reduce the lockout duration for
user accounts.

B. Increase the lockout duration for
user accounts.

C. Decrease the minimum length of
passwords.

D. Configure Windows NT auditing to track failed logon attempts.

44. Some users belonging to (trusted)
domain DM_Sales need access to files
on a member Windows NT Server
that belongs to (trusting) domain
DM_Mktg. How can you facilitate
access for the global group belonging
to DM_Sales to the member server
belonging to DM_Mktg?

A. Create a local group in
DM_Sales, add the required user
accounts, and assign the appropriate rights to the server in
DM_Mktg.

B. Create a global group in
DM_Sales, add the required user
accounts, create a local group in
the local account database on the
server in DM_Mktg, assign the
appropriate rights to the local
group, and add the global group
from DM_Sales to the local
group on the target server.

C. Create a global group in
DM_Sales, add the required user
accounts, create a local group on
a domain controller in
DM_Mktg, assign the appropriate rights to the local group, and
add the global group from
DM_Sales to the local group on
the target server.

D. Create a local group on a domain controller in DM_Mktg,
assign the appropriate rights to
the group, and add the required
users from DM_Sales to the
local group.

45. To how many global groups can a
single user account belong on a
Windows NT network?

A. 32

B. 16

C. 8

D. None of the above.

46. What Windows NT Server tool
creates local groups?

A. User Manager

B. User Manager for Domains

C. NET.EXE

D. All the above

47. User accounts that you use to back up disk drives on domain controllers should be members of what group?

    A. Domain Admins.

    B. Server Operators.

    C. Administrators.

    D. Backup Operators.

    E. None of the above. These users should simply be granted Full Control rights to all volumes on the domain controller.

48. What functions are members of the local group Print Operators able to perform on a Windows NT member server? Choose all that apply.

    A. Manage print jobs

    B. Create new printers

    C. Create print shares

    D. All the above

49. Your company's human resources department wants to place several documents on the network and make them available to users only on your single domain Windows NT network. These documents should be read/write access for the local group HRDept and read only access for all other users. How should you set the NTFS permissions for these files?

    A. You should assign Change permission for the local group HRDept and Read permission for the special group Everyone.

    B. You should assign Change permission for the local group HRDept and Read permission for the global group Domain Users.

C. You should assign Full Control permission for the local group HRDept and Read permission for the Global group Domain Users.

D. You should create a local group on the target server, add the global group Domain Users to that local group, assign Read permission to the local group, and then assign Change permission to the local group HRDept.

50. What special attribute does a user account known as a service account have?

    A. A service account is a user account that is assigned the right to logon as a service.

    B. A service account is a Windows NT service that emulates a user account.

    C. A service account is a user account that is a member of the built-in local group Service Admins.

    D. Service accounts are system-level objects used by the special group System and are not accessible by any user accounts.

51. You configured your Windows NT network so that all user profiles for Windows NT Workstations are stored on a shared network drive. A user modifies her desktop and then logs off the Windows NT Workstation. After logging off, she realizes that she was not connected to the network when she modified her desktop. Has she lost the changes that she made to her desktop?

    A. No. A copy of the modified profile is saved on the Windows

NT Workstation's local hard drive. When the Windows NT Workstation boots, the system automatically uses the newest user profile.

B. Yes. If a Windows NT Workstation is configured to store profiles on a shared network drive, any changes made while the workstation is not connected to the network are lost.

C. No. A copy of the modified profile is saved on the Windows NT Workstation's local hard drive. When the Windows NT Workstation boots, the system prompts the user to update the profile stored on the shared network drive.

D. No. A copy of the modified profile saves to the shared network drive whether or not the user is logged on.

52. By default, where is the policy file NTCONFIG.POL stored in a Windows NT network?

A. On the local hard drive of the workstation.

B. In the NETLOGON share directory.

C. In the user's home directory.

D. None of the above.

53. Which of the following Windows NT Workstation actions can you control using system policies? Choose all correct answers.

A. The boot sequence of the workstation.

B. Customized logon screen.

C. Remove the last logged on name from the logon dialog box.

D. Standard Startup menu.

54. What is the name of the file in which Windows 95 policies are stored on a Windows NT network?

A. POLICY.CFG

B. NTCONFIG.POL

C. CONFIG.POL

D. WIN95.POL

55. When a Windows NT Workstation reads a user policy file, how does it store the information?

A. The policy file is stored in a policy file on the local hard drive.

B. The Windows NT Workstation does not store the information, but the workstation reads the policy file from the network each time Windows NT starts.

C. It is stored in the Default User directory.

D. The information merges into the HKEY_CURRENT_USER subtree of the Windows NT Workstation Registry.

56. What are the four explicit share permissions available in Windows NT file share security?

A. Read, Execute, Full Control, No Access

B. Read, Change, Full Control, No Access

C. Read, Change, File Scan, Full Control

D. Read, Write, Execute, File Scan

57. A user belongs to two groups that have permissions assigned to a file share. One group is assigned No Access permission, the other group is assigned Full Control permission.

Which of the following file-related functions can the user perform within the share?

   A. Can change the share permissions.

   B. Can read, write, and create files and directories.

   C. Can only view files and directories.

   D. Has no permission to perform any file access functions within the share.

58. A user belongs to a local group that is assigned Read rights to a file share on a domain controller. The user also belongs to another local group on the domain controller that is assigned Change rights to the same file share. What is this user's effective right(s) to the file share?

   A. Read

   B. Change

   C. Change and Read

   D. Full Control

59. What is the maximum number of users that can connect simultaneously to a file share on a Windows NT Workstation?

   A. 32

   B. 16

   C. 8

   D. 10

60. What NTFS directory permissions are required to view only directory contents and navigate only subdirectories?

   A. View and Execute (VX)

   B. List (RX)

   C. Read

   D. All the above.

61. Assuming NTFS, which of the following file permissions can be assigned under the Special permission? Choose all correct answers.

   A. Read

   B. Take Ownership

   C. File Scan

   D. Add

62. NTFS file permissions are:

   A. Mutually exclusive

   B. Hierarchically exclusive

   C. Cumulative

   D. Collective

63. Some data files are stored on a Windows NT Server in the (NTFS) directory C:\INVENTORY\DATA. These files are assigned Read permission for local group Accounting and Change permission for local group Management. They are moved to (NTFS) directory C:\INVENTORY\SECRET, which is located on a different server. The target directory for these files has Read permission for both Accounting and Management. What access permissions will Management have to these files after they move to the target directory?

   A. Read

   B. Change

   C. Access Denied

   D. List

64. Some data files are stored on a Windows NT Server in the (NTFS) directory C:\INVENTORY\DATA. These files are assigned Read permission for local group Accounting and Change permission for local group Management. They are moved to (NTFS) directory C:\INVENTORY\SECRET, which is located on the same server. The target directory for the files has Read permission for both Accounting and Management. What access permissions will Management have to these files after they move to the target directory?

   A. Read

   B. Change

   C. Access Denied

   D. List

65. Bryan has been asked to create a local group named Sales on a Windows NT Server named ACCTG and to assign Change permission for Sales to a large, complex directory on ACCTG. Several different NTFS permissions already are assigned for other local groups to numerous subdirectories within this directory. How can Bryan add the NTFS permissions Sales without disturbing the existing permissions?

   A. Bryan has to work through the entire directory manually with Windows NT Explorer to add the new permissions.

   B. Using the Add feature of Windows NT Explorer.

   C. Using the NET.EXE utility.

   D. Using the CACLS.EXE utility.

66. When calculating effective permissions for a file share on an NTFS directory, Windows NT compares the file share permissions and the NTFS permissions. As a result of this comparison, what is the effective access permission?

   A. The least restrictive permission is the effective permission.

   B. The most restrictive permission is the effective permission.

   C. The permissions are cumulative.

   D. The least restrictive permission is the effective permission except when No Access is assigned to either the share or the NTFS directory.

67. To assign a user NTFS permissions to a volume in a trusting domain, you should:

   A. Directly assign permissions to the user with Windows NT Explorer.

   B. Create a local group in the trusted domain, add the user to the local group, and make the local group a member of a global group that has the appropriate NTFS permissions for the target volume.

   C. Add the user to a global group in the trusted domain, and add the global group to a local group in the trusting domain that has appropriate NTFS permissions.

   D. None of the above solutions works because the domains do not have a full-trust relationship.

68. A user's *credentials* that facilitate access to resources on a Windows NT network are called:
    A. Access Control Lists (ACL)
    B. Access Control Entries (ACEs)
    C. Security IDs (SIDs)
    D. Access tokens

69. What utility do you use to set auditing policies for domain controllers on a Windows NT network?
    A. User Manager for Domains
    B. Server Manager
    C. Server Manager for Domains
    D. User Administrator

70. You suspect that one or more of the users on your Windows NT network are attempting to hack into unauthorized resources. What audit policy do you use to look for these users?
    A. File and Object Access: Look for failed attempts to access unauthorized resources.
    B. Process Tracking: Look for attempts to access unauthorized resources.
    C. Logon and Logoff: Look for excessive failed logon attempts.
    D. Use of User Rights: Look for failed attempts to perform a task.

71. What Windows NT utility do you use to view the log file where audit information is stored? Choose all correct answers.
    A. Event Viewer
    B. User Manager for Domains
    C. Server Manager
    D. NotePad

72. You configure auditing for all files stored in directory C:\DATA\SENSITIVE on a Windows NT Server. Files from directory C:\DATA\SENSITIVE are moved to directory D:\SENSITIVE. Auditing is disabled for directory D:\SENSITIVE. What is true about the auditing configuration for these moved files?
    A. The audit settings for the files does not change.
    B. The audit settings for the files does not change; however, you must change audit settings in Event Viewer for audit information to be logged correctly.
    C. Auditing is disabled for these files; however, you can restore their original audit settings with the Windows NT command-line utility NTAUDIT.EXE.
    D. Auditing is disabled for these files.

73. What is the purpose of a print spooler?
    A. A print spooler is responsible for receiving, distributing, and processing print jobs.
    B. A print spooler formats print jobs before they are sent to the printer.
    C. A print spooler queues jobs for distribution to Print Manager.
    D. A print spooler is responsible for managing printer shares.

74. To monitor disk drive activity using Performance Monitor, you must first:
    A. Create a service account that has full access to the physical drive you want to monitor, and then

assign the service account to Performance Monitor.

B. Configure the target drive(s) as striped sets.

C. Start the Disk Monitor service.

D. Run the command-line utility DISKPERF.EXE.

75. Which of the following is a valid Class B address?

A. 197.18.87.114

B. 131.255.25.10

C. 255.255.15.67

D. 127.19.181.78

76. What service do you use to provide printer access to Windows NT network printers for UNIX (IP) print requests?

A. TCP/IP printing support

B. LPD

C. LPR

D. UNIX Gateway for Windows NT

77. What utility do you use to manage and configure WINS on a Windows NT network?

A. Server Manager

B. WINS Manager

C. WINS Administrator

D. Protocol Manager

78. What command do you use to add routes to a multihomed Windows NT Server?

A. ARP

B. ROUTE

C. RARP

D. NET

79. What line protocols does Windows NT Remote Access Service support? Choose all correct answers.

A. PPP

B. PPTP

C. SLIP

D. TCP/IP

80. When analyzing the performance of a Windows NT Server, what are the two types of memory you should monitor? Choose two answers.

A. Virtual Memory

B. Chip cache memory

C. Memory with parity

D. Physical memory

81. A multihomed Windows NT Server can provide improved performance over a single-homed Windows NT server because:

A. It can serve as a router between networks, eliminating the need for an additional hop between networks (in the form of a router).

B. It can simultaneously process network requests.

C. It can run more protocols on a single network.

D. There is no performance advantage to a multihomed server.

82. What tool would you use to view user connections on a Windows NT Server?

A. User Manager

B. Server Manager

C. NET.EXE

D. Windows Diagnostics

83. What Windows NT utility do you use to log system resource utilization?
    A. Performance Monitor
    B. Resource Manager
    C. Windows Diagnostics
    D. Task Manager

84. Which of the following Windows NT Server objects is not an object that you can monitor using Performance Monitor?
    A. Paging file
    B. Memory
    C. Network adapter
    D. Redirector

85. What Windows NT program do you use to initialize the physical disk counters for use with Performance Monitor?
    A. NTFSCVT.EXE
    B. DISKPERF.EXE
    C. FDISK.EXE
    D. NET.EXE

86. What might a steady increase in Pool Nonpaged memory usage without an increase in server activity indicate?
    A. Not enough physical memory on the server.
    B. Memory errors.
    C. A *leaky* process or thread.
    D. Excessive network traffic.

87. What is the maximum length of a NetBIOS name?
    A. 16 characters.
    B. 15 characters.
    C. 32 characters.
    D. Unlimited, but you use only the first 15 characters.

88. Under what circumstances does a browser election take place?
    A. When a master browser announces that it is being shut down.
    B. When a client cannot find a master browser.
    C. When a domain controller is being initialized.
    D. All the above.

89. What Windows NT utility do you use to create an emergency repair disk?
    A. RDISK.EXE
    B. FDISK.EXE
    C. ERD.EXE
    D. NET.EXE

90. How can you create a Windows NT boot diskette?
    A. Format a diskette from within Windows NT, copy NTLDR, BOOT.INI, NTDETECT.COM, and NTBOOTDD.SYS (if required) to the diskette.
    B. Run the FORMAT /S command from a DOS session.
    C. Run RDISK, and then delete the non-system files from the emergency repair disk.
    D. Copy all the files (including hidden and system files) from the root directory of the Windows NT system partition to a formatted floppy diskette.

91. Which of the following statements are true about performing an emergency repair on a Windows NT Server? Choose all correct answers.
    A. RISC systems do not require a boot disk.

B. Intel systems with FAT system partitions boot with an MS-DOS diskette.

C. RISC systems can boot with an MS-DOS diskette.

D. Intel system with NTFS system partitions can boot with an MS-DOS diskette.

92. You installed Windows NT Server on a new computer and configured it as a Backup Domain Controller. When the new server boots, it fails to connect to the Primary Domain Controller. You confirm that all hardware, protocol drivers, and configurations are correct. Why might the Backup Domain Controller not connect to the Primary Domain Controller?

A. You failed to assign the same password to the local user Administrator on the new BDC as the password of the local administrator on the PDC. The two computers, therefore, fail to make a valid RPC connection.

B. You did not create the share IPC$ on the new PDC before attempting to join the domain.

C. You installed the BDC while it was not connected to the network or while the PDC was not available to the new BDC.

D. You did not enable the Server service on the new BDC.

93. Hardware detection is not required when Windows NT boots on a RISC computer because:

A. All RISC computers have exactly the same hardware configuration, and Windows NT for RISC-based computers is already configured for RISC.

B. Hardware information is stored in non-volatile memory on RISC computers.

C. RISC computer manufacturers provide a machine-specific Hardware Abstraction Layer (HAL) with each computer.

D. None of the above. Hardware detection is required on RISC computers.

94. Which of the following statements are true concerning TCP/IP? Choose all that apply.

A. TCP/IP is a connectionless protocol.

B. FTP uses TCP/IP to transfer files over a TCP/IP network.

C. TCP/IP transmits and receives data in frame format.

D. TCP/IP transmits and receives data as byte streams.

95. What utility do you use to monitor RAS connections from the Windows NT or Windows 95 RAS client side?

A. RAS Admin

B. Network Monitor

C. Dial-Up Networking Monitoring

D. Windows Diagnostics

96. Which of the following are RAS security features? Choose all that apply.

A. PPTP filtering

B. Callback security

C. Encryption

D. All the above

97. Which of the following is a utility that you can use to change a DHCP-assigned IP address on a Windows NT Workstation or Server?

   A. CONFIG

   B. RELEASE

   C. IPCONFIG

   D. RARP

98. You are the network engineer for a single-segment Windows NT network that uses the TCP/IP protocol. You are asked to break the network into two segments by adding another network adapter to one of the Windows NT Servers, and then configuring the server as a router. For the two network segments to communicate correctly, which of the following statements are true? Choose all that apply.

   A. The IP address range for both segments must be the same.

   B. The server that is used as a router must be a domain controller.

   C. The subnet masks on both segments must be the same.

   D. You must define the IP address on each card in the router/server on hosts as the default gateway for the respective segments.

99. The protocol used to translate MAC addresses to IP addresses on a TCP/IP network is:

   A. RARP

   B. ARP

   C. FTP

   D. DNS

100. The backup schedule used on your Windows NT Server is as follows:

Sunday night through Friday night: Incremental backup

Saturday night: Full backup

Your server has a volume named ACCTDATA. Data is modified every day on this volume. If all data on ACCTDATA is lost after the Wednesday backup completes, how many backup data sets must you restore to recover the volume?

   A. 2

   B. 4

   C. 1

   D. 5

Answers and Explanations

1. **B**   Members of the Administrators local group have full access to the server's resources. (Managing Resources.)

2. **B**   The rationale for the other two answers is incorrect. When operating in a full-trust domain environment, the user does not automatically have a logon ID for each site (site is synonymous with domain in this example), and logon requests are processed by the nearest domain controller that belongs to the user's domain, not simply the nearest domain controller. (Managing Resources.)

3. **D**   Domain trust relationships are nontransitive. (Planning.)

4. **B**   The two domains involved in a trust relationship establish a password-secured communication link. You must have administrative rights to set up a trust relationship, but you don't

use the Administrator password. Either domain in a trust relationship may break the trust. (Managing Resources.)

5. **A**   The global group is automatically added to the local group Administrators after a Windows NT Server or Workstation joins a domain. (Installation and Configuration.)

6. **B**   The standard for assigning permissions is AGLP: Account to Global group to Local group to Permissions. (Managing Resources.)

7. **D**   A complete-trust domain is not the ideal directory service structure for a large network. (Planning.)

8. **B**   Disk striping with parity enables you to regenerate lost data, if a physical disk drive fails. (Installation and Configuration.)

9. **B**   Disk duplexing is disk mirroring in combination with independent disk controller cards for each physical disk drive. (Installation and Configuration.)

10. **C**   Data, along with parity information, is stored in blocks across at least three physical disk drives. Because parity information is stored, data on any one drive can be regenerated, if the drive fails. Without parity information, you cannot recover any data from the striped set. (Installation and Configuration.)

11. **D**   NetBEUI is not routable—TCP/IP is the Internet standard—and NetBEUI offers only limited scalability. (Connectivity.)

12. **B**   You exclude a Windows NT Server from functioning as a master browser by setting the Registry entry MaintainServerList to False. (Installation and Configuration.)

13. **A, B**   Use both WINNT.EXE and WINNT32.EXE to install Windows NT Server. (Installation and Configuration.)

14. **B**   The default installation directory for Windows NT Server is \WINNT on the system partition. (Troubleshooting.)

15. **D**   Neither the built-in Administrator nor the local group Administrators can be deleted. The global group Domain Admins is automatically added to the local group Administrators when you install a domain controller. (Installation and Configuration.)

16. **C**   Both Primary and Backup Domain Controllers handle Windows NT network logon requests. (Troubleshooting.)

17. **B**   The software interface that communicates between system hardware and Windows NT is called the Hardware Abstraction Layer (HAL). (Troubleshooting.)

18. **B**   "At least" is the key phrase. You can have more than one browser per network segment, depending on the number of hosts on the segment. (Installation and Configuration.)

19. **A**   Use a TCP/IP subnet mask to define the host and network portions of an IP address. (Connectivity.)

20. **C**   You might answer A; however, remember that you can add static addresses to a WINS database. (Installation and Configuration.)

21. **B**   The Windows NT domain name and the DNS name do not have to be the same on a Windows NT network. (Installation and Configuration.)

22. **B**   DHCP clients look for a DHCP server via BOOTP broadcasts. (Installation and Configuration.)

23. **B** Although C will work, B is the best solution because it requires only a single network adapter and a very limited configuration. Answer D seems to be a viable option except the bridges do not route; therefore, the network still is a single segment. (Connectivity.)

24. **C** NWLink is an implementation of the Novell IPS/SPX protocol. It is used to facilitate communication between Windows NT and NetWare hosts. (Connectivity.)

25. **A** The binding order of network services on a Windows NT Server determines the order in which the system services network requests. (Monitoring and Optimization.)

26. **D** The best server service optimization setting for a Windows NT Server running Microsoft Exchange is the Maximize Throughput for Network Applications setting. (Monitoring and Optimization.)

27. **A, D** By default, Windows NT Servers act as browsers; browsers maintain information only about the domain to which they belong. (Managing Resources.)

28. **D** The criteria used to elect a browser are: the operating system type, the operating system version, and whether the computer is currently a browser, master browser, or able to become a browser. (Managing Resources.)

29. **A** To facilitate directory replication, you must assign a user account permission to log on as a service (service account). (Installation and Configuration.)

30. **A** Use Server Manager to configure import and export servers to be used with Directory Replication service. (Installation and Configuration.)

31. **D** The system partition on a Windows NT Server is not extendible. To increase the size of the system partition, you must reinstall Windows NT defining both physical drives as a single volume. (Installation and Configuration.)

32. **D** Use Disk Administrator to extend a volume set. (Installation and Configuration.)

33. **B** Disk striping with parity is the most secure disk fault-tolerance supported by Windows NT Server. (Installation and Configuration.)

34. **B** Assigning multiple printers to a single print queue is called printer pooling. (Managing Resources.)

35. **A** Network Client Administrator creates client startup disks. (Managing Resources.)

36. **C** Server Manager creates a domain account for a Windows NT client system. (Managing Resources.)

37. **A** You install Network Services for Macintosh by selecting the Services tab in the Network applet in Control Panel. (Managing Resources.)

38. **A** User Manager is used to create local user accounts. User Manager for Domains can create either local or global user accounts. (Managing Resources.)

39. **A** Services for Macintosh uses the Primary Group property of a user account. (Managing Resources.)

40. **D** To limit the use of the user accounts to their intended role as training tools, limit account access to the training workstations and set logon times to office hours at the home office. (Managing Resources.)

41. **C** The Rename option is on the User menu in User Manager and User

Manager for Domains. (Managing Resources.)

42. **C** Use User Manager for Domains to set user account policies for domain user accounts. (Managing Resources.)

43. **B, D** Increasing the lockout duration for failed logon attempts and tracking failed logon attempts can enhance network logon security. (Monitoring and Optimization.)

44. **B** The recommended AGLP standard applies here: Account to Global group to Local group to Permissions. (Managing Resources.)

45. **D** A user account can belong to an unlimited number of global and/or local groups. (Managing Resources.)

46. **B, C** User Manager is not a Windows NT Server tool. (Managing Resources.)

47. **D** User accounts that you use to back up disk drives on domain controllers should be members of the local group Backup Operators. (Managing Resources.)

48. **D** Print operators can manage print jobs, create new printers, and create print shares. (Managing Resources.)

49. **D** Following the AGLP rule, you should create a local group on the target server, add the global group Domain Users (actual users that belong to the domain) to the local account, and then assign Read permission for the target files. Remembering that NTFS permissions are cumulative (except for No Access), when you assign Change permissions to the local group HRDept, users have Read/Write permissions to the target files. (Managing Resources.)

50. **A** A service account is a user account that you assign the right to logon as a service. (Installation and Configuration.)

51. **C** A copy of the modified profile is saved on the Windows NT Workstation's local hard drive. When the Windows NT Workstation boots, the system prompts the user to update the profile stored on the shared network drive. (Installation and Configuration.)

52. **B** The Windows NT policy file is stored in the NETLOGON share directory because all clients connect to the NETLOGON share during authentication to check for a system policy. (Installation and Configuration.)

53. **B, C, D** You can control whether or not a workstation can boot from the A drive, but the boot sequence is set in the workstations CMOS configuration. (Installation and Configuration.)

54. **C** Windows 95 policies are stored as CONFIG.POL. (Installation and Configuration.)

55. **D** After a Windows NT Workstation reads a user policy file, the information merges into the HKEY_CURRENT_USER subtree of the Windows NT Workstation Registry. (Installation and Configuration.)

56. **B** Read, Change, Full Control, and No Access are the four explicit share permissions available in Windows NT file share security. (Managing Resources.)

57. **D** The No Access permission on a file share overrides any other assigned permissions. (Managing Resources.)

58. **B** Change includes the Read permission, so the effective permission is Change. (Managing Resources.)

59. **D** The maximum number of users that can connect simultaneously to a

file share on a Windows NT Workstation is ten. (Installation and Configuration.)

60. **B**   List (RX) directory permissions are required to view only directory contents and navigate only subdirectories. (Installation and Configuration.)

61. **A, B**   File Scan and Add are not valid NTFS permissions for creating Special Permissions. (Managing Resources.)

62. **C**   NTFS file permissions are cumulative. (Managing Resources.)

63. **A**   If a file is moved from one directory to another across NTFS volumes, the files inherit the permissions from the target directory. (Managing Resources.)

64. **A**   The files are moved to a directory on the same volume. When files move to a new location on the same NTFS volume, they retain their original permissions. (Managing Resources.)

65. **D**   CACLS.EXE is a Windows NT command-line utility that can edit (rather than replace) permissions on files and directories. (Managing Resources.)

66. **B**   The most restrictive permission between NTFS and file share permissions is the effective permission. (Managing Resources.)

67. **C**   Answer C follows the AGLP rule. (Managing Resources.)

68. **D**   Access tokens are a user's *credentials* that facilitate access to resources on a Windows NT network. (Managing Resources.)

69. **A**   Use User Manager for Domains to set auditing policies for domain controllers on a Windows NT network. (Managing Resources.)

70. **A**   File and Object Access: By looking for failed attempts to access unauthorized resources, you can identify attempts to access unauthorized resources. (Monitoring and Optimization.)

71. **A**   Use Event Viewer to view the log file in which audit information is stored. (Monitoring and Optimization.)

72. **D**   Auditing information associated with files and directories works the same as NTFS permissions; when the files are moved from one NTFS volume (C:) to another (D:), the files inherit the auditing information from the target directory. (Managing Resources.)

73. **A**   A print spooler is responsible for receiving, distributing, and processing print jobs. (Managing Resources.)

74. **D**   To monitor disk drive activity using performance monitor, you must first run the command-line utility DISKPERF.EXE. (Monitoring and Optimization.)

75. **B**   The first octet in answer A is a Class C number, the first octet in C is an invalid number, the first octet values in D are reserved for local loopbacks. (Connectivity.)

76. **B**   LPD (Line Printer Daemon) enables UNIX to access Windows NT printers; LPR enables the Windows NT network to access UNIX printers; and TCP/IP printing support is the LPD and LPR services. (Connectivity.)

77. **B**   Use WINS Manager to manage and configure WINS on a Windows NT network. (Installation and Configuration.)

78. **B**   You use the ROUTE command to add routes to a multihomed Windows NT Server. (Installation and Configuration.)

79. **A, B, C**   RAS supports TCP/IP, but TCP/IP is a network protocol, not a line protocol. (Connectivity.)

80. **A, D**   You should monitor virtual and physical memory when analyzing the performance of a Windows NT Server. (Monitoring and Optimization.)

81. **B**   Answer A is true, but B is the better answer. (Connectivity.)

82. **B**   You use Server Manager to view user connections on a Windows NT Server. (Monitoring and Optimization.)

83. **A**   Use Performance Monitor to log system resource utilization. (Monitoring and Optimization.)

84. **C**   You cannot directly monitor network adapters by Performance Monitor. (Monitoring and Optimization.)

85. **B**   Use DISKPERF.EXE to initialize the physical disk counters for use with Performance Monitor. (Monitoring and Optimization.)

86. **C**   A steady increase in Pool Nonpaged memory usage without an increase in server activity often indicates a *leaky* process or thread. (Monitoring and Optimization; Troubleshooting.)

87. **A**   You are limited to 15 characters by Windows NT because the system internally uses the 16th character. (Managing Resources.)

88. **D**   A browser election takes place when a master browser announces that it is being shut down, when a client cannot find a master browser, and when a domain controller is being installed. A browser election can also take place when a master browser fails to respond to other hosts on the network for a predetermined period of time (the default is 12 minutes). (Troubleshooting.)

89. **A**   You use RDISK.EXE to create an emergency repair disk. (Troubleshooting.)

90. **A**   To create a Windows NT boot diskette, format a diskette from within Windows NT, and then copy NTLDR, BOOT.INI, NTDETECT.COM, and NTBOOTDD.SYS (if required) to the diskette. (Installation and Configuration.)

91. **A, B**   When performing an emergency repair on a Windows NT Server, RISC computers do not require a boot disk. You can boot Intel computers FAT system partitions with an MS-DOS diskette. (Troubleshooting.)

92. **C**   The successful installation of a Backup Domain Controller requires that a PDC is already installed and available over the network to the new BDC. (Installation and Configuration.)

93. **B**   Hardware detection is not required when Windows NT boots on a RISC computer because hardware information is stored in non-volatile memory on RISC computers. (Troubleshooting.)

94. **B, D**   TCP is a connection-oriented protocol that utilities, such as FTP, use. TCP transmits and receives data as byte streams. (Connectivity.)

95. **C**   Use Dial-Up Networking Monitoring to monitor RAS connections from the Windows NT or Windows 95 RAS client side. (Troubleshooting.)

96. **D** PPTP filtering, callback security, and encryption are all RAS security features. (Monitoring and Optimization.)

97. **C** You can use IPCONFIG to change a DHCP-assigned IP address on a Windows NT Workstation or Server. (Connectivity.)

98. **C, D** Subnet masks on a Windows NT Server that you configure to route must all be the same; in this example the Windows NT Server serves as the default gateway for both network segments. (Installation and Configuration.)

99. **B** ARP (Address Resolution Protocol) is used to translate MAC addresses to IP addresses on a TCP/IP network. (Connectivity.)

100. **D** Because both incremental and full backups reset the file archive bit, you must restore all data sets beginning with the last full backup. (Troubleshooting.)

Glossary

$ character—A character used to create a hidden share.

10Base-2—A method of network cabling commonly associated with Ethernet networks. Uses coaxial cabling between systems with T-connectors linking each system. Must be terminated at either end of the cable.

10Base-T—A method of network cabling also known as *twisted-pair*. This cabling is the most common implementation today and can be used for Ethernet and token-ring networks. It involves a central wiring center.

Access Control Entries (ACEs)—Entries within the Access Control List. ACEs are the individual security assignments within the ACL. There will be one ACE entry for each individual permission set on the object under NTFS.

Access Control List (ACLs)—The master list of access controls. Each object under NTFS has an ACL and each object contains ACEs that determine the access to the resource with one ACE for each security assignment. The ACEs are sorted with No Access entries at the top.

Account lockout—You can specify to lock out an account after a given number of unsuccessful logon attempts.

Account Operators group—A group that holds the right to administer user accounts.

Account policy—A way to administer security for accounts (such as password age, account lockout, and more).

Administrators group—A group that holds the right to administer the local server.

Advanced RISC Computer (ARC)—A non-Intel x86-based computer. Windows NT support includes MIPS, PPC, and Alpha.

AGLP—Stands for accounts, global groups, local groups, permissions. It is the methodology used for assigning permissions in a multidomain environment.

Application Event log—The Application event log contains error messages specific to applications installed on a Windows NT system. These include services such as the DHCP service and BackOffice applications such as Microsoft Exchange Server.

AT.EXE—An executable file used to start or stop services using the NET START and NET STOP commands, as well as to start other executables such as NTBackup.

Auditing—Logs access to files and directories. Helps to track object usage and security credentials. Generally used to determine use of rights successes and failures, object access, process tracking, logons and logoffs, shutting down the server, and so on.

AutoDial—A Windows NT feature that automatically associates network connections with phonebook entries. If a resource is needed that is only accessible via a dial-up connection, Windows NT attempts to make the connection.

BackOffice support—MS BackOffice applications most often require NT Server as the underlying operating system.

Backup browsers—The backup browser gets a copy of the browse list from the master browser (on the subnet) and distributes the browse list to subnet clients who request it.

Backup Domain Controller (BDC)—Any server with a copy of the account database that is not the Primary Domain Controller. Added as a load-balancing mechanism to validate users to the domain. The BDC can also serve as a file, print, and application server. In addition, the BDC receives regular updates from the PDC of the domain accounts database so that it may validate users logging onto the domain.

Backup Operators group—A group that holds rights to back up and restore servers.

Baseline—A set of measurements of performance to which subsequent measurements can be compared.

BDC—See *Backup Domain Controller*.

Bindings—Software interfaces between network cards, protocols, and services. The Bindings tab enables you to tweak the arrangement of bindings to increase performance on your NT machine. The tab also enables you to configure the order in which protocols are to be used when attempting to negotiate connections with the server and workstation services.

Boot—The process of initializing the operating system.

Boot partition—A partition that contains the NT operating system files.

BOOT.INI—On Intel-based Windows NT systems, the menu of selectable operating systems is stored in this text file.

Bottleneck—A resource snag that limits the rate at which a task can complete. Any component that restricts the performance of a computer.

Bridge—Links networks and is commonly used to overcome node per-segment limitations.

Built-in accounts—When Windows NT is installed, two built-in accounts are created, the Administrator and Guest accounts. Neither can be deleted, but both can be renamed.

Built-in groups—Groups that are created when Windows NT is installed. Includes both global and local groups; these groups cannot be deleted.

Cache—A temporary storage area in memory where data waits to be transfered from one location to another.

Call-back security—RAS Service enables an Administrator to configure whether the office network is to call back users after they have authenticated with the network. The options include using no call back, calling the users at a number they enter, or calling the users back at a preconfigured phone number.

CDFS (CD File System)—Implemented on CD-ROMs.

Centralized user management—User information (such as logon information) that is stored in a central location.

Characterization file—Contains all the printer-specific information, such as memory, page protection, soft fonts, graphics resolution, and paper orientation and size. It's used by the two dynamic link libraries whenever they need to gather printer-specific information.

Client Services for NetWare (CSNW)—Enables Windows NT Workstation to access file and print resources on a NetWare server. Used in conjunction with NWLink IPX/SPX protocol. After clients have been authenticated, they can use file and print services on the NetWare server.

COMPACT.EXE—Utility used to compress files from the command prompt on NTFS partitions.

Complete trust domain model—A trust model with two or more domains. Each domain has a mixture of accounts and resources. All the domains trust the other domains with two-way trusts. These trusts allow the users in any domain to access resources in any of the other domains.

Compression—Used to minimize the storage space needed for files on NTFS partitions.

Control set—A set of controls used to determine the configuration.

Counters—Statistical measurements used to track levels of performance on system and hardware components in Performance Monitor.

Creating groups—The task of creating new groups, either local or global.

Creating users—The task of adding new user accounts to an account database.

Creator Owner group—A special group representing the owner of a resource.

CSNW—See *Client Services for NetWare*.

Cyclic Redundancy Check (CRC)—Determines whether a file has been corrupted during an Emergency Repair Process. If the CRC value of a file does not match the CRC value stored in the SETUP.LOG file, the file is assumed to be corrupted and is replaced during an Emergency Repair Process.

Data Link Control (DLC)—A protocol that provides support for connections to HP network printers—as well as IBM mainframe and AS-400 computers.

Decentralized user management—User information is spread across different machines and changes have to be made to all machines when a user account is being changed.

Deleting groups—The task of deleting a group. You cannot delete built-in groups.

Devices—Control Panel applet used to start, stop, or disable device drivers.

DHCP (Dynamic Host Configuration Protocol)—A service that works with TCP/IP to automatically assign IP addresses to clients, relieving administrators from the burden of manually configuring IP addresses on all the clients on the network.

DHCP Server Service—Service that facilitates the assignment of IP addresses to clients.

Dial-Up Networking—Connecting to a network through phone lines. This is the client version of the software used to connect to a RAS server.

Directory Replication—A facility that enables you to configure Windows NT Servers to automatically transmit updated versions of important directories to other computers on the network. This is commonly the NETLOGON share. It maintains the identical version of the directory contents on all import servers based on contents at the export server.

Directory Services—The Windows NT components that enable users to log on with an account in the SAM database and then use that account to access resources throughout the enterprise.

Directory Synchronization—Any changes to the SAM database are copied from the PDC to all the BDCs at regular intervals. (See also *Security Account Manager (SAM)*.)

Disabling users—The task of disabling a user account that doesn't delete the account, but prevents the use of it.

Disk Administrator—A graphical utility used in Windows NT Server to manage all aspects of drives.

Disk duplexing—Like disk mirroring, but in addition each drive in the mirror has a separate disk controller. This provides redundancy for both a disk failure or a controller failure. (See also *disk mirroring*.)

Disk mirroring—Known as RAID 1. Copies a complete logical drive to space on another physical disk. If the original drive fails, the mirror can be used.

Disk striping—Known as RAID 0. Combines equal areas from several physical disks into one logical drive. Data can be written to or read from the disks simultaneously. This provides both faster reads and writes. This scheme does not provide fault-tolerance, so if one drive fails, the data on all the drives is lost. It supports disk sets of 2 to 32 disks.

Disk striping with parity—Known as RAID 5. Combines equal areas from several physical disks into one logical drive. Data can be written to or read from the disks simultaneously. This can improve read and write performance. Data on one disk is devoted to redundant information, so if one disk fails, the data on the array can still be recovered. Supports disk sets of 3 to 32 disks.

DNS (Domain Name System)—The name system used for the Internet, such as www.microsoft.com. Runs as a service on an NT Server to resolve this type of name to an IP address. Whereas WINS maps computer names to IP addresses, DNS maps Fully Qualified Domain Names to IP addresses.

Domain—A network model in which user management is done in central locations. Also a collection of computer accounts. Only NT Workstations and Servers can be true members of a domain.

Domain Admins group—A global group of users who administer a domain. Initially contains the Administrator account.

Domain controller—Maintains a copy of the account database for the domain providing central management of all accounts and resources.

Domain Guests group—A global group of guests.

Domain master browser—The domain master browser requests subnet browse lists from the master browsers and merges the subnet browse lists into a master browse list for the entire domain. The computer functioning as the domain master browser is always the Primary Domain Controller.

Domain name—The name of the networking entity.

Domain Users group—A global group of users. Includes all users except the Guest account; all new users are automatically members of this group.

DUMPCHK—Used to verify that the contents of a memory dump file are valid and not corrupted.

DUMPEXAM—Used to write the key contents of a memory dump file to a text file named MEMORY.TXT. It can only be used with STOP 0×0000000A and STOP 0×0000001E errors.

DUMPFLOP—Used to copy the contents of a memory dump file to a series of floppy disks. It copies the file in a compressed format.

Enhanced Integrated Drive Electronics (EIDE)—Common hard drives found in computer systems. When multiple EIDE drives are installed on a computer, ensure that the proper master/slave settings have been configured on the drives.

Event Viewer—Program used to view system, security, and application events.

Everyone group—Special group of which everyone is automatically a member.

Exclusive OR function—Function used in disk striping with parity to calculate the parity information.

Export server—The machine that makes information available to be replicated.

Extended partition—A partition that can be subdivided into logical drives; there can only be one extended partition on a drive.

FAT (File Allocation Table)—The primary file system used for DOS. Alternative format for media to NTFS. FAT32 is an enhanced FAT introduced with Windows 95.

Fault tolerance—Capability to recover from hardware errors, such as a failing drive. Data on a disk array is protected from loss if a single disk in the array fails.

File Delete Child—Special security option available for POSIX compliance. If you have Full Control permissions to a directory, you can delete any file in the directory (even if the file has been assigned the No Access permission).

File and Print Services for NetWare—This service makes a Windows NT Server emulate a NetWare 3.12 server. Using this service enables Novell NetWare clients to use file and print services on the NetWare server without installing Microsoft networking client software.

File and Print sharing—The services for defining how resources are shared. Enables other users to connect to resources on your computer.

FQDN (Fully Qualified Domain Name)—The common name used to refer to locations on the Internet (such as www.mcp.com).

Frame types—NWLink uses varying frame types to transport information across the network. For communication to be successful, the client and server must be using the same frame type.

FTP (File Transfer Protocol)—The protocol for sending and receiving files across the Internet.

Gateway Services for NetWare (GSNW)—Enables Windows NT Server systems to access NetWare files and print resources directly, and to act as a gateway to NetWare resources. Non-NetWare clients on a Windows NT network then can access NetWare resources through the gateway as if they were accessing Windows NT resources, without any need for NetWare client licensing.

Gopher—A means to create a set of hierarchical links to other computers. An Internet protocol that provides hierarchical links to Telnet and FTP sites.

Global group—Used to contain collections of like users. Global groups can only contain accounts from the same domain. Used to group accounts together (must be from the same domain). Not used for permission assignments.

Group—Logical grouping of user accounts that performs similar tasks and needs the same rights and permissions.

GSNW—See *Gateway Services for NetWare.*

GuardTime—A REG_WORD value that defines how long a directory must be stable before its files can be replicated. The range of acceptable values is 0 to one half of the Interval value.

Guests group—Local group of guests that can log on to the server.

Hardware Compatibility List (HCL)—All hardware on this list has been tested and proven to work with the Windows NT operating system. When purchasing a system, be sure that all hardware is on the HCL or has its own NT 4 drivers.

Hardware profile—A method of configuring what devices and services should be started upon start-up time depending on the location of the hardware or the tasks to be completed. Enables a user to configure which devices are to be available for use when starting up the computer.

Hardware Quantifier Tool—On Intel systems, this utility can be used to identify all installed hardware on a system. It is found in the \Support\HQTool directory on your Windows NT installation CD-ROM.

Hardware requirements—The requirements your computer must meet to be able to run specific software or hardware components.

Hive—A subkey in the Registry that is stored entirely in a dedicated file in the %SystemRoot%\System32\Config directory.

Hot fixing—Automatic error correction implemented in NTFS for moving data from bad sectors on a hard disk and permanently marking the bad sectors as unusable.

HTML (Hypertext Markup Language)—The language of HTTP documents.

HTTP (Hypertext Transfer Protocol)—A client/server protocol used on the World Wide Web for the transmission of web documents.

Import server—A machine configured to receive information from export severs.

Information events—Informational messages or problems of noncritical nature of which you should be aware. Shown in the Event Viewer as blue "I" icons.

Integrated Services Digital Network (ISDN)—A digital media provided by telephone companies that provides faster communications and higher bandwidth than traditional phone lines.

Interactive group—A special group everyone becomes a member of when logged on locally.

Internet—International wide area network using the TCP/IP protocol.

Internet Information Server (IIS)—Installed on an NT Server, runs with TCP/IP. Provides web server, FTP server, and Gopher server capabilities.

Internet Service Manager—The main utility for administering and configuring IIS.

Interrupts/sec—Performance Monitor counter that measures the amount of interrupts the processor handles per second.

Interval—A REG_WORD value that defines how often an export server checks for updates. The range is from 1 to 60 minutes, and the default is 5 minutes.

IP address—Dotted decimal notation of unique address per host. This is a 32-bit address composed of both a network address and host address within that network.

IPCONFIG— The command used to retrieve current IP information about a host. The IP Configuration utility can be used to view a client's TCP/IP configuration. It is also used to renew and release DHCP IP address leases.

IPX/SPX—Network protocol used by NetWare servers. It stands for Internetwork Packet Exchange/Sequenced Packed Exchange and provides both connectionless and guaranteed delivery of information.

ISDN—See *Integrated Services Digital Network.*

Kernel debugger—Enables a system technician to investigate the state of a system after a STOP error has occurred. It enables the technician to perform stack traces and investigate what drivers were in use at the time of the STOP error. The kernel debugger can also be invoked when there is no STOP error.

Last Known Good configuration—During a Windows NT boot-up, the Last Known Good configuration can be selected so that the last successful boot sequence is used instead of the current configuration information. It is often used when a configuration change has been performed incorrectly.

Local groups—Windows NT provides the administrator with local groups with which to manage users' rights and permissions. By adding users to local groups, those users inherit the rights and permissions of the group.

Local user profiles—The default type of profile assigned to users by Windows NT. They reside on the local machine (in the file NTUSER.DAT) and are available only when the user logs on to that machine. Includes users Start menu entries and desktop settings.

Log—Documentation of what has occurred. In the case of Performance Monitor, a log file is used to record objects and counters on a server.

Logical disk—A means of dividing a physical disk into multiple partitions that appear to be separate disk drives.

Logon scripts—Scripts that run when users log on to a Windows NT computer. Commonly implemented as BAT for CMD files. They are stored in the %Systemroot%\system32\ repl\import\scripts directory.

LPD (Line Printer Daemon) service—Enables a Windows NT Print Server to control a TCP/IP network interface printer. It also enables UNIX clients to send print jobs to a Windows NT printer using the LPR command.

LPQ (Line Printer Query) tool—Enables a UNIX host or Windows NT client to check where a job is in the queue for a printer controlled by the LPD Service. The Windows NT client must install the TCP/IP Print Services to have access to the LPQ command.

LPR—Command that enables Windows NT computers to print to printers managed by UNIX hosts. It also is used by UNIX hosts to print to a Windows NT printer controlled by the LPD service.

Managing shares—Usually done with Server Manager and enables you to fine tune shares (involves setting permissions and connection limits to the shares). Also performed from the NT Explorer on the local computer.

Mandatory profile—User profile that can't be changed by a user. Created by renaming the NTUSER.DAT file NTUSER.MAN.

Master Boot Record (MBR)—The primary boot record used at each boot.

Media Access Unit (MAU)—The central wiring center for a token-ring network.

Member Server—An NT server computer that plays no part in maintaining the domain's account database and does not authenticate user's logons to the domain. It does not act as a domain controller. May exist in a domain or workgroup environment.

Memory Dump file—An option that can be configured to dump the contents of memory at the time of a STOP event. The contents of memory are initially stored into the page file and then are copied into the configure memory dump file when the system is restarted.

MEMORY:PAGES/SEC—Performance Monitor counter that measures the number of times that a memory page had to be paged into memory or out to disk.

Migration Tool for NetWare—Uses a relatively simple method to transfer file and directory data, along with user and group account data and directory rights from a NetWare server to a Windows NT domain controller.

Mirrored set-fault tolerance RAID Level 1—Requires two hard drives in NT Server. Data written to a mirrored partition on Disk 0 will be mirrored on a partition, equal in size, on Disk 1.

Multilink—Combines multiple physical links into a single logical link to increase bandwidth when using Dial-Up Networking. Can be used for bundling multiple ISDN channels, or two or more standard modems. The multilink protocol enables a client to use multiple phone lines to connect to a remote network. Users are able to increase their total bandwidth using this technology.

Multiple master domain model—A trust model with two or more domains containing user accounts and one or more domains with resources. In this model, all resource domains trust each of the master domains with one-way trusts. The master domains also trust each other with two-way trusts.

Multiprocessor—Term relating to the capability of an operating system to use more than one processor.

Multiprotocol routing—Using more than one protocol and routing them across a network.

NBTSTAT—A TCP/IP utility that can be used to determine what NetBIOS names your computer has registered. It also can be used to list all NetBIOS names that your client has resolved to IP addresses and stored in the NetBIOS name cache.

NETSTAT—A TCP/IP utility is used to determine what ports are in use during a TCP/IP session.

Net share—Command to share a directory from the command prompt.

NetBEUI (NetBIOS Extended User Interface)—NetBEUI is a nonroutable protocol stack that ships with Microsoft LAN Manager. It was developed for LAN Manager and ships with NT. NetBEUI is suited for small networks.

NetBIOS (Network Basic Input/Output System)—System that defines a software interface and a naming convention, not a protocol. The NetBEUI protocol provided a protocol for programs designed around the NetBIOS interface.

NetBIOS name—Each computer in Microsoft networking must have a unique name. This name is used to identify the computer and its services that are offered on the network.

NetWare—Novell's network operating system.

NetWare Directory Service (NDS)—A distributed database of network resources primarily associated with NetWare 4.x systems.

Network Client Administrator—A utility that creates the NT client-based administration tools setup directory. Also enables the configuration of a network installation point for the installation of client software. Client software that can be installed includes MS-DOS, LANMAN DOS, LANMAN, and OS/2.

Network group—A special group that everyone becomes a member of when connected to a network share on a server.

Nonpaged memory—Data that is written to a specific location without being written to or read from a physical disk first.

Nontransitive trusts—Trusts do not flow from one domain to another through a middle domain. A trust always involves only two domains. (See also *trust relationships*.)

Novell NetWare—Server software from Novell.

NTBackup—The NTBackup utility can also be used to back up the Windows NT Registry of the computer where the backup is being performed. Ensure that at least a single unit from the Boot partition is included in the backup set for this option to work.

NTFS—NT file system. A file system designed for Windows NT that is fault-tolerant and can be used to set permissions for files.

NTFS partitions—Disk partitions formatted with NTFS rather than FAT.

NTFS permissions—Permissions of files and directories on an NTFS volume. Can be assigned to directories and to files. NTFS permissions affect both local and remote users.

NTLDR—The load program\routine for the Windows NT operating system on the Intel architecture.

NWLink—The NWLink IPX/SPX compatible transport provides support for IPX/SPX Sockets and NetBIOS APIs. NWLink is a routeable protocol and requires little configuration.

Objects—System and hardware components tracked by counters in Performance Monitor.

One-way trust—A trust relationship with a single trusted domain and a single trusting domain. (See also *trust relationships*.)

Operating system—The software required to run any other programs such as word processors or spreadsheet applications.

Optimal performance—Getting the best performance from the software and hardware currently in place.

Orphan—A remaining disk from a broken mirror set.

Paged memory—Virtual memory that all applications use when the applications believe that they have the full memory range available.

Paging file—This is where pages are stored when they are not active in RAM. Windows NT, by default, controls the size of the paging file.

Parity—Redundant information, such as a checksum. If a piece of data is lost, parity can be used to recalculate the original piece of data.

Partitioning—The method of dividing a physical hard disk into smaller units. A partition is a unit of storage on a disk.

PC Cards (PCMCIA)—A Control Panel applet used to add and configure PCMCIA device drivers. Also used to identify cards that NT does not support.

PDC (Primary Domain Controller)—The first NT Server online in a domain. It maintains the master database of all user account information in the domain.

Per-seat licensing—Each computer that accesses a Windows NT Server requires a separate client access license. Clients are free to connect to any server, and there are unlimited connections to the server. Each client participating in the network must have a per-seat license.

Per-server licensing—For each per-server license that you purchase, one concurrent network connection is allowed access to the server. When the maximum specified amount of concurrent connections is reached, NT returns an error to a connecting user and prohibits access. An administrator, however, can still connect to the server to increase the amount of per-server licenses.

Phonebook entries—In essence, the Address Book for all established telephone links is assigned in the Dial-Up Networking dialog box. Also the bundle of information that Windows NT needs to establish a specific connection.

Ping—A tool used to test the validity of an IP address and verify a client's TCP/IP configuration. It tests the connectivity between two systems.

Platform-independent—NT is platform-independent as it exists in versions for Intel, Alpha, and others.

Point-to-Point Protocol (PPP)—A protocol normally used in conjunction with TCP/IP routers and PCs for communicating over a dial-up or a leased line WAN link. Used for connecting dial-up clients to a RAS server; provides encrypted authentication credentials.

Point-to-Point Tunneling Protocol (PPTP)—Similar protocol to PPP but encapsulates enhanced security through encryption. Provides secure connections to a network attached to public network by encapsulating information with PPP packets.

Policy file mode— A mode of operation for the System Policy Editor. It edits the system policy file that is used for different users and computers in your domain.

Policy templates—Template files used for System Policy Editor when creating system policies.

Ports—A Control Panel applet that lists the available serial ports. It also is used to add a port under Windows NT.

Power Users group—A group of servers that are almost as powerful as Administrators.

Preferred server—A NetWare (3.x) server selected from a list of available NetWare servers in conjunction with GSNW and CSNW during the NT logon process. The Preferred Server indicates which NetWare server you want to validate your NetWare logon process.

Primary Domain Controller—The first server installed in a domain. The PDC maintains the master copy of the directory database and provides logon validation for users.

Primary partition—A partition that can't be subdivided. NT supports up to four primary partitions on a single drive or three primary partitions and one extended partition.

Print drivers—The software that determines the capabilities for the print device to which printers send print jobs.

Print job—Data destined for a print device.

Print Operators group—A group that holds rights to administer printers.

Print processor—Responsible for completing the rendering process. The tasks performed by the print processor differ depending on the print data's data type.

Print router—The print router receives the print job from the spooler and routes it to the appropriate print processor.

Print spooler—The software responsible for receiving, distributing, and processing print jobs.

Printer—The software between the operating system and the physical printing device.

Printer graphics driver DLL—This dynamic link library consists of the rendering or managing portion of the driver; it's always called by the Graphics Device Interface.

Printer interface driver—This dynamic link library consists of the user interface or configuration management portion of the printer driver; it's used by an administrator to configure a printer.

Printer pool—A collection of identical printing devices configured as one printer to increase printing productivity by printing jobs on the first available printing device.

Profiles—Stored information about a user's settings for desktop, network neighborhood, program files, and more. Profiles can be local or roaming.

Priority—An arbitrary ranking that places one process ahead or behind another in a processing order.

Promiscuous—A program that is not limited to just monitoring the network traffic going in and out of one computer, but all the traffic on the network.

Queue—A series of print jobs waiting to be printed.

RAID (Redundant Array of Inexpensive Disks)—A system used for fault-tolerance. Windows NT Server provides software implementations of RAID 1, disk mirroring, and RAID 5, stripe sets with parity. A combination of two or more disks that can provide performance gains by enabling data to be written to or read from several drives at once. Other RAID arrays enable redundant data to be written to one of the disks in the RAID array to protect the data from a single disk failure.

RAS (Remote Access Server)—Provides dial-up connectivity to remote users over phone lines, X.25, or ISDN links. Comprised of a server component (Remote Access Server) and a client component (Dial-Up Networking). It extends the power of NT networking to a remote user via dial-up connectivity.

RDISK—The RDISK utility is used to backup all hives in the Registry except the SAM and SECURITY hives. These hives can be backed up using this utility if the /S parameter is used.

REGEDIT—The Windows 95 Registry Editor is also included with Windows NT. It provides greater search capabilities than REGEDT32 but cannot edit the REG_MULTI_SZ data type.

REGEDT32—The native Windows NT Registry Editor. It contains native editors for all supported data types in the Windows NT Registry.

Registry mode—The mode of operation for System Policy Editor, which edits the local registry.

Remote Access Service—See *RAS*.

Remote server—A server remotely connecting to the network.

Renaming users—The task of renaming a user account. It doesn't affect the SID assigned to this account.

Replication service—The service that performs replication for export and import servers.

Replicator group—Special group associated with the directory Replicator service.

RIP for IP—A routing protocol available for NT.

RIP packets—Data transferred across routers.

Roaming profile—A profile that is located on a network server share and is downloaded to every computer to which a user logs on.

Router— A router helps LANs and WANs achieve interoperability and connectivity and can link LANs that have different network topologies (such as Ethernet and Token Ring).

Scope—A series of IP addresses available for distribution by the DHCP server. Options can be set in DHCP Manager on a scope-by-scope basis.

SCSI adapters—A Control Panel applet used to install SCSI adapter drivers and IDE drivers.

Sector sparing—Data in a fault-tolerant array is automatically written to a good sector if NT detects a bad sector as the data is written to the drive.

Secondary cache—(Also called Level 2 (L2) cache.) Internal cache is called Level 1 cache (L1) and can generally outperform L2 cache. The real factor with cache is the cache controller and system design.

Security Account Manager (SAM)—The database in which user accounts, group accounts, and computer accounts is stored. The read/write copy is stored on the Primary Domain Controller, whereas a read-only copy is stored on all the Backup Domain Controllers in the domain.

Security Event log—Contains error messages related to auditing. This event contains success and failure events based on the audit setting policy set in the User Manager for Domains.

Security log—One of the major NT logs that tracks security-related events.

Serial Line Internet Protocol (SLIP)—A protocol that carries IP over an asynchronous serial communications line.

Server Manager—A utility to remotely manage servers on the network.

Server Message Block (SMB)—A file-sharing protocol jointly developed by Microsoft, Intel, and IBM. SMB specifies a series of commands utilized to pass information between computers using the following four message types: file, printer, session control, and message.

Server Operators group—A local group that holds rights to administer a server.

Service Advertising Protocol (SAP)—A NetWare protocol that enables servers to advertise their services to the network.

Services for Macintosh—A service that enables the system administrator to create shares for Macintosh users as well as creating printer queues for Macintosh.

SETUP.LOG—This file is a listing of all files and their CRC values installed by the Windows NT installation process.

Share permissions—Permissions that are applicable to share points. Includes Full Control, Change, Read, and No Access. They enable the administrator to set security levels on file shares. File shares enable an administrator to create an entry point into the file system of a server. Share permissions are the only security that can be applied to FAT partitions.

Sharing—Creating an entry point on a server that can be accessed from the network.

SID (Security ID)—The SID is what Windows NT uses to uniquely identify each user and group account.

Single domain model—A trust model with only one domain. All accounts and resources are in one domain.

Single master domain model—A trust model with one domain containing user accounts and one or more domains with resources. All the resource domains trust the account (master) domain with one-way trusts, which enables users in the master domain to access resources in any of the resource domains.

SLIP (Serial Line Internet Protocol)—A line protocol that can be used to access TCP/IP networks. Windows NT can act as a SLIP client, but not as a SLIP server, because SLIP does not support encrypted authentication.

Small Computer System Interface (SCSI)—High performance hard disks commonly found in high-end server computers. SCSI enables larger quantities of hard disks to be installed into a system.

Special groups—Groups that cannot be administered but are used by NT for local or remote users based on the task users are performing or where users are performing the task from (Network versus Interactive).

Spool—Temporary holding place for jobs waiting to print. This operates in the background to manage the printing process.

STOP error—The most critical type of error possible in NT. Prevents the Windows NT operating system from continuing to operate. It is also known as a Blue-Screen error.

Stripe set—Hardware solution to increase performance by writing data to multiple drives (2–32 drives in NT Server and Workstation) in 64 K segments. Stripe sets may enhance performance because data is written across multiple disks concurrently. However, stripe sets offer no faulttolerance; if a single disk were to break down, all data would be lost. (See also *stripe set with parity*.)

Stripe set with parity—RAID Level 5 hardware and software solution to increase performance by writing data to multiple drives (3–32 drives in NT Server) in 64 K segments. Information is written across the disk set in a 64 K stripe. For each stripe, parity data is written to one of the disks so that if a single disk were to cease working, the missing information could be rebuilt using the remaining data and the parity information for the stripe. Stripe sets with parity offer faulttolerance support because parity information is written to each disk in the stripe set in rotation.

Striping—Combining equal areas from several disks into one logical drive. When the data is written to these disks, it is striped in 64 K units and written to each disk simultaneously. The data can also be read simultaneously from the disks. This scheme improves read/write performance.

Subnet—A division of network into subnetworks. Used to break up a larger pool of IP addresses into smaller pools, most often due to performance or physical separation of the network.

Subnet mask—Used to mask a portion of the 32-bit IP address so that the TCP/IP protocol can distinguish the host portion of the IP address from the network portion.

SYSDIFF—A utility used to assist in deploying applications to multiple computers.

System Event log—Contains all error messages related to the Windows NT operating system. This includes startup errors that may occur.

System partition—A partition that contains the files necessary to boot the Windows NT operating system.

System Policy Editor—Enables a user either to edit the local Registry or to create a system policy file that can be merged into configured user's, group's, and computer's registries.

System policies—Rules governing system use and templates of the Registry that are merged with the user's existing Registry. These can be implemented as a computer, user, or group policy and stored in the file NTCONFIG.POL for NT and CONFIG.POL for Win95.

Take Ownership—Permission allowing a user of the network to take ownership of a file or directory.

Target computer—The computer that is suffering from the STOP errors. This computer has its BOOT.INI edited to enable a kernel debugger to investigate its memory space after a STOP error has occurred.

TCP/IP (Transmission Control Protocol/Internet Protocol)—A suite of protocols used to connect dissimilar hosts on a network. This is the primary protocol used on the Internet.

Telephony Application Program Interface (TAPI)—TAPI is a device driver for the PCs phone system. It provides a standard interface with telephony applications. TAPI manages communications between the computer and the phone system.

TRACERT—A TCP/IP utility that can be used to determine the route that packets take when being transferred to a remote network.

Trust relationships—A secured communication link between two domains implemented as a Remote Procedure Call, or RPC. One of the domains acts as the trusted domain, and the other is the trusting domain. The trusting domain permits users from the trusted domain to access its resources.

Twisted-pair—See *10Base-T*.

Two-way trust—Two one-way trusts. In a two-way trust, both domains are trusted domains and trusting domains. (See *trust relationships*.)

Universal Resource Access—Users can access all resources with a single account, regardless of physical location.

User—An account representing a person allowed to log on to a domain.

User Manager—Program to manage user and groups, as well as user rights, account policy, and trust relationships.

User Manager for Domains—The main utility for user account administration on an NT Server. It is used to maintain the domain's account database making any updates to the copy on the PDC. A Member Server only runs User Manager.

User policies—Rules governing users that are merged with the HKEY_CURRENT_USER Registry and stored in the file NTCONFIG.pol.

User profiles—Individual settings maintained for a user. They can be local (stored only on the system where users are working) or roaming.

User rights—Specific rights to which users have been assigned.

Virtual Private Network—A wide area network existing through virtual connections. Makes use of existing network connections to create secure tunnels enabling a secure, wide-area network to be implemented over an existing network such as the Internet.

Volume sets—Areas of free space combined into a single logical drive. Provided by Windows NT to enable 2–32 areas of free space to be combined into one logical disk partition.

Warnings—Problems that create NT Server conditions to be alerted about. They are indicated by a yellow exclamation mark in the Windows NT Event Viewer.

Web Administration Tools—Tools used to administer your network through the web.

Windows 95—An operating system created as a successor to Windows 3.1.

Windows 95 clients—Computers running Windows 95 in a network environment.

Windows NT clients—Computers running Windows NT in a network environment.

Windows NT Server—The server operating system version of NT optimized for file sharing and server applications.

Windows NT Workstation—The workstation version of NT optimized for single-users.

WINNT.EXE—A 16-bit installation program used to install Windows NT.

WINNT32.EXE—A 32-bit installation program used to install Windows NT 4 from a previous version of NT.

WINS (Windows Internet Naming Service)—A service installed on Windows NT that dynamically registers and records NetBIOS names and the IP addresses associated with them. This database is then used to resolve NetBIOS names to IP addresses for WINS clients.

Workgroup—A network model in which each computer manages its own resources (including user accounts).

All About the Exam

The exam incorporates a variety of questions from a question bank intended to determine if you have mastered the subject. Here are some tips to keep in mind as you prepare for your exam:

- Make sure you understand the material thoroughly.

- Go through all the practice problems. Reread those sections with which you were having trouble.

- Make sure you are comfortable with the style of the scenario questions. These will probably be the most challenging part of the exam.

- Review the exam objectives.

The Microsoft Certification Process

Microsoft has a variety of certifications available for their products. You can find out more about their certifications on the web page: http://www.microsoft.com/train_cert/.

How to Become a Microsoft Certified Product Specialist (MCPS)

The Microsoft Certified Product Specialist is the entry level of Microsoft's certifications, and requires passing a minimal number of exams. Microsoft Certified Product Specialists are required to pass one operating system exam, proving their expertise with a current Microsoft Windows desktop or server operating system, and one or more elective exams from the MCSE or MCSD tracks. The operating system exam choices eligible are in the following list:

- Exam 70-073: Implementing and Supporting Microsoft Windows NT Workstation 4.02
  OR Exam 70-042: Implementing and Supporting Microsoft Windows NT Workstation 3.51

- Exam 70-067: Implementing and Supporting Microsoft Windows NT Server 4.0
  OR Exam 70-043: Implementing and Supporting Microsoft Windows NT Server 3.5

- Exam 70-030: Microsoft Windows 3.1

- Exam 70-048: Microsoft Windows for Workgroups 3.11-Desktop

- Exam 70-063: Implementing and Supporting Microsoft Windows 95

- Exam 70-160: Microsoft Windows Architecture I

- Exam 70-161: Microsoft Windows Architecture II

All exams for Microsoft's premium certifications (Microsoft Certified Systems Engineer and Microsoft Certified Solution Developer) are available as electives and provide further verification of skills with Microsoft BackOffice products, development tools, or desktop applications.

How to Become a Microsoft Certified Systems Engineer (MCSE)

The Microsoft Certified Systems Engineer is probably the most rapidly growing certification in the world. It proves that you are knowledgeable in advanced operating systems such as Windows 95 and Windows NT, that you excel in networking-related skills, and that you have a broad enough background to understand some of the elective products.

MCSE candidates need to pass four operating system exams and two elective exams. The MCSE certification path is divided into two tracks: the Windows NT 3.51 track and the Windows NT 4.0 track.

Table B.1 shows the core requirements (four operating system exams) and the elective courses (two exams) for the Windows NT 3.51 track.

Table B.1   Windows NT 3.51 MCSE Track

Take These Two Required Exams (Core Requirements)	Plus, Pick One Exam from the Following Operating System Exams (Core Requirement)	Plus, Pick One Exam from the Following Networking Exams (Core Requirement)	Plus, Pick Two Exams from the Following Elective Exams (Elective Requirements)
Implementing and Supporting Microsoft Windows NT Server 3.51 #70-43	Implementing and Supporting Microsoft Windows 95 #70-63	Networking Microsoft Windows for Workgroups 3.11 #70-46	Microsoft SNA Server 3.0 #70-13
AND Implementing and Supporting Microsoft Windows NTWorkstation 3.51 #70-42	*OR* Microsoft Windows for Workgroups 3.11-Desktop #70-48	*OR* Networking with Microsoft Windows 3.1 #70-47	*OR* Implementing and Supporting Microsoft Systems Management Server 1.2 #70-18
	OR Microsoft Windows 3.1 #70-30	*OR* Networking Essentials #70-58	*OR* Microsoft SQL Server 4.2 Database Implementation #70-21
			OR Implementing a Database Design on Microsoft SQL Server 6.5 #70-27

Take These Two Required Exams (Core Requirements)	Plus, Pick One Exam from the Following Operating System Exams (Core Requirement)	Plus, Pick One Exam from the Following Networking Exams (Core Requirement)	Plus, Pick Two Exams from the Following Elective Exams (Elective Requirements)
			OR Microsoft SQL Server 4.2 Database Administration for Microsoft Windows NT #70-22
			OR System Administration for Microsoft SQL Server 6.5 #70-26
			OR Microsoft Mail for PC Networks 3.2-Enterprise #70-37
			OR Internetworking Microsoft TCP/IP on Microsoft Windows NT (3.5-3.51) #70-53
			OR Internetworking Microsoft TCP/IP on Microsoft Windows NT 4.0 #70-59
			OR Implementing and Supporting Microsoft Exchange Server 4.0 #70-75
			OR Implementing and Supporting Microsoft Internet Information Server #70-77
			OR Implementing and Supporting Microsoft Proxy Server 1.0 #70-78

Table B.2 shows the core requirements (four operating system exams) and elective courses (two exams) for the Windows NT 4.0 track. Tables B.1 and B.2 have many of the same exams listed, but there are distinct differences between the two. Make sure you read each track's requirements carefully.

Table B.2   Windows NT 4.0 MCSE Track

Take These Two Required Exams (Core Requirements)	Plus, Pick One Exam from the Following Operating System Exams (Core Requirement)	Plus, Pick One Exam from the Following Networking Exams (Core Requirement)	Plus, Pick Two Exams from the Following Elective Exams (Elective Requirements)
Implementing Supporting Microsoft Windows NT Server 4.0 #70-67	Implementing Supporting Microsoft Windows 95 #70-63	Networking Microsoft Windows for Workgroups 3.11 #70-46	Microsoft SNA Server 3.0 #70-13
AND Implementing and Supporting Microsoft Windows NT Server 4.0 in the Enterprise #70-68	*OR* Microsoft Windows for Workgroups 3.11- Desktop #70-48	*OR* Networking with Microsoft Windows 3.1 #70-47	*OR* Implementing and Supporting Systems Management Server 1.2 #70-18
	OR Microsoft Windows 3.1 #70-30	*OR* Networking Essentials #70-58	*OR* Microsoft SQL Server 4.2 Database Implementation #70-21
	OR Implementing and Supporting Microsoft Windows NT Workstation 4.02 #70-73		*OR* Microsoft SQL Server 4.2 Database Administration for Microsoft Windows NT #70-22
			OR System Administration for Microsoft SQL Server 6 #70-26
			OR Implementing a Database Design on Microsoft SQL Server 6 #70-27
			OR Microsoft Mail for PC Networks 3.2- Enterprise #70-37

Take These Two Required Exams (Core Requirements)	Plus, Pick One Exam from the Following Operating System Exams (Core Requirement)	Plus, Pick One Exam from the Following Networking Exams (Core Requirement)	Plus, Pick Two Exams from the Following Elective Exams (Elective Requirements)
			OR Internetworking Microsoft TCP/IP on Microsoft Windows NT (3.5-3.51) #70-53
			OR Internetworking Microsoft TCP/IP on Microsoft Windows NT 4.0 #70-59
			OR Implementing and Supporting Microsoft Exchange Server 4.0 #70-75
			OR Implementing and Supporting Microsoft Internet Information Server #70-77
			OR Implementing and Supporting Microsoft Proxy Server 1.0 #70-78

How to Become a Microsoft Certified Solution Developer (MCSD)

The Microsoft Certified Solution Developer (MCSD) program is targeted toward people who use development tools and platforms to create business solutions. If you are a software developer or programmer working with Microsoft products, this is the certification for you.

Table B.3　Microsoft Certified Solution Developer Program

Take These Two Required Exams (Core Requirements)	Plus, Pick Two Exams from the Following Elective Exams (Elective Requirements)
Exam 70-160: Microsoft Windows Architecture I	Exam 70-021: Microsoft SQL Server 4.2 Database Implementation
AND Exam 70-161: Microsoft Windows Architecture II	*OR* Exam 70-027: Implementing a Database Design on Microsoft SQL Server 6.5
	Exam 70-024: Developing Applications with C++ Using the Microsoft Foundation Class Library
	Exam 70-065: Programming with Microsoft Visual Basic 4.0
	OR Exam 70-165: Developing Applications with Microsoft Visual Basic 5.0
	Exam 70-051: Microsoft Access 2.0 for Windows-Application Development
	OR Exam 70-069: Microsoft Access for Windows 95 and the Microsoft Access Developer's Toolkit
	Exam 70-052: Developing Applications with Microsoft Excel 5.0 Using Visual Basic for Applications
	Exam 70-054: Programming in Microsoft Visual FoxPro 3.0 for Windows
	Exam 70-025: Implementing OLE in Microsoft Foundation Class Applications

How to Become a Microsoft Certified Trainer (MCT)

MCTs are product evangelists who teach Microsoft Official Curriculum (MOC) courses to computer professionals through one or more of Microsoft's authorized education channels. MCTs have special access to current Microsoft product information and invitations to Microsoft conferences and technical training events. This certification is designed for those who want to teach official Microsoft classes. The process for becoming a certified trainer is relatively simple and consists of both a general approval for the MCT program as well as an approval for each course you want to teach.

MCT Application Approval

The three steps to the MCT application approval process are

1. Read the MCT guide and the MCT application at `http://www.microsoft.com/train_cert/mct/`.

2. Send a completed MCT application to Microsoft, including proof of your instructional presentation skills.

3. Send proof of your MCP status to Microsoft.

After you have done these steps, you will have satisfied the general part of the MCT application process. You only have to do this the first time.

MCT Course Certification Approval

The second part to becoming an MCT is that MCTs must be separately certified for each individual class they teach. Four steps are required to become certified to teach a Microsoft Official Curriculum course:

1. Pass any required prerequisite MCP exams to measure your knowledge.

2. Study the Official Microsoft Trainer Kit for the course for which you seek certification.

3. Attend the MOC course for which you seek certification.

4. Pass any additional exam requirement(s).

After you've completed both the MCT application and the MCT course certification, you'll be authorized to begin teaching that MOC class at an official Microsoft Authorized Technical Education Center (ATEC).

Registering and Taking the Exam

When you are ready to schedule your exam, contact the Sylvan Prometric test registration center that is most convenient for you from the following table:

Country	Telephone Number
Australia	1-800-808-657
Austria	0660-8582
Belgium	0800-1-7414
Canada	800-755-3926
China	10800-3538
France	1-4289-8749*
Germany	0130-83-9708
Guam	001-61-800-277583
Hong Kong	800-6375

continues

continued

Country	Telephone Number
Indonesia	001-800-61571
Ireland	1-800-626-104
Italy	1-6787-8441
Japan	0120-347737
Korea	007-8611-3095
Malaysia	800-2122
Netherlands	06-022-7584
New Zealand	0800-044-1603
Philippines	1-800-1-611-0126
Puerto Rico	800-755-3926
Singapore	800-616-1120
Switzerland	155-6966
Taiwan	008-061-1142
Thailand	001-800-611-2283
UK	0800-592-873
United States	800-755-3926
Vietnam	+61-2-9414-3666*

If this is your first time registering for a Sylvan Prometric exam, Sylvan assigns you an identification number. They ask to use your Social Security or Social Insurance number as your identification number, which works well for most people because it's relatively easy for them to remember. You also have the option of having them assign you a Sylvan ID number if you prefer not to disclose your private information.

If this is not your first exam, be prepared to give Sylvan your identification number. It's important that you use the same identification number for all your tests—if you don't, the exams won't be credited to your certification appropriately. You have to provide Sylvan Prometric with the additional information: mailing address and phone number, e-mail address, organization or company name, and method of payment (credit card number or check).

Sylvan requires that you pay in advance. Microsoft certification exam prices are related to the currency exchange rates between countries. Exams are $100 in the United States, but certification exam prices are subject to change, and in some countries, additional taxes may apply. Please verify the price with your local Sylvan Registration Center when registering. You can generally schedule exams up to six weeks in advance, or as late as the day before the exam.

You can always cancel or reschedule your exam if you contact Sylvan Prometric at least two working days before the exam, or by Friday if your test is scheduled on Monday. If you cancel, exams must be taken within one year of payment.

Same-day registration is available in some locations if space is available. You must register at least 30 minutes before test time. The day of the test, plan to arrive a few minutes early so that you can sign in and begin on time. You will be provided with something to write notes to yourself on during the test, but you are not allowed to take these notes with you after the test.

You are not allowed to take in books, notes, a pager, or anything else that may contain answers to any of the questions.

Hints and Tips for Doing Your Best on the Tests

The Microsoft Certification exams are all between 75 and 90 minutes long. The more familiar you are with the test material and the actual test's style, the easier it is for you to concentrate on the questions during the exam. Note that a score of 784 or higher is considered passing (minimum 40/51 questions).

You can divide your time between the questions however you like. If there are any questions you don't know the answers to, mark them to come back to later if you have time. You will have 90 minutes for the actual exam and it has 51 questions. Make sure that you think about whether you want to try out the practice test before you sit down to take it—some people find that the additional familiarity helps them, but other people find that it increases their stress level.

Things to Watch for

Make sure that you read each question and all its possible answers thoroughly. This is especially important for the scenario questions. Many people lose points because they select the first answer that looks correct to them when a better answer is lurking on their screens.

After you've made sure that you understand the question, eliminate those answers which you know to be wrong. If you still have two or three choices, consider which of them would be the *best* answer and select it.

Marking Answers for Return

In the event that you aren't quite sure of an answer, you have the option of marking it by selecting a box in the upper-left corner and returning to the question at the end when you are given the option of reviewing your answers. Pay particular attention to related questions you find later in the test in case you can learn enough from them to figure out the answer to the question you were unsure of before.

If you pay close attention, you will probably find that some of the other questions help to clarify questions of which you were uncertain.

Attaching Notes to Test Questions

When you finish a Microsoft exam, you are allowed to enter comments on the individual questions as well as on the entire test. This feature enables you to give the team that reviews Microsoft exams some feedback. If you find a question that is poorly worded or seems ambiguous, this is the place to let them know about it.

Index